The Self-Care Toolkit: Self-Therapy, Freedom From Anxiety, Transform Your Self-Talk, Control Your Thoughts, & Stop Overthinking

by Nick Trenton

www.NickTrenton.com

Table of Contents

BOOK 1: THE ART OF SELF-THERAPY: HOW TO GROW, GAIN SELF-AWARENESS, AND UNDERSTAND YOUR EMOTIONS 9

TABLE OF CONTENTS 11

PART 1: GETTING TO KNOW YOUR DEEPER SELF 13

CHAPTER 1: WHAT IT MEANS TO MASTER SELF-EXPLORATION 16
CHAPTER 2: TAKE A WALK ON THE DARK SIDE WITH SHADOW WORK 23
CHAPTER 3: GESTALT TECHNIQUES—BE PRESENT, BE RESPONSIBLE, BE WHOLE 29
CHAPTER 4: UNDERSTANDING INTERNAL FAMILY SYSTEMS 37

PART 2: SO, HOW DID YOU GET HERE? 43

CHAPTER 5: WHAT IS YOUR ATTACHMENT STYLE? 44
CHAPTER 6: HOW TO REPARENT YOUR INNER CHILD 51
CHAPTER 7: REWRITE THE STORY OF YOUR LIFE 57

PART 3: THOUGHTS ARE THE CODE THAT PROGRAMS YOUR LIFE 63

CHAPTER 8: IDENTIFY AND CHANGE YOUR CORE BELIEFS 63
CHAPTER 9: THE ABCD MODEL 71
CHAPTER 10: THE TRIPLE COLUMN TECHNIQUE 77
CHAPTER 11: COGNITIVE DEFUSION 83

PART 4: BUILD THE LIFE YOU WANT ONE ACTION AT A TIME 89

CHAPTER 12: SYSTEMATIC DESENSITIZATION 89
CHAPTER 13: BEHAVIORAL ACTIVATION 95
CHAPTER 14: BEHAVIORAL EXPERIMENTS 101

SUMMARY GUIDE 107

BOOK 2: ANXIETY IS THE ENEMY: *29 TECHNIQUES TO COMBAT OVERTHINKING, STRESS, PANIC, AND PRESSURE* 111

TABLE OF CONTENTS...113

CHAPTER 1. YOUR ANXIETY MANAGEMENT TOOLKIT 115

1. LABEL YOUR EMOTIONS 115
2. BUILD SELF-AWARENESS 117
3. QUESTION YOURSELF USING SOCRATIC METHOD 119
4. TEST YOUR FALSE BELIEFS 121
5. MAKE A MIND MAP 124
6. PLAY MIND GAMES 127
7. USE THE ABC MODEL TO UNDERSTAND YOUR STRESS 129

CHAPTER 2. AN ANXIETY-FREE LIFESTYLE 133

8. LIMIT CAFFEINE INTAKE 133
9. SCHEDULE YOUR "WORRY TIME" 134
10. CULTIVATE GRATITUDE 136
11. USE "MENTAL ANCHORING" 139
12. HAVE A SOLID MORNING ROUTINE 141
13. START A HOBBY 143

CHAPTER 3. ENTER YOUR MIND 147

14. BELLY BREATHING 147
15. THE 5-4-3-2-1 GROUNDING TECHNIQUE 149
16. HAVE A MANTRA 150
17. SCAN YOUR BODY 152
18. LAUGHTER MEDITATION 155
19. LOVING-KINDNESS MEDITATION 156

CHAPTER 4. THE FIRST STEP IS SEEING IT 159

20. GUIDED IMAGERY 159
21. METAPHORIZE YOUR ANXIETY 161
22. TALK ABOUT YOURSELF IN THIRD PERSON 163
23. ROLE-PLAYING 164
24. HAVE AN ALTER EGO 166

CHAPTER 5. REFRAME AND SHIFT 169

25.	ACCEPT YOUR ANXIETY	169
26.	TELL YOURSELF YOU'RE JUST EXCITED	171
27.	WRITE TO YOUR FUTURE SELF	173
28.	LEARN HOW TO SAY "I DON'T"	175
29.	HAVE NO OPINION	177

SUMMARY GUIDE 181

BOOK 3: TRANSFORM YOUR SELF-TALK: *HOW TO TALK TO YOURSELF FOR CONFIDENCE, BELIEF, AND CALM* 185

TABLE OF CONTENTS 187

CHAPTER 1. THAT VOICE INSIDE YOUR HEAD 189

THE SCIENCE OF SELF-TALK 191
SELF-TALK AS AN AMPLIFIER 194
EENIE, MEENIE, MINIE, MOE 196

CHAPTER 2. GOOD VERSUS EVIL 201

POSITIVE VERSUS NEGATIVE SELF-TALK 201
A SIMPLE COST-BENEFIT ANALYSIS 206
MEET YOUR INNER CRITIC 208
FIVE LEVELS OF SELF-TALK 211

CHAPTER 3. ALL YOU NEED TO DO IS LISTEN 215

THE KEY TO SELF-AWARENESS 215
ASSESSMENT TOOLS AND TIPS 220

CHAPTER 4. REPLACE, TRANSFORM, EVOLVE 227

THREE-STEP COGNITIVE BEHAVIORAL THERAPY 228
STEP 1: OBSERVE 228
STEP 2: CHALLENGE 229
STEP 3: REPLACE 232

CHAPTER 5: MORE THAN WORDS 241

EVERYDAY REINFORCEMENT 241
A SELF-EMPOWERMENT HABIT 244
THE CULMINATION OF REWRITING YOUR SELF-TALK 246

SUMMARY GUIDE 251

BOOK 4: ANTI-ANXIOUS: *HOW TO CONTROL YOUR THOUGHTS, STOP OVERTHINKING, AND TRANSFORM YOUR MENTAL HABITS* 257

TABLE OF CONTENTS 259

CHAPTER 1: REFRAME YOUR INTERNAL DIALOGUE AND TAKE CONTROL OF YOUR SELF-TALK 261

PROBLEM 1: THE ALL-OR-NOTHING DISEASE 263
PROBLEM 2: "OUT OF POWER" LANGUAGE 265
WHAT TO DO ABOUT IT 267
HOW TO IDENTIFY YOUR COGNITIVE DISTORTIONS 270

CHAPTER 2: ANALYZE THYSELF: THE ABC METHOD AND THOUGHT JOURNALS 279

STEP 1: HOW TO KEEP A THOUGHT JOURNAL 282
STEP 2: RETHINK . . . AND REDO 283
DECENTER, SHIFT PERSPECTIVE, AND CREATE DISTANCE 286
HOW TO TAKE A STEP BACK 287
A WORD ON THE MOST USELESS HABIT IN THE WORLD 290
TRY A COGNITIVE DEFUSION EXERCISE 292

CHAPTER 3: MASTER THE ART OF DISTRESS TOLERANCE AND SELF-SOOTHING 301

HOW TO SELF-SOOTHE 303
TIPP SKILLS 304
WHAT RADICAL ACCEPTANCE REALLY MEANS 307
THE ACCEPTS SKILL 309
BRAIN DUMPING, MENTAL NOTING, AND SCHEDULED WORRY TIME 311

CHAPTER 4: UPGRADE YOUR PSYCHOLOGICAL TOOLKIT WITH STOIC *AMOR FATI* PHILOSOPHY 317

BEYOND RADICAL ACCEPTANCE: AMOR FATI 317
NEGATIVE VISUALIZATION 320
WHAT IS YOUR ORIENTATION: SOLUTION OR PROBLEM ORIENTATION? THOUGHT OR ACTION? 326

CHAPTER 5: AVOID THE TRAP OF TOXIC POSITIVITY AND FEEL YOUR FEELINGS 333

THE POSITIVE IS POWERFUL, BUT 334
GOOD VERSUS WHOLE 336
LETTING GO OF TOXIC POSITIVITY 337
ONE UNDERAPPRECIATED WAY TO GENUINELY FEEL BETTER 339
EMOTIONAL REGULATION 339
THE LIFE CYCLE OF AN EMOTION 341

CHAPTER 6: BUT WHERE DOES NEGATIVE THINKING REALLY COME FROM? 349

YOUR NEGATIVITY MAY BE "HARDWIRED" 350
COUNTERING THE BIAS FOR THE NEGATIVE 352
RETHINK TOXIC RELATIONSHIPS—INCLUDING THE ONE YOU HAVE WITH YOURSELF 354

SUMMARY GUIDE 361

BONUS 10 MENTAL HEALTH WORKSHEETS AND 30-DAY MENTAL HEALTH ACTION PLAN 366

Book 1: The Art of Self-Therapy: How to Grow, Gain Self-Awareness, and Understand Your Emotions

Table of Contents

THE ART OF SELF-THERAPY: HOW TO GROW, GAIN SELF-AWARENESS, AND UNDERSTAND YOUR EMOTIONS

TABLE OF CONTENTS

PART 1: GETTING TO KNOW YOUR DEEPER SELF

CHAPTER 1: WHAT IT MEANS TO MASTER SELF-EXPLORATION
CHAPTER 2: TAKE A WALK ON THE DARK SIDE WITH SHADOW WORK
CHAPTER 3: GESTALT TECHNIQUES—BE PRESENT, BE RESPONSIBLE, BE WHOLE
CHAPTER 4: UNDERSTANDING INTERNAL FAMILY SYSTEMS

PART 2: SO, HOW DID YOU GET HERE?

CHAPTER 5: WHAT IS YOUR ATTACHMENT STYLE?
CHAPTER 6: HOW TO REPARENT YOUR INNER CHILD
CHAPTER 7: REWRITE THE STORY OF YOUR LIFE

PART 3: THOUGHTS ARE THE CODE THAT PROGRAMS YOUR LIFE

CHAPTER 8: IDENTIFY AND CHANGE YOUR CORE BELIEFS
CHAPTER 9: THE ABCD MODEL
CHAPTER 10: THE TRIPLE COLUMN TECHNIQUE
CHAPTER 11: COGNITIVE DEFUSION

PART 4: BUILD THE LIFE YOU WANT ONE ACTION AT A TIME

CHAPTER 12: SYSTEMATIC DESENSITIZATION
CHAPTER 13: BEHAVIORAL ACTIVATION
CHAPTER 14: BEHAVIORAL EXPERIMENTS

SUMMARY GUIDE

Part 1: Getting to Know Your Deeper Self

Therapy is a wonderful thing. A trained mental health professional can help you explore psychological blind spots, set goals, and work with you through tricky thought patterns so you can gently change them.

But what if you don't want therapy, or can't access it?

Here's a question to ponder: In conventional therapy, what do you think is the *main factor* that determines success for the person seeking help?

Is it the skill or experience level of the therapist?
Is it the kind of therapy they're doing—i.e., their theoretical approach and techniques?
Is it the duration and intensity of therapy?

You may be surprised to learn that one of the most influential factors for success in therapy is "therapeutic alliance"—with the factors listed above being almost negligible (Strupp, 2001; Ardito, 2011; Lynch, 2012). Think about that for a moment: The kind of therapy you get, with whom, and for how long has *less* of an impact than does the relationship between the therapist and their client.

This is a big deal. It means that with sufficient empathy, goodwill, and emotional connection (all of which make up a sense of "therapeutic alliance"), you can still find success in therapy even if your therapist is completely unskilled and using techniques that are not actually suitable for you. On the other hand, it also means that you can go to the best practitioner there is, but if you don't connect emotionally with them, your chances of success with them are slim.

What does all this mean for those of us who want to explore the concept of self-therapy? Well, it means that theoretical knowledge is not a pre-requisite for psychological growth and insight. And that means that we can still help ourselves even if we lack the kind of training that mental health professionals possess.

"Self-therapy" is a way to recreate some of the benefits of conventional therapy, but on your own terms. This book is all about giving you the tools you need to gain better self-awareness, build emotional maturity, and learn to change your behavior so that you can start creating the kind of life you want for yourself.

The tools we'll explore in the chapters that follow are the very same ones used by cognitive behavioral therapists, counselors, and psychologists the world over. By adapting them for your own use, you can start cultivating more contentment with who you are, challenge limiting thought patterns, and zoom out to gain a broader view of the narratives on which your life is structured. From there, you can *consciously* choose what you want for your life, rather than passively being at the mercy of these forces.

But, keep in mind the power of "therapeutic alliance"—the real reason that people succeed in therapy at all. What does it look like to have a good therapeutic alliance with yourself? Imagine all the qualities and characteristics of a warm, understanding, and empathetic counselor, and imagine treating yourself with the same positive sense of compassion and interest. To be a good "self-therapist" is not solely about what you know, but about:

- Self-empathy
- Self-respect
- Self-trust
- Self-awareness
- Having "positive regard" for yourself
- Being committed to the process
- Being positive and hopeful about the process as a whole

If these things are in place, then you can embark on a journey of self-therapy that may be every bit as beneficial as a more conventional therapeutic relationship.

In the pages that follow, we'll start at the very beginning: your deepest self. In Part 1, we'll look at helpful techniques and mindset shifts that will help you master self-exploration and gain deeper awareness into how you actually tick. Then, in Part 2, we'll take a look into the past and investigate how your family and early experiences shaped who you are today. After all, if you want to rewrite the story of your life, you need to understand the story as it is so far, and how it got that way.

In Part 3, we shift our attention to the cognitive manifestations of our core beliefs and inner emotional realities: our thoughts. Using evidence-based cognitive behavioral techniques, we'll look at our thought processes and take charge of them, asking whether they're genuinely helping us achieve the kind of life we want. Finally, once all this groundwork has been laid, we can dive into the practical work of Part 4, where we explore ways to start taking action and changing our behavior in the world day after day.

Self-therapy isn't learned overnight, and it can be challenging at times, but rest assured that no matter where you are now or where you want to be, these techniques will bring improvements to your life. Whether you are looking for more direction and purpose, want to improve your relationships, or simply need to get a handle on who you are and what you really want in life, there's something in this book for you. Let's jump in.

Chapter 1: What It Means to Master Self-Exploration

What you'll learn in this chapter: why and how to improve your self-awareness, as well as a six-part process for learning more about what makes you tick.

Here's a good question to begin with: WHO ARE YOU?

The first and arguably most important of the three maxims inscribed at the Temple of Apollo at Delphi is *nosce te ipsum*, or "know thyself." Though nobody is entirely sure who first insisted these words be carved (they were already ancient history by the time of Plato), what's clear is that humankind's fascination with self-knowledge is not new.

According to professor emeritus at California State University, author, and psychologist Dr. Tom Stevens, mastering self-exploration can provide us with a sophisticated, nuanced answer to this question. But we cannot even begin to answer the question until we have something crucial: self-awareness.

Too many people go through life on autopilot or in a kind of distracted haze. They are not really sure what they feel, what they want, or who they are. They are unclear about their values, have fuzzy boundaries, or have never really stopped to consider why they behave as they do.

If you've ever asked yourself . . .

"Why do I do that?"

"What do I really want?" or

"Why am I unhappy?"

. . . then chances are you can benefit from more self-exploration. When you have explored yourself in enough depth, you can identify who you are as a person (both strengths and weaknesses), take responsibility for what you need, and then make informed decisions about the choices you want to make in your life.

If you embark on any plan for personal development without self-awareness, though, you are merely going through the motions. Perhaps you end up doing what you think you "should" be doing, or substitute other people's desires and values for your own. Not only does self-awareness make you happier, more resilient, and more accepting of who you are, it also allows you to live authentically and create a life that is right for *you*.

Imagine you fall ill and consult a doctor. The doctor examines you and conducts some tests to check out your condition, then makes a diagnosis. With the *inner* world, though, things are not so simple. If you consult a psychologist or counselor, all they have to help them reach a "diagnosis" of your condition is . . . whatever you tell them. They have diagnostic tools like doctors do, but these are often just lists of subjective symptoms and experiences that rely on your self-report.

Therefore, if *you* don't really know what your experience is, they can't help you much. If you lack self-awareness, you may simply wander into someone else's guess for what your experience is. Self-knowledge and self-awareness are not only important for genuine growth, they're non-negotiable.

So what exactly is self-exploration? According to Ryan Howes, PhD, psychologist, writer, and professor in Pasadena, California, it involves "taking a look at your own thoughts, feelings, behaviors, and motivations and asking **why**. It's looking for the roots of who we are."

The idea is that if you can understand why you do something, you *empower yourself to do something different*. If you don't truly understand what is going on in your heart and mind, you only have a dim hope of fulfilling your potential, overcoming obstacles, or connecting fully with others in your relationships.

Beginner Strategies: Make Self-Exploration a Habit

Self-awareness is like exercise—the more you practice, the better you become!

The best way to gain more self-awareness is to build it into your life as a regular, consistent habit. This can be as simple as asking yourself, whenever you remember, "What do I notice about myself right now?"

Simply pause, become aware, and *be* with yourself for a moment. Try just ten minutes to start (what about trying right now, as you read this book?). Notice if you get distracted and your mind wanders. Notice what you're feeling and where that experience sits in your body. Notice the thoughts in your mind. Notice what you're doing. Notice what came just before. Even notice thoughts like, "I'm bored. Am I doing it right?"

Unplug and check in with yourself. Importantly, you don't have to *do* anything about what you notice. You don't have to judge, interpret, cling to, avoid, or analyze what you notice. Just notice. For example, you might be having a shower and suddenly notice that you're in a really bad mood. Why? You pause and decide to become aware for a moment.

You sit somewhere quietly and notice that you're annoyed. You notice your thoughts and how they're rushing ahead to an imagined future encounter at work. You realize you were rehearsing a hypothetical argument in your mind. You notice how you're actually scowling a little, your jaw is tense, and you're not paying much attention to anything else. Without awareness, none of this would have been noticed. Let's take a closer look.

Tom Stevens' Six-Step Self-Exploration Process

Once you've gained some practice with the above exercise, you can challenge yourself to go further and follow Dr. Stevens' six-step approach for digging a little deeper.

Step 1: Switch on Your "Inner Noticer"
As we did in the previous exercise, just get into the habit of observing yourself neutrally and without judgment—like a scientist taking a step back and recording data from afar. See if you can notice thoughts, feelings, physical sensations, and actions—and the difference between them.

Example: You notice your bad mood in the shower, your tense jaw muscles, and the mini argument you seem to be holding in your head.

Step 2: Notice Any Problematic Situations?
This step may happen automatically, but see if any patterns begin to emerge.

What is the "problem" exactly?

When did it start?

What came before it? Does this sequence of events usually happen this way?

What typically comes after this experience?

What is going on in your environment when this happens?

Example: You realize, with repeated moments of awareness, that you actually feel this way most mornings, during most showers. You realize this may be a problem for you and is setting the day off on the wrong foot.

You look more closely at yourself for a few days and notice that you don't wake up irritable, but seem to feel that way only after your mind wanders in the shower and starts to entertain certain thoughts and "predictions."

Step 3: Notice the Strongest Emotions and Where They Lead
Notice not only what you feel but the intensity of those feelings. There may be some emotions that you become aware of that you are actually quite uncomfortable with. If you can notice that you are trying to resist or avoid them, see if you can keep maintaining awareness anyway. In fact, become most curious about the strongest, most difficult, or most uncomfortable emotions.

Keep asking more questions of this emotion—what came before? What happened next?

Example: The strongest emotion, even though you try to avoid it, turns out to be *anger*. You say you're annoyed and find yourself blaming random occurrences that come after your shower, but the more awareness you bring to the situation, the more you see that you are in fact very angry at something. What? This is difficult to admit because you don't consider yourself an angry person. But you keep being aware.

Step 4: Try to Notice Any Emerging Connections
Now's the time to really put on your scientist cap and bravely investigate those strong feelings, rather than avoid or deny them.

What images, ideas, thoughts, or memories seem to most often be connected with the strong emotion?

What strengthens these emotions and what seems to make them fade?

Can you connect this experience or emotion with something similar in the past?

If there are many situations that produce this emotion, what do those situations have in common? What connects them?

Example: You are aware that you keep rehearsing imaginary conversations in your mind, where you envision your work colleagues are criticizing you, and you are angrily defending yourself, as well as venting off a long list of hidden resentments of your own.

In these conversations, you find yourself saying things like, "Oh, so I suppose you think you're perfect, then?" and, "If you're such an expert, then why do you pay me to do it for you, huh?" In time, you notice that this reminds you of something very interesting: the way you feel is very similar to arguments you used to have with your father growing up, where he would criticize your work no matter how hard you tried.

Step 5: What is the underlying core belief, value, or theme behind this emotion?
Keep going and you should eventually uncover the bigger picture that connects everything together—thought, feelings, behavior. The magic of self-awareness is this ability to see the overarching patterns and themes that are playing out in your life.

You've become aware of all the surface details; now, what is the bigger underlying theme that brings them all together? In what ways are all the separate issues you're experiencing alike?

Example: You realize that the bigger picture is that you're feeling insecure about your performance at work and are assuming that people are judging you. You play out imaginary conversations in your own mind, but this is not an accurate reflection of what is actually happening in your workplace right now, but an echo of something from your deeper childhood.

Step 6: Use Your Insights to Identify Your Boundaries, Then Take Control
Self-awareness is not just something we do for the sake of it. It's something we develop and then *put to use*. Once you've gained greater insight into your problem, there's one of two ways forward:

1. Identify the external cause of the problem and take responsibility for acting, given what we know
2. Identify the inner cause of the problem (i.e., us!) and take responsibility for that, whether that means changing our thoughts, emotions, or behaviors.

As you can see, in both options, we need to own up to our portion of the problem and take responsibility for acting in our own best interests. After all, self-awareness that doesn't lead to any concrete changes in the real world is not much more than navel-gazing!

Example: You ask yourself honestly if there's any objective reason to believe that people are critical of you at work. When you're content there aren't, you deliberately choose to become aware any time you catch yourself getting stuck in imaginary "replay" conversations. Then, you rehearse a mantra: "I'm competent and capable, and I'm doing the best I can. I am proud of myself."

Now, the above example may seem insignificant on the surface, but imagine if such a problem was allowed to run its course without ever being revealed by the light of awareness. You may have gotten out of the shower *every single morning* in a bad mood, never really knowing why. Maybe one day you went into work feeling grumpy and sensitive and snapped at a colleague, assuming they were being rude. This could set off a whole cascade of negative outcomes—all of which could be avoided if you knew yourself better.

On the other hand, while this is happening, other things are *not* happening: You are not giving yourself the opportunity to fix the real problem, which is the unresolved issues you have with your father and with your own sense of self-worth. Maybe you even assume the problem is that you feel angry "for no reason," so you start trying to solve the problem in all the wrong ways—i.e., reading a self-help book about anger or taking up Tai Chi.

These things are great, but they probably won't work because they are not addressing the real root of your problem, which is more accurately low self-esteem. This is why it's so important to start with awareness and self-exploration as the first step.

Becoming aware is a simple, free, and easy thing that any of us can do right now, in this moment.

As our example shows, what started out as simply curiosity and awareness of the most ordinary daily activities can yield valuable insight into who you are as a person. All that's needed is time, patience, and the willingness to know ourselves better.

Something else that's needed is *radical honesty*. When you start down the path of "noticing" all the sensations you ordinarily wouldn't, you may become aware of certain things that make you uncomfortable. If, with growing awareness, you get close to an unflattering truth about yourself, the tendency may be to flee this realization. But this is just about as useful as pitching up to a therapist's office and telling white lies about what is going on in your life—it may avoid discomfort in the short term but will make things worse in the long run.

For a different example, let's say you notice an increasingly uneasy feeling in the shower every morning before work. You zoom in on the emotions, look for patterns, and gradually realize what the problem is: you. The truth is, you are no longer challenged by your work, and each morning, the dread you feel at the thought of going into the office is coming from a creeping sensation that you are not using your talents properly, and that for your own good, you need to leave and find a more appropriate job.

However, because facing this fact is so uncomfortable, you don't quite allow yourself to see it. You know you are overqualified for your role and that you should leave . . . but you are terrified of starting over, and as unwilling as you are to admit it, you are pretty content with how cushy your job is. So you don't leave, and you don't allow yourself to think of leaving. You say to others, "Oh, I'm just stressed right now because we're dealing with a difficult client," but this is not really the truth.

On some level, you are aware of your own self-deception, and it's *this* that makes you feel bad every morning. You are not even irritated with the job anymore, but with yourself—and this is an insight that you can only reach if you are honest and willing to face up to what you are really thinking, feeling, and doing.

In the chapters that follow, we'll be taking this foundation of self-exploration and awareness and building on it as we go. But if that foundation is to serve us well, it has to be *real*. Next, we'll take a closer look at the power of refusing to avoid or flee uncomfortable emotions, and turning to face and accept them head-on instead.

Chapter 2: Take a Walk on the Dark Side with Shadow Work

What you'll learn in this chapter: what the shadow is and how and why to embrace it with acceptance and compassion.

When most people experience uncomfortable emotions, they want to do one thing and one thing only: get away from them. In fact, they may turn to therapy with precisely this attitude: "Make it go away!"

However, this is the opposite of the mindset you need. As we saw above, what's required is a willingness to tolerate, accept, and be with emotions, **all our emotions**, no matter how uncomfortable they are and without judgment.

If you start to make awareness and self-exploration a bigger part of your life, sooner or later you're going to encounter parts of yourself that you really, really don't like. And your tendency will be to run as far away from them as possible! However, this is where the technique of shadow work comes into play—and this is essential work if we hope to evolve and grow as human beings.

Carl Jung was the psychiatrist, author, and theorist who first introduced the idea of the shadow. In *Psychology and Religion*, he wrote,

> *"Unfortunately there can be no doubt that man is, on the whole, less good than he imagines himself or wants to be. Everyone carries a shadow, and the less it is embodied in the individual's conscious life, the blacker and denser it is. **If an inferiority is conscious, one always has a chance to correct it.** Furthermore, it is constantly in contact with other interests so that it is continually subjected to modifications. **But if it is repressed and isolated from consciousness, it never gets corrected**"* (1938, pp. 131).

In simple terms, the shadow is our psychological blind spot—it contains everything that we can't "see"— i.e., that is outside our awareness. When it is made unconscious, a fact, feeling, or idea about ourselves is cut off from our sense of self and assumed not to exist.
Every person has a shadow, but the idea is that if we can acknowledge it, accept it, and integrate it back into our awareness as something that rightly belongs to us, we

enjoy greater mental health, authenticity, creativity, energy, and maturity. It is not the fact of the material in the shadow itself—it is neither good nor bad as it is—but rather that the material is unacknowledged, unintegrated, and unregulated into conscious life. In Jung's words, "blacker and denser."

Where does the shadow come from? When we are young, we have certain experiences that teach us that some parts of ourselves are acceptable and others aren't. In order to survive in the world as dependent beings and get our needs met, we unconsciously decide to disown those "bad" parts of ourselves and disidentify with them. We push them out of awareness.

For example, as children, your parents may have punished you when you yelled or expressed frustration. This doesn't have to be a major crisis point, either; let's say you kicked the wall once when you lost your temper, and your mom scowled at you and said, "Don't do that!" At the same time, maybe your parents responded with warmth and approval whenever you expressed feelings of calmness and self-control. Conclusion? There must be something wrong with anger. So, you put "anger" into the shadow. It hasn't gone anywhere; it's just that we don't see it anymore.

After a lifetime of this, you achieve adulthood and believe that you have a mild, even temperament and that you never get angry. Except, mysteriously, sometimes when you're alone in the car and someone cuts you off in traffic, you are stunned at the tirade of enraged abuse you can fling at the driver . . . Where did all that come from? The answer is your shadow.

This "dark side" of our conscious awareness doesn't contain just bad things, by the way. We can also disconnect from and disown positive feelings, attributes, or thoughts. We may put into the shadow things like excitement, hope, silliness, and so on because of early experiences that taught us these things were bad.

Consider this famous quote by Marianne Williamson:

> *Our deepest fear is not that we are inadequate. Our deepest fear is that we are powerful beyond measure. It is our light, not our darkness, that most frightens us. We ask ourselves, 'Who am I to be brilliant, gorgeous, talented, fabulous?' Actually, who are you not to be? You are a child of God. Your playing small does not serve the world.*

While it's true that the shadow contains primeval and ancient human feelings like rage and lust, that's not all it contains. Imagine a little girl who quickly solves a complex math problem, to the astonishment of her father. Her father, perhaps projecting his own issues, immediately says, "Big whoop, so you solved it. Don't boast." The little girl nods and quickly decides inwardly that pride in her abilities is not acceptable. She stuffs down any belief in her own talent, along with any hope that she might be admired or praised for the things she is gifted at doing. In adulthood, she has pushed these feelings so far into her shadow that intelligence and brilliance are no longer a part of her identity at all.

While most people can agree that disowning your hope, talent, joy, pride, etc. is a sad loss, isn't it a good thing to section off the worst parts of ourselves? Is that really a problem? The trouble is that the shadow is never completely hidden. It still shows itself; however, it may do so in sneaky ways. Our shadow may express itself in strange behaviors we don't understand—in dreams, in slips of the tongue, or in behavior others can see but we don't ourselves recognize.

One day, when the little girl from the earlier example grows up and learns a friend of hers earned a PhD in science, she scoffs and thinks secretly to herself, "Big whoop! Who does she think she is, anyway?"

How does your shadow express itself?

Perhaps your anger comes out in passive aggressiveness. You may say, "I'm the least angry person in the world!" Yet somehow, others can *feel* the anger radiating off you anyway. It's because it's still there, in the shadow. As long as we have a shadow, we will remain at least partly unconscious of our deeper motivations and may be trapped in behaviors that are not good for us, without really understanding why.

On top of this, there's a sneaky phenomenon called projection, in which we end up incorrectly ascribing to others the feelings and thoughts we ourselves have but have disowned and relegated to the shadow. The classic example is the person who is being dishonest but has pushed that fact out of awareness. The shadow seeps out, however, in the form of them constantly accusing *others* of hiding something or being dishonest. They're projecting when they say, "The problem isn't in me, it's in you!"

In this way, what we are unconscious of can harm us. It can threaten our relationships, jeopardize our work, and weaken our potential. It can also leave us confused, immature, and fragile people who lack wisdom and self-knowledge. The solution? Again, it's awareness! According to Jung, **we improve our lives and heal when we integrate the shadow.**

That may sound like a good idea, but nobody wants to look at their shadow. Nobody wants to face up to the things they cannot face in themselves, by definition! So how exactly do we see what we can't see?

Accepting the Shadow

First things first, what you *don't* want to do is continue to judge and condemn the "bad" parts of yourself—after all, this is precisely what caused it to be shoved out of awareness in the first place. No, we cannot be whole and integrate the shadow by heaping on more scorn or shame. Instead, we need to be curious, compassionate, and open-minded.

To engage our shadow, we need a few things:
- Patience
- A genuinely accepting and nonjudgmental attitude
- Honesty
- The willingness to be brave enough to face things we don't like about ourselves

Here are a few ways to do that.

Technique 1: Pay Attention to Your Emotional Reactions

Imagine someone has a drinking problem that they can't quite admit to themselves. In their shadow is everything they deny about themselves: a lack of self-control, frequent reckless behavior, even the habit of denial itself. They are unwilling to face up to the fact that they behave in ways they don't like when they drink too much, and unwilling to accept the shame they feel because of it. In fact, they could go for years never acknowledging this problem.

One day, this person notices themselves feeling extremely judgmental about a friend who smokes marijuana. They say, "It's totally irresponsible. Don't they care about what they're doing to their health? So reckless. They obviously lack self-control! I'm so disappointed in them . . ." Others might be puzzled at this outburst. Why such a strong reaction?

The answer probably lies in the person's shadow. Read through their thoughts again, and you'll see that this is in fact what they think of *themselves*. The shadow can hide from awareness, but it often shows itself as judgment of others, or strong and disproportionate reactions that don't quite fit the situation at hand.

It's a good idea to become aware of anything that seems to "push your buttons" and cause a reaction that is bigger than it should be. Prick your ears if you seem to have been "triggered" automatically by something, and become curious why. What bothers you in others is often something you've disowned in yourself!

Technique 2: Embrace Imperfection

While rage, jealousy, and lust are all understandably relegated to the shadow, much of what we put there isn't really so bad when you think about it. The shadow may feel big and scary and overwhelming, but it's often like the monster under the bed—when you peek to check, there's nothing there.

If you can learn to embrace flaws and imperfection and accept that **you are a complex person with both good and bad qualities**, then you weaken the power of the shadow. One way to do this is to consciously decide you will judge and condemn others less often (hint: to the extent you judge them, you also judge yourself). Another idea is to deliberately ask, "What's so wrong with being a flawed human being?"

Here's an exercise to try.

1. Identify the attributes, ideas, thoughts, or feelings you most often judge in others.
2. Write them down ("I hate stupid people").
3. Now rephrase the sentences so they apply to you ("I can be stupid sometimes").
4. Read through these new sentences and notice how you feel. Ask yourself, is it *really* the end of the world if they're true? Does it mean that you're not worthy of love, or that you don't also possess good qualities? You may notice that the more forgiving you are about other people's stupid mistakes, the easier it is to accept occasional stupidity in yourself, and vice versa.
5. If you're having trouble, try to imagine a loved one who has that attribute, yet whom you still adore and respect anyway (maybe you realize that your pet Labrador is the stupidest being on the planet, but that doesn't stop them from also being the one you love most!). Imagine that you, too, are perfectly acceptable as you are, warts and all.

Technique 3: Ask for Feedback

Your shadow is a bit like the back of your head—you can't see it, but it may be very visible to everyone else!

Asking someone you trust and respect to help you see your blind spots takes some courage, but it's well worth it. Identify someone who you believe knows you well—the last thing you want is to ask someone who will accidentally project their own shadow onto you! Ask someone who themselves has been able to demonstrate emotional maturity, and who will be happy to help you look objectively at your shadow without bringing judgment into the equation.

Since this may be a tall order, another option is to enlist the help of a therapist, counselor, or psychologist to help you work through the more sensitive parts of your shadow. They'll be able to hold you accountable while keeping a "safe space" that won't trigger more defensiveness in you.

If both of these options are not feasible, you can always sit down and carefully consider the feedback you've already received from others. Can you find any themes or patterns in what you've been told by ex-partners, old bosses (or current ones!), friends, family members, or even random people? You may already have been given heaps of feedback that consistently points to your shadow, only you haven't been courageous enough to take it fully on board.

Notice if you repeatedly find yourself angry with people's appraisals of who you are (again, it's about noticing *disproportionate* reactions) and ask honestly if they may have a point. Think back to disagreements you may have had or recall criticisms or advice others may have repeatedly given you. You may have dismissed it in the past, but could it be that others have said similar things? Could there be a pattern?

The important thing about shadow work is that you are not trying to play "gotcha!"

You are not attempting to catch yourself out or punish yourself. If on reflection you notice that more than a handful of people have mentioned how over the top you can be at times, just own and acknowledge that. Avoid getting lost in shame or embarrassment about it—just accept it gracefully and be proud of yourself that you're able to be aware.

If that fails, one technique always works: humor. Laugh at yourself a little. "Oh, there I go again! What a drama llama I am. How do you put up with me?"

Chapter 3: Gestalt Techniques—Be Present, Be Responsible, Be Whole

What you'll learn in this chapter: how to open yourself more fully to the present by putting the past to rest.

As you embark on more self-exploration and become more aware of yourself in the present, you may notice something interesting: that so much of your experience is actually all about the **past**.

Gestalt therapy is a kind of psychotherapy first introduced by Fritz and Laura Perls in the 1940s and addresses this issue of "letting go of the past."

You may start to notice that what keeps you from living in the present or planning for the future is the fact that you have unresolved conflicts and patterns that are living on from the past. Gestalt therapy, then, is all about healing that past so you can focus on the present moment and your responsibilities in that moment. If you can do that, the theory goes, you can make better decisions and greatly improve your resilience, self-knowledge, and well-being.

In a 2018 Good Therapy article on Gestalt principles, licensed counselor Jodi Clarke puts it this way: *"Gestalt therapy is a humanistic, holistic, person-centered form of psychotherapy that is focused on an individual's present life and challenges rather than delving into past experiences."* The idea is not to endlessly rehash the past, but to *resolve* and *release* it so we are free to take responsibility for our lives right now.

What do we need to begin Gestalt therapy techniques? As you might have guessed, it's awareness.

First, let's look at this word "gestalt," which is a German term that roughly translates to "whole." Its meaning suggests that "the whole is greater than the sum of the parts." A gestalt is then the meaningful form or shape that we give to all our collected experiences. **With our perception, we make sense of the world with our narrative and our identity—this is a gestalt.**

However, every person is connected to and influenced by their environment and others. So, it follows, then, that if we want to understand ourselves and fulfil our potential, we need to also understand our context. To change, we have to become aware of what is, and also accept it. In this way, we relieve suffering and anxiety and free ourselves to seek growth and development instead.

Gestalt therapists believe the reason we are unhappy in life is because there is a gap between our present and our future. In other words, our mind may travel faster and further into the future than the concrete circumstances of our lives can keep up with! Thus, we create worry, anticipation, and a whole world of expectations and interpretations that cause us trouble. We also cause ourselves trouble when we use our minds to travel back to the past.

But here, the Perls have some advice: *all we can ever experience is the present.* The perception we have of the past or the future is not "objective" because it is actually a reflection of how we're living right now.

So far so good, but how can we apply any of these insights into our own lives? Below, we'll look at five popular Gestalt therapy strategies that you can try for yourself.

Strategy 1: Pending Issues

A pending issue is an event in the past that continues to have an influence on the present. These issues are like knots, blocks, or mismanaged perceptions that linger—for example, a grudge against a family member or an unresolved issue with an old friend. According to the Perls, we resolve these issues by engaging them and refusing to avoid them anymore. We need to construct an imaginary encounter in which we face this issue now, in the present, and put it to bed.

Maybe we say a final farewell to someone who died before we could share what we wanted to. Maybe we address an unspoken resentment or ask someone for forgiveness.

How? Close your eyes and go quiet within yourself, then mentally evoke the person, issue, or event. Don't flee any uncomfortable emotions. Do what you need to do to "close the circle." We'll look at this idea in more detail when we talk about "re-parenting the inner child," but for now, just rehearse in your imagination any act or words that will help you find closure.

Here's an example. Katie has an extremely critical and judgmental father. Growing up, he complained relentlessly about everything and was never satisfied—not with himself or with others or with life in general. He was definitely not satisfied with *her*. No matter what she did, he found fault with it and would even openly mock or belittle her efforts.
Katie is now an adult and has a whopping "pending issue"—her self-esteem is non-existent, she self-sabotages, and she never speaks up or shares herself with the world (why would she when she has been trained to assume that nothing she does will ever be acknowledged and respected, let alone valued?). She's begun to realize that this is

an outstanding pattern *from the past*—it doesn't reflect what is going on right now since she is surrounded by encouraging friends, a doting husband, and a boss who believes in her talents.

Katie is now using Gestalt techniques to recognize when the voice of the Inner Critic is really just the voice of her father from the past. When she recognizes herself saying things like, "Is that all?" or, "Why bother trying? It won't work," or, "Shut up. People are not interested in what you have to say," she goes quiet inside herself and visualizes her father as a little person standing on her shoulder, whispering negative thoughts in her ear. She vividly imagines picking him up by the scruff of his collar, and pressing him firmly between the pages of a photo album labeled *Ancient History*. Doing this, she says, "No. It IS worth trying. I have something to say, and people are interested in hearing it. I have talents. I've done well. I have a lot to be proud of. I don't have to hide myself away . . ."

Strategy 2: Addressing the Empty Chair
This is a familiar technique, but some people aren't aware that it comes from Gestalt therapy. Here, you take your mental and emotional perception of a person or event and **externalize** it so you can then engage with it or have a dialogue. This gets unresolved issues moving again and allows trapped feelings to be acknowledged and then released.

For example, you may imagine that your childhood bully is sitting in the chair opposite you. Really visualize them there, and now imagine everything you wish you had said back then. Speak your mind.

"You know what? I couldn't say anything back then because I was just a kid, and I was scared. I had nobody looking out for me, and you took advantage of that. I couldn't say anything, but I'm saying it now. You took something from me that wasn't yours to take. You were wrong."

Perhaps you even imagine the childhood bully responding to you from the empty chair:

"Oh, get over yourself! It wasn't that bad. You were a crybaby then and you're a crybaby now. Are you still whining about what happened all those years ago? I forgot about you . . ."

You reply:

"Well, I used to believe that. But it's a lie. I was a really strong, brave kid, and I'm still surprised to this day what I put up with all on my own. Here's the thing—I couldn't walk away from you then, but I'm doing it now. You don't deserve any more of my attention, because I have a good life now and I don't want you here in my mind, ruining all that."

You may notice that as you speak, things shift. Conversations (even imaginary ones!) move issues forward. By processing the bullying you endured in the past, you can gradually release it. You may one day find yourself having a very different conversation with your imaginary bully:

"I've realized something. Perhaps I need to *thank* you. You taught me how to value myself and how to put up rock-solid boundaries. You taught me who I *didn't* want to be! You made me stronger. In a strange way, you helped me be the bigger person—and now that I'm older and wiser, I'm grateful for that lesson."

The empty chair technique can be more abstract than this, though. For example, put your fear itself into the chair, and personify it. What does it want? What is it telling you? More importantly, what do you have to say to it?

"Fear, we've been through a lot, you and me. Maybe in the past you seemed like a good idea, but these days, I'm not so sure that you're working in my best interests anymore. On the one hand, you're so comfortable to have around, and you kind of get me off the hook for a lot of things, if I'm honest! But on the other hand, I'm beginning to get restless with you hanging around all the time, and nothing ever gets to change with you second-guessing me . . ."

On the other hand, if you're feeling anxious and afraid, you could also put your *strength* into the chair and talk to that. Ask what it needs to be stronger. Ask why it's hiding away right now and letting fear take over.

"Hello, strength. It was really, really weird to meet you the other day. You were so small—at first, I wasn't even sure it was you at all. But actually, it felt good to have you around. What made it possible for you to make an appearance at that moment?"

As you can see, there is a lot of flexibility and creativity in how you use this technique! Just remember that the goal is to bring the past into the present *so you can actively process it, engage with it, and release it.* If you merely dredge up the past so you can wallow in it, you are reinforcing the very patterns you're trying to liberate yourself from.

Strategy 3: "I'm Responsible"
When you are burdened with past issues, you are in truth absolving yourself of the responsibility to live dynamically and spontaneously in the present. This is something that many of us may not want to fully admit to ourselves: that our unresolved issues are a kind of security blanket and an excuse for not living up to our potential right now, in the lives we live in the present.

If we can become aware of and accept our own duty to the present, however, we can start embracing our responsibility and begin making conscious, proactive choices. In other words, we **make the shift from, "This is who I am/was," to, "Who do I want to be right now?"**

There are a few phrases, mantras, or ways of speaking that will help put you into the responsible, present-focused mindset:

"I'm responsible for that."

"I accept that it's my job to change things."

"I have a choice in what happens next."

For example, you may find that you're wracked with guilt and shame about how you behaved in the past. You may be carrying that embarrassment and regret around with you, but by doing so, you only limit your ability to make good decisions right now, in the present.

Using the "I'm responsible" strategy, you teach yourself to say, "I can't change the past, but I am in charge of what I do and say now, and I choose to do better." Just remember to make sure your responsibility is anchored in the only place that you genuinely have it: the present.

But this is not just about regret over mistakes we've made. It's more about how being trapped in the past can prevent us from being one hundred percent present right now. Consider Jake's example. Jake was dating Emma for nine years in total, but they had a prolonged and dramatic breakup after years of infidelity and betrayal. Jake left the relationship in tatters, feeling completely consumed with bitterness and resentment. He decided he needed to get himself into therapy and start healing his broken heart . . .

. . . and that was four years ago. Jake is *still* in therapy, still heartbroken, and still telling anyone and everyone about how vicious Emma was, how bad the breakup felt, and how difficult it was to put the pieces back together again. Jake has half-heartedly attempted to meet new women, but he only ends up telling them on the second date that he isn't over his ex yet, he can't trust women, and he is still processing the pain.

One day, while Jake is in the therapist's chair yet again, ranting about the psychological complexes Emma left him with, bemoaning his fate, and wishing that women weren't so two-faced, his therapist calmly asks him, "Who is making decisions for your life *right now*—is it you or is it Emma?"

This stuns him. It's true—for the last four years, he has been blaming a woman who is not even around anymore. By dwelling for years on Emma's culpability, he robbed himself of his own agency and his right to act right here and right now. By wallowing in what had been in the past, he didn't allow himself to ask what *could* be in the future. By holding so tightly on to "Emma wrecked my life," he conveniently avoided the trickier question of, "What am I going to do to build up my life the way I want it?"

We are never responsible for what other people do. But we always have the gift of responsibility for what we do right now regardless of what has come before.

Strategy 4: Continuum of Consciousness
This technique is about shifting focus from the WHY of your experience to the HOW.

How are you responding to life's challenges, experiences, and problems?

How does it feel?

How are you personally carrying this experience?

Too often, we allow our self-exploration quest to be dominated by the question, "Why is this happening?"

But this question can only take you so far. Asking "how" questions actually gives you deeper insight into the unique ways that your experience is unfolding **for you**. No psychological theory can tell you what that is. No amount of reading about other people's experiences will give you a true understanding of your own.

So, before you leap in with "why?" take the time to simply observe and be curious about "how?" Flesh out your experience. Describe it. Take a moment to really perceive what that feels like. For some people, their experiences are better grasped by imagery, metaphor, poems, art, or other non-verbal expressions.

Let's imagine that it's 2020 again and you are battling a raging anxiety demon during the heart of the Covid-19 pandemic. You were always a little OCD about germs, but within a few months, the panicky news coverage has you in a tailspin of full-blown health anxiety.

You're petrified that you'll catch the big bad bug and die, and you can't seem to stop your mind from racing everywhere. Nothing seems to get clean enough. You're lying awake at night, thinking of gnarly worst-case scenarios. Concerned friends and family tell you that you're having a mental health crisis and that your perceptions are distorted.

You ask, "Why is this happening?"

Your already over-anxious brain tries to answer the question. You go back online and fall down rabbit holes, self-diagnosing with exotic psychiatric disorders you've never heard of before. You read journal articles attempting to understand the genetic basis for anxiety disorders. You read opinion pieces from people exploring the political and cultural aspects of the Covid hysteria. Why is this happening? Is it state-funded propaganda on YouTube? Or do they just *want* you to think that? Or are you just anxious because your mom exposed you to too many chemicals during pregnancy?

You can see the problem. "Why" is a question that could potentially provide insight, but it's always of the intellectual kind. For the person with a debilitating germ obsession, delving further into theories and explanations and justifications only fuels the anxiety fires. After all, who ever felt *calmer* after a two-hour Google session that begins with the search "less known signs of cancer"?

Instead, you could ask *how*. Exactly how does your experience go from mild anxiety in the morning to full-blown panic by the afternoon? Well, you might see that you feel worse after hours online doing "research" to help find answers. Forgetting about sensationalist newspaper pieces or what talking heads are saying on the news, you ask *how* your experience is unfolding. Yes, it's a global phenomenon and you're not the only one with anxieties, but what does it all look like for YOU as the unique person you are?

Going down this path, you are actually able to uncover the process and mechanism that is maintaining your anxiety in the present—too much exposure to doom and gloom online. Had you only focused on *why*, you would not have seen what was actually unfolding for you. In fact, you would have stayed in your panic spiral and maybe added a few more anxieties to obsess over ("Oh no! I've just seen an article about how lack of sleep weakens the immune system and makes you more vulnerable to viruses . . . This news is going to keep me up at night!")

Strategy 5: Change Questions into Affirmations
This is a technique that will help you firm up your internal reality and get you into the proactive, responsible mindset. It's a simple but powerful approach that brings both unresolved issues from the past and unreal hypotheticals from the future *into the present*, where they can flow and move again.

Simply take your questions and turn them into affirmative, true statements.

For example, one day you become aware of yourself thinking, "Why do I feel so depressed today?" So, you convert it to: "I feel depressed today."

That's not all, though. Once you definitively make this statement, follow it up with responsible, proactive behavior in the present. Embrace how you feel and face up to it, but then move on, asking what you can do about it *right now*. "I feel depressed today, so I'm going to go for a walk in the sunshine and make sure I get an early night tonight."

As you can see, there is the brave acknowledgment of your present reality, as well as the commitment to taking action—again, in the present reality. If you keep dwelling on questions ("What's wrong with me? Why did she say that? Why am I having so much trouble right now?"), you are actually trapping yourself in a state of mind that exacerbates your suffering rather than addresses it. It's passive, and it encourages a victim mindset.

On the other hand, in stating something outright, you might actually convince yourself of how inaccurate it is. In this case, you can consciously choose to let the statement go and refuse to have it take up any more room in your mind.

Here's an example: You've signed up for a new coding course, but the other students are way more advanced than you and are quickly managing with material you can't make head or tail of. You notice yourself thinking, "Why do I suck at everything I try?"

Here, you pause and decide to make this into a firm statement instead. "I suck at everything I try." Now just pause again and notice what this feels like. Allow your heart and mind to catch up with this new reality. What does that feel like?

"Oh wait, that does sound a bit dramatic. I'm new and haven't had as much experience as those other students, but I take responsibility, and I'm going to keep practicing without getting discouraged." In this way, emotions and perceptions are kept alive and flowing rather than left to stagnate passively.

To understand this, merely consider what would have happened if you had carried on with the train of thought inspired by the question, "Why do I suck at everything I try?"

There are lots of answers to this.

"You're not as good at coding as they are."

"This course isn't right for you."

"Maybe you're just not as smart."

Even though asking such a question *seems* on the surface like a reasonable thing to do, the truth is that it doesn't solve any problem, resolve any issue, or move anything forward. It brings no real insight. But when you say something definitive in the present, you turn a hypothetical into something real, and then you have two options: Either it's true or useful, or it isn't. Maybe you go another way:

"I suck at everything I try. No wait, that doesn't sound right. I don't suck at *everything*, but boy do I seem to suck at coding right now! I'm giving this course a few more weeks, and then I'm going to make a decision on whether to continue." And just like that, you are not wrestling and agonizing over whether you suck or not—you have acknowledged that you do, accepted it, and already made a conscious plan for what to do about it.

Chapter 4: Understanding Internal Family Systems

What you'll learn in this chapter: that there are many parts of you, but well-being occurs when all those parts find a way to live together.

In reading the above technique, you may have noticed that there were seemingly *two* versions of yourself, and these two were in dialogue:

One part of you was critical, stuck in the past, and acting on autopilot.

The other part was wiser, kinder, and able to step in with a more objective rebuttal.

This theme is expanded on in Internal Family Systems, or IFS. The idea is that **everyone is made of several smaller subpersonalities—i.e., the mind is like a mini family.** This means we can talk about and deal with the different inner parts of ourselves in much the same way as we would with a literal family. The roles of each of these parts are not set in stone; we can evolve and change. IFS therapy, then, is about bringing all your separate parts together to work as a whole.

IFS was first introduced by family therapist Richard Schwartz. He described the patterns he noticed in his patients: "What I heard repeatedly were descriptions of what they often called their "parts"—the conflicted subpersonalities that resided within them." He set about trying to understand these parts as well as how they related to one another. If the mind is a family, what does a "happy family" look like?

The theory states that there are probably infinite aspects within each person, but they tend to fall into three main groups:

Firefighter – These are protectors who step in to help when triggered, i.e., "put out the fire" in whatever way possible (healthy and sustainable or not!).

Manager – Manages emotions and situations via planning and control.

Exile – The exile is basically what both the managers and firefighters are working to contain. The exile's job is to hold difficult feelings of shame, pain, or hurt from previous unresolved experiences.

These parts of us all have a purpose. Even the "bad parts"! When you work with an IFS therapist, your goal is to find out what that purpose is.

As an example, you may have experienced a trauma in your childhood that created feelings of anger and rage in you. These feelings are exiled when the manager steps in to suppress and contain them. Furthermore, when these feelings of rage and anger do break free, the firefighter is ready to step in and manage the emergency. This may be in the form of addictive behaviors that numb and distract, or projection onto someone else so that you don't have to face the exile too closely.

An IFS therapist will typically walk you through a six-part process, but you can replicate the same thing on your own:

Step 1: Find

As with so many of the techniques we'll discuss in this book, begin by becoming aware. Notice all sensations, as well as how your body and mind are connected. Perhaps you notice a tightness in your stomach.

Step 2: Focus

Instead of avoiding or fleeing these sensations, put your focus more intently on them. Notice this feeling of stomach tightness, for example, without letting your mind wander somewhere else.

Step 3: Flesh Out

Once you have sustained attention on a sensation or a part of yourself, try to expand on it.

What emotions are connected to it? Do any other ideas or associations come to mind? For example, maybe you realize that this stomach tightness feels a little like anxiety, but a particular kind of anxiety. Maybe certain colors and images spring to mind, or you imagine a person, symbol, or image that embodies this specific sensation.

Step 4: Feel Toward

Become aware of how you feel toward this fleshed-out sensation. What kind of a role does it play in your life? How do you respond? Maybe you notice that this is a regular sensation for you, and that when it comes up, you tend to panic and do what you can to ignore it or distract yourself.

Step 5: Befriend

Here's where the hardest work happens: instead of ignoring or distracting yourself, you decide to get to know this part better.

Imagine it literally is a long-lost friend or estranged family member you are welcoming back into your life. Now, you don't have to embrace it or pretend that it feels better than it does. All you have to do is see it, acknowledge it, and accept it for what it is. Also, accepting it doesn't mean you necessarily want that feeling to stay there forever!

Step 6: Explore Your Fear

Many of these parts of us are there for one reason: fear. So now, ask this part of yourself: "What are you afraid will happen if you're not here?" Try to imagine what this part of yourself is trying to achieve, and what role its presence plays for you. Maybe you notice that this anxious knot in your stomach is actually, in its own strange way, trying to protect you.

What this six-step process does is normalize your reactions and bring them all together as one. IFS has much in common with Gestalt therapy since it's all about holistic wellbeing. It also relates to Jung's shadow work because in engaging the different parts of ourselves, we are re-claiming previously disinherited aspects with acceptance and compassion.

IFS therapy works because it encourages awareness and invites us to look at ourselves with kindness and as *wholes*. Also, instead of pathologizing parts of ourselves, we accept them and become curious.

What role is this part playing? If we can understand its purpose, we can choose to fulfil that purpose in a healthier, more conscious way. We can say, "Thank you, stomach pain, for trying to keep me safe, but there is nothing to fear."

Finally, IFS is a great way to deepen body-mind connection, and so may help with issues like chronic pain or the physical sides of depression and anxiety. That's because rather than seeing any sensation as a problem, we simply embrace it and welcome it into the "family"!

Here are a few more things to keep in mind:

- As you become aware, try personifying parts of yourself and literally asking, "Who needs attention right now?"
- Often, "reactive" parts of us (i.e., those acting up with pain or unpleasant sensations) simply need validation and attention. You don't necessarily have to **do** anything, just **be with** the feeling.
- Set aside judgment by continually asking what this part's "job" is. How did it get that job (i.e., what early experiences brought it into being)? If it didn't have to do this job, what would it prefer to do instead? What would happen if it stopped doing its job?

These kinds of questions may feel a little corny at first, but they can be powerful. You may find out, for example, that, "If I let go of this fear, I'm afraid everything will go wrong," or, "It's my job to keep the other parts safe by controlling everything."

And so here we arrive at the three types again. The managers and firefighters will typically work hard to keep the exile at bay. For example, part of you may be sincerely depressed and hopeless, but another part is valiantly trying to put on a brave face and not let on how scared the other parts feel.

In other words, the parts of yourself are *in relationship*. One part of you may be trying to manage the others, a second part may be hiding away in shame, and a third part may be trying to pull everything together.

The goal of IFS is not to eliminate these different parts of yourself and pick the winner. Rather, it's the same goal as conventional family therapy: to get all the parts working in healthy, happy harmony. Some parts may release on their own once they realize they are no longer needed, or they may evolve and update, but this is not because they have been shunned or forced out of awareness.

The IFS model doesn't see people as just a mess of different sub-personalities, though. There is a Core Self at the center of it all, and in fact, it's this part that recognizes the existence of the other parts, observing and identifying certain triggers and reactions and consciously deciding to be more productive and more accepting.

The healthy, balanced Core Self is

- Confident
- Calm
- Creative
- Clear
- Curious
- Courageous
- Compassionate
- Connected
- Present
- Patient
- Persistent
- Playful
- Able to have perspective

To the extent that you are able to feel the above is the extent to which your Core Self is developed, and the degree to which you are consciously engaging with the present. Our goal with IFS, then, is to

1. Free certain parts of ourselves from extreme and unproductive roles
2. Rekindle trust in our Core Self
3. Harmonize all parts of ourselves in awareness and acceptance so they can work as a whole

If all of this sounds complicated, it needn't be. We can use this model any time we become aware of a difficult or unpleasant sensation. Turning inward, we can ask, *What part of me is this? What is its function?*

Consider the example of Jessie, who is gradually becoming aware of her habit of choosing cruel, emotionally distant boyfriends. She is beginning to see a pattern and recognize a recurrent feeling: When her boyfriend gets angry, raises his voice, and starts to express his temper around her, she gets a sickening feeling in the pit of her stomach.

She instantly starts to soothe and placate him, smiling, trying to help . . . Only, her fussing often seems to make him angrier. One day when this happens, she decides to pay attention instead to what is going on with *her*. She takes a moment for herself, paying attention to the weird feeling in her gut. She doesn't flee this feeling. Ordinarily, she'd smile and try to act like everything was fine, attempting to quickly pacify and soothe other people—not just her boyfriend. But now, she sits with the feeling in her gut instead. She doesn't smile or rush in to quickly give people whatever they want to make them calm down again.

Fleshing this feeling out, she realizes that she is afraid—*very* afraid. She sees a vision of herself as a little girl desperately trying to get angry grown-ups to stop fighting and yelling. She then sees a vision of herself as a little lap dog rolling over on her back to expose her belly to an angry wolf. The feeling in her gut seems to say, "If I'm sweet and kind and helpful and never get angry, then you can't hurt me."

It takes a few separate occasions for Jessie to become more and more familiar with this feeling—and comfortable with just exploring it rather than defaulting to her usual placating behavior. Every time she does, she gains more insight. She starts to connect this gut feeling with her mother, who had a violent temper. And she then starts to see that these two experiences—the need to placate and the feeling in her stomach—are actually two parts of her.

The fear in her gut is a young, vulnerable child whose primary caregivers are behaving in scary and unreliable ways—this is the IFS "exile" feeling. Her knee-jerk tendency to calm down and placate angry people is more of a "manager" helping to protect and take care of the fearful child part. It's this manager part that steps in, saying, "Okay, where's the threat? Let's do whatever we can to calm this person down so we'll be safe. Let's smile and fuss and tell them whatever they want to hear."

Once she does this, Jessie can see the reason that *both* these parts exist in her life. She can accept and love that frightened child, but she can also thank the part that rushes in to smile and placate—it is only doing its best to help. Jessie begins to understand something else: When she was young, being small and vulnerable, the "placating manager" was all she had. That part was brave and did its very best to help her, even though the strategy doesn't work so well as an adult.

There is another part in Jessie that is growing stronger. It's a calm, confident part of her that is all grown up and confident in its ability to set boundaries and assert them when people go too far. One day, when her boyfriend loses his temper and starts yelling in a threatening way, the familiar pang in her gut appears. But this time, Jessie allows her Core Self to step in and take charge of the situation.

Internally, she tells that frightened, exiled child, "Don't worry, I'm here to look after you." She tells the fretful manager, "Thank you for all you've done for me, but we don't need to do that placating and simpering and smiling anymore. You can relax now."

Then, to her boyfriend, she squares her shoulders and says calmly, "You're angry. But don't ever speak to me in that tone of voice again. I'm going out now. We can talk about this later, when you've calmed down." While there may still be some drama in Jessie's immediate future, it's clear that she has taken the first giant step toward releasing those old patterns and opening the way for something better.

How you use this technique in your own life is up to you. You could keep a journal or combine this approach with some of the techniques already discussed above, especially the empty chair technique. You could draw a diagram illustrating your different aspects, or even play around with creating dialogues between all the parts—as you do so, you are strengthening your Core Self.

As you can imagine, IFS isn't appropriate for those who are dealing with delusions, psychosis, or schizophrenia, for obvious reasons. If you find that engaging with the separate parts of yourself is an overwhelming, threatening, or just plain weird idea, then give it a miss. There are plenty of alternative techniques to try.

Takeaways

- No matter who you are, it is possible to improve your life with the same evidence-based techniques used by cognitive behavioral therapists all over the world, i.e., self-therapy can help you live the life you want to live.
- Begin with asking who you are—that is, engaging in self-exploration. With practice, the habit of asking, "What do I notice about myself right now?" will become easier.
- Use Dr. Tom Stevens' six-step approach for cultivating self-exploration: 1) turn on your "inner noticer" and observe yourself without judgment, 2) zoom in on "the problem", 3) follow the strongest emotion, 4) allow yourself to notice any emerging patterns or overarching themes, 5) see what core beliefs are linking everything together, and 6) use these insights to inspire new, more conscious behavior.
- Carl Jung was the first to talk about the shadow, which is an archetype containing all the unconscious and disowned parts of our psyche. We reintegrate the shadow with patience, non-judgmental acceptance, honesty, and the willingness to face our dark side. We can do this by noticing disproportionate emotional reactions that may hint at the shadow's presence, mindfully embrace our imperfections and weaknesses (humor helps), as well as ask others for their honest feedback on what we can't see in ourselves.
- Gestalt therapy is about understanding how your perception shapes your world, as well as releasing the past so you are more fully available to respond to the present. Some ways to do this include 1) rehearse acts of closure, 2) try the empty chair technique, 3) claim responsibility for your life, 4) shift from the WHY of your experience to the HOW, 5) change questions into affirmations.
- Internal Family Systems posits that the mind is made of many parts in relationship: firefighters, managers, and exiles. Befriend and feel into difficult emotions and normalize them by asking the role they play in your life.

Part 2: So, How Did You Get Here?

As you practice growing your self-awareness, as you engage your shadow and bring it into the light, and as you use various Gestalt techniques to strengthen your conscious living in the moment, you may start to encounter something ironic. You may discover that increasing awareness in the present tends to show you just how much is unresolved and unacknowledged in the past!

In Part 2, we expand our awareness to take a broader view of our context, our history, and all those early life experiences that shaped the people we are today. Again, the goal is not to dwell or to passively bemoan everything that went wrong. Rather, we are looking to understand, with a purpose to rewrite, release, or even challenge those early experiences.

Let's begin by considering one of the biggest influences on the way we think: the earliest bond we developed with our primary caregivers.

Chapter 5: What is Your Attachment Style?

What you'll learn in this chapter: how your attachment style influences everything in your life, how to identify it, and how to work around it as a conscious, proactive adult in the present.

It's not a surprise that our environment and the formative relationships of our childhood years play a big part in who we are as adults. Yes, it is our responsibility to face ourselves as we are, warts and all, in the present. But you've also probably wondered more than once, "Where did all of this come from?"

Before we embark on questions of early childhood attachment and the inner child, we should note one important caveat: we seek to understand our childhoods not so we can blame others, get trapped in pessimism, or dwell in perpetual victimhood. We seek to understand so that we can reclaim conscious, responsible control over ourselves in the present.

British psychologist John Bowlby was the first to pioneer the theory of attachment styles. He suggested that all children come into the world with an evolutionarily programmed and innate need to form attachments to primary caregivers because that is the only way they can survive. During the critical period from infancy to around five years old, the developing child is sensitive to the quality of this primary attachment.

In 1952, together with researcher James Robertson, Bowlby observed that children demonstrate distress whenever their mothers are separated from them. They initially protest, then they experience despair, and finally they appear to detach altogether, even rejecting the primary caregiver.

He also noticed that during experiments, infants had different responses to being separated from their mothers. Some were upset but could be soothed on the mother's return, others were upset but continued to be upset despite the mother's return, and still others appeared completely disinterested by either the mother's presence or absence—as though they had already detached. Some babies showed no discernable pattern at all and were anxious one moment, aloof the next. Why?

For Bowlby, the reason is that each of these children was working from a unique "internal working model" inspired by their early attachment experiences. This model is a cognitive framework that helps them understand themselves, other people, and the world at large. Not only did Bowlby think that this was evidence for the way that early childhood experiences shape children's experience, but that these early models were in fact prototypes for adult relationships, too.

For him, the attachment bond is the emotional connection you develop with a primary caregiver—usually your mother. **The nature of this bond serves as an early template or model, influencing all other relationships you have in your life**. It becomes the single biggest influence for how you handle intimacy as an adult—and it's on a physiological level, too, since the infant's developing brain will literally take shape to adapt to the environment it finds itself in.

People's attachment styles vary according to what they've learned in those early relationships to caregivers. The idea is that if you had a stable, caring, and responsive bond with your caregiver, you developed a **secure attachment style**. When a caregiver responds to a helpless child's nonverbal cues for their needs to be met, those children grow up to be confident, self-aware, trusting, and able to form good relationships with others. These were the children who were distressed at their mother's absence but able to be comforted when she returned.

Other characteristics and behaviors resulting from secure attachment include:

- Empathy skills
- Good boundaries
- High self-worth
- More satisfying relationships
- Good communication skills
- The ability to express needs honestly
- Trust
- Ability to be alone, but valuing connection
- Mature, able to manage conflict and bounce back from disappointments

You don't need perfect care one hundred percent of the time to have formed a secure attachment. Similarly, just because you are securely attached doesn't mean you never experience relationship difficulties. But good-enough parenting most of the time may have convinced you of some very lasting core beliefs about the world being a generally safe place, and that you and other people are largely good and can be trusted.

Without consistently responsive caregiving, however, you would develop an **insecure attachment style**. This is characterized by difficulties around intimacy, and connections that are too distant, too clingy, too anxious, or a little of all of these—hence too chaotic!

There are three main types of insecure attachment:

1. **Ambivalent**

Also called "anxious," this attachment style is characterized by neediness, uncertainty, and low self-esteem. Intimacy is desired, but there is a constant fear that others don't want to provide it. This is the person who can't help but worry whether their partner loves them, and is often embarrassed by their own clinginess. These were the children who were upset to be left alone, but who could not be comforted even after the mother returned. At the core of this experience may be the anxious belief, "You're here now ... but for how long? When will the other shoe drop?"

Such a person may make their partners the center of their world and have difficulty trusting them or letting them have their own space, feeling that the distance provokes panic. They may have trouble with boundaries and feel worthless unless validated in a relationship. They may be jealous or even manipulative, or simply ask for constant reassurance.

The reason makes sense: this person's early caregiver relationship was inconsistent, which means the child learned to be anxious, never quite knowing if their needs would be met or not.

2. **Avoidant-Dismissive**

This style, however, is the opposite. People with this attachment style don't crave intimacy but resist it, feeling that closeness is threatening, so they'd prefer to meet their own needs and never rely on others. These are the people who value their independence, but they can feel claustrophobic in relationships and so uncomfortable with emotions (their own and others') that they appear cold and aloof.

Can you guess which infant group this was in Bowlby's experiments? It was the group of infants who were indifferent either by the mother's presence or their absence. Bowlby knew that all children moved through stages of distress after separation: First, they cried, then they became quiet but filled with despair, and eventually, perhaps because they realized they were alone, they stopped fretting and simply ignored the mother, seeking out other caregivers or perhaps attempting to do without a caregiver at all.

This makes sense from an evolutionary perspective. An abandoned young animal in the wild will first call in distress for its mother, but if she doesn't come, it will stop drawing attention to itself and go quiet—but not without some dejection. Finally, it learns to just do without. Remembering that baby animals are entirely dependent on their primary caregivers, we know the resulting core belief here is naturally, "Well, if you can't care for me, then I'm just going to have to make sure I don't need you anymore and can take care of myself."

Such a person may prefer shallow, fleeting connections where they can maintain their freedom, and they may cause damage when they dismiss others' emotions or even are unfaithful. As much as they resist it, they may still pine for connection but not know how to initiate it.

Their early caregiver relationship was one where they felt rejected. Rather than inconsistent care, there was very little care at all. This means that such a child would have been forced to intentionally disconnect to protect themselves, self-soothing with the idea that they could meet their own needs instead.

3. **Disorganized or Chaotic**

If your early caregiver relationship was abusive, traumatic, or neglectful, you may develop complex feelings around relationships, and even believe that you are undeserving of love or intimacy. You might not have had your needs met, yet still not have learned to meet them yourself, so your world and the people in it can feel unsafe and unpredictable. These are the children who displayed chaotic and unpredictable responses to being separated from their caregivers.

As adults, they may find relationships distressing and confusing and swing from one extreme to the next. They may experience addiction and show other destructive behaviors like aggression, violence, or drug use. They may deeply crave connection but violently push it away when it happens, alternatively controlling or feeling controlled. Relationships for those with disorganized attachment styles can feel scary and disorienting.

In each of the three styles above, the initial relationship echoes into adulthood. A person may have a mix of styles, and importantly, it's not about a caregiver's behavior so much as the infant's *perception* of that behavior.

Consider Lydia and Mike.

Lydia is the child of teenage parents who divorced when she was young. Being passed back and forth from mother to father to concerned family members, Lydia felt unwanted as a child, and consequently, she is now the type to cling tightly to anyone who shows her a shred of affection. She has low self-esteem and is never single; typically, she seeks out people who are unsuitable and emotionally unavailable, and unconsciously tries to "convince" them to stay with her.

Enter Mike, who is the child of an overachieving single mother who depended heavily on him for emotional support. His mother was demanding, intrusive, and emotionally intense, but it was all about her. Mike felt that she never really cared about or understood *him* as a person, and he left home as soon as he could.

When Lydia and Mike meet, it's as though their issues click into one another like terrible puzzle pieces. He is distant and avoidant, fleeing emotional demands and intimacy—but the more he does this, the more Lydia feels that she ought to pursue him and win him over. Without knowing it, echoes from their past are playing out in their current adult relationship. They are both unconsciously replaying the old dynamics—Lydia being the pursuer, and Mike fleeing (while on some level, secretly wanting to be pursued).

Because attachment styles are all about relationship dynamics, it's often something that people first become aware of in the context of a relationship with someone else. Both Lydia and Mike need to figure out healthier, more conscious ways of connecting if their relationship has a chance of surviving.

Knowing all this, how can we use attachment theory to improve our own lives?

The first step is to identify what attachment style you might have. Then, crucially, realize that this can change—you are not doomed to stay that way forever! The more you understand about how your relationship mindset came to be, the more you can empower yourself to take steps to correct it. Here are some simple ideas.

Tip 1: Become Aware of Your Nonverbal Communication Patterns

Our earliest communication with our primary caregivers was nonverbal. Whenever you interact with others, you are (unconsciously) replicating that same dynamic in your gestures, tone, eye contact, and word choice.

For example, Lydia might notice that whenever she is with Mike, she talks the most. It's as though she is afraid that if she isn't talking, his attention will wander and she'll lose him. Mike might notice that he has a tendency to physically remove himself from interactions, especially those he sees as making emotional demands on him. He'll be present, but with arms crossed, body turned sideways, and minimal eye contact. He'll also give monosyllabic answers or allow himself to be distracted by his phone during conversations.

You can immediately improve your relationships with others by consciously paying attention to the unconscious messages you may be sending. The next time you enter a conversation, deliberately relax and open your body, take deep belly breaths, and smile. Be in the moment, right now, rather than continuing on with momentum from the past. It makes an enormous difference!

Tip 2: Develop Your Emotional Intelligence

The good news is that by applying some of the techniques in this book, developing your emotional intelligence is precisely what you're doing. Emotional intelligence, or EQ, is the ability to understand and regulate your own emotions so that you can empathize, communicate, and manage conflict. Improving your EQ will take a lifetime, but you can take a few easy first steps by making sure you are being present in every interaction you have with others.

Go calm and quiet in yourself and bring awareness to what is actually going on in an interaction. Truly listen. Bring your focus to everything the other person is communicating, not just the words they're saying. Notice how you feel in response. The start of any emotionally intelligent response is simply to have the presence of mind to ask, "What is going on with me emotionally right now? What about the other person?"

For Lydia, she is learning to recognize when she is in "clinging" mode and instead choosing not to pursue. She is trying to train herself to realize that Mike's tendency to withdraw is *not* a reflection of her value as a person. When he pulls back, she sits with her feelings and learns to soothe herself.

By doing this, she stops pursuing Mike, who is then free to figure out for himself what intimacy is, whether he wants it or not, and how it looks when expressed in a healthy way. He creates distance, but when Lydia doesn't come chasing him, after a while, he realizes that he *does* value emotional closeness—but the healthy kind. He takes the initiative and discovers for himself the value of vulnerability and of Lydia herself.

Tip 3: Find a Role Model

Sometimes, secure attachment is easier to feel than it is to understand. If you befriend people who have a secure attachment style, you can learn from them, modeling your behavior based on theirs. If you try to relate to someone who is also insecurely attached, then you can both destabilize one another and cause more pain and confusion. But a securely attached person can regulate and calm the interaction.

It may take a little time, but a securely attached partner or friend can gradually show you what it means to trust, to have boundaries, to accept with compassion, and so on. It's so much easier to spot your own unhelpful patterns of behavior if it's in the context of a normal, safe relationship. Alternatively, you might decide that for this issue, seeking a therapist or other mentor can help you "practice" what it means to live as someone who is comfortable and competent with intimacy.

In Lydia and Mike's case, their complementary attachment issues allowed them to work *together* on creating a more securely attached relationship in the present. In fact, some therapists believe that this is precisely why we are drawn to the people who most push our buttons this way—it is because through them, we have a chance of facing and finally releasing our respective old patterns from the past. If you are in a challenging relationship right now, take heart; with a little conscious intention and the willingness to do the emotional work, the relationship can be a precious opportunity to break old patterns once and for all—and experience the kind of healthy connection you were both craving all along.

Tip 4: Challenge Yourself

Finally, if you are aware that you have certain tendencies in relationships, you can consciously choose to challenge yourself to do something different. If you know that you have issues with trust, for example, ask if you can push yourself to go out of your comfort zone and trust anyway, just to see what happens. Pay attention to the result and then adjust. In this way, you construct behavioral experiments that teach you to test out different mindsets (we'll cover more on behavioral experiments in a later chapter).

All humans need and crave healthy connections with others, but our early experiences can interfere with the way we seek out, maintain, and provide intimacy with others. Perhaps it doesn't ultimately work out with Lydia and Mike. But fast forward a few years, and maybe Lydia has realized that the surest path to her development is to remain single and learn to be confident and secure in her own self-love before thinking of starting another romantic relationship.

Perhaps Mike unconsciously orchestrates a subsequent relationship that he *cannot* leave—his next relationship is with a woman who falls pregnant almost instantly. The responsibilities of fatherhood and the chance to explore the issue of attachment but from "the other side" are precisely the challenges he most needs to grow as a person.

All of the above doesn't just apply to romantic relationships, however. Any connection we have to other human beings, in any capacity, is a reflection of our attachment style. Our attachment style can affect everything in life because relationships are such a core part of the human experience. It can influence our self-concept and our perceptions and determine the behaviors we choose.

If you notice repeated patterns in your relationships, become curious about what early dynamics you may be repeating. You were helpless and dependent as a child when you first adapted to your caregivers and formed your attachment style. But right now, you are an adult who has the power of awareness and conscious responsibility, so you can choose to re-work those patterns into something that helps you connect to others in the ways you want to.

Chapter 6: How to Reparent Your Inner Child

What you'll learn in this chapter: what your inner child is, how it affects your life as an adult, and six ways you can begin meeting needs that originally went unmet in your childhood.

The theory of the inner child (originally introduced by psychotherapist Carl Jung) rests on the idea that right now, we are all every age we have ever been. As we grow, we add more layers onto our psyches, but at the very core is still the little child we once were. The inner child was once vulnerable and impressionable, and during its earliest experiences with caregivers, its emotions and core beliefs were put in place.

Depending on our earliest childhood experiences, that inner child may be feeling alone, afraid, hurt, or confused. Resolving and healing this pain is what inner child work is all about. By going back to "reparent" ourselves, we put to rest unresolved issues from the past and free ourselves to engage with the present in a more whole, happy, and healthy way.

What do you think your inner child would say to you if it could speak?

Would it cry or throw a tantrum? Play and be carefree? Ask for reassurance?

You may never have considered actively engaging this emotional, unconscious part of yourself, but doing so may be one of the most powerful forms of self-therapy you'll ever try. That's because when your inner child is happy and well, you are able to move on in life with more energy, creativity, authenticity, and contentment.

Though your childhood is over, its effects can live on in the present in the form of learned behavior and attitudes. For example, if we learned in early childhood that the world was an unsafe place and that it was useless to ask others to meet our needs, we may grow up to be quite pessimistic and independent, never quite trusting others.

We may see this childhood pain reflected in all our adulthood relationships—that is, until we can go back to that inner child and resolve the issue ourselves. The idea is that ignoring or repressing this pain won't make it go away. It is only by acknowledging, accepting, and healing it that we move on.

If you're wondering whether this kind of work is difficult, scary, or time-consuming, well, it can be! It's also usually something that is done with the help of a trained therapist. However, you may be surprised at just how intuitive these exercises are and how much you enjoy them once you try them for yourself.

Reparenting Yourself

In the seventies, Dr. Lucia Capacchione used art therapy to help her clients access and heal their inner children. The goal is to reclaim and reconnect with parts of yourself that have been neglected, much like the process for shadow work described above. The principles are simple because they are not all that different from the way we parent children normally: by making sure they feel loved, safe, valued, and seen.

When, how, and how often you do the following techniques and exercises is up to you. Try them when you're feeling emotional, overwhelmed, or confused. At times like these, there's a good chance your wounded inner child has been activated, so it's an opportunity to step in and engage with them directly. Alternatively try them daily, either in the morning or evening as part of your everyday routines, or incorporate them into other techniques like journaling and visualization.

Reparenting yourself can be summed up very simply: **it's the act of recognizing what needs went unmet for your childhood self and committing to giving that to yourself, right now in the present.**

This idea alone can be liberating. It's never too late to give yourself what you once needed, and the results can be miraculous! If adult problems stem from unmet childhood needs, then meeting those needs in the present has the effect of releasing us from that childhood pain and allowing us to move on, healed.

Here are some practical exercises to try for yourself. Be patient, be kind, and be creative because your inner child is just that—a child. That means they're unique, and what they need most is love and understanding.

Prompt 1: Meet Your Inner Child

Center yourself with a few deep breaths, close your eyes, and try to imagine yourself as a child. See the younger you. What do they look like, what are they doing, and how are they feeling? Relax and let images bubble up for you. Do any particular conversations emerge, or are you reminded of any particular events or memories? Imagine what your inner child is saying or asking for.

If you like, imagine introducing yourself to them. A great way to do this is to find old childhood pictures to jog your memory and give you a visual anchor. "Hello, I'm you but older. It's nice to meet you." Try not to self-censor or judge what comes up for you (i.e., don't tell yourself, "This is silly").

Prompt 2: Start a Dialogue

You want to earn your inner child's trust and let them know that you want the best for them. In your visualization, avoid barging in to tell that inner child what to do, or judging them. Instead, let them speak for themselves in an open-ended dialogue.

Write a letter from your childhood self to your adult self, or vice versa. Remember that facts and details don't matter—feelings do. No perception or perspective is wrong, and you are not on a fact-finding mission.

Simply ask, what did you miss out on as a child? What did you need to hear? What did you wish the adults around you could have provided for you? Then listen with a kind and open heart to the answers that emerge.

Prompt 3: Connect the Past with the Present

Inner child work can take time. To process the past, look for recurrent emotional themes in the dialogues you have with your inner child. Then ask yourself if you feel similarly now as an adult. Can you see any connections or patterns linking the present with the past?

A good idea is to ask, "In what ways did I have to adapt as a child to survive not having my needs met?" Look at your adult life and see if you can identify that learned pattern. For example, as a child, you might have had an insecure attachment style. This led you to adapt by creating a certain core belief about yourself: "If I am perfect and serve everyone's needs, then I can be useful to people and they won't abandon me."

Looking at your adult life, you can see how this core belief impacted your relationships. Now you have a reason to let go of this ingrained pattern and start to engage with others in healthier, more authentic ways.

Prompt 4: Give Yourself Now What You Needed Then

You can come right out and ask, "Inner child, what do you need?"

You could then ask the adult version of yourself to step in and parent the child version of yourself. Do this by:

- Visualizing an encounter with your inner child—for example, in a guided meditation.
- Writing a letter to your inner child to reassure them.

- Writing down or rehearsing a dialogue—try using the Gestalt empty chair technique.
- Literally giving your inner child a little gift or taking them somewhere special. For example, if you felt that your creativity was dismissed as a child, you could go buy some craft supplies and gift wrap them for your inner child. "This is for you—I can't wait to see what you create!"
- Using the insight you gain from a dialogue with your inner child, agree to make changes in your life that reflect your commitment to healing that most vulnerable part of yourself. For example, you may set new boundaries at work, book a long-overdue doctor's appointment, or enjoy a little self-care.

Prompt 5: Use Affirmations

Depending on what your inner child most needed to hear growing up, craft a few sentences that affirm your love and compassion for them:

"You belong."

"You deserve love and respect."

"You are safe."

"You are great just the way you are."

"It's okay to play, to explore, and to express yourself."

"There is enough, and you are enough."

Say these affirmations to yourself whenever you remember. Try writing them at the top of each page of your journal or weave them into meditations and visualizations where you talk to your inner child. By doing so, you are gently re-writing the script you learned all those years ago.

Back then, you were small, defenseless, and completely dependent on your caregivers. But now, as an adult, you are stronger, more self-aware, and able to consciously choose whether to hold on to these self-limiting beliefs or create something better.

Prompt 6: Go on a Playdate

This may feel awkward at first but may be the easiest activity of all. Your inner child loves to play and have fun! So, dedicate some time in your schedule to letting them do just that. Forget what you *should* be doing and just be creative, playful, and light. Have ice cream on top of your cereal if you want to, run as fast as you can through a field, paint faces on rocks you found on the beach, or sing at the top of your lungs without a care for what it sounds like!

For just a moment, put down your burdens; let go of shame, guilt, and anxiety; and reconnect with that childlike part of you that is briming with optimism, hope, and possibility.

Chapter 7: Rewrite the Story of Your Life

What you'll learn in this chapter: that you are the author of your own life, and that it's never too late to rewrite the story.

When you practice self-therapy and re-parent your inner child, you are doing something special: re-writing your life script.

"I'm so shy; I could never do something like that."
"I was a wild child!"
"I'm pretty unlucky."
"I'm not a math person."
"Women always leave me eventually."

Every time you repeat statements like the ones above, you reveal the unconscious narrative you have taken on for your life.

Imagine two friends go out to an Ethiopian restaurant that serves cuisine none of them are familiar with. Friend A says, "Oh, I'm such a foodie. I love all these interesting new dishes. Don't you?"

Friend B says, "Nope! I can't even pronounce these names . . . Do you think they serve just normal things?"

Friend A orders something exotic and unpronounceable, and Friend B manages to convince the waitress to bring her a plate of fries. The fries come, and she discovers a deep-fried Band-Aid hidden amongst them. "That's typical! It'll always be me . . ." she says.

Friend A looks at Friend B and says, "You always were fussy!"

Friend B retaliates. "It's because I'm a *supertaster*. I can't handle certain textures; it's just the way I am."

Friend A rolls her eyes and thinks to herself, *I'm way more adventurous and open-minded than she is.*

A self-narrative is exactly like a movie script, telling us the role we play and what kind of story we're living. Friend A and Friend B have, essentially, *typecast themselves* in their own life movies. Friend B always plays the role of fussy stick-in-the-mud, and Friend A always plays the role of adventurous, open-minded gourmand. They always have the same type of conversation, too (B: "Oh my God, you did *what*?" A: "Oh, come on, live a little!").

The thing is, although the script may feel like it's written in stone, it isn't—it was put there by our life experiences and can absolutely be changed. After all, neither of these women were born this way. And there is nothing at all stopping either of them from waking up tomorrow and behaving in completely different ways.

We all play roles and work our way through the same old scripts. But first, we need to be aware of the fact that we are doing it in the first place.

Our self-perception can become so automatic and ingrained that we don't see it anymore and simply assume it's fact. We may have been given a narrative as children when we were too young to really understand it, either by our caregivers or society at large, and then internalized that perception and took it on as our own.

In your narrative, you may be the villain, the hero, or the victim. You may be an introvert or a black sheep or a playboy or a . . . supertaster. This narrative shapes everything in your life—how you engage with others, how you feel about yourself, your identity and sense of purpose, your choices and how you interpret events—EVERYTHING!

In our very trivial example, Friend B is consciously making choices in accordance with who she thinks she already is—she refuses to try something new and orders French fries. It may sound far-out to say that our thoughts create our reality, but this is precisely what Friend B does. In her case, the reality she creates for herself is one without interesting new foods!

What's more, when she discovers the Band-Aid, she voluntarily announces that she is precisely the kind of person this *always* happens to. This belief, too, will affect her life as surely as her habit of ordering the safest thing on the menu. Consider, for example, that every time she encounters something disappointing, uncomfortable, or unjust, she will essentially tell herself, "This is normal. This is just how it goes for me."

The attitude that Friend B displays in the restaurant may be just the same attitude that allows her to stay in a dead marriage, forego her fitness goals, or blandly accept inconsiderate treatment at work. After all, it's only a matter of time until she meets someone who agrees with the role she's assigned herself, right? Friend B might wonder why she's constantly passed over for promotions or new opportunities at work, but fails to see that people are only responding to the invisible sign she's wearing on her head: "I don't like new things! I take zero risks and prefer being passive!"

But, if you change the narrative, everything else changes, too. Your entire life can be transformed if you can transform the story that your life runs on.

This is where narrative therapy can help. Devised by therapist Michael White, narrative therapy is a way of consciously reclaiming your life's meaning. Instead of living *inside* the script, you step *outside* of it and look at it objectively. Narrative therapy tells us:

- We are all unique, and our experience and perception matters. We are enough as we are.
- We don't need to blame or point fingers; the idea is to understand and take ownership of stories, not condemn them.
- We are not our thoughts, and we can externalize our problems. Our stories can change.
- We are each the experts on our own lives, and *we* are the authors.

There are many useful narrative therapy techniques out there, but one exercise is especially suited for those wanting to practice self-therapy. The My Life Story exercise is based on the principles of narrative therapy and encourages a holistic perspective on your past and present.

The goal is to create an outline of your life that does not revolve around negative memories and pain as much as moments of intensity or growth. By doing so, you cultivate a broader, richer perspective of your life. When we internalize a narrative, we tend to pay more attention to evidence that confirms our beliefs, thus forming a self-fulfilling prophecy. We also tend to exaggerate the negative while overlooking the positive. The My Life Story exercise works to counterbalance this tendency.

My Life Story Exercise:

Step One

Begin with a title (and maybe a subtitle), something that you feel captures the essence of your life. For example: *"To the Top of the Wrong Mountain, a story by Sarah Jones."*

Step Two

Write at least six chapter titles that reflect significant moments in your life history. Focus on life stages or key pivotal events. Then, write one or two sentences to describe each chapter.

For example, "Chapter 4: The Work Tunnel. *For four years, I worked hard on that PhD, and when I came up for air, I realized that my whole life had changed around me while I was stuck with my nose in a book. Still, I relished the fact that during that period, I seemed to have been christened The Clever One."*

Continue with all the chapters.

Step Three

Write the final chapter of your life, which includes future dreams, aspirations, goals, and a game plan. This chapter should be longer and more detailed than the others because it is closest to the present and will likely contain themes and issues that are most relevant to you right now.

For example, you could write, "Chapter 10: Finding My Truth. *In the future, I learn more about my own values and make my life according to what I want rather than what is conventionally deemed 'successful.' I find my happily ever after—on my own terms!*"

Step Four

After writing the final chapter, you can go back and add more sentences to the earlier chapters if you would like, but it's not necessary. Remember that this exercise is not about accurately documenting memories or creating a biography for someone else to read. It's more about making an outline or framework to help you identify patterns and gather the emotional checkpoints of your life.

To help you reflect, try using these questions:

- Are there any recurring themes, symbols, or ideas in my chapters?
- Is there a progression or development across all these chapters or events?
- Does the story fit with how I think of myself today? Does it align with how other people view me?
- Is there anything about myself that I used to think or believe but no longer do?
- What do I want to change about my story moving forward? How would I prefer to think of myself?
- If I were rewriting this story, how would I do it?
- Where did this story or this theme come from? When did I first start thinking of myself this way?
- What chapters need to be added in order to bridge the gap between today and the final conclusion?
- Are there different ways to interpret or understand these events? Can I look at them through a different lens now that they are in the past?

For some people, overarching narrative themes become clear when they are made visual—for example, in a diagram. Another way to do the above exercise is to draw out a map or graph of your life so far. Put time along the x-axis, and emotional intensity or happiness/well-being on the y-axis.

Now, as you move through your life, chart the "beats" or main events where things changed. For example, the line may go up sharply after your marriage, but then, after an illness or financial trouble, drop down again. Sometimes, seeing everything on one page can reveal patterns that look so obvious in hindsight but were nevertheless hidden from your awareness.

For example, you may notice that every single one of your major life transitions has centered around the ups and downs of romantic relationships. Seeing it all laid out this way gives you the insight that you have been unconsciously defining your identity and self-worth according to your relationship status.

Narrative therapy is a post-modern approach, which means that one of its principles is that there is no underlying "objective reality" and that our memories, our self-concept, and our stories are all social and psychological constructs. However, that doesn't mean we cannot gain more insight by finding a "trusted editor" as a second pair of eyes.

If you have a close friend or confidante, you might choose to run your story past them to see what they think. They may be able to spot things that you've missed (if there's something in your shadow, for example, you may unconsciously omit it). They may also prompt you with alternative explanations or suggest a point in your story that doesn't align with their perception of you.

It's up to you to decide what to do when you encounter these discrepancies. It may be that if everyone sees you differently from how you see yourself, you ultimately reject those perceptions and lean into your own. Or it may be that you are able to accommodate their perspectives and let them enrich and balance your own.

What ultimately matters is not the story per se, but the fact that you are consciously engaging with the story *as its author*, not merely a mindless enactor.

Ask for feedback with the understanding that it may be difficult to hear, but also that you don't necessarily have to take it as gospel. Your life is one hundred percent unique, and it's your responsibility to define yourself in a way that aligns with your values and deepest truth. That said, we are all growing and evolving, so don't be afraid to learn something from others, to let them help you see blind spots, or to admit when you've taken too narrow a view on things.

As you can imagine, narrative therapy takes a little bravery, honesty, and creativity. But if you can, it's a great way to take control over your life and start living the story you want to live.

Takeaways:

- To better understand how you are, it's worth understanding your early childhood experiences. Your attachment style becomes the model on which all your subsequent relationships are based, and it influences your self-concept, core beliefs, and behavior. If our needs were met by primary caregivers, we develop a secure attachment style and healthy attitudes toward intimacy. However, if our needs were not met or met poorly, we may develop insecure attachment styles.
- There are three insecure attachment styles: ambivalent (where care was inconsistent and we end up too "clingy"), avoidant (where care was lacking and so we overdeveloped our sense of independence, shunning intimacy), and

- disorganized (where abusive early dynamics created a chaotic attitude toward relationships).
- We can improve our relationships by consciously challenging old patterns, seeking out positive role models, and paying attention to our emotional intelligence and nonverbal communication.
- We can resolve many past issues by re-parenting the inner child. The inner child is the younger version of yourself that still lives on in the present. Reparenting is the act of recognizing what needs went unmet for your childhood self and committing to giving that to yourself right now in the present. Dialogues, affirmations, and playdates can also help!
- Narrative therapy tells us that we are not our thoughts, we can externalize our problems, and stories can change. Use the My Life Story exercise to become aware of overarching patterns and themes in your life. Plot out your life as a story, but reflect on ways you might like to change that story. A trusted "editor" could also provide feedback and help you think about different ways to frame or reframe your life narrative.

Part 3: Thoughts are the Code That Programs Your Life

Chapter 8: Identify and Change Your Core Beliefs

What you'll learn in this chapter: what your core beliefs are, where they come from, and what you can do to gently challenge them.

The underlying assumptions we have about ourselves, others, and the world in general are known as **core beliefs**.

They are "core" in that they are so deeply ingrained, they may feel like a part of us, like our own name. In the previous chapters, we've already encountered some examples of these, as well as seen how they can stem from early childhood experiences.

Core beliefs emerge in childhood when we learn to interpret the world around us based on our connections with caregivers and our personal experiences. While these mental shortcuts can be beneficial in many circumstances, they can become ingrained patterns of thought, feeling, and behavior that are ultimately self-sabotaging.

If you've ever felt caught in a habit that you can't seem to break, or stuck with a behavior you'd like to change (such as addiction or poor communication), you've probably had a core belief working behind the scenes. For example, in your self-therapy journey, you might have gradually come to recognize a pattern of undervaluing yourself. Digging into it, you see a core belief at the center of it all: "I am not as worthy as other people."

Once you identify this core belief, you see how it manifests itself everywhere—in negative self-talk, in choices that keep you playing small and avoiding risk or exposure, and in relationships with people who seem to unconsciously agree that you are not worth much!

Identifying your core beliefs and assumptions is critical because it allows you to establish the connection between your beliefs and how you're feeling in each passing moment. This insight allows you to take a step back and consider the problem from a different perspective. You get to ask yourself, "Wait, is this how I want to approach this moment? Do I want to keep playing out this tired old loop, or do I want to choose something different?"

A big part of cognitive behavioral therapy (CBT) is learning how to identify and challenge your core beliefs so that limiting perceptions can be reshaped and you can live the life you want to live, experience more happiness, and fulfil your potential. *A core belief is like an internalized "rule" that guides the creation of your personal narrative. We behave in ways to confirm these rules*, i.e., if we encounter something that affirms it, we cling to that and focus on it, whereas if we encounter something that disproves our belief, we dismiss it.

The more we affirm a belief, the more entrenched it gets, which is why it can take time and effort to challenge. Ultimately, we interpret everything through the lens of this belief. If we believe, for example, that we are unworthy as people, when someone smiles at us on the street, we may think, "I wonder why they're laughing at me?" Or perhaps we don't even notice their smile in the first place.

Core beliefs can vary in both their accuracy and their usefulness—our goal in self-therapy is to transform our unconscious, maladaptive, and inaccurate core beliefs into alternatives that genuinely support our wellbeing and growth as people. We can't do this, however, if we're unaware, or unwilling to gently challenge what we "know." We need to constantly remind ourselves that **core beliefs are not facts**. They are just thoughts and ideas that we have repeated so often that we believe them to be true.

Core beliefs can create negative automatic thought patterns. Therefore, when we challenge these so-called "cognitive distortions," we gently loosen the core belief and give a healthier alternative the chance to take root instead.

Let's return to our example core belief—"I am not as worthy as other people"—and see how it inspires negative thought patterns.

1. **Early experiences** – as a child, your father compares you unfavorably to your siblings, and you are routinely interrupted or dismissed since you are the youngest child.
2. **Core belief** that arises to "explain" this painful feeling and help you survive it—"For people to treat me this way, I must be inferior somehow. I must be worth less than others."
3. **Critical incident later in life** – the loss of a job.
4. **Automatic cognitive distortion** – "I lost my job because I'm the worst employee and they all hate me and think I'm stupid. I won't get another job because I'm worthless."
5. **Consequences of those thoughts** – low self-esteem, depression, guilt, shame, and the inability to seek out new work because of the assumption that you will only be rejected anyway. Perhaps even physical symptoms like insomnia and addictive eating.

This sounds dramatic, but core beliefs can also be set up in subtler, seemingly innocuous ways. For example, if you routinely expressed doubt and fear to your caregivers, and they said, "Oh, don't be silly! There's nothing to be afraid of. You're big and strong!" their intentions might have been noble, but you still internalized the core belief that it's shameful to be afraid and that to be considered strong, you need to hide how you really feel.

This core belief may play itself out in all sorts of patterns in adulthood. You may get trapped in the habit of never truly expressing yourself to others, never admitting when you need help, and feeling deep down that if others knew how scared you sometimes felt, they'd think you were "silly." One day you could be having an argument with your spouse when you realize the problem: you cannot honestly tell them that you're afraid, so you're expressing anger instead and causing all sorts of misunderstandings.

The general CBT process is as follows:

1. Identify your core belief
2. Ask whether this belief is really serving you in the present
3. If not, challenge the belief, soften it, or invert it
4. Consciously choose to cement this alternative belief by taking action

For example:

1. Core belief is "it's wrong/weak/silly to feel or express fear"
2. This belief is making your relationships feel shallow and inauthentic; you don't need or want it anymore.
3. You decide to challenge it by inverting the core belief ("expressing your true feelings takes integrity and strength of character") or soften it ("people may sometimes be uncomfortable with others expressing fear, but that doesn't mean I can't safely share my true feelings with those closest to me").
4. Action: decide in the moment to make small steps to admitting fear and doubt. Is it really so bad as you predict? Do people respond as you assumed they would?

The "Downward Arrow" Technique
Here's another strategy that will help you uncover and rework automatic thoughts that are no longer serving you. Remember, of course, that not all enduring, fundamental beliefs about yourself are harmful—but if you find that the cost of this belief is too high, you can change it.

Step 1: Pick a situation that generates negative feelings for you—for example, public speaking.

Step 2: Identify the thoughts that this situation encourages—for example, "I'm weird and awkward and people can tell."

Step 3: Now ask, **what does this negative thought actually *mean* to you?** "It means I have failed to live up to people's expectations of me." You could also ask, "If this were true, why would that be so bad?"

Now, continue asking the questions from step 3.

"If I don't live up to people's expectations of me, why would that be so bad?"

Answer: "Because then they'll disapprove of me and judge me."

"And what does that mean to me?"

"It's means that I don't belong."

"And what does that mean to me?"

"That I'll be a bad person."

And that's it—your core belief: *In order to be a good person, I need to behave like other people.*

You may need to dig a lot, or your core beliefs may be close to the surface, but keep going until you hit something that feels like a deep, fundamental "rule" on which your life is based. Here's another example:

You have begun to notice that you always get to a point in the dating process when you start to feel uncomfortable and want to dump them and run away. You pay close attention to these negative feelings and allow them to coalesce in your mind. You dig until you find a negative thought that inspires and maintains these feelings: "Don't get too close!"

You start the downward arrow technique by asking, "If this were true, why would it be so bad?" In other words, if people did get too close, then what?

Answer: "Then it would mean that we were in a full-blown relationship."

"And what does that mean?"

"It means that there's a kind of agreement to be together."

"And what does that mean?"

"It means that you can't just easily decide not to be together anymore..."

"And what does that mean?"

"It means you're basically trapped!"

"And...?"

"It means that you're no longer allowed to live your life the way you want to live it, but have to be part of a couple, and that means everything you do has to take them into consideration..."

There's the core belief: Getting close equals loss of freedom.

You could dig even deeper than this and uncover some very general beliefs underlying this one, such as "people are untrustworthy" or "the world is not really safe." This may tie in neatly to any insights you've gained from examining your attachment style (can you imagine Mike from the earlier example discovering this exact core belief in himself?). It's no wonder, then, that such a person would get uncomfortable the moment any relationship started to get more serious!

Now, identifying core beliefs is obviously just the start—what you *do* with this insight is what matters. But by taking the time to tease out the deep and unconscious way you're making sense of your world, you are giving yourself a real chance of taking action that will genuinely benefit you.

Core beliefs tend to fall into three categories: ideas about yourself, ideas about other people, and ideas about the world. Some common ones include:

- I am defective somehow
- I only have worth if other people like me
- The world is an unsafe place, and you can't trust anyone
- I am fundamentally unable to cope
- Life is unfair
- I can only relax if I have total control
- The course of my life is determined by other people's choices

Once you've identified core beliefs, now what? Continue to gently challenge them, invert them, or soften them. The idea is to replace what is automatic, unconscious, maladaptive, inaccurate, and irrational with something that is deliberate, conscious, helpful, accurate, and rational. For example, you could deliberately remind yourself that getting close to another human being does indeed require certain compromises and occasionally not getting what you want, but it's not exactly a self-annihilating "loss of freedom"—especially given the many benefits involved, too!

If this was Mike's core belief, he could consciously work to replace it with something like, "Being in a mature adult relationship requires a little give and take, but in the right relationship, I will never be less of myself, but the very best version of myself."

The great thing about working with core beliefs is that they offer a doorway to genuine transformation. *Any time we transform in life, it is because we've managed a shift in perspective.* So it's not really just about identifying a belief and turning it on its head, or just doing the opposite. It's about completely reframing the way you see things—or thinking about the issue on an entirely different level. In Mike's example, he may grow and heal as a person when he begins to see that he doesn't need to frame his needs *versus* Lydia's at all—that relationships do not have to be zero-sum, or built on a kind of threatening either/or tension. In fact, as he matures, he may come to regard other people's "demands" on him as a welcome opportunity to grow, an invitation to challenge himself, and a way to be, ironically, even more authentically himself than ever before.

But you cannot make transformations of this kind without first fully understanding where you are now. If Mike never saw his core belief as a core belief, he would be trying to solve his life's problems in a very, very different way, i.e., from *within* that core belief. He would merely notice himself feeling uncomfortable with increasing intimacy, and then ask, "How can I make this feeling go away?" The answer, from within the logic of the core belief, is obvious: "Get away from this new relationship as fast as you can!"

How can you uncover and begin to challenge your own core beliefs?

Tip 1: Soften Absolutist, All-or-Nothing Language

If you discover words like *never*, *forever*, and *everyone*, or strong words like *hate, impossible*, and *failure*, try to rephrase them to make them more nuanced and less black and white.

"I always mess up." Do you really? Always? It's probably more accurate to say that sometimes you don't achieve what you want, but that you also have some things to be proud of, and not being perfect doesn't mean you can't learn or try again and do better next time.

The sentiment behind these words can be there even if the literal word itself isn't. Consider:

"That's women for you!" (All women are XYZ.)

"Why is the world like this?!" (The whole entire world is wrong.)

"That's it for me now." (It's impossible to change how I feel, now or ever again.)

You could gently scale these absolutist thoughts down to a more realistic size:

"I'm having a difficult time with my wife at the moment." (Just *one* woman!)

"I get so frustrated with these kid-proof locks!" (Not, ahem, the whole world.)

"I'm too tired to think about it this very instant." (You are feeling bad now, but tomorrow that may change.)

Tip 2: Face Your Fears

Cognitive distortions and negative self-talk often revolve around catastrophic thinking. For example, imagine your marriage is on the rocks, but you are afraid of divorce so late in life. You're terrified you're too old to start over. You think, "If I lose my partner, that's it for me. I'll never find anyone else again, and I'll be lonely and miserable for the rest of my life." You create suffering for yourself because you are assuming the worst possible outcome.

Now, one way people attempt to deal with fears is to deny them outright. A concerned friend might hear the above and respond, "Oh, that's ridiculous! Of course you'll find someone new! I bet if you put yourself out there, you'd find the perfect catch in a month!" Why does something like this so seldom make people feel better? That's simple: We don't believe it.

The fact is, there is some grain of truth in almost all the fears people have now and again. And we don't get a better handle on that fear by pretending that this isn't the case. In a way, denying fears like this can actually make them stronger. Consider that one possible response to the above is, "A month? It took me more than four years to find my current partner, so I *know* that's not true . . ."

Do you see what's happening? You're grabbing hold of your cognitive distortion and following it down a potentially dark rabbit hole—a rabbit hole that only ends in catastrophe. You are allowing your fear to push you around and to balloon out of shape and take over. When you face your fears, however, you do the opposite:

You ask yourself, *Even if this thing I'm afraid of did happen, would it really be so bad? And is it really true that I can't cope with it?*

Imagine you really did lose your partner and never dated again. Then what?

Really sit with that potential outcome and avoid fleeing from it. It would be heartbreaking, yes. It would be extremely difficult. But would it really be the *end of your life entirely*? It might take a long, long time to recover . . . but couldn't you recover eventually?

Taking it further, is it true that a partner is the *only* path to happiness in life? Aren't there many other things that bring you joy and purpose? If you face the absolute worst possible outcome, you'll often find that you are exaggerating how bad it is and underestimating your own ability to handle it. The truth is, finding someone else is a possibility for you. But even if you didn't, well, even this outcome is manageable—it may even be preferable!

And again, we see that bravely engaging with fears, just like challenging core beliefs, is a path to better things. It's what allows us to "level up" our thinking and shift perspective. In this example, by properly engaging with this fear, the person may discover something interesting and unexpected: that there actually *would* be some benefits to being single for a long time . . .

On the other hand, if they had only catastrophized and then fled from those imagined disasters and anxieties, this insight would never have had the chance to take root.

Chapter 9: The ABCD Model

What you'll learn in this chapter: how to use the ABCD model to identify and re-engineer your ingrained thought patterns and cognitive distortions.

Albert Ellis, one of CBT's pioneers, devised the popular ABCD model, which is a classic cognitive behavioral therapy (CBT) technique and one we can make use of in self-therapy. When used correctly, Ellis's approach can help us address a wide range of emotional issues, including anger, depression, or anxiety.

In ABCD,

A stand for **Activating Event** ("trigger").

B stands for **Belief System** (how you interpret your trigger, whether a core belief is at play or not).

C stands for **Consequences** (the emotional and behavioral consequences that result).

D stands for **Dispute** (where we examine, challenge, or reframe our underlying core beliefs, assumptions, and expectations).

The ABCD framework is a great way to structure your efforts to identify and change cognitive distortions, and in so doing change your entire life. While the techniques described in the previous sections are good for uncovering deep and lasting core beliefs, the ABCD technique is more suited for everyday thoughts and self-talk.

While it's always good to understand the deeper emotional and psychological roots of your self-concept, you can also make strides by dealing with cognitive distortions purely on the cognitive level. In fact, many people think of CBT this way—with your brain being a kind of computer and your thoughts being the programming that results in certain emotional and behavioral outputs.

Change the program, change the outputs!

Our minds work so fast that our responses can seem automatic at times. The ABCD model helps us slow things down and take control. We can run through the acronym in the heat of the moment or do a kind of "thought postmortem" after the fact, when we're trying to understand why things happened the way they did. At first, reflecting on events that have already passed may be easier, but with practice, you should be able to start noticing certain thought patterns as they occur.

To begin using the ABCD model, simply run through each of the four letters of the acronym in turn. The magic happens at D, dispute, where you give yourself the chance to act and choose a different way forward for yourself. Many people find the process very calming and grounding, and it can certainly help you dial back strong emotions and see a more sensible, clearer, and simpler way forward.

Here's how.

Get a journal or pen and paper and start making notes (if you're doing this process in the moment, you will obviously frame this process in the present tense and do it somewhat quicker, without writing anything down).

Step 1: Start with the **Activating Event**
What happened?

What is the event, thought, feeling, gesture, situation, or dynamic that triggered the present situation?

Bear in mind that a trigger can be *anything*, from **external** events to **internal** sensations, such as:

- The smell of the tobacco your grandfather used to smoke.
- Being in the car.
- Having to be appraised and graded by superiors.
- Seeing a particular kind of violence in a movie.
- The memory of something that happened in school thirty years ago.
- Feeling sick or unwell.

Step 2: Identify Your **Beliefs**
What are you saying to yourself about this trigger?

What is your interpretation of events?

What style of thinking or cognitive distortion are you applying?

What core belief is activated?

Remember that this can be lightning fast and so automatic you don't give it a second thought. You might smell tobacco, be unconsciously reminded of your grandfather, and suddenly find your thoughts running away with you, leading to the belief, "I am alone in this world." Or the thought could be a knee-jerk, "I never told him how much I loved him; it's my fault."

Step 3: Identify the Resulting **Consequences**
What do your thoughts and beliefs make you feel?

How do you behave, given your thoughts and beliefs?

What does this thought or belief imply, cause, or bring about for you?

In our example, the thought, "I am alone in this world," triggered by the smell of tobacco, could cause a feeling of sadness or despair. The thought, "I never told him how much I loved him," could lead to feelings of guilt, remorse, and regret.

On the other hand, consequences are not just feelings. A consequence can also be a behavior, a decision or choice, or even an adjustment to your attitude or self-concept. Though not much appears to have changed on the outside, you may quietly make an adjustment to your self-concept to reflect and accommodate your belief, such as, "I always let people down."

Step 4: **Dispute** the Belief
Once you've explored these beliefs in detail, it's time to challenge your thoughts, beliefs, and resulting consequences.

In what ways can you adjust your belief?

Can you make it softer, more rational, more accurate, or more useful?

Is there a more realistic alternative?

Having followed the ABCD process, you're probably well aware of how bad it can feel to hold certain thoughts and beliefs. But now is the time to try out something that feels better. Pay attention to how alternative possibilities *feel*—it's not just about finding something that is more rational and realistic. It's also about finding a perspective that feels comfortable and positive. Something that will inspire and enable you to take positive action.

For example, the ABCD process can show you how limiting and self-sabotaging it is to keep beating yourself up for not properly saying goodbye to your grandfather before he died. It simply isn't rational to keep regretting a thing that can't be changed, and it's not exactly fair to carry that guilt forever.

So, you reflect and write down an alternative: "I loved my grandfather and he knew that. I'm not perfect, and I could have treated him better while he was alive, but I can always honor his memory right now by choosing to remember the fond memories instead and not be so hard on myself."

Here are a few more simple examples:

Example 1

Activating event – finding out that two friends have spent time together without inviting you.

Belief – "Maybe they're both talking about me."

Consequence – Feeling suspicious, left out, and hurt; withdrawing socially; and being a little aloof the next time you encounter them.

Dispute – There's no reason to think that two friends spending time together is in any way a problem. There are many benign and reasonable explanations for why they didn't invite you. New alternative thought: "I can trust that my friends like and appreciate me."

Example 2

Activating event – A receptionist has just been rude to you.

Belief – "Nobody knows the meaning of service in this country anymore."

Consequence – Feeling powerless, angry, and apathetic, as well as tempted to be rude in return.

Dispute – This receptionist *is* rude, but not every receptionist in the entire country is rude. In any case, getting angry won't help the situation, so there's no point raising your voice and putting her on the defensive.

The real power of this technique comes in the final step, where we are given the chance to consciously choose something different.

Now, just because you completed the process and wrote it down doesn't mean that you won't encounter the same automatic thought again, or that the core belief is gone forever. Remember that this sort of technique is more suited to the more superficial aspects of daily life. But that doesn't mean it doesn't have value. *That's because you unlearn distorted thinking in exactly the same way as you learned it: slowly, day by day, over a long period.*

The good news is that every time you become aware of your triggers and notice your response and the way your core beliefs influence your feelings and behaviors, you weaken old patterns and strengthen new ones. But that does mean that you have to be patient and consistent and not get too discouraged if you cannot make an overnight transformation.

Let's say that you repeatedly notice yourself feeling left out of social situations, and that, when you pay attention, you often notice that you have suspicious thoughts or assume that you've been slighted. As you continue to "dispute," you may gradually dig away at the deeper causes for this experience. When combined with some of the exercises described previously (for example, the downward arrow technique that asks, "What does that mean to you?" or using the Gestalt empty chair technique and placing your primary caregiver in the seat), you gain more depth and understanding.

In this example, the ABCD process helps you identify recurrent superficial patterns that you can then follow and investigate further with more in-depth techniques. Perhaps by using some of these tools, you identify broader ways of behaving in your life in general. Maybe you realize that your feelings of being left out come from an overall low self-esteem. By working on the "dispute" part of the ABCD approach, you solve this issue in a top-down way, while at the same time, you may experiment with some inner child work to tackle the issue from the bottom up.

One day, after practicing both these techniques, you may be pleased to discover that the thought, *I can trust that my friends like and appreciate me*, actually occurs to you all on its own, without you needing to sit down and run through the ABCD model.

Finally, though you don't have to write down your ABCD process, it's a good idea to keep a kind of "thought journal," at least in the beginning, for a few reasons:

- By writing, you slow your thought process down and give yourself less of a chance to slip into default unconscious patterns.
- You collect a log of triggers, behaviors, and consequences, which will show you overarching themes and patterns over time. This can yield incredible insights.
- With practice, you will learn to better recognize triggers and your responses to them until they disappear completely. You'll know the process is working when you're able to say, "Aha! I've seen this trigger, and I can see myself going down that path. But I feel strong enough to choose my alternative belief, instead."

Chapter 10: The Triple Column Technique

What you'll learn in this chapter: a simple but useful technique for homing in on your cognitive distortions—the filters you place over objective reality.

So far in this book, we've spoken about "thoughts" as though they're always a clear and easy thing to identify. What is one thought, exactly?

Here's a peek into someone's stream of consciousness:

Okay, just smile, just look natural. You know most people here already, so it'll be fine. It'll be okay. Oh, God, there's what's-her-name in the corner. Just avoid her. Why does she always come to these events, anyway? So annoying! You really need to be less judgmental; you're such a mean person sometimes. Ooh, peanuts! Ugh, not very good peanuts. Still, stand here and mind your own business for a while. You're getting fat again, you know. Was this shirt a bad idea after all? Why can't you ever stick to an exercise regime? Like, ever? Peanuts are high in protein, though. Oh no, there's Andrew. Damn. Just look at how he's looking at you . . . Are peanuts all that high in protein, though? Still, probably shouldn't eat too many . . .

Every moment of every day, your mind is whizzing along. Some thoughts are banal and completely neutral observations. Some are based in the present, and some only *seem* like they're based in the present but are really old thought patterns that are still echoing from a time in the past. A thought can be an explanation, a justification, a question, a denial, a memory, an expression of desire, a complaint, a placation, a lament, a criticism, a compliment . . .

Mostly, though, thoughts are one thing: unconscious. When you first start to be conscious of your thoughts, you might well look at this immense volume of thought traffic and wonder where to start! It can be tricky, but as you watch your mind and what it does, try to look for thoughts that seem **distorted, automatic,** and particularly **emotional**.

"Peanuts are high in protein" is not likely to warrant much further attention, but a thought like "you really need to be less judgmental; you're such a mean person sometimes" does. Anytime a thought seems like it appears from nowhere in a knee-jerk way and comes with an emotion that doesn't quite match what's going on in the present, then it's likely that this thought is a cognitive distortion.

Some people say that your thoughts influence your reality, but this is not exactly true—in a big way, your thoughts *are* your reality.

What you tell your mind to believe, it believes.

That means if you fill your mind with negative self-talk all day every day, your life will be shaped by that negativity. If you say, completely unconsciously and without even realizing that you've done it, "You're a judgmental and mean person," then why shouldn't you eventually come to believe it? So many of us think that our inner self-talk is just a neutral narrator casually perceiving events, but really, our inner talk *shapes* our perception, and then our perception works to confirm what we have already decided we believe.

The goal is to become aware of our self-talk and be more discerning about the effect it is having on our perception and therefore our lives. We don't have to take our self-talk's word for it! Instead, we can check to see whether it's distorted, and ask the more conscious, healthier, and more realistic part of us to *talk back* to that negative self-talk and correct those distortions.

This is what the triple column technique can help you do. Using this technique, you can zoom in on cognitive distortions so you can moderate them. Here's a step-by-step process.

Step 1: Create Your Table
On a piece of paper, draw two lines to make three columns, each labeled:

1. Automatic thoughts
2. Cognitive distortion
3. Rational response

Step 2: Write Down Your Self-Critical Thoughts
In the first, far left column, begin by writing down the negative self-talk you've become aware of. This will be a mix of core beliefs, emotions, expectations, assumptions, biased, guesses, judgments, interpretations, and reactions. For example:

This is a complete, total disaster.

This always happens.

I'm to blame.

I bet he's angry with me.

I was supposed to do better.

As you gain more practice, it will become easier and easier to pay attention to your thoughts. Meditation can help you tune into the contents of your mind, but you can also get an inkling of your self-talk by your regular talk and what you say to others. Do you ever talk to yourself out loud as you go about your daily life? Pay attention to what you say.

Step 3: Identify Cognitive Distortions

Some of your thoughts may be positive, hopeful, inspiring, kind, and rational. But if you're reading this book, chances are your self-talk tends to be more critical and negative! In the middle column, for each of the thoughts you noted in step 2, identify any cognitive distortions that apply (more on this in just a moment).

Step 4: Explore rational alternatives

In the final column, try to find more accurate, useful, and positive alternatives for each thought. Now, it's important that this alternative thought is still realistic. You don't need to tell yourself comforting lies or unbelievable platitudes. You don't need to "cheer yourself up" or pretend that things are better than they are.

So, for example, a good alternative for, "I'm fat and out of shape and completely unattractive," could be, "I have many positive attributes, and if I'm unhappy with my health or appearance, I can always make positive changes." The alternative, "You are the most attractive person to ever live," is just as distorted—plus, you're unlikely to believe it, anyway.

Once you've identified these alternatives, the hard part begins—you need to consistently remind yourself to counter every negative bit of self-talk with a more positive rebuttal. Again, it takes time and practice. In the beginning, you may be quite surprised just how much negative self-talk you engage in!

Let's now take a look at cognitive distortions—which are exactly what they sound like—inaccurate, twisted perceptions that don't properly reflect the reality they are observing.

It's worth noting that having rational and adaptive thoughts won't absolve you from ever having to suffer. But they will ensure that you are not unnecessarily adding to your own suffering with your thoughts. The goal of any CBT-inspired self-therapy is not to be completely rid of negative emotion—that's impossible!—but rather to have a healthier, more mature, and grounded response to life's inevitable challenges.

Here are a few common cognitive distortions:

Disqualifying the Positive

When something positive threatens to disprove a negative core belief or automatic assumption, then the tendency is to discount it.

"I know I received a positive performance review last week, but that was probably just a fluke. What matters is the fact that my work was questioned this morning. *That's* the more accurate reflection of my professional capabilities."

Rational alternative: *We are all complex individuals who contain both good and bad attributes, and we are okay just as we are.*

Mind-Reading or Fortune-Telling

This is when we act as though we can tell with one hundred percent accuracy what other people are thinking, or that we absolutely know what events will unfold in the future.

"He thinks I'm an idiot, I know it."

"I can't share my idea because I'll just be shut down."

Rational alternative: *We cannot read minds or predict the future. The only way to be sure is to communicate or wait to see what the future brings!*

Magnifying or Minimizing

Blowing something way out of proportion or minimizing it into nothing depending on what the prevailing core belief requires.

"I made a typo on page three and that basically means my boss will fire me on Monday, I'm sure of it."

"I wouldn't want to worry those poor doctors with my broken leg. It's really not that bad . . ."

Rational alternative: *The truth usually lies somewhere in the middle of extremes. Whatever I encounter, big or small, positive or negative, I can cope with it.*

Personalization

This is when we interpret events as though they always necessarily connect back to us somehow, making us take on more responsibility, blame, or even praise for things that really have nothing to do with us.

"My son wouldn't have failed math if only I had pushed him a little more."

"She's in such a bad mood; I wonder what I did."

Rational alternative: *Even though I care, I cannot be responsible for other people's emotions or actions.*

Labeling

This is what it sounds like—putting labels, often harsh ones, on experiences or perceptions. When you label yourself, you're assigning yourself a fixed role in your narrative. The trouble is, this is usually limiting or inaccurate.

"I'm a moron."

"I could never relax with my OCD tendencies."

Labeling can range from the obvious ("You're an idiot.") to the more subtle ("Well, I'm half-Italian—I'm just hot-blooded."), but in each case, it acts to remove you from spontaneous, conscious choice in the moment and instead makes you behave in automatic, stereotyped ways.

Rational alternative: *I am many things, but in every moment, I can make new choices, and I'm not bound forever to keep making the same choices I made yesterday.*

All-or-Nothing Thinking

This is easy to spot if only you look. Black-and-white thinking poses just two extremes, when reality is usually a lot more nuanced.

"They didn't hire me for the job, so they must think I'm incompetent."

"If it rains on the last day, our whole vacation will be ruined."

"You're with me or against me."

Rational alternative: *There are endless shades of gray between two extremes, and there are usually more than just two options in life.*

Generalizations

One very common cognitive distortion is to over-extrapolate, i.e., to take one isolated instance and assume that this implies something about every other instance, everywhere, at all times. Like so many of the other distortions on this list, the effect is to flatten out nuance, simplify reality, and give us a picture of the world that is easier to manage—the price is that this simplified picture is usually wrong!

"Men just don't care about marriage as much as women do."

"She's a lawyer; don't trust a word she says!"

Rational alternative: *Life is complex. I encounter each situation, person, and event individually. I am always willing to question my biases and be proven wrong.*

"Should" Statements

We may sometimes overestimate our knowledge and assume we perfectly understand the "rules" on which our world runs. That's why we can boldly state what "should" and "shouldn't" happen—and get upset when it *doesn't* happen that way.

We miss out on the fact that we seldom have the perfect and complete information needed to make such pronouncements. When you examine why you believe something ought to have been the case, you may find nothing more than a few flimsy assumptions and expectations that are not really based in reality.

"You are X years old; you should have this all figured out by now."

"This should not have happened."

Rational alternative: *I may have a preference for a particular outcome, but how the world unfolds is largely not under my control. There is no point arguing with reality, but I know that whatever a situation's outcome, I can cope and make choices according to my own values.*

You may have noticed in our original example that there were plenty of *should* and *shouldn't* statements—you shouldn't be so judgmental, you shouldn't eat too many peanuts, you should smile and look natural . . .

Cognitive distortions are easy to grasp when written on the page, but it takes awareness and practice to identify them in your own life. After all, the most impactful distortions are likely to be the ones that are most entrenched and most invisible to you.

Luckily, we have a flag that signals that cognitive distortions may be at play: every time we feel overwhelmed emotionally, whether that's anger, sadness, anxiety, or confusion, we can stop and say, "What's going on with my thoughts right now? And how are these thoughts making me feel?"

Write them down (there may be many!), identify any distortions, then go in and re-engineer those thoughts.

The next time you encounter the same trigger, the idea is to remember the alternative and deliberately revert to that instead. Yes, it will take time for these updated, more moderate versions to take hold, and at first, they may not feel easy or natural. But with consistent practice, you will find it easier. You will reach a point one day where it is the old, maladaptive thought that feels unnatural, while the more rational one feels better!

Chapter 11: Cognitive Defusion

What you'll learn in this chapter: three techniques to quickly gain distance, control, and perspective when you feel overwhelmed by thoughts and feelings.

Identifying core beliefs and using the ABCD model and triple column technique can all feel pretty exhausting!

Especially if anxiety and overthinking are a problem for you, it may seem like all these techniques and models only add to the stress of trying to manage and untangle your thoughts. Even though CBT is NOT about forcefully stopping certain thoughts, it can sometimes feel like you're playing "whack-a-mole" with intrusive, negative, or self-critical thoughts.

If this is the case and you often feel like your head is a big mess of knots and tangles, you might enjoy the approach suggested by ACT, or Action Commitment Therapy. One goal of ACT is not to change, fight, repress, or battle thoughts and feelings. Instead, **we change how we relate to those thoughts and feelings**. Big difference.

To put it another way, the idea is that the *content* of our thoughts is never the problem. Rather, it's our attitude and *response* to that content that can create trouble for us.

Person A may have the thought, "Nobody loves me," and respond to that thought by completely identifying with it. They focus on it fully, believe it, and allow it to drag them down a rabbit hole of similarly dark thoughts.

Person B also has the thought, "Nobody loves me," but they are not identified (or what ACT calls "fused") with this thought. They don't take this thought as one hundred percent absolute truth.

Person A is experiencing being unloved.
Person B is experiencing the *thought* that they are unloved.

Person A is fused with their experience, feeling it as absolute reality, whereas Person B understands that they are in fact just having an experience and that reality and thoughts about reality are not necessarily the same thing.

Person B is practicing cognitive defusion and detaching themselves from their experience rather than identifying with it. No, they are not emotionless robots—the thought, feeling, and experience is still there. The only difference is that they are not lost and drowning in it. They look at thoughts from the outside rather than at the world from inside their thoughts.

They are aware and can notice what is happening to them.

Sometimes, when we **battle** our thoughts, we only end up creating more of the same problem. Importantly, being "fused" this way can entail both clinging to an experience or desperately avoiding and denying it. Either way, we are still being pushed around by the thought! It is our response to the thought that is creating problems, not the thought. So unless we change our response, we stay tangled.

Returning to our example in the previous chapter, recall the person at the work party who discovered the thought, "You shouldn't be so judgmental of others." Now ask yourself, what is the *cause* of this person's negative feeling—is it that they had a fleeting negative thought about someone else, or is it that they have a more lasting belief that there is something wrong with this thought in the first place?

Look at the following thoughts:

"Ugh, I don't like that person."
"You're judgmental and mean not to like that person."

Which one causes more trouble?

The ACT defusion techniques we will look at below all work because they achieve the following:

- Increase psychological distance from strong experiences, reducing negativity
- Remind us that our thoughts are not the same as reality
- Remind us that we are not slaves to the influence of our thoughts
- Help us stay flexible, open-minded, and creative
- Keep us in the present moment when we can respond to our experiences spontaneously
- Stay connected to our power to choose what we do and how we respond

ACT is essentially a way to develop metacognition, i.e., to **think about your thinking.**

Set aside the content of whatever thoughts, feelings, and experiences you're having and look at them *as thoughts*—are they actually helping you in any way? Are they causing you to suffer? Is this thought in control of you or are you in control of it? Is it helping you achieve the kind of life you want for yourself, or is it getting in the way?

Even if you don't actually answer these questions, the mere fact of asking them puts you in a completely different frame of mind—calmer, more rational, and more proactive.

Defusion Technique 1: "I'm noticing that . . ."

Try saying these words: "I'm noticing that I'm having the thought of/the feeling of/the experience of . . ."

You gain psychological distance. You are not the thought; you are just *having* the thought. If the thought comes, then it will go again. It's just a temporary experience that you can observe in yourself. It's important not to judge or interpret the experience. Your only job is to notice it.

"I'm having that same old cognitive distortion again . . ."

"I'm experiencing a strong feeling of sadness right now."

"I notice my mind wanting to follow each of these anxious thoughts. I also notice that when I do this, there's an instant tightness all along my shoulders."

Defusion Technique 2: "Thanks, mind."

You are not your mind. Your mind may whirr along automatically and generate all sorts of thoughts, which cause an endless conveyor belt of feelings. But your mind is just one part of you, like your circulatory system or your middle toe.

Consider that when you have allergies, your immune system is trying to do its job but has made a kind of error in perceiving something harmful as a threat. The problem is the response itself. Your immune system can be in overdrive, but you are not your immune system, and luckily you know that there really isn't any threat. That's why you can safely take an antihistamine to deal with the symptoms, effectively saying, "Thanks, immune system, but everything's under control" (not unlike what we do with the "manager" or "firefighter" in IFS—Internal Family Systems).

Similarly, your mind's job is to think, process, plan, create, and so on. Like the immune system, it gets carried away sometimes, though. Overthinking, anxiety, and negative self-talk are not actually helping you in any way, even if they feel like they are. So in these instances, you can consciously thank your mind for trying its best to do its job—and choose not to believe it!

"Thank you, fear, for trying to keep me safe. I'm going to take a chance, anyway."

"Thank you, mind, for bringing that to my attention. I'll consider it later."

The trick is not to take your thoughts as gospel, and sometimes, even use a little humor or sarcasm. If you like, give your recurrent unhelpful beliefs names and identifies. For example, you can imagine your anxiety as a comically melodramatic panda holding a sign saying, "The end is nigh." You can notice it, smile, and say,

"Thanks, Doom Panda. I know you're trying to help. But sit down and relax because I'm busy living my life!"

Defusion Technique 3: Leaves on a Stream
When we are fused with our experience, it seems to expand and fill all our awareness. For example, we feel anxious and worried, and it suddenly seems like this is how we have always felt, and we can't imagine feeling any different in the future. We forget that sensations and perceptions are *fleeting*—they come and they go again.

The Leaves on a Stream exercise is very simple meditation to try when you feel the relentless onslaught of too many thoughts and sensations. What it helps you do is realize that sensations are not permanent. Too often we prolong suffering because we either cling to or resist certain experiences. However, if we only relaxed and let them go, they would move and flow of their own accord without us having to fight or cling to them.

Here's how to do the exercise:

1. Take a few deep breaths; close your eyes; and imagine a peaceful, calm, and clear stream flowing gently past your feet.
2. Just enjoy this stream and notice how it is always moving—never hurrying or dawdling, but just moving along with ease as it goes.
3. When a thought pops into your mind, imagine taking this thought out of your head and gently placing it on a leaf floating by on the river. Watch the thought gently bob out of view as the river carries it away.
4. When another thought emerges in you (or the same one!), put it on another leaf and watch it, too, float by.
5. You are not resisting any of these thoughts. You are just allowing them to come and then go.
6. When you are feeling a little calmer, open your eyes again. You can repeat this exercise any time you feel overwhelmed by thoughts and feelings.

That's a nice little stream, so clear and smooth the way it flows . . . the way it ripples a little without the surface of the water breaking . . . pretty . . . Don't forget you have to sort out that direct debit with the bank . . . Ooh, there's a thought. Okay, I'm imagining it as a little pebble. Onto a leaf it goes, just like that. Look how the leaf dips a little into the water under the weight of the stone . . . but it still goes! There it goes, slowly on its path . . .

. . . but seriously, you need to sort that out and check to see that that refund thing has been sorted out. The last thing you want is for that account to be overdrawn . . . Oh, wow! There it is again. That's a thought that can go on a leaf, too. This is lame, though. I'm bored. Lalalala, so bored. You never did get on well with meditation, and this is why . . .

Hey, wait, that's a thought, too! A lot of them. Onto a leaf you go. And you, and you. Hey, you're getting the hang of this now . . . You idiot, don't be so proud of yourself for doing the exercise correctly for, like, two minutes. It's just a silly little meditation thing that will . . . aha! That's a thought too. Here comes the next leaf . . .

Even if you have the thought, "Oh no! I have a million thoughts. My stream is going to get clogged up for sure!" it doesn't matter. Just place *that* on a leaf and keep going. The moment you come to awareness, you are at the beginning again. It doesn't matter how long you were distracted for or how far your mind wanders, only that it comes back and you find that distance and presence again (hint: a little humor helps, too).

If you like, you can combine all three of these defusion techniques into one and make any adaptations you like. For example, you could imagine that there is a tiny person sitting on top of your head, and every time you have a thought, a little party balloon emerges. You imagine the little person tying a knot in this balloon and then releasing it into the air where it floats away until it becomes a pinprick on the horizon.

As you visualize all this, you say things like, "I'm noticing a feeling of shame. Thank you, mind, for this balloon, but I won't need it. Goodbye!" Perhaps you picture each thought as a different-colored balloon, or imagine putting tiny, shrunk-down versions of your problems and worries into the balloons, where they become harmless and inconsequential.

Whichever way you choose to practice defusion, just remember some key principles:

- Gain distance
- Stay present
- See your thoughts *as thoughts*
- Stay flexible and choose not to respond
- And most importantly: **don't fight** sensations; simply let them flow on.

Takeaways

- A core belief is a deep and fundamental assumption or idea that impacts our identity and behavior, as well as the life narrative we create for ourselves. We can transform our unconscious, maladaptive, and inaccurate core beliefs into alternatives that genuinely support our wellbeing and growth as people. In CBT, we identify, challenge, and rework core beliefs. We can identify core beliefs with the downward arrow technique.
- Our goal is to replace what is automatic, unconscious, maladaptive, inaccurate, and irrational with something that is deliberate, conscious, helpful, accurate, and rational.
- The ABCD model stands for Activating event, Belief, Consequences, and Dispute. We can use it to identify and re-engineer your ingrained thought patterns and cognitive distortions. By identifying the four parts, we can discover more rational alternatives to habitual thought patterns.
- Cognitive distortions are like a filter placed over objective reality. The triple column technique can help us identify and address these distortions. Write down

a thought, identify possible distortions, then soften, invert, or moderate that thought and revert to it next time you have that thought again.
- Cognitive defusion is a way to quickly gain distance, control, and perspective when you feel overwhelmed by thoughts and feelings. We suffer not because of our experiences, but our responses and attitudes toward those experiences, i.e., our over-identification with them.
- Defusion techniques include using the phrase, "I'm noticing that..." thanking our mind for trying to help and using the Leaves on a Stream meditation to let thoughts flow on without resistance or clinging.

Part 4: Build the Life You Want One Action at a Time

Chapter 12: Systematic Desensitization

What you'll learn in this chapter: how to systematically face your fears and break old limiting associations so you can build new ones.

In Parts 1, 2, and 3, you delved deep into your own psyche, carefully considered your core beliefs, integrated your early childhood experiences, engaged your shadow, and reconsidered your personal life narrative.

This kind of work is invaluable, no doubt. However, it's incomplete unless it's combined with deliberate **action** in the world.

Much self-help advice out there takes the reverse approach and starts with goals, actions, and behaviors with the hope that it will inspire positive internal changes. However, you're more likely to succeed if you work "from the inside out" and allow your actions and behaviors to emerge from a strong, healthy sense of self.

Systematic desensitization is an evidence-based therapy that combines relaxation techniques with gradual exposure to help you overcome a phobia, such as fear of flying, heights, or public speaking. However, the principles and techniques are useful even if you don't have a specific phobia you'd like to challenge.

The power of systematic desensitization is that it allows your inner world to interface with the outer world—it creates an arena where you can literally *test out* your core beliefs, assumptions, biases, and expectations. This real-world practice can be far more powerful than merely talking or thinking about the changes you'd like to make in your life.

Here's how it's practiced: you work your way up through increasing levels of emotional intensity, which explains the other term this technique is known by: progressive exposure therapy. You start with the least intense and consciously and deliberately dial up the intensity.

There are three key processes involved for the process to work:

1. A **hierarchy** of intensity (in the classic case, the emotion in question is fear or panic)
2. Slow and **incremental or graded** exposure

3. Relaxation techniques used to **desensitize** you to progressive levels of exposure

For a very basic example, you have a fear of spiders. You set up a hierarchy that begins with thinking about spiders and looking at pictures of them (scored as Level 1), to letting a full-grown tarantula walk all over your hand without feeling any fear (scored as Level 10!). You start by thinking about spiders. When you do, you feel panicked. You pause and quickly use a breathing technique to calm yourself down. Then you think about spiders again.

In fact, you think about spiders *while* doing your calming breathing exercise. After some time, Level 1 doesn't cause any panic. So you move to Level 2 and do the same thing. This, in a nutshell, is the procedure for systematic desensitization.

The overall goal of this technique rests on classical conditioning. You create new associations between relaxation and what is normally threatening or frightening (for example, spiders). Over time, a stimulus or situation will stop producing the same negative reaction in you as you gradually "teach" yourself a new way of responding. You will start to associate spiders with neutral feelings or feelings of calm.

There are a few different ways to practice systematic desensitization, but here is a simplified approach you can follow on your own.

Step 1: Choose Your Favorite Relaxation Technique
You need to find a way to induce feelings of calmness and control in yourself. There are many ways to do this:

Visualization

For example, closing the eyes and imagining in vivid detail a beautiful, serene place that makes you feel calm, such as a garden or peaceful beach.

Deep Breathing

Slow and regulate your breathing so that your heart rate drops and your nervous system is calmed down and regulated. Take a few deep, slow belly breaths and deliberately imagine yourself relaxing both physically and mentally.

Progressive Muscle Relaxation

Your muscles can access deeper states of relaxation if they tense up first. Lie down somewhere and, moving through the different parts of your body, tense up a muscle for a few seconds, then very slowly release the tension as you breathe and relax fully. Repeat a few times before moving on to the next area, paying close attention to places where tension often occurs: the neck, jaw, and shoulders.

Meditation

The Leaves on a Stream technique above is very calming and focusing, but you can also use other mindfulness techniques such as mantras, chanting, or simply bringing your mind back to the present moment when it wanders.

Step 2: Create Your Hierarchy of Emotions
Next, you need to set up a framework so that you can pair relaxation with those situations, ideas, or phobias that normally trigger negative reactions. This is the "systematic" part of systematic desensitization.

How you do this will depend on what you're trying to achieve—there are no rules, except that the levels have to genuinely represent an increasing hierarchy of intensity *for you*. The classical approach to tackle phobias might look something like this:

1. You identify the most frightening level of fear and what that would be—for example, speaking in public in front of a big crowd of people for more than five minutes. This is set at "Level 10."
2. You identify the lowest level, "Level 1," which might be merely imagining talking in front of a crowd of people.
3. You fill in the gaps between Level 1 and Level 10 so that you have progressively more fear-inducing situations, such as talking in front of only two people, or talking to a crowd but for just thirty seconds. There are no rules here—it rests purely on your personal perceptions.
4. For each level, devise a practical, real-world activity. If giving practice speeches to a small room of seated people is at Level 5, then you might sign up for a public speaking course so you can literally do this.
5. You're finished with this step of the process when you have a kind of ladder of progressing intensity.

Step 3: Move through Gradual Exposure
Now you have to climb that ladder. Before you do, though, the first thing to remember is that **you are in control.** There is no force; you choose how fast you move up the ladder.

The second thing to remember is that as you move through the activities for each level, you need to pay careful attention to pairing your experience with the relaxation technique you chose in Step 1. You are not needlessly exposing yourself to stressful or unpleasant things for the sake of it! Rather, you are trying to break your fearful associations by creating new experiences around that stimulus. Without the relaxation element, you may in fact be reinforcing negative patterns, not breaking them.

The process is simple. Start at Level 1. Let's say this is thinking about your fear—spiders. As you do this, notice your anxiety levels. When they get unmanageable, use your relaxation technique to calm you down again. Keep going.

How do you know when you can progress to the next level? That's easy: when you are comfortable at the current level. So, if you are able to think about spiders comfortably, then you can try Level 2, which is where you look at cute cartoon pictures of spiders.

Again, when you notice anxiety, you use your relaxation technique again. Try to closely pair the relaxation with the exposure. In other words, try to summon up feelings of calm *while* you're engaged in the unpleasant sensation. When you have reached the final and highest level, congratulations—you have cured yourself of your phobia.

You're probably wondering how this technique can be applied to conditions other than public speaking or fear of spiders. Granted, the approach doesn't work for every single issue out there, but as long as you can build in the three components (hierarchy, graded exposure, and desensitization with relaxation techniques), then you'd be surprised how versatile it can be. Let's take a look at some less common applications of this technique.

Systematic Desensitization Example: Social Anxiety

This could encompass a whole range of behaviors, feelings, situations, challenges, and thoughts. Let's say you're a painfully shy person who has been working on their self-esteem and core beliefs, but realizes that at some point, you have to go into the world and take risks. You construct the following "ladder" of graded exposure and pair each step with deep breathing and visualization.

1. Think about greeting one person in class
2. Think about greeting a group of people in class and striking up a conversation with them
3. Smiling at someone in class
4. Greeting someone in class
5. Greeting a group in class; striking up conversation
6. Smiling at a stranger in the street/ in a supermarket
7. Greeting a stranger
8. Striking up a conversation with a stranger
9. Introducing yourself to a group of strangers
10. Striking up a conversation with a group of strangers

Depending on how you use it, the approach can be adapted for anger management, generalized anxiety, bad habits, or addictions. If you are trying to *create* a new conditioned response as opposed to just getting rid of one, you might choose to use both relaxation techniques and affirmations to cement new core beliefs. For example, if you are trying to develop better eating habits and a healthier relationship to food, you could gradually expose yourself to situations you know trigger certain unwanted behaviors, such as buffets.

The next time you're at a buffet (let's say that's Level 4), you quickly do a visualization where you see yourself calm, happy, and in control, and you also bring out some pre-chosen mantras and affirmations ("I make choices to support my health and wellbeing. I can binge if I want to, but I choose instead to eat in a way that makes me feel good about myself.")

If you have a genuinely stubborn or debilitating phobia or issue, it may be wise to consult a therapist who can at least guide you and set you off on the right foot. Those with more serious PTSD, for example, may not benefit from systematic desensitization. Likewise, you may need some help in setting appropriate targets (for example, it isn't advisable to use the approach to help you become progressively desensitized to things that are in fact bad for you, like an abusive relationship).

Remember that even though the process may be scary and uncomfortable at times, you are always in control, and you can always choose how fast to go, where to go, and when. That's the beauty of self-therapy!

Chapter 13: Behavioral Activation

What you'll learn in this chapter: why staying active and engaged in life is so important, and how to create a life that best reflects your deepest values.

The premise of behavioral activation is pretty simple: when you're depressed, you're less active. That means you're not out there in the world, encountering new potentially rewarding experiences. Therefore, you end up more depressed!

Without realizing it, you are stuck in a cycle of low mood and negative feelings. In this situation, staying at home to dwell forever on reflection and "self-therapy" may be precisely the thing that is keeping you feeling bad.

Instead, according to behavioral activation theory, you need to **do something.**

With all this talk of inner children, shadows, and invisible core beliefs and narratives, you could be forgiven for forgetting you have a body at all. But you do, and there is a close relationship with your mood and what you do with that body. While therapy is great, some of the best things you can do for yourself include the obvious: spend time with loved ones, move your body, learn something new, or go on an adventure. By acting, you give yourself the chance to create three important things:

1. Pleasure
2. Mastery
3. Connection

Break the cycle of inactivity and depression by being proactive. Because you're breaking a cycle, though, and because there may be very little initial momentum, you have to take the first step *even when you don't necessarily feel like it.* It's a mistake to think that motivation is needed for action—sometimes it's the other way around, and action inspires motivation!

There are a few components to master when introducing behavioral activation into your life:

Step 1: Monitor Your Activity

You need to first understand your activity levels and patterns, as well as how that affects your mood day to day. To do this, keep a record that tracks what you are doing for literally every hour of your waking life. You might think you already know how you spend your time, but prepare to be surprised. Sometimes, visually seeing your schedule on one page can give you a more accurate and unexpected sense of what you're actually doing with your time . . . i.e., your life!

You can easily create a chart for yourself in Microsoft Excel or simply draw up your own table by hand, leaving enough space to jot down a word or two, such as "watching TV" or "working." You might also like to present the data in different ways and list how many hours go to each activity (a pie graph can be insightful!).

One important thing to do: simultaneously track your mood. For example, you could use a ten-point scale or simply assign a word to each day, like "calm" or "grumpy." Here's an example:

	Activity	Mood
17:40 – 18:00	Drive home, audiobook	Excited and happy
18:00 – 19:00	Cooking dinner with Ally	Stressed out
19:00 – 22:00	Watching TV, some YouTube	Exhausted, bored
22:00 – 22:30	Pre-sleep ritual and yoga	Calm, neutral
22:45 – 00:09	Browsing Reddit in bed	Irritable, depressed

Step 2: Analyze Your Activity
Once you've gathered such data for around a week (more is better), it's time to look at the bigger picture and ask yourself: **Are there any patterns between my activity levels and my mood?**

Maybe you notice that despite most people disliking their commute, you actually really enjoy yours because it gives you a chance to spend some quality time with yourself and listen to inspiring and motivating audiobooks. Maybe you've been telling yourself how important it is to cook together with your girlfriend every evening, but that you consistently find the whole thing more stressful than you thought you did.

Some more questions to guide your analysis:

Which activities were associated with the best mood? And vice versa?
Is there any connection between activity level/intensity and mood?
How did you feel on days when you didn't leave the house or talk to another person?

Depending on your answers, you can now compile a list of activities that you know create good feelings, and a list of those you know that don't.

On your list of Activities that Make Me Feel Good, you might include a daily walk, talking to a friend on the phone, or eating a healthy home-cooked meal.

On the list of Activities that Make Me Feel Bad, you could include a Netflix binge, scrolling social media, or getting out of bed at noon.

The point of monitoring and analyzing your own data is to prove to yourself, to literally *see*, the connection between your activity levels and mood. There may be a few surprises in there—for example, you may discover that talking to friends on the phone makes you feel better, but only certain friends! In our example, so-called quality time with your girlfriend actually makes you more stressed, not less.

Step 3: Reflect on Your Values

You may be the kind of person who says, "My family means everything to me," and yet when you look at how you actually spend your time, you realize that you devote more hours to TV, mindlessly browsing junk on the internet, and shopping than you do spending quality time with loved ones. In other words, your life is not reflecting your deepest and truest values.

Our values are those things that add genuine meaning to our lives. They influence how we engage with others, our priorities, how we see ourselves, and what choices we make. A happy and balanced life is one guided by our values; an unhappy one is where our goals, actions, and priorities have nothing to do with our values.

Take some time identifying what your values are, i.e., your "big why" guiding all your actions. Some examples:

Family life, children, and parenting
Your romantic relationships, marriage, connection
Spirituality
Fun, adventure, new experiences
Education and learning
Personal development, healing
Service, community, charity
Financial success, professional development, career
Creativity
Physical wellbeing and health

Discovering your values is, sadly, not something you can quickly do in an hour, but with consistent self-inquiry, you can start to understand those things that drive your world and move it forward. If you're finding it difficult to identify your values, you could ask questions like:

When have I felt most fulfilled? When has life felt most meaningful, and what was I doing at those points? What am I most proud of? Who do I admire most, and why exactly? What am I most ashamed of or disappointed with in life, and what does this tell me about what I value instead?

In the above example, after gathering weeks of data, the person may discover that they sincerely value personal growth, their spirituality, and living a conscious and purpose-driven life. They come to this conclusion because their mood and behaviors consistently point them in this direction.

They feel amazing when they're learning something new, listening to wise or intelligent people giving inspired advice, or challenging themselves to be better. Almost always, they feel good when having interesting conversations with others and trying new things out there in the world. They also feel completely *not* amazing when they're at home alone, past their bedtime, staring at a harsh smartphone screen while absorbing a steady stream of pessimism and bitterness on some obscure Reddit forum.

When a hypothetical person's life is laid out like this, it all seems so blindingly obvious. And yet, how many of us are oblivious to the ways our everyday actions influence everything? We may spend all night hunched over in bed, doomscrolling, and then wake up in the morning and wonder why we feel so awful. It's not because we are randomly suffering from some mental illness. It's not even because we have bad habits (although both of these things could be true also). Rather, it's that our actions are not aligned with our stated values.

Your values can change throughout life, and you may hold several values, each with a different level of priority. As you reflect on your values, though, ask yourself, "**Have I lived my life in accordance with my values?**" Luckily, the previous activities and exercises will have given you additional insight into what really matters to you fundamentally.

Step 4: Activate Value-Driven Activity

Now that you know how you spend your time, what you value, and the degree of overlap between these two things, you can take informed, conscious action to improve. Simply acting isn't good enough—it needs to be activity that speaks to your values. Remember, too, that you might not necessarily feel like it in the moment, but that if you have monitored your routines and identified your values, you *know* that certain activities will benefit you.

Consult your list of Activities That Make Me Feel Good and devise some tasks to try according to your values. Sometimes feel-good activities are exactly the same as value-aligned activities, but sometimes you may have to make some tweaks. Try creating an "activity menu" of options you know you enjoy and which are important. For example:

Yoga

Eating or cooking a good meal
Movie night with spouse
Volunteering
Reading a good book
Taking the dog for a walk
Sports with friends
Enjoying a solo hobby
Tidying the house

The person in the example may enjoy motivational speakers, watching interesting documentaries, or journaling. Note that just because they realized they enjoy listening to audiobooks on the drive home from work, it doesn't mean that this is the *only* activity that can speak to their underlying value. They can meet their need for learning new things or for personal growth in a host of different ways.

Now, don't dive in and try to do every single one of your listed activities immediately. Instead, just as you did with systematic desensitization, rank the activities from easiest to hardest. Each takes different amounts of energy and yields different levels of benefit. Rank them according to ease, then pick the easiest ones first. This way, you build momentum and work your way up to more intensive activities over time.

Schedule some activities for the coming week, being specific about what you plan to do, when, with whom, and so on.

Finally, an important last step: continue to monitor how you feel. During this week, keep track of both your activity levels and your mood. Note how you felt afterward so that you have enough data to make any necessary adjustments for the week after that.

Step by step, you design your life consciously and in accordance with your principles. You don't just take any old action, but action that is aligned with your values. You may be surprised at just how effective such a data-driven approach can be!

A few tips as you master this strategy:

- Go slow and take baby steps. You want to gradually build up to more activity—doing too much too quickly can burn you out.
- Consider breaking bigger and more energy-intensive tasks into smaller, easier ones first. This makes things much less overwhelming and more manageable.
- Give yourself a reward when you successfully make positive changes, and take time to acknowledge the progress you've made.
- Have self-compassion and don't beat yourself up if you end up procrastinating or canceling activities. At the same time, challenge yourself and don't let yourself get away with saying, "I'm too tired. I'll do it when I'm feeling better."
- Finally, make sure that you're paying attention to tasks that are absolutely necessary and prioritizing those. These are things like showering, filling an important prescription, or making sure the grocery shopping is done.

- So many of us want to change but lose focus when it comes to making real-world plans and goals. It can be difficult to know exactly how to convert insights from self-therapy work into practical changes for yourself. Behavioral activation is a useful framework that can help you stay organized as you make meaningful, lasting changes to your daily routines.

Chapter 14: Behavioral Experiments

What you'll learn in this chapter: how to test out your beliefs and assumptions, and design experiments to help you identify healthier, more rational alternatives instead.

Our final chapter is all about challenging our misconceptions, biases, and assumptions in the best way possible: empirically. "Behavioral experiments" are a way to deliberately examine our beliefs and preconceived ideas and is a big part of self-directed CBT.

In a previous section, we looked at cognitive distortions and how to argue against them. We also closely examined our core beliefs and our personal narratives and how we might challenge these so they can be rewritten. However, the mind is extremely powerful, and many people are masters at fooling themselves, clinging to irrational beliefs despite lacking any shred of evidence!

Behavioral experiments are a great way to get around our own cognitive illusions and see things the way they really are. An experiment is set up in such a way that we can trust our conclusions to be accurate. Knowing that your beliefs are logical, reasonable, and sound (instead of based on superstition, habit, fear, or assumption) is incredibly liberating.

Conducting a behavioral experiment is not difficult, but it does take some honesty. We have to be willing to drop our filters and be open-minded enough to adjust our perceptions when faced with evidence. We all have mental models that encourage us to focus on what fits our narrative, dismiss what doesn't, and distort everything else so that our prevailing belief is preserved. But we also have the power to challenge those models.

A classic example is imposter syndrome. This is where a person holds a belief in their own unworthiness, and that filter colors everything they perceive. They are unable to acknowledge any praise, awards, or promotions as valid, and instead interpret them in the context of their unworthiness: any achievement must be a mistake, and they'll be found out as frauds any day now.

When we conduct behavioral experiments, though, we put our beliefs to the test, committing to holding only those views that have a basis in reality.

How to Test Your Own Cognitive Hypothesis

A hypothesis is a guess or prediction about what will happen in the future, or a tentative explanation. It's not unlike the "mind-reading" or "fortune-telling" cognitive distortion, though, because often these hypotheses have very shaky foundations, indeed. Using the scientific method, we pose a hypothesis and then test it. We devise an experiment, gather data, interpret that data, and then check to see if the result allows us to reject our hypothesis or not.

There is an infinite number of ways to conduct experiments, but they all follow this basic pattern of hypothesis testing. The next time that hypothesis pops into your head, you can argue against it very effectively—because you have already proven to yourself that it isn't true! What matters is that we approach our hypothesis as scientists do: with curiosity, neutrality, and a genuine desire to understand the phenomenon at hand. That means no shame and blame!

Step 1: Identify the Belief You Want to Test
Try to write this belief or prediction down as a single sentence, looking for things that could be cognitive distortions. For example:

"I can't join the dance class because other people will laugh at me."

"Everyone at work feels sorry for me."

"If I were to share my true feelings with others, I'd lose everyone."

Step 2: Assess the Strength of Your Belief
This is simple: how strongly do you believe the above on a scale of one to ten?

You might also like to separate out how much you "believe" it logically versus how much you believe it emotionally. For example, you may know on a rational level that people aren't conspiring against you, but it may nevertheless feel like that sometimes.

Step 3: Design Your Experiment
This part might require a little creativity, but here are three ideas to get you started:

Create a survey. For example, if you think your nose is absolutely hideous and people hate it, then submit your picture to an anonymous forum and ask people what they think—there are places online designed for precisely this purpose! If eighteen out of twenty people didn't even notice your nose, then you have pretty compelling evidence that the hypothesis "my nose is hideous" can be rejected.

Be brave, try it, and see what happens. For example, there's one very obvious way to find out if the hypothesis "I can't join the dance class because other people will laugh at me." Join the class and see! For this to work, though, you need to be brave but also honest.

Try out something new in earnest and avoid self-sabotaging or deliberately interpreting events to support your foregone conclusion. If this sounds extreme, take some inspiration from systematic desensitization and try out a smaller, less risky experiment first, like taking a Zoom dance class where people won't be focusing much on you.

Do the opposite. Sometimes, the only way to test your hypothesis is to stop doing something you have convinced yourself you need to do. For example, the hypothesis "if I don't keep micromanaging my employees, they'll mess up" can be tested by choosing not to micromanage, and waiting to observe if your employees really do mess up. Again, a little courage is needed!

Step 4: Proactively Identify Potential Obstacles

Depending on what you're trying to achieve, plan ahead and make sure that you're giving your experiment the best chance of success. Ask for help if you need it, get advice from others, or see what friends, family, or even a therapist can do to help set up the right scenario. Obviously, you want to avoid any experiments that are dangerous, inappropriate, or liable to backfire.

Step 5: Do the Experiment and Record Your Result
Play out the experiment you've designed and immediately record the results as neutrally as possible. Even better if you can gather hard numerical data about what you find since it's very difficult to argue against cold facts and figures!

In the same way as you identified and adjusted distorted beliefs in an earlier chapter, take the time now to see how your findings compare to your original hypothesis. On the rare occasion, your prediction may actually be confirmed, but it's more likely that you have to make some adjustments. Take the time to literally rewrite the sentence you started with.

"I can't join the dance class because other people will laugh at me" becomes "Nobody seems to care what others do in a dance class."

"Everyone at work feels sorry for me" becomes "On doing an anonymous 360 assessment, ninety percent of people have no strong feelings about me either way, and ten percent expressed genuine concern about my stress levels but deny feeling sorry for me."

"If I were to share my true feelings with others, I'd lose everyone" becomes "When I share how I feel, people have a range of reactions, but I have not discovered a single piece of evidence that these reactions mean I will be abandoned completely."

Look at the rating you gave your hypothesis in Step 2 and see how you feel now after the experiment is concluded. In most cases, you won't magically reduce this number to zero and be completely free of worries and issues. But you're almost certain to see that number drop.

As you read through the process for behavioral experiments, you might have thought, "Well, that sounds fine, but *my* beliefs and assumptions really are true. I know they are, and I don't need to test them."

It's important to recognize that this is most likely just the voice of fear. If you are terrified at the prospect of being hurt or embarrassed when your worst fears are confirmed, become curious about this fear itself.

Let's be honest: life is complex, and our perceptions are likely to be a *blend* of fact and fiction, truth and illusion. It may in fact be true that you don't have an especially nice nose. But what is *not* true is that your nose is "disgusting," that you are unattractive, that other people notice or care about this feature, and that because of it, you are completely incapable of living a happy and successful life!

Behavioral experiments, then, are not some feel-good way to reassure yourself. Rather, it's about anchoring in reality and embracing your world as fully as you can without distorting biases, expectations, assumptions, and interpretations.

The particular conclusion you arrive at is irrelevant; your sense of *clarity* is the goal. So, after a behavioral experiment, you can change your belief to something a lot more comfortable, mature, and resilient: "I don't have the best nose in the world, but it doesn't seem to matter much because there are so many other great things about me, especially beyond my appearance."

Combined with the other techniques discussed in this book, behavioral experiments can be a powerful way to own your experience, take control, and anchor your perception in the real world.

If this all seems like too much effort, then you can start by simply asking this one question: **do I have evidence for this belief?**

Feelings are not evidence!

If you honestly cannot say you have any hard proof for a particular belief, then try to understand that you are choosing to believe something that may be completely wrong. A possible alternative: just withhold judgment. Who says you have to always have an opinion, an answer, or a conclusion? Delay making a pronouncement either way.

If you don't have any evidence for or against, there's nothing wrong with saying, "I just don't know." If you were dumped without an explanation, you could easily get carried away with all sorts of reasons for why it happened. But if you ask yourself, "Do I have any evidence for these beliefs?" you will probably find that the answer is *no*.

In this case you cannot do an experiment to find out the "truth," but you can decide not to play a guessing game. Sometimes, the most rational thing we can do is to admit that there are simply things in life we can never understand!

Takeaways:

- Systematic desensitization is an evidence-based therapy that combines relaxation techniques with gradual exposure to help you overcome a phobia, but it can also be used to address other issues like social anxiety or anger management.
- First, choose a relaxation technique, such as progressive muscle relaxation, mindfulness techniques, or deep breathing. Then, create a hierarchy of levels, from activities that are least intense or fear-inducing to most intense. Devise an activity to try for each level. Then, move through each level and gradually expose yourself, using the relaxation technique when your emotions feel overwhelming.
- When you're depressed, you're less active. Behavioral activation is a way to take action and create pleasure, mastery, and connection to others. Take action even if you don't feel like it.
- Start by monitoring your mood and how you actually spend every hour in a single week. Then analyze that activity and represent it visually, looking for patterns and connections between activity and mood. Ask yourself if the way you spend your time reflects your deepest values, whatever they are. Then choose to activate those activities that will speak to your values by scheduling them in, observing the result, and adjusting as you go.
- Behavioral experiments allow you to test out your beliefs and assumptions and design experiments to help you identify healthier, more rational alternatives instead. First, identify the belief (hypothesis) you want to test, assess its strength, design an experiment to test that hypothesis, run the experiment, and then decide whether the results support your hypothesis or not.
- A simple way to bring a more rational mindset to our thought processes is just to ask, "Do I have evidence for this belief?"

Summary Guide

PART 1: GETTING TO KNOW YOUR DEEPER SELF

- No matter who you are, it is possible to improve your life with the same evidence-based techniques used by cognitive behavioral therapists all over the world, i.e., self-therapy can help you live the life you want to live.
- Begin with asking who you are—that is, engaging in self-exploration. With practice, the habit of asking, "What do I notice about myself right now?" will become easier.
- Use Dr. Tom Stevens' six-step approach for cultivating self-exploration: 1) turn on your "inner noticer" and observe yourself without judgment, 2) zoom in on "the problem", 3) follow the strongest emotion, 4) allow yourself to notice any emerging patterns or overarching themes, 5) see what core beliefs are linking everything together, and 6) use these insights to inspire new, more conscious behavior.
- Carl Jung was the first to talk about the shadow, which is an archetype containing all the unconscious and disowned parts of our psyche. We reintegrate the shadow with patience, non-judgmental acceptance, honesty, and the willingness to face our dark side. We can do this by noticing disproportionate emotional reactions that may hint at the shadow's presence, mindfully embrace our imperfections and weaknesses (humor helps), as well as ask others for their honest feedback on what we can't see in ourselves.
- Gestalt therapy is about understanding how your perception shapes your world, as well as releasing the past so you are more fully available to respond to the present. Some ways to do this include 1) rehearse acts of closure, 2) try the empty chair technique, 3) claim responsibility for your life, 4) shift from the WHY of your experience to the HOW, 5) change questions into affirmations.
- Internal Family Systems posits that the mind is made of many parts in relationship: firefighters, managers, and exiles. Befriend and feel into difficult emotions and normalize them by asking the role they play in your life.

PART 2: SO, HOW DID YOU GET HERE?

- To better understand how you are, it's worth understanding your early childhood experiences. Your attachment style becomes the model on which all your subsequent relationships are based, and it influences your self-concept, core beliefs, and behavior. If our needs were met by primary caregivers, we develop a secure attachment style and healthy attitudes toward intimacy. However, if our needs were not met or met poorly, we may develop insecure attachment styles.

- There are three insecure attachment styles: ambivalent (where care was inconsistent and we end up too "clingy"), avoidant (where care was lacking and so we overdeveloped our sense of independence, shunning intimacy), and disorganized (where abusive early dynamics created a chaotic attitude toward relationships).
- We can improve our relationships by consciously challenging old patterns, seeking out positive role models, and paying attention to our emotional intelligence and nonverbal communication.
- We can resolve many past issues by re-parenting the inner child. The inner child is the younger version of yourself that still lives on in the present. Reparenting is the act of recognizing what needs went unmet for your childhood self and committing to giving that to yourself right now in the present. Dialogues, affirmations, and playdates can also help!
- Narrative therapy tells us that we are not our thoughts, we can externalize our problems, and stories can change. Use the My Life Story exercise to become aware of overarching patterns and themes in your life. Plot out your life as a story, but reflect on ways you might like to change that story. A trusted "editor" could also provide feedback and help you think about different ways to frame or reframe your life narrative.

PART 3: THOUGHTS ARE THE CODE THAT PROGRAMS YOUR LIFE

- A core belief is a deep and fundamental assumption or idea that impacts our identity and behavior, as well as the life narrative we create for ourselves. We can transform our unconscious, maladaptive, and inaccurate core beliefs into alternatives that genuinely support our wellbeing and growth as people. In CBT, we identify, challenge, and rework core beliefs. We can identify core beliefs with the downward arrow technique.
- Our goal is to replace what is automatic, unconscious, maladaptive, inaccurate, and irrational with something that is deliberate, conscious, helpful, accurate, and rational.
- The ABCD model stands for Activating event, Belief, Consequences, and Dispute. We can use it to identify and re-engineer your ingrained thought patterns and cognitive distortions. By identifying the four parts, we can discover more rational alternatives to habitual thought patterns.
- Cognitive distortions are like a filter placed over objective reality. The triple column technique can help us identify and address these distortions. Write down a thought, identify possible distortions, then soften, invert, or moderate that thought and revert to it next time you have that thought again.
- Cognitive defusion is a way to quickly gain distance, control, and perspective when you feel overwhelmed by thoughts and feelings. We suffer not because of

our experiences, but our responses and attitudes toward those experiences, i.e., our over-identification with them.
- Defusion techniques include using the phrase, "I'm noticing that…" thanking our mind for trying to help and using the Leaves on a Stream meditation to let thoughts flow on without resistance or clinging.

PART 4: BUILD THE LIFE YOU WANT ONE ACTION AT A TIME

- Systematic desensitization is an evidence-based therapy that combines relaxation techniques with gradual exposure to help you overcome a phobia, but it can also be used to address other issues like social anxiety or anger management.
- First, choose a relaxation technique, such as progressive muscle relaxation, mindfulness techniques, or deep breathing. Then, create a hierarchy of levels, from activities that are least intense or fear-inducing to most intense. Devise an activity to try for each level. Then, move through each level and gradually expose yourself, using the relaxation technique when your emotions feel overwhelming.
- When you're depressed, you're less active. Behavioral activation is a way to take action and create pleasure, mastery, and connection to others. Take action even if you don't feel like it.
- Start by monitoring your mood and how you actually spend every hour in a single week. Then analyze that activity and represent it visually, looking for patterns and connections between activity and mood. Ask yourself if the way you spend your time reflects your deepest values, whatever they are. Then choose to activate those activities that will speak to your values by scheduling them in, observing the result, and adjusting as you go.
- Behavioral experiments allow you to test out your beliefs and assumptions and design experiments to help you identify healthier, more rational alternatives instead. First, identify the belief (hypothesis) you want to test, assess its strength, design an experiment to test that hypothesis, run the experiment, and then decide whether the results support your hypothesis or not.
- A simple way to bring a more rational mindset to our thought processes is just to ask, "Do I have evidence for this belief?"

Book 2: Anxiety is the Enemy:
29 Techniques to Combat Overthinking, Stress, Panic, and Pressure

Table of Contents

CHAPTER 1. YOUR ANXIETY MANAGEMENT TOOLKIT

1. LABEL YOUR EMOTIONS
2. BUILD SELF-AWARENESS
3. QUESTION YOURSELF USING SOCRATIC METHOD
4. TEST YOUR FALSE BELIEFS
5. MAKE A MIND MAP
6. PLAY MIND GAMES
7. USE THE ABC MODEL TO UNDERSTAND YOUR STRESS

CHAPTER 2. AN ANXIETY-FREE LIFESTYLE

8. LIMIT CAFFEINE INTAKE
9. SCHEDULE YOUR "WORRY TIME"
10. CULTIVATE GRATITUDE
11. USE "MENTAL ANCHORING"
12. HAVE A SOLID MORNING ROUTINE
13. START A HOBBY

CHAPTER 3. ENTER YOUR MIND

14. BELLY BREATHING
15. THE 5-4-3-2-1 GROUNDING TECHNIQUE
16. HAVE A MANTRA
17. SCAN YOUR BODY
18. LAUGHTER MEDITATION
19. LOVING-KINDNESS MEDITATION

CHAPTER 4. THE FIRST STEP IS SEEING IT

20. GUIDED IMAGERY
21. METAPHORIZE YOUR ANXIETY
22. TALK ABOUT YOURSELF IN THIRD PERSON
23. ROLE-PLAYING
24. HAVE AN ALTER EGO

CHAPTER 5. REFRAME AND SHIFT

25. ACCEPT YOUR ANXIETY
26. TELL YOURSELF YOU'RE JUST EXCITED
27. WRITE TO YOUR FUTURE SELF
28. LEARN HOW TO SAY "I DON'T"
29. HAVE NO OPINION

SUMMARY GUIDE

Chapter 1. Your Anxiety Management Toolkit

Whether stress is just an occasional occurrence for you or you're battling a more entrenched anxiety disorder, there are thankfully countless scientifically proven methods for cultivating a calmer, happier, and more balanced life. We'll start this chapter with a few key strategies that will help you understand your anxiety so you can consciously take control.

The first step is always to become aware of where we stand. Only then can we start to challenge our beliefs, put labels on our experiences, and start to pick apart the stress response as it plays out in our day-to-day lives. Let's dive in.

1. LABEL YOUR EMOTIONS

When you're stuck in an anxiety spiral, it can be hard to even put a finger on what's happening to you. All you know is one thing: it feels bad! Your thoughts are racing all over the place, and you may even feel physically ill. It's like overthinking, worry, and anxiety are an overwhelming flood that completely washes over you, and you can't escape or defend yourself. Think about the last time you felt completely swamped with anxiety and overthinking—what did it feel like? If you find it difficult to find the right words to describe the intense feelings, then this following tip will help you.

Dan Siegel is a professor at the UCLA School of Medicine, and teaches people how to "name it and tame it." According to Siegel, when we label our strong emotions, we create distance between us and them. Giving how we feel a name is one way we can almost step outside of that flood of anxiety, rather than being swallowed up by it!

It's a question of controlling your feelings or allowing yourself to be controlled by them. Or a handy way to think of it is: if you can *see* an emotion, you don't have to *be* an emotion.

Psychological distance is the feeling of perspective we gain over our ourselves. The thing is, when we're caught in an overthinking loop or anxious rumination, we lack awareness. We may feel a rush of strong negative emotions, but we lack perspective or the ability to say, "I'm experiencing some anxiety right now."

Much of our fear comes from our inbuilt fight-or-flight response instilled in us by evolution. Based in the amygdala of the brain, this reaction is completely unconscious, automatic, and physiological. To step out of this instinctual, knee-jerk response, we need to pause long enough to realize that we are actually having that response in the first place, and this realization brings us into our "higher brain," the prefrontal cortex.

Clinical psychologist Dr. Mitch Abblett explains how strong emotions like anxiety can be like a handheld right in front of our faces. We are so fixated on that hand that we cannot see anything else in front of us. Simply acknowledging what is going on by giving a label to your emotions, however, reminds you that this hand in front of your face wasn't always there, and that it won't be there forever. When you do this, something special happens: you create a little gap in which you get to choose what you do next.

Matthew Lieberman and colleagues published a paper in *Psychological Science* back in 2007, where they found that "affect labeling" (i.e., putting feelings into words) actually alters the brain. When Liberman's test subjects underwent fMRI scans while experiencing strong emotions, simply labeling these emotions decreased activity in all the regions of the brain associated with emotional regulation, particularly the amygdala. This is the little gap. Once the strong emotional response is dampened, then we can go in and allow our rational brains to step in and solve problems for us.

And this is the lesson that mindfulness practitioners have been teaching for years. When we label an emotion, it is no longer something we *are* but something we *are aware of*. And so we disengage. And when that strong anxiety is not so firmly attached to us, we can make decisions from a calmer, more deliberate place psychologically.

How do we name emotions as we're experiencing them? It can be difficult in the heat of the moment—but that's exactly when we need to learn to do it! Here's a step-by-step guide:

- First, simply become aware of what your *body* is doing. Your body is in the moment and will be the first to alert you to strong emotions. Let's say you've just gotten off the phone with your father, and a few minutes later, you become aware of an awful antsy feeling around your shoulders and chest and a horrible tight lump in the back of your throat.
- When you notice this physical response, stop. Just pause and bring awareness to it. Let's say you excuse yourself and go and sit quietly in your room for a moment.
- Next, breathe a little more slowly and focus on the physical sensation while you try to identify what you're feeling. You are only looking for a label—not an accusation, diagnosis, or judgment. Maybe after a few breaths, you say to yourself out loud, "I am feeling anxiety . . . I'm having worried and panicky thoughts . . ."

- At this point, you can literally imagine the word "anxiety" as separate from you. Visualize the word "anxiety" in letters that you hold in your hands or which you can pin to your clothing.
- Keep breathing and notice how you feel after you give your experience a name.

Here, you might be wondering if you need to get away from the anxiety, or somehow visualize yourself destroying it. But you don't! Simple awareness is enough to create distance. You don't have to fight with what you feel or analyze it or rush to find a solution. You just need to be aware and feel what you feel.

Before any meaningful action can take place, you need to be able to see what you're feeling. So just focus on that for a moment. Try not to say, "I am stressed." *You* are not stressed, you're just you, and you're experiencing stress. There is stress. Stress is occurring. As you breathe in and out, try simply saying "stress"—because once you can identify the phenomenon unfolding, you can see that it is not especially attached to you . . . if you don't want it to be. It is just something that is happening.

Sometimes with anxiety, we can get caught in a trap feeling anxious about how anxious we feel. So, for this exercise, don't fight anything. Our awareness is not a "solution" to anything; it's simply an emergency stop on a runaway thought process. It allows us to gently remove the hand from in front of our face.

2. BUILD SELF-AWARENESS

To be able to label our emotions and to question our beliefs and thoughts, there is one thing we cannot do without: self-awareness. Anxious rumination can *feel* like we're thinking, like we're being aware, but it's usually an illusion. We're not really solving any problems, clarifying the situation, or getting anywhere—we're just going round in circles and making ourselves feel bad.

A moment of self-awareness in the midst of an anxiety spiral can be a life raft, but it also pays to cultivate an overall greater sense of self-awareness in everyday life. It's almost as though you're inoculating yourself against runaway thoughts in the future. Self-awareness is not just a skill but a stable long-term trait. It is about knowing and understanding yourself, including your strengths, weaknesses, triggers, and joys.

Greater self-awareness is not some abstract quality—it results in real self-esteem, greater calm, and a more internal locus of control (i.e., the feeling that *you* are in charge and not merely reacting to outside forces).

Here are three practical tips to try in order to deepen your self-awareness.

Tip 1: Keep a thought diary

This an easy, accessible way to constantly monitor/tune into your feelings and plans. Eventually, you internalize the ability to notice what you're feeling and when without pausing to put pen to paper. When you write your thoughts down, you practice labeling (and the distance it brings) and you also see more clearly your own self-talk—what effect does it have on you to think these thoughts? When you're flustered, sit down and pour everything onto the page. But rather than ruminating, use the journal to go on a fact-finding mission.

How are you feeling? What came before these feelings? What are you thinking? What is in your control here and what isn't? How accurate are your appraisals? What resources do you have right now? What are you trying to achieve and is your approach working? What action can you take?

You'll know a journaling session has been successful when you close the pages and feel like you've reached an end and gained some insight into where to go next. One tip: focus on the *what* rather than the *why*.

Tip 2: Engage in mindfulness practices

You don't need to have a full-blown yoga practice or a daily meditation session to benefit from mindfulness. Remember, the key is to gain awareness—and even a moment of awareness can bring distance, control, and a sense of relief from overthinking.

Practice strengthening the body-mind connection by doing some deep breathing and stretching exercises, or spend some time in quiet contemplation. The only goal is to stay present in your body, in your breath, and in the moment. You are not trying to accomplish anything, play "gotcha!" with your thoughts, or judge how mindful you're being. Try to aim for a few seconds of still, calm awareness peppered all throughout the day whenever you can remember.

Tip 3: Take a personal inventory

When trapped in anxious overthinking, your mind can convince you that everything is awful and that you're completely hopeless. But the truth is that you have many strengths, skills, and resources at your disposal. You always have options. Beyond that, you can strengthen your self-esteem by frankly acknowledging your limitations and weaknesses. When you're aware of your flaws, you can own them.

There are many ways to learn more about yourself and what makes you tick—good and bad. An easy example is to simply acknowledge the fact that you have a tendency to ruminate. If you know this about yourself, then you're instantly empowered to work around these limitations. You're never caught off guard, unaware of why you do what you do. You recognize your triggers when they emerge, and you know the ways to manage them.

You could take psychometric tests or do self-assessments like the MBTI, which will help you better understand your personality. You could also ask those closest to you to share what they understand about your strengths and weaknesses as people looking from the outside in. One interesting exercise is to make a list of what you think your ten best and worst traits are (for example, "dedicated" or "aloof") and then compare them to a list you ask a close friend or family member to compile. You may be surprised!

Alternatively, ask mentors or work colleagues to give you (considerate) feedback to help you better appreciate aspects of your behavior you might not see clearly. A therapist is another person who can help you gain a clear, balanced, and accurate view of yourself that can help moderate the tendency to overthink.

One big caveat about self-awareness and introspection, however: we do not necessarily gain any self-awareness by simply turning inward and contemplating our navels. There is, in fact, a wrong way to be self-aware! It's easy to imagine why: you only replicate any bias or blind spots you have, and never get to test your theories against reality.

There are actually *two* kinds of self-awareness—internal and external. The former is about how well we know our own needs, goals, and feelings, and the latter is about understanding how others see us. Introspection typically only helps us with internal self-awareness, but we need *both* types to be balanced, well-functioning people.

Simply being aware of what we think and feel doesn't mean that these thoughts or feelings are right or helpful. In fact, research by organizational psychologist Tasha Eurich has shown that people who introspect a lot may actually be *worse* at self-awareness! Seeing that ninety-five percent of people claim to be self-aware when just fifteen percent are, Eurich said that "eighty percent of us are lying to ourselves about whether we're lying to ourselves."

Anxiety and overthinking thrive in the private spaces in our own minds. If we can open up those spaces, shine some light on them, and invite in others' perspectives to moderate our own, we can reshape the thought patterns that cause us anxiety.

For example, you could argue with yourself for years about whether people secretly dislike you at work, writing fruitlessly in a diary under the guise of gaining awareness about why you're so unlikable. But if you go out there and gather genuinely given feedback from your colleagues and discover that you are in fact not disliked at all, you gain real, usable self-awareness that will diminish your anxiety, not increase it!

3. QUESTION YOURSELF USING SOCRATIC METHOD

If you suffer from anxiety and overthinking, you can sometimes start to think of your brain as an enemy. You might start to view thinking of any kind as stressful and exhausting. But the truth is, your brain and the rationality it is capable of is a wonderful thing. The mind is a terrible master and a wonderful servant, as they say. Borrowing some cognitive tools from the philosopher Socrates can help us train our faculties to work for us rather than against us.

Socrates once said, "I know you won't believe me, but the highest form of human excellence is to question oneself and others." For people who find their ruminating takes on an endless, compulsive quality, questions can act as a clarifier, cutting away at useless rumination and allowing us to see ourselves and our thought processes more clearly.

Using the Socratic method, you will be able to assess the credibility and logic of your own thoughts, and this can be a powerful antidote to the illogic of our most anxious obsessions. You will also be able to identify your own thought patterns and recognize inconsistencies and assumptions.

First of all, let's make a distinction:

Here is an anxious question: "What if something goes wrong? What if *everything* goes wrong?"

Here is a more useful question: "What evidence do I have that this is a problem?"

Both are questions, but they act in very different ways. The first one is open-ended, vague, and, actually, when you look closely, cannot have a real answer. This is the kind of question that encourages, you guessed it, more overthinking. The second question, however, is focused, deliberate, and intended to bring clarity. It has an answer. And that answer can be acted upon.

When you practice Socratic questioning, you are emptying your mind and assuming you know nothing, then proceeding methodically and logically. What do you really know? Instead of running away with assumptions, guesses, and foregone conclusions, you *discover* the answer step by step. The usual outcome is that you realize your anxiety was an illusion created by faulty assumptions, not objective reality.

Let's say you do the exercise from the previous section and uncover an anxious thought: "My elderly father is really ill and may not last the rest of the year." This leads to, "He's probably going to die any day now, and I won't be able to cope when it happens . . ."

But if you can open that gap by pausing, you can ask questions. According to Clark & Egen (2015) the Socratic method survives in modern-day psychology in the form of Cognitive Behavioral Therapy, which focuses on examining thoughts and beliefs so they can be consciously modified. A good question can help you untangle thoughts that are creating anxiety for you. A "good question" is concise, open (yet purposeful), curious, and neutral—i.e., there is no judgment or an assumed right answer.

Conventionally, Socratic dialogues (and CBT therapy) takes place between two people having a conversation. But with practice, you can have a conversation with yourself, or more accurately, with your anxious thoughts. Let's return to our example and look at a few questions that can help guide us out of confusion and stress:

Clarification questions: What do you mean by "really ill?" What exactly will happen if you "can't cope"?

Questions that challenge assumptions: Do you have reason to believe he will die soon? Are you making assumptions about his illness?

Uncovering evidence: Can you find any proof that death is imminent? Do you have all the information you need to reach that conclusion?

Exploring alternatives: Is it possible that he may in fact live? How are his doctors framing his illness?

Exploring implications: What effect is this fear having on your life? How does this impact others?

By asking these questions, the person in our example could soon realize that although his father's illness is serious, there is actually very little evidence to suggest that he will die. He can look again at his original thought: "He's probably going to die any day now and I won't be able to cope when it happens . . ." This thought causes anxiety and launches a whole avalanche of other equally anxious thoughts. But can it be modified?

After gently questioning himself, he can arrive at a milder idea: "There is always a chance that he could die, and that is the case for any of us at any time, but he is alive and well now, and there is absolutely no reason to overthink it." What's more, in the calm that this more balanced idea creates, he could start to see that he actually has very little information and can take action by talking to his father or his father's doctor to better understand the situation rather than passively panicking about it.

When it comes to overthinking, Socratic dialogue can help us slow down and not simply take our own word for it! Your brain can be your worst enemy or your best friend. Commit to using your brainpower for good, and you can actually reduce anxiety by finding clarity and useful ways forward. The next time you've identified a stressful thought in yourself, put it under the microscope and ask it to defend itself. Why should you allow an irrational, inaccurate, or flat-out wrong idea to torment and bother you? Try this process:

Step 1: Put your anxious thoughts or ideas into a sentence.

Step 2: Ask, is there any evidence to believe it? Also ask what you one hundred percent know and what is merely bias, expectation, fear, assumption, exaggeration, or catastrophic thinking.

Step 3: Challenge yourself. If something seems a little shaky, look closer. Deliberately look for alternatives or counterexamples to challenge what you currently think.

Step 4: Rewrite this thought into something more moderate.

Even if you can remember none of these steps in the heat of the moment, just remind yourself to challenge your assumptions, ask questions, and look for evidence. Decide that you won't grasp hold of a thought until it has stood on trial to justify itself!

4. TEST YOUR FALSE BELIEFS

The funny thing about anxiety is how *unreal* it is. You can convince yourself that something is really a Very Big Problem, but if you look at it with another perspective, all you can see is a person sitting safely and comfortably in their living room, having a series of electro-chemical signals run through their brain. That's literally it. The Very Big Problem is simply a story they're telling themselves.

When we worry and ruminate, we can take any old story and behave *as if it were true.* We can start with "what if they were laughing at me?" and end with "I'm an awful human being and everyone hates me for sure," all with zero correction or input from the objective world around us. The brain has an amazing capacity to entertain thoughts and ideas that simply aren't true. This is an amazing ability that allows us to be creative, to plan, to dream, and to think up new solutions that don't yet exist. But it also allows us to dream up awful hypotheticals and fictitious theories that act like mental torture devices we make for ourselves.

There's one blindingly obvious way to counter this tendency of the brain to run off unchecked into the unreal—test it. Do an experiment. Compare what's in your head with what's out there in the world and see if your anxious model of reality actually stands up to scrutiny. It sounds like an odd way to go about it, but how often have you worked yourself up into a froth over an idea that you never once stopped to check the veracity of? How often have you told yourself a mental story and simply assumed it was true without ever checking to see if it was?

Much research is now focused on revealing the relationship between anxiety disorders, perception, and the inability to tolerate uncertainty. Psychologist Aaron Beck and his colleagues claimed that anxiety *"is an uncontrollable affective response dependent upon the **interpretation** of a situation and the appraisal of a possible threat of negative events."* Basically, the anxiety is not a result of the stimulus itself but our interpretation of that stimulus as a threat. We decide how anxious we feel based on:

- How likely we think the threat is to occur
- How bad we think it'll be when it happens
- How well we predict we can cope
- How much help we can expect from the outside

As you can see, all of the above are about *perception* of reality, not reality. If we appraise something as a threat (for example, people laughing when we walk into a room), we may respond with a racing heart, a blush, and a flood of negative thoughts, i.e., "they're laughing at me." Almost without knowing you're doing it, you could create a rich inner theory about this experience designed to deal with the perceived threat and uncertainty. Your anxiety, once started, seems to feed on itself so quickly that you never stop to ask, "Are they actually laughing at me?"

Testing our false beliefs can act like a safety valve that breaks the anxiety cycle. For a simple example, you could straight out ask in the moment if people are laughing at you, or pull someone aside and ask them in private what their interpretation of events was. "Oh no, Emma just told a really funny joke the moment you walked in!"

Using Socratic dialogue, too, is a way to test our assumptions before we get carried away with them. True, sometimes you really don't know—but this is where tolerance of uncertainty comes into play. If you have no way of knowing whether people were in fact laughing at you, for example, you could still conclude, "Well, I have no evidence either way." Sometimes, you may have a more vague and general belief, such as, "My whole friend group secretly dislikes me." This belief, too, can be tested.

See if you can ask yourself questions to test this potentially false belief:

- How likely we think the threat is to occur—How likely is it really that people you consider friends all secretly dislike you? Is it really all that possible, given how often they choose to spend time with you?
- How bad we think it'll be when it happens—Even if your friends occasionally didn't get on with you, would that be so bad? Is it the end of the world if someone doesn't like you one hundred percent? Does one person disliking you mean that others won't or that you're completely unlikable?
- How well we predict we can cope—Is being a little concerned about this really such a big deal? Is it really crucial that you find out how others feel deep down, or can you handle a little ambiguity?
- How much help we can expect from the outside—"If you struggle with this idea, isn't it possible you can talk to your friends about how you feel? Could you sort out your feelings with a therapist or someone else you trust?"

Another very direct way to test our potentially false beliefs is through **exposure therapy**. Traditionally, psychologists have used this approach to help people overcome specific phobias. The idea is that if you repeatedly expose yourself to a stimulus you firmly believe you can't tolerate, you show yourself that you *can* tolerate it—you give yourself proof that the thought "I can't get on a plane because I'll crash" is actually not true.

Your brain makes an interpretation of a stimulus and decides it's a threat. But when you repeatedly encounter this "threat" and nothing bad happens, your brain soon has to adjust its appraisal.

Importantly, this isn't something that happens abstractly in your head. It's something you **do** out there in the world. To make exposure therapy work, however, you have to tolerate the stimulus until it no longer provokes a fear response. Quit before this point and you only reinforce that the stimulus is a bad thing to fear and avoid. How can you use exposure therapy in your own life when dealing with overthinking?

First, identify a thought or story you're telling yourself that is causing you to feel anxious; for example, "I'm incapable of public speaking." Let's say the thought of public speaking causes a major anxiety response.

The next step is to see if this can be tested in reality. Sit down and write a list of graded steps you can take to gradually expose yourself to the idea of public speaking. Remember to tolerate the stimulus until it doesn't cause a fear response anymore.

Maybe you sign up for an amateur acting class and practice, in baby steps, getting on stage and speaking a few lines, then gradually increasing the time you spend on stage. Work up to offering to give a presentation at work where you have to speak for a longer period. Every time you expose yourself to the stimulus, challenge yourself to observe what is happening: is it *really* as bad as you thought? Are you absolutely "incapable," or do you just find it a little unfamiliar and uncomfortable?

Finally, keep going and allow your experiences to gently challenge your original thought. Maybe you eventually arrive at a more balanced view. "I don't really enjoy public speaking, but it's something I can do if I need to, and I'm sure I could get better if I practiced."

Not all beliefs and thoughts can be challenged with exposure therapy. If that's the case for you, try to embrace the uncertainty rather than rush in with a story or theory to help counter the perceived "threat." It can take practice to simply say "I don't know yet what kind of situation this is" instead of "this is a bad situation." The next time you encounter an ambiguous or unresolved situation, choose to deliberately interpret it as *unknown rather than threatening*. "That girl from last night's date hasn't replied to my text. I don't know how she feels about me yet," is far less anxiety-provoking than, "She hasn't replied. She's definitely not interested. I hate dating!"

Researchers are now wondering whether intolerance uncertainty is a kind of personal characteristic or trait that predisposes us to anxiety. Gentes & Ruscio published a meta-analysis in 2011 in *Clinical Psychology Review* exploring this trait in detail, and through statistically analyzing the data, they found definite and significant links between mental illness and what has been called "paralysis of cognition and action in the face of uncertainty."

How well a person can tolerate uncertainty has even been implicated in things like OCD, social anxiety, depression, and even eating disorders, so if this is something you recognize in yourself, learning to tolerate the unknown could make a drastic difference to many areas of your life, stress included.

5. MAKE A MIND MAP

What does anxiety and overthinking *look like*?

Close your eyes right now and visualize how rumination and stress look. If you're like most people, you might imagine one thing: chaos. Anxious thoughts are characterized by never-ending loops, knots, tangles, and too many thoughts piled up on top of each other in a complete mess, right?

Brain dumping is a seriously useful tool for cutting through this mind clutter and finding sweet, sweet **clarity**. Think of it as an organized brain dump. Instead of letting that plate of crazy mental spaghetti swirl around in your head, you put it down on paper. From there, you can get some relief, start to organize things, claim back a little control, solve problems, take action to improve what you can, and let go of those things you can't change.

It's as though you are in a crowded and chaotic train station, running around, getting freaked out about every tiny detail. But when you make a mind map, you zoom out and get a bird's eye view of everything. Suddenly, you don't feel so overwhelmed, and you can also start to see how things can be simplified, decluttered, and slowed down.

The technique is very simple. First, get out a piece of blank paper and a pen or pencil and sit somewhere you'll be undisturbed for a while. Begin with a focus word or phrase—you don't have to nail down the single Big Issue that's worrying you; just put down the first main problem that springs to mind. Importantly, you don't want to get distracted by doing it "right" or analyzing at this stage. Just give yourself permission to put everything you're thinking of onto the page. Don't overthink it.

For example, you sit down and imagine your head is a jug and you're pouring everything out. The first word that comes out is DEADLINE. You scribble this in dark, menacing letters at the center of the page, then draw some branches around it. On these branches, you explore different aspects of this main nub of anxiety. You could explore, for example:

- How you feel about it
- The people involved
- Physical sensations
- The history of this idea or feeling
- Events in the past
- Thoughts about this idea
- Related areas of concern
- Why it's a problem
- Other complicating factors

From each of these branches, you extend more details. For example, branching from DEADLINE could be "I feel resentful and obliged" and "exhausted" as feelings about an upcoming tight deadline. Off of the "resentful" branch, however, you may discover you have even more mental material to dump, and draw more sub-branches: "I agreed to this when I knew I shouldn't have." This may lead to some other branches to do with your job or boundaries that need strengthening (more on this in a later chapter).

Now for the second part. Once you've put everything down, just pause for a moment and see if there's anything else in there. Remember that you are not in problem-solving, judging, or organizing mode just yet. You are in brain-dump mode. And yes, it will be messy (that's the point!).

How do you organize the mess? Well, take a breath and consciously ask your brain to go into a different mode. When we overthink and ruminate, we are in a state of mind where we are constantly distracted by endless detail and irrelevant minutiae. To get out of anxiety, we need to stop being at the mercy of these meaningless details and start instead to take control of them. Cut through the clutter with these four questions:

- **What can I control?**
- **What can I not control?**
- **What can I DO to improve my situation?**

- **What really matters to me most?**

When we focus on control, concrete action, and our values, it's as though we have a sword that cuts through mental confusion and overwhelm. Let's go back to our example. You look at the resulting mind map and ask first what you can control. You see that you cannot change the fact of the deadline, or the fact of what you have already done in the past. But you see that you can control what you do right now. You have a look at your mind map and see some patterns (in previous maps you might have made, too).

You keep turning these questions over and over again, and the issue begins to take a simpler, clearer shape. It seems that every time you agree to act against your own principles or values, and any time you take on the work you think you should be doing rather than the work you can realistically do, then you feel stressed and resentful. Still, what to actually do with this insight? Well, you can make sure you act differently next time. But what about now?

Perhaps you take a yellow highlighter and highlight only those parts of the mind map that you can reasonably do anything about. When you are literally staring at a page of clutter with only one or two yellow lines through it, you can see for yourself how much of your thoughts are useful, and how much is pure distraction, stress, and overthinking!

It sounds too simple, but sometimes, if we can visually see how much of our stress is unnecessary, we can more easily let it go. The stressed mind loves vague, general visions of doom. But if you can narrow things down to specifics, put words to them, and start ordering your thoughts, you start to see how insignificant most of your thought traffic actually is.

Mind mapping takes a little practice. Be careful that you don't inadvertently give yourself another tool for rumination! If you're feeling overwhelmed, go back to the four questions above. If you feel a little lost, look for patterns. For example, even though it feels like you have three dozen separate things to worry about, could they really all be versions of the same thing? And if you're feeling bad, try to find specific words to describe it. "Everything is wrong and I hate my life" is so big and overwhelming, but "I am overwhelmed right now by the number of tasks I feel people expect me to do" is smaller and more manageable.

Once you've gotten the hang of mind maps for stress management, you can incorporate other techniques covered in this book. For example, you can use a mind map to help you identify false beliefs you want to rewrite, ask questions of yourself, or put labels on the emotions you're feeling.

Finally, it's worth remembering that sometimes, a mind map alone won't magically solve all your problems or shine a light out of a dilemma. But what it will always do is put you in a proactive, rational, and conscious frame of mind. And *this* will make you feel calmer and more in control whether you solve the problem or not!

6. PLAY MIND GAMES

One powerful weapon we have against useless overthinking is distraction, or, as T.S. Eliot phrased it, "distracted from distraction by distraction." Here's the thing: if you already know logically that your rumination does not serve you in any way, then you know you can safely ignore it.

Fighting with overwhelming thoughts just makes them stronger. What you need instead is a complete break and to completely take your mind off things. Being distracted is sometimes the perfect (and only!) way to short circuit rumination and give yourself enough of a break to gain mental serenity again.

Yes, "distraction" has a bad reputation. But if we use it consciously and deliberately, it can be a way to quickly escape a runaway brain when things like mindfulness are just not going to work.

Playing "mind games" with yourself is a little like catching an unhappy child's attention by waving a stuffed toy around. You can't rationalize with a two-year-old having a tantrum about something that makes no sense in the first place. All you can do is cleverly pull attention away long enough to get them to calm down! Think of your anxious brain the same way—it's just a child having a tantrum. It's just gotten stuck in the mud and needs a quick shove to loosen it again. Here are a few ideas to help you do just that:

Game 1: Fantasize about the perfect day

If there were absolutely nothing to stop you, what would your perfect day look like? If you had all the money, time, and energy in the world, what would you get up to from the moment you opened your eyes in the morning? Have fun with it. If you like, you can construct your own imaginary hypothetical society, or dream up the perfect home—it doesn't have to be realistic or make any sense. It just has to be entertaining.

Game 2: Get lost in questions

Anxiety and curiosity are mutually exclusive experiences—you cannot be both at the same time.

Imagine you're a child again and looking at the world with completely fresh eyes. What stands out to you? What's really weird when you start thinking about it? What have you always secretly wondered but never actually investigated?

You don't have to come up with any profound insights or do anything to find out the answers to big questions. Just playing around with being open and loose. Like, who decided where the borders of countries go? What was it like when there were no "countries"? When was the first time they even used that word? Has there ever been someone born exactly on a boundary?

Game 3: Go on a mental walk

One sneaky way to distract yourself is simply to give your poor overworked brain a job that is pretty simple yet engrossing. You can "displace" anxious thoughts with neutral or pleasant ones that require your full attention.

Close your eyes and picture a favorite place, a holiday you've gone on, or a well-known route you've traveled in the past. Now mentally walk through this visualization, taking plenty of time to flesh out the details on each of the five senses. See how much you can remember from your childhood home or classroom. Or try to reconstruct the layout of the supermarket you used to go to in another town. This is a great exercise when you're trying to fall asleep.

Game 4: The alphabet game

This one is simple. Pick a broad category, like animals, food, or movies, then move through the alphabet thinking of an item that starts with that letter. For example, "aardvark, baboon, camel, dinosaur..."

You could make yourself think of three items before moving on, or make a special rule where you can avoid tricky letters like Q, if you want to. Or, when you get to Z, go around the alphabet again and repeat the process with new items.

Game 5: Build your mental museum

This is a little like going on a mental walk, except instead of fleshing out a memory you already have, you build something from scratch. Start by imagining that you're in a completely empty room with bare white walls—or go a step further and imagine no walls at all (remember that scene in *The Matrix*?). Now assemble a collection of things exactly as you want them.

Maybe you could gather up a few favorite images or paintings, or make an exhibition of all your favorite items—or for that matter, your favorite people! Collect little mementoes that remind you of happy memories or of things you care about. You can make the theme of the museum anything you like. It can be personal or simply a fantastical vision of a hypothetical museum you'd love to visit.

Game 6: Memory game

Give your brain the task of remembering a speech, poem, pattern, or sequence. Challenge yourself. You could also play counting games where you count backward or skip ahead in fixed intervals—or go backward in fixed intervals!

Game 7: People watch

If you're feeling anxious when away from home and need a distraction in a public place, try people watching. Watch people walk by and try to guess their names, their occupations, their ages, or even their deepest secrets. See if you can imagine what each person is thinking at that very moment, or where they may be headed to.

It's true that distraction can be harmful if done compulsively or unconsciously, but it can certainly be a clever way to manage stress if used wisely. You can even try inventing your own distraction games. The only aim is to find a mental activity that is absorbing enough to pull your mind away from compulsive rumination. The idea is that once you've played the game for a while, you'll come back to the "real world" and discover you're feeling much more relaxed.

7. USE THE ABC MODEL TO UNDERSTAND YOUR STRESS

You're probably beginning to notice a few themes here. It seems that for all methods for tackling anxiety, we need to do the opposite of what our stressed and ruminative mind wants us to do!

For example, where it wants to be general and vague, we can be specific.

Where it wants to jump to conclusions, we can slow down and look at the facts.

Where it wants to be irrational and panicky, we can be deliberate, conscious, and in control.

One great framework for understanding a whole range of approaches to stress reduction is called the ABC model. It pulls you out of the reactive, unconscious frame of mind that is anxiety and puts you in a position to move forward.

A is for Adversity (or sometimes Activating event or Antecedent, i.e., what came before)

B is for Beliefs (that are triggered by the Adversity)

C is for Consequences (our behavioral and emotional response)

Very generally, if we can understand the events that trigger certain thoughts and beliefs, and how these then in turn create consequences for us (i.e., stress!), we can work backward to create a life that is closer to what we want.

Let's start with the activating event. This can be internal (for example, a headache) or external (for example, a comment from someone else). Now, these stimuli in themselves mean nothing. We come in with certain beliefs and interpretations about them, and these can be rational or irrational. Let's say you have a headache, and this activates certain (usually automatic) beliefs: *Just my luck. I'm not going to be able to do my work today. This is bad, and it's going to get worse . . . I can't believe this is happening to me.* These thoughts then trigger certain emotions, in this case fear and worry. Importantly, it's not the event itself but our interpretation of it that creates anxiety.

But as you can see, the beliefs above are not exactly based in objective reality. They are distortions.

When we are stuck in anxious rumination, we think we are solving a problem by dwelling on our beliefs themselves; for example, we might think at length about how bad the headache is and how we are going to deal with the catastrophe it will turn out to be. But with the ABC model, what we do is examine the beliefs themselves. Who says the headache will be a catastrophe, anyway? We don't take for granted that our beliefs are always accurate!

If we feel anxious, it is usually because we hold beliefs, assumptions, and biases that trigger and maintain this anxiety. Change those beliefs and we remove the anxiety.

Here's another example. You find out that two of your friends are hanging out but didn't invite you to join them (activating event). You think, "They've excluded me on purpose. Maybe they're talking about me right now" (beliefs), and as a result, you have trouble falling asleep that night, and the next morning, you are rude to both of them, causing upset (consequences).

Now, the ABC model helps us understand what has happened, but it also helps us go back and re-engineer situations so that we get the outcomes we want.

1. First, identify the **activating event**, trigger, or antecedent (not being invited)
2. Next, **identify how you feel** about this event or situation (ashamed, excluded, rejected)
3. Then, see if you can **find the belief** behind this response ("If they didn't invite me, it must be because they dislike me.")
4. Take a close look at this belief and ask whether it's really true. **Is it rational?** (The belief is not really rational since they could fail to invite you while still liking you. You realize that you have also spent time with them individually without inviting the other without intending any offense. You also realize that they are actually closer to one another than to you, and that this isn't the end of the world—other people can have close connections without it threatening you in any way!)
5. Try to recognize alternative interpretations of the situation, or **modify your belief** (Your friends have not done anything *to* you. There isn't really a problem. In fact, seeing as they're doing a hobby you don't really like, you're a little relieved they didn't invite you . . .)

Everyone has different reactions to stress, and we may ourselves vary in our responses over time. But we can always become aware of and moderate these responses.

The ABC model helps us identify and change those irrational beliefs that cause anxiety. It's worth starting with emotions because they are usually at the forefront of our experience. If you feel angry, investigate whether a boundary or right has been violated. If you're sad, look at what has been potentially lost. Fear and anxiety can point to beliefs that dwell on threat—real or imagined (let's be honest, it's often imagined!). Guilt comes from the knowledge that we've violated someone's boundary.

Now, laying out examples on paper like this can make it seem fairly straightforward, but life is usually a bit more complicated. There are many ways we can use the ABC model. We can use it for small, individual scenarios as they unfold in the moment, or we can use it retroactively to dissect recurring overall themes and patterns in our lives. Or both!

When you're exploring antecedents, bear in mind that there could be many. It could be a person, an event, or just a situation. Consider the setting/environment, timing (the hour, day, time of year . . .), what sensory information is coming in, what *isn't* happening, people's behaviors or words, memories, (sometimes we don't even realize a memory has triggered us and instead think our anxiety has to do with what is happening in the present) or certain relationship dynamics.

Likewise, there may be many resulting beliefs and thoughts that are triggered. You may find that a surface level belief ("they've excluded me") sometimes conceals a deeper, more lasting core belief ("there is something wrong with who I am"). It's worth taking your time to dig a little.

Finally, consequences can be varied and play out on different time scales, too. We can ask what effects our beliefs have on us either in the short term or the long term. In our example, the short-term consequence is to lash out at the two friends, but in the longer term, you may discover that your core beliefs are actually getting in the way of your relationships in general.

How you use insights gained from the ABC model is up to you. But here are three questions that can help you reprogram your conditioned response from each level, A, B, or C:

A: Is it possible to change or remove certain triggers and antecedents? How?

B: If your resulting belief is irrational, how can you modify or completely replace it?

C: Can you change the consequences of your behaviors so that you reinforce the more rational beliefs?

If the ABC model doesn't quite work for you, take a look at the RAIN framework created by Michele McDonald, a renowned meditation teacher. It's simple:

RECOGNIZE/RELAX into what is emerging in your awareness (for example, your anxious feelings).
ACCEPT/ ALLOW it to simply be what it is.
INVESTIGATE the thoughts and emotions that emerge (this includes bodily sensations, too).
NOTE what is unfolding from one moment to the next.

Here's how that could look written as an inner self-dialogue: *So I feel some stress coming on. I know this feeling. That's okay. I can let it happen, and it's not a problem. It really isn't. I'm going to relax and let this wave just pass. And it will pass. What is happening to me? I feel a weirdness in my chest. I recognize those core beliefs coming up in me, but I also notice that I'm not following that path into fear, either . . . I'm having an anxiety experience right now, and it's okay. In fact, I notice that it is already waning . . .*

The reason this RAIN technique works is because it puts us in a frame of mind that cannot co-exist with anxiety. When we are open, curious, and relaxed, we simply *can't* feel anxiety. So, what happens if we relax into our stress response and just become curious about it rather than fearing it and resisting it? Most of us know what it feels like to fear the fear. What does it feel like to be curious about it, instead?

Summary:

- Whatever form stress and anxiety take in your life, it's worth having some psychological tools to help you manage it mindfully. Build more self-awareness by learning to label your emotions and noting how they feel on your body in the moment. We can also build self-awareness by keeping a regular thought diary, or by taking psychometric tests.
- We don't have to accept our anxious thoughts as gospel. The Socratic questioning method asks us to look for evidence, become curious, and deliberately seek out alternative interpretations. We can likewise test our false beliefs by reappraising our assessment of the situation and the "threat" we see.
- Making a mind map gives us perspective and clarity on the chaos that may be in our minds. Start with a single word or phrase and do a "brain dump," then look for patterns and themes, asking what you can control and what you cannot. One of the best cures for anxiety is to ask what you can realistically **do** about your situation.
- The ABC model helps us understand the antecedents, beliefs, and consequences of our stress reaction, and allows us to re-engineer our perspective and behave differently.
- One option is to simply distract yourself by giving your brain an engaging "mind game."

Chapter 2. An Anxiety-Free Lifestyle

8. LIMIT CAFFEINE INTAKE

Now, you might not want to hear what comes next, but if you're consistently battling anxiety, caffeine could be the hidden culprit. Did you know that the DSM—the *Diagnostic and Statistical Manual of Mental Disorders* used by the American Psychiatric Association—contains *four* separate disorders related to caffeine? Caffeine is the world's most commonly used psychoactive substance.

But Dr. Julie Radico is a clinical psychologist who reminds us that caffeine is not a problem per se—after all, it can boost concentration levels and give us a shot of energy. Not to mention it's delicious. "But I encourage people to know healthy limits and consume it strategically because it is activating and can mimic or exacerbate the symptoms of anxiety."

Because of the ubiquity of coffee in modern life, many of us (doctors included) simply never think of coffee as something that could be adding to our anxiety behind the scenes. So, we valiantly plug away at mindfulness and do our breathing exercises, conveniently forgetting the four cups of espresso we had that morning!

So, how much is too much? Well, there is variation in individual tolerance levels. The standard advice is not to exceed four hundred milligrams daily, or risk overstimulation, anxiety, and a range of fun physical effects such as nausea, gastrointestinal distress, and heart palpitations. For perspective, a normal cup of coffee brewed at home contains around one hundred milligrams of caffeine, but drinks sold in coffee shops and things like energy drinks or supplements can contain as much as four hundred milligrams in one cup. Cola can contain about thirty to fifty milligrams per can, and even tea and decaffeinated coffee can add to your overall caffeine intake, so don't assume that you're in the clear just because you don't drink coffee.

So, is the solution to quit caffeine cold turkey? Probably not. Unless you are extremely sensitive to it or are battling a pronounced anxiety disorder, it's more about *moderation* and drinking coffee strategically than it is about quitting completely. A 2007 study by Sergi Ferré in the *Journal of Neurochemistry* explains exactly *why* coffee has the effects it does. Caffeine blocks the neurotransmitter adenosine, which results in us feeling more alert. But the same process also triggers adrenaline release. This process is not dissimilar from the one that unfolds in the HPA axis during the fight-or-flight response. Beyond a certain point, in other words, "alertness" turns into "anxiety."

A 2018 study by Winston et. al. in the journal *Advances in Psychiatric Treatment* found that a too-high caffeine intake can actually mimic the symptoms of a range of psychiatric disorders—including anxiety. This is important: it means that there are at least some people out there who have been diagnosed with an anxiety disorder, when the real story is that they are suffering from excessive caffeine intake.

If this sounds like you, the solution is obvious. Before you consider behavioral or lifestyle change, and before you think about anti-anxiety medication or therapy, check to see that your morning cup of coffee is not to blame. Trying to stop abruptly may lead to caffeine withdrawal, which can be counterproductive. Instead, taper off gradually, find a comfortable dose that's right for you, and don't exceed it.

9. SCHEDULE YOUR "WORRY TIME"

Stress is a part of life. And we've already explored the power of acceptance and acknowledgement without resistance. If worrying has been a constant part of your life that it almost seems like a day job, maybe it's time to turn things around and be the boss. How? One counterintuitive way is to deliberately dedicate time in your schedule to worry. In other words, give yourself permission to worry . . . but do it on your own terms.

If you're used to thinking of your anxiety as some annoying, difficult, or even shameful tendency, then it might feel strange at first to "worry more effectively." But let's start with an assumption: you will probably worry at least somewhat some of the time. So choose *how* you do it. Here's a suggestion:

Step 1: Be aware of when you're worrying.
Step 2: Acknowledge that you're "allowed" to feel worried—but that you'll merely delay worrying for later.
Step 3: Pick up your worry again later at some pre-planned, limited time window in the future.

That's all there is to it. You cannot do this process if you're not first mindful of what's happening, but don't be too hard on yourself if you slip into unconscious rumination now and again—practice makes perfect. Simply be glad when you "come back" to awareness and carry on without beating yourself up for getting trapped in a loop.

Next, say to the worry, "I see you. I'll give you all the attention you need . . . but not right now." Then, perhaps jot down some notes to help remind you later. Have a "worry book"—once a thought is in there, it's safe and you don't need to return to it until the designated worry time. Your mind will want to return there, but politely remind it, "You don't have to do anything right now, mind. Nothing is outstanding, and there is no problem to solve right now. For the time being, we only have to relax. You can worry as much as you like . . . later."

If you are having particular trouble with delaying worries, simply write *that* worry down in the book too! For example, "I'm really worried that this stupid technique is actually going to ruin my life." Your brain will play a trick on you. It will try to argue that worrying is a useful thing, and that by not worrying, you're doing something wrong or allowing everything to go haywire. Just notice this and give yourself permission to put all that rumination aside for the time being. You can catastrophize later as much as you want!

Okay, so when do you actually worry?

Allocate a time (around twenty minutes) once a day when there are no restrictions, and you can worry to your heart's content. In fact, during this time, you're not allowed to do anything other than go through your worry book and worry. Completely focus on your worries. Note how it feels to worry now after a day spent not worrying. You may notice a few unexpected things:

- The thoughts you believed were really, really important a few hours ago don't quite seem as urgent now
- We are capable of "sitting with" anxiety
- Our worrying doesn't actually change anything—because we can stop doing it and life just carries on as it did before
- Worrying actually doesn't feel very good (this sounds obvious, but it can be a lightbulb moment for some people—why spend so much time deliberately making yourself feel bad—especially when it doesn't achieve a single thing?)

The next time an "urgent" worry comes up, you might find yourself wondering, "How is this going to look to me a few hours from now? Is it really as urgent as it feels?"

Sometimes, you'll look at a thought you've written down and be comfortable completely crossing it off the list. It's no longer relevant, so congratulations, you spared yourself some unnecessary worry! But sometimes you'll put something in your worry book that *is* genuinely a problem. Then what? As before, we need to become aware of what we can control, what we can't, what we value, and what action we can take. Worry can serve a purpose—it can alert us to problems and inspire us to solve them by taking action.

There is an Erma Bombeck quote: "Worrying is like a rocking chair. It will give you something to do, but it won't get you anywhere." Instead of just going back and forth, commit to busting worries by *doing* something about them.

Your scheduled worry time can be used to simply worry, but you can also take it a step further. Look at everything you've written down and categorize it. What is in your control and actionable? What isn't? What is you trying to people-please or solve problems that are not your business to solve? Can you see any items that are just mindless what-if questions, regrets, or distorted beliefs?

Once you've had a look at the actual content of your worrying mind, it's a great idea to take one simple next step: look at all the problems you can actually do something about and identify only the very next small step you need to take to get started.

For example, if you've been worrying about how you're going to manage catering for a massive party at the end of the week, your very next action might be to confirm the actual guest numbers so you know how many you're catering for. Don't think beyond this, just identify this next step and then take it. Often, your very next step will simply be planning some time in your schedule for when you'll work on the issue at hand. Once you've scheduled blocks of time this way, put the issue out of your mind. If you're someone who gets worried about forgetting things, then set a reminder that will work for you and then forget about it.

This "forgetting about it" is where the real work takes place. You'll gradually learn to trust yourself. If you've done what you can, you can rest. Eventually, with practice and with using the above techniques, you will actually prove to yourself that your worry is kind of useless, and that you can manage your life perfectly well without it!

Think of it as developing an attitude of healthy boundaries. Imagine your worry is like a pushy relative who never shuts up and never leaves you alone. You need to learn to say no to them! You also need to learn to tell yourself that worrying is not the same as problem solving. **Do** something to solve the problem, and if you can't, then it's not worth worrying about, right? Scheduling worry teaches you an important lesson: that *you* are in control of your thoughts. They are not in control of you.

10. CULTIVATE GRATITUDE

By now, there is so much evidence for the value of being thankful for the positive things in our lives that you'll see gratitude practice suggested as a solution for just about anything. But did you know that being grateful can also help you lower stress levels? It's easy to understand why. When you're anxious and overthinking, your brain is hyper aware of everything that's wrong, exaggerating perceived threats and dwelling on all the bad things that could potentially happen. But when you are grateful, your brain does the opposite—it zooms in on what's important, what's right, and what's going well.

Being grateful is not just a box we tick or something we do once and never again. It's a habit. A 2008 longitudinal study by Wood et. al. published in the *Journal of Research in Personality* found that gratitude improved relationships, strengthened mental resilience, and lowered anxiety. When we are grateful, we are:

- Less self-critical and easier on ourselves
- More compassionate with others
- Able to give support and seek it from others
- Better equipped to bounce back from adversity

Being grateful doesn't mean we don't experience stress. It just means we deal with it better. A 2019 German study by Heckendorf et. al. (*Behavior Research and Therapy*) discovered a significant reduction in anxious negative self-talk when study participants used an app that helped them cultivate more gratitude day to day. It's this ability to think differently about adversity that helps us stress less about it.

You might be tempted to think of keeping a gratitude journal as a kind of trendy fad that couldn't possibly help combat all the genuinely terrifying things in your life. But practicing gratitude can literally change your brain. Anxiety can cause us to release stress hormones and neurotransmitters that teach us to look for the negative in our lives. And when we look, we can usually find something to worry about! And the cycle continues.

But if we're grateful, we create a neurochemical environment that primes us to see the good instead. And the more good we see, the better we are at seeing it.

You cannot be grateful and anxious at the same time. If we choose gratitude, it displaces stress. After all, stress is not just a response—it's a perspective and an attitude. And attitudes can change. You can choose to focus on the thought, "Look how blessed I am!" instead of, "Look how much is wrong with everything." You don't literally change reality, but you do choose which parts to take in, to focus on, and to make bigger.

Sounds good, but how do you actually practice gratitude and switch away from anxiety (an ungrateful state)? First of all, don't fake it! Going through the motions will get you nowhere. The first step is just to become aware. Human beings tend to enjoy the good things in their lives at first, but quickly become numb to them over time, taking them for granted precisely because those good things are so abundant.

Instead, consciously look around your life and really see all the great things you have. Find beauty around you. Even if you're having a hard time with the rose-tinted glasses, pause and appreciate the fact that you are a completely unique human being who is doing their best to be their best. Isn't that wonderful in itself? That you're trying?

What have you achieved that you're not giving yourself full credit for?

What is working well for you right now?

Who has helped you or supported you, even when they could have easily not done so?

In what ways are the people around you actually quite awesome?

Can you see how your life has a lot of good in it, even though there are always problems, too?

The conventional advice is to "write five things in a notebook you're grateful for every day," and this is great advice. But gratitude is not just singling out this and that, but a complete mindset switch. When you adopt this frame of mind, everything looks different. It's not that you are tasked with thinking of the nice things in your life—it's that you change your attitude in such a way that *everything* in your life looks a little nicer than it did before. You know—the opposite of what anxiety does!

Gratitude takes practice. It takes time to shift your mindset, but it can be done. Author of *Emotional First Aid* Dr. Guy Winch claims that gratitude acts like a kind of mental immunization against stress. When we are grateful, we flood our brains with calm-inducing serotonin and dopamine. We feel happier and more at ease. We are better able to tolerate uncertainty. "Gratitude is an emotion that grounds us and is a great way to balance out the negative mindset that uncertainty engenders," he says.

Gratitude is a daily habit as important as eating right and exercising. And it all comes down to *focus*—i.e., where we choose to put our attention. Have you ever noticed if someone you know is pregnant, suddenly all you seem to see around you are pregnant women? It's the same with gratitude. When you deliberately put your attention on the good, you will suddenly seem to find it all over the place.

Gratitude Tip 1

Wake up every morning and, first thing, pause and reflect on everything you have to be grateful for. Take stock of your blessings. What are you learning every day? What opportunities are there? What have you taken for granted? What beautiful things surround you? What is better today than it was a year ago? What has someone done for you that you're happy about?

Dwelling on the answers to these questions will help you set your emotional tone for the day. You don't need to do anything special, just pause and deliberately appreciate how great some things actually are. Do it every morning before you even step out of bed.

Gratitude Tip 2

Keep a journal. First thing in the morning or last thing at night, use journaling to reflect on the day and what went well with it. Really dwell on the positive emotions. Write a love letter to your life telling it how glad you are that it is what it is! Try not to mechanically write the same things over and over again. The exercise is about more than making a list. You want to give your brain time to genuinely experience all those happy neurotransmitters!

Even if you're having a hard time, try to focus on the positive within that. You've come down with the flu? Well, at least you have someone to take care of you, and time to catch up on some trashy reality TV! You got some bad feedback for a work project? But thinking about it, hasn't your critic also kind of done you a favor by drawing your attention to what can be improved? Looking for the silver lining sounds cheesy, but there almost always is one.

Gratitude Tip 3

Don't just keep all those warm, fuzzy feelings to yourself, though. Whenever you can remember, ask if there's someone in your world who you could show a little more appreciation to. Demonstrating how thankful we are for other people not only makes us feel amazing, it'll do the same for them!

Too often we don't say just how much we love and appreciate those around us. Why keep it a secret? Think of someone you haven't spoken to in a while but who you'd be devastated to never hear from again. Reach out to them and be earnest and complimentary. Write a sincere thank you note to someone who's made a difference in your life. Give gifts, leave little encouraging notes for others to find, or simply make a point of telling the barista at the coffee shop that they've made your day with their incredible mocha.

11. USE "MENTAL ANCHORING"

If anxiety, rumination, and overthinking are like powerful overwhelming waves, then "mental anchoring" is a way to grab hold of something and stay stable in the flood. Mental anchoring is a popular technique used to manage panic attacks, but can help any time we need to ground ourselves.

It works because of the brain's tendency to create links and associations. The technique is based in NLP, or Neurolinguistic Programming, and allows us to grab hold of a kind of primary experience and create a path back to it so we can access it later when we need it—i.e., in moments of anxiety or panic.

Michael Carroll is the founder of the NLP Academy and teaches people the simple four-step process: first, you access a particular state; then, you find an anchoring stimulus in that state, and then you exit that state. When you're done, you can test the anchor if you like.

Before we explain what this means, let's consider the type of anchors you can have—all are based in our sensory perception:

Visual anchors – something you can see internally (like the image of a peaceful beach) or externally (like a red string tied round your wrist).

Auditory anchors – something you can hear internally (repeating to yourself a mantra) or externally (ringing a bell, whistling, or clicking your fingers).

Kinesthetic anchors – something to do with touch or movement (such as drawing a shape on the back of your hand or pressing the soft spot of flesh between index finger and thumb).

Olfactory anchors – something you can smell (for example, a little spritz bottle of lavender essential oil).

Gustatory anchors – something you can taste (for example, mint chewing gum).

Now, let's say you were feeling anxious and wanted to feel calmer and in control. You would think back to a moment in the past when you felt how you'd like to feel now. For example, you might choose a peaceful memory you have of camping with your family in the forest. Take your time sinking into this memory, reliving it on all the sensory channels you can—dwell on what you smell, see, touch, etc.

As you relive this memory, you start to relive the feelings of calm and control you felt then. Really dig deep into these feelings and how they connect to your sensory memories. See the beautiful green trees swaying around you, smell the fresh air, feel the warmth of the sun on your skin. When you are at the "peak" of this emotional state, quickly connect it to your chosen anchor. For example, you might rub your fingers over a smooth polished quartz stone you can keep in your pocket. This quartz stone now becomes an anchor back into this peaceful moment. The anchor does not have to relate to the memory for the association to work.

You can test to see if this association has cemented itself by later running your fingers over the smooth stone in some other context. Are you immediately reminded of the forest and the sun again? Bear in mind that making the link may take a few attempts. Anchoring is essentially reprogramming your brain. For it to work best, be consistent and keep repeating the stimulus with the anchor to tie them together. Remember to pair the anchor to the *peak* of your emotional experience. This takes a little practice, so be patient.

Later in this book, we'll explore other ways to use our senses to anchor in the present moment and cut anxiety as it's happening. But for now, the NLP mental anchoring technique is a great way to prepare yourself ahead of time to better manage overwhelming feelings as they emerge.

The great thing about anchoring is that your body and mind are already doing it. After all, your anxiety response might be nothing more than a series of negative associations you've made. For example, you might catch a whiff of the scent your awful ex used to wear and suddenly be reminded of all the negative feelings you have around that breakup. Or you could hear certain words or phrases that remind you of painful, traumatic, or just embarrassing moments from your past—like a magic spell, it almost seems to transport you right back into that state of mind!

With this technique, you are taking your brain's propensity to make associations and using it for good. The technique can be used to break certain associations *and* make new ones. There is no limit to the kind or number of associations you make—all you need to do is be aware of the rules your brain follows to make those associations and consciously choose to make them in a way that helps you live the life you want to live.

It is as though we take a "button"—i.e., a stimulus or anchor—and wire it up to a desired mental state; for example, calmness. We want to connect our brains in such a way that when we push the button, we feel the state of mind we want to feel.

Here's a summary of the steps you need to follow to do this wiring-up process. It's not enough to simply read about them and intellectually grasp the idea—you need to try these steps for yourself and literally *experience* the associations in your own brain. The experience is what strengthens the connection.

Step 1: Choose a desired state of mind

Step 2: Choose an anchor

Step 3: Explore in full detail a memory where you felt the desired state

Step 4: At the emotional peak of the memory, capture the feeling with your anchor

Step 5: Repeat—as many as five or ten times—to cement the association

Step 6: Test the connection by engaging the anchor and noticing whether you conjure the desired emotion

Step 7: If it doesn't work, drill the association a few more times, or pick a stronger memory to work with

12. HAVE A SOLID MORNING ROUTINE

Anxiety and overthinking are about the individual distorted thoughts we have and the anxious actions we choose in one moment or another. But anxiety is also an overall attitude that colors everything in life like a filter. Similarly, to tackle anxiety, we need to take specific actions, but we also need to put a different filter over our entire lives.

We need consistent daily habits, routines, and ways of seeing that shape our every moment. This is why a morning routine is so important. A good morning routine sets the pattern for the rest of the day. Your ideal stress-busting routine will not be exactly the same as everyone else's, but it turns out that there are a few scientifically proven activities that will definitely boost your mood and ward off anxiety. How you include some of these ideas is up to you.

Drink water

Amanda Carlson is a registered dietician and director of nutrition at Athletes' Performance, which is responsible for training world-class athletes. "Studies have shown that being just half a liter dehydrated can increase your cortisol levels," she says. And more cortisol means more stressed feelings. "When you don't give your body the fluids it needs, you're putting stress on it, and it's going to respond to that." But being stressed itself can also lead to dehydration . . . which can make you more stressed, creating a vicious cycle.

One simple way to fend off dehydration is to always keep a glass of water next to your bed. Drink water first thing in the morning.

Enjoy nature

You don't need to go outside into the woods for a walk first thing in the morning (although if you can, great!). But do take some time to enjoy the natural, non-manmade world to ground yourself in the morning. This could be:

- Opening your window the moment you wake up to take deep breaths of fresh morning air
- Having your breakfast in your garden, maybe even putting bare feet in the grass
- Play some soothing nature sounds (oceans, birdsong, rainstorms, etc.) as you get ready for the day, or enjoy a few YouTube videos of relaxing nature scenes, cute cats, or beautiful scenery.
- Really enjoy something wholesome and natural to eat, like some fresh fruit
- Get outside in the sunshine, smell the rain, or take a moment to enjoy the birds on your windowsill

Eat well

According to the National Institute of Mental Health (NIMH), chronic stress can increase your risk for developing obesity, heart disease, depression, type 2 diabetes… and anxiety. Everyday Health ran a survey in 2019 of 6,700 Americans, where thirty-five percent rated their stress levels as a six or a seven on a scale from one to seven. And that was before the pandemic! The most common way of dealing with stress? Food. And you can guess that the foods chosen were not fruit smoothies and broccoli.

Ali Miller is a dietician and author of *The Anti-Anxiety Diet* and claims that the key to a stress-busting diet is to maintain stable blood sugar levels. This means avoiding refined carbs that can spike blood sugar and insulin levels, then crash, exacerbating stress on the body. Instead, choose high-fiber foods and whole grains, and avoid fasting or binging. Likewise, healthy fats slow digestion and increase satiety, so eat things like eggs, avocados, and nuts to help balance stress hormones and regulate your mood.

Commit to having a light but wholesome breakfast every morning; for example, some oatmeal with raisins and cinnamon, a mushroom and spinach omelet, or some whole grain toast with peanut butter. Choose foods that make you happy, like a single block of dark chocolate (yes, a 2009 study by Martin et. al. in the *Journal of Proteome Research* found that modest daily chocolate intake lowered stress hormone levels). Have some coffee but not too much, or try tea—a 2013 study in the *Journal of Psychopharmacology* discovered that chamomile actually alters the body's stress response and stimulates the release of feel-good neurotransmitters.

One tip is to add a banana to your breakfast. A preliminary study in *Neuropharmacology* found that depression and anxiety could be a result of magnesium deficiency. Bananas are rich in magnesium, not to mention potassium and B vitamins, which regulate the nervous system and ease fatigue. Other foods to include are oily fish (rich in brain healthy Omega 3), milk (calcium deficiency has been associated with poor mood), and fruit (vitamin C may lower cortisol levels).

Avoid too much caffeine, refined sugar, and alcohol, and don't allow yourself to get too hungry, nor to have meals that are too big and heavy. Eat mindfully, go easy on yourself when you're not perfect, and remember that food is a source of joy and wellbeing.

The best way to get a solid morning routine going is to be realistic and start small. Don't try to completely makeover your life in twenty-four hours. If you make it enjoyable, you're more likely to stick to it, so choose small changes that will actually work for your lifestyle and the kind of person you are. For example, if you hate cooking and have a tiny kitchen and a busy job, don't go and buy a giant smoothie maker and force yourself to concoct elaborate breakfast smoothies in the morning—you'll only increase stress, not lower it!

Be consistent and patient. Know that slipping up here and there is not the end of the world. Be flexible so that if something isn't really working, you don't have to completely give up—just become curious about what *will* work. Always remember that self-care is about loving your body and enjoying life; it shouldn't feel like hard work or a punishment!

Here are a few more things you can build into your morning routine, but again, don't feel pressured to do all of them. Sometimes, the small changes make the biggest difference if they are changes that fit, that are chosen mindfully, and that are done consistently.

- Don't look at your phone first thing in the morning. Keep it in another room.
- Meditate, read a few pages from an inspirational book, pray, or do a contemplative exercise.
- Take a few deep breaths.
- Stretch or do some quick yoga.
- Do a visualization for the day ahead, or say some affirmations.
- Indulge in a self-care treat like a special bath, some lovely music, or a delicious snack you reserve for mornings only.
- Drink water, tea, or coffee, and really savor it along with your healthy breakfast. Don't eat while distracted.
- Be mindful with everything you do. Get up early so you can take your time. Feel the bubbles of your shampoo in your hair. Dress with care. Enjoy the quiet, private ritual of drinking some tea, sit down with a gratitude journal, or make some goals for the day ahead.

A morning routine, whatever it looks like, does one important thing: it tells your body and mind that whatever happens, you're in calm control. You're the boss. You set your intention, and you follow through. Every day.

13. START A HOBBY

A 2013 study in the *Mental Health Review Journal* found that "gardening-based interventions for people experiencing mental health difficulties reported that benefits include a reduction in symptoms of depression and anxiety and an increase in attentional capacity and self-esteem. Key benefits include emotional benefits such as reduced stress and improved mood." A *Frontiers in Psychology* paper published in 2021 also found that people who indulged in their cooking hobby during the Covid-19 lockdowns experienced stress reduction and better resilience.

So, does this mean we have to take up gardening or baking to beat our stress? Nope! It may simply be that hobbies—whatever they are—can improve our overall wellbeing and make us more resilient to everyday stress. Having a pastime is a great way to ease your mind and just focus on something else. A hobby can also give you a sense of pride when a goal is accomplished, and if it's a social hobby, you get all the benefits of friendly interaction with others.

If you have a project that you've been putting off, it might be time to pick it up again. But if you're in the market for a new hobby, the golden rule when it comes to hobbies is that they should be fun! If you're not really enjoying something, give yourself full permission to drop it. If cooking and gardening seem like torture to you, don't force yourself. Sometimes, those of us with tendencies toward anxiety can put a lot of pressure on ourselves to do things "right" or get hung up on the outcome rather than just enjoying the process as it unfolds.

You'll know a hobby is the right one for you when you feel pleasantly distracted and look forward to picking it up again. You should feel refreshed and relaxed by it rather than seeing it as another thing on the to-do list. Here are a few things to try:

Arts and crafts: Drawing and painting, compiling scrap books, collage making, knitting and crochet, sewing clothing and quilt making, woodwork, metalwork, mosaics, making candles or soap, flower arranging, jewelry making, interior design, or leatherwork.

Music: Either listening to it or making it. Join a choir or sign up for drumming lessons, or just tinker with your ultimate playlist. You can do official classes with a teacher or just get a simple instrument to play around with.

Writing: Write stories, poems, novels, letters, or articles, or keep a journal. Think about joining a writing group or a flash poetry club. Why not enter competitions?

Physical activity: Exercising, dancing, swimming, hiking or walking, surfing, martial arts, extreme sports, spending time with animals, camping, or gymnastics.

Reading: There's a whole world of things to read! Subscribe to a new magazine, try a classic novel, consider joining a reading club, or go to talks by famous authors.

Everything else: Cooking, gardening, photography, wild foraging, pottery, calligraphy, building puzzles, flying kites, decorating cakes, keeping chickens, baskets and weaving, car restoration, dog and cat breeding, standup comedy or improv, collecting comic books, horse-riding, glass-blowing, hang-gliding, or joining an amateur drama group.

Be honest about which hobbies genuinely make you feel good, which ones are a good fit for you personally, and which ones are likely to make you feel happier and more relaxed. Sometimes, we can get caught up in a hobby because we're very competitive, or feel like we should do it because we have some talent in that area, or simply because it's what others expect of us. Maybe we feel that we need to have hobbies for others to find us interesting. But drop all of these assumptions and choose something that genuinely makes you feel good. If your ideal hobby is buying air-dry clay from the craft store and making random misshapen animals for a few hours on the weekend, then do that!

Try to choose hobbies that have other benefits, too. For example, joining a gym and doing Pilates is a hobby that may make you feel good, but it also improves your physical fitness and floods your body with endorphins, building long-term stress resilience. So you benefit from *two* forms of anxiety management. Or you could volunteer at an animal shelter because you love cats, but get the additional feel-good benefits from knowing you've helped animals in need. And by learning to cook better, you de-stress, improve your nutrition, and do something for your family that bolsters your relationship with them. All of this indirectly improves wellbeing and reduces stress.

As with all other routines, start small and be consistent. It's better to experiment a little at first to see if you like something, then ramp it up as you go. Avoid spending too much money on equipment at first, and don't get too hung up if you skip a few lessons or don't do especially well in the beginning. The goal is not to become a virtuoso, but to enjoy yourself. So, if you've given it a good shot and find that you're not getting much from a new hobby, don't worry about quitting and looking for something you like better.

Summary:

- Easy, everyday lifestyle changes can make a big difference with anxiety and overthinking. An obvious area to examine is whether you're having too much caffeine. Try to limit yourself to four hundred milligrams daily.
- Everyone worries, so at least do it strategically by scheduling worry time. Keep a worry journal so that instead of fighting worry, you postpone and contain it, tackling it on your own terms.
- Practice gratitude daily to gently shift your perspective to focus on everything that is going well in your world. Use a journal or write thank-you notes to people who have shown you kindness.
- Mental anchoring is a technique that, once established, can be used as often as you like to help ground and calm you. Choose an anchor, choose a desired state, then connect the two during visualization so that revisiting the anchor brings you back to that state of mind.
- Have a consistent morning routine where you focus on good food, nature, healthy habits, and quiet contemplative time where you set your intention for the day. Make sure you're hydrated, since dehydration can elevate cortisol levels.
- Finally, choose a hobby that can act as a pleasant distraction—but make sure you're choosing something you genuinely enjoy.

Chapter 3. Enter Your Mind

No book on stress management and anxiety reduction would be complete without a section on meditation and mindfulness. In fact, meditation is rightly considered one of the best and most effective ways to regulate your stress response and access a more tranquil and controlled state of mind.

However, don't worry if you have never really enjoyed formal meditation or feel like you may lack the time or wherewithal. The mindfulness techniques discussed in this chapter are easy and accessible and can be done anywhere, anytime, with very little practice. The great thing about them is how easily they can be combined with other strategies covered in this book!

14. BELLY BREATHING

One excellent technique to start with is a deceptively simple one: belly breathing, also known as diaphragmatic breathing. Instead of breathing from the chest, belly breathing is about deeper, fuller breaths that originate from the diaphragm, which is a large dome-shaped muscle in your abdomen. When you breathe in, the diaphragm tightens and moves down, creating more space in your lungs that draws air in. When you exhale, the diaphragm relaxes, and this contracts the lungs, expelling air out.

This type of breathing encourages full oxygen exchange, which in turn slows the heartbeat and lowers blood pressure. All of this spells more relaxation of your entire body, less physiological arousal, and a more balanced stress response.

The next time you're feeling ultra-stressed, pause and notice what your breath is doing. Often, we breathe incorrectly without even knowing we're doing it. Anxious breathing tends to be shallow and rapid—it's part of our fight-or-flight response. Even though we were all born with the knowledge of how to breathe deeply (watch how a baby breathes!) we can learn bad habits as we grow up and favor smaller, tighter chest breathing. But if we relearn this skill, we give ourselves a tool to quickly relax our bodies via our breath.

By slowing our breath, we slow our thoughts and bring ourselves into a more relaxed frame of mind.

So how do you do belly breathing? Thankfully, it's something anyone can learn to do, and it can be done anywhere, anytime.

1. Find a comfortable spot to sit or lie down, checking to see that you're not slouching or holding tension in your muscles.
2. Close your eyes or, if you're more practiced, keep them softly gazing in the middle distance.
3. Put one hand on your belly and the other on your chest.
4. Breathe normally and notice the movement of your hands with your body. Try to breathe deeply so that the hand on your belly is moving up and down more than the hand on your chest.
5. Take more deep breaths, focusing on keeping the breath in your belly. Breathe in through your nose and imagine you're blowing yourself up like a balloon. Exhale slowly through the mouth, almost like you're whistling but without sound.

And that's it! When we are deeply relaxed, we tend to breathe like this anyway. But if we can pause during stressful moments and train ourselves to breathe like this on purpose, we encourage ourselves to relax and slow down. Shallow chest breathing is unfortunately the norm, but it is associated with tension, both muscular and psychological. Just practice shallow, quick breathing at the "top of your lungs" for a minute or so and then notice what emotions you feel afterward!

Belly breathing is a wonderful thing to do first thing in the morning, almost as though you are waking your lungs up and filling every cell in your body with fresh clean air. As you breathe, you could even use visualization to imagine that you're exhaling stress and worry and inhaling peace, calm, and happiness (we'll look at visualization techniques in more detail later on).

A 2017 paper published in *Frontiers in Psychology* by Xiao Ma and colleagues found that belly breathing triggers the body's natural relaxation response, which then has positive benefits on the psychological experience of stress. The researchers took forty participants and randomly assigned them either to a control group or a group that completed a belly breathing intervention. This intervention included twenty intensive breathing training sessions over eight weeks. These participants learned to breathe at an average rate of around four breaths per minute.

All forty participants completed tests for attention, mood, and cortisol levels, both before the eight-week period and after. The results showed that the intervention group had better moods, better attention, and lower salivary cortisol levels, suggesting they were less stressed overall. If these participants could achieve all that in just eight weeks, what could you do if you had the rest of your life to master deep belly breathing?

Now, as with all mindfulness techniques, not every approach is going to work for everyone. For some, focusing so closely on the breath can actually exacerbate anxious feelings. If you notice yourself feeling awkward, panting, holding your breath, or getting worried about whether you're doing it right, pause and come back to the exercise later. It doesn't mean that breathing exercises are not right for you; it just means that something else might work better; for example, yoga breathing.

You could also use an app to help guide your breathing practice, or even seek out the help of a therapist. It may work for you to pair breathing exercises with another relaxation technique like guided imagery, chanting, or singing, or something like Tai Chi. That said, it's worth noting that diaphragmatic breathing may feel strange at first, so don't worry if it takes a little while to become familiar with it.

15. THE 5-4-3-2-1 GROUNDING TECHNIQUE

Anxiety has a funny way of fueling itself. We can get caught in loops, and a negative thought or sensation, when focused on, seems to grow larger and larger . . . and soon we're panicking about how much we're panicking. This is in effect what happens in a panic attack. Isn't it strange how a person can be in the grips of the most terrifying experience of their lives, convinced they're about to die, even though they're *in reality* just sitting in a mall where nothing is going on and they're perfectly safe? Such is the power of the mind!

Grounding techniques work because they recognize that anxiety is about detaching our senses from the real world. Ordinarily, our fight-or-flight response is there to keep us safe from real dangers in the present moment. But with anxiety, the danger is only imagined. We respond to something that actually isn't happening to us.

There is one sure-fire way to come out of this mental loop: get back into our bodies. The mind can carry us to the past to stress about things that have already happened, or to the future to things that haven't happened yet (and may never happen), but when we stay in the *present*, we notice how little there is to actually fear right in front of us. Your brain can rush around in a million directions, but your body can only ever be in one place—the present. So connect to that present by anchoring in your body's senses.

Here's how to do the 5-4-3-2-1 grounding technique. Unlike some techniques, it's quite easy to remember, and you can mix it up a little without changing the effectiveness. Try it any time you're feeling stressed and overwhelmed, or when your mind is getting caught up in a reinforcing loop. You only need a few minutes.

First, just take a few deep breaths and orient yourself. Then:

Find FIVE things around you that you can SEE. Completely immerse yourself in the sense of sight. Find something in your environment and focus on it. Its precise texture, its color, its shape—just explore the object with your eyes. Do this for four more things.

Then, find FOUR things that you can TOUCH. Maybe you notice the feeling of the fabric on the chair you're sitting on, or the feeling of your hair against your cheek.

Next, find THREE things that you can HEAR. There's no need to identify positive or negative, good or bad. Just listen. You might hear the low hum of a computer, birds outside, or chatting next door.

Then, find TWO things you can SMELL. Some people can find this difficult, but if you pay attention, you may notice there are actually plenty of smells all around you!

Finally, find ONE thing that you can TASTE. This may simply be the lingering taste of coffee on your tongue, or you may detect a faint taste of toothpaste. If you can and you want to, nibble on something nearby or take a sip of something, even if it's just water.

What's the point of all of this? Well, when you try it out for yourself, you'll notice that after just a few minutes, you feel calmer and more grounded. Sometimes, all you need is to break the anxiety spiral and distract yourself long enough to calm down. You're also doing something else with this technique, and that is inviting your body to notice just how little danger there really is. Our minds can be screaming, "Danger, danger, danger! This is bad!" but if we pause a moment and check in with what is actually happening, we realize that things are . . . fine.

Sure, we may still have a problem to deal with, but we may be feeling far calmer and more in control about it than before. You can try this technique anywhere and at any time. You can even do it in public without people being aware that you're actively calming yourself down. If you're having a hard time and feel overwhelmed at work, for example, you can always excuse yourself to the bathroom and take a few minutes to gather yourself with this exercise.

One twist on the usual 5-4-3-2-1 exercise is to finish off with finding one positive thing about the present situation, or about yourself. Often, when we're lost in anxiety, we can feel like we're being ridiculous and getting worried over nothing, and this can leave us with a strong sense of embarrassment or even shame. Feeling so out of control can be a knock to the confidence and make us feel vulnerable and unsure of ourselves.

That's why it's so useful to ask yourself, "What good thing can I see in this situation right now?" or "What one good thing can I recognize in myself right now?" It may be that at the end of the exercise, you become aware of a possible solution, and that the problem doesn't seem so bad anymore. Maybe you simply remind yourself that you've been in tough situations before, and you've coped with it just fine. Or you realize that you have had the presence of mind and mental strength to recognize your anxiety and take control of the situation. Well done! You can feel proud about that!

16. HAVE A MANTRA

Being trapped in anxious overthinking can feel very lonely and scary, as though you're completely adrift. But really, you have plenty of anchors, emergency switches, and escape routes to help you halt the stress spiral and gain calm control again. One way you can put a speed bump in rumination is to use a mantra.

Mantras are a commonly overlooked form of meditation. Basically, a mantra is any word, phrase, or meaningless sound that you chant out loud in order to slow the mind, focus your thoughts, and come to awareness in the moment. Mantras have a long, religious, devotional history in many different ancient cultures, but you needn't fully immerse yourself in the spiritual aspects to benefit from the mind-calming power of a mantra.

In 2016, Perry et. al. published a paper called "Chanting Meditation Improves Mood and Social Cohesion." In the researcher's experiment, they examined forty-five inexperienced chanters, as well as twenty-seven experienced chanters and discovered that simply chanting "om" for ten minutes can relieve anxiety and depression, focus the mind, boost mood, and even improve social bonding if done in a group.

A similar 2017 paper by Jai Dudeja wanted to understand the biochemical basis of this effect, suggesting that mantras may work because they boost the overall levels of nitric acid in the body, which regulates the nervous system, relaxes muscles, and increases blood flow. When we chant, we calm our autonomic nervous system and lower our breathing rate, our blood pressure, and our heart rate. And we breathe more deeply and slowly too!

What mantras should we use, and how?

First of all, classic Sanskrit mantras have very specific meanings, and you may or may not like to explore some of these. For example, the sound "om" is meant to evoke the primordial sound of creation itself, and chanting it is a contemplative practice on the nature of reality. Alternatively, you can use what's more commonly thought of in the West as an affirmation, and chant it like a mantra. Here are some excellent mantras in English that can help dissolve anxiety and worry:

- *This too shall pass* (reminds you that how you're feeling now won't last forever!)
- *One thing at a time* (just focus on what's in front of you, and you'll feel less overwhelmed)
- *I am not my thoughts* (to give some distance from negative self-talk)
- *I'm only human* (mistakes are normal)
- *I'm right here, right now* (reminds you to anchor in the present and in your body)
- You may simply like to repeat a calming word over and over, such as "peace, peace"
- You could also use a poem, a quote, a saying, or a favorite prayer that's personally meaningful to you

- You can use a nonsense made-up phrase if you want to use mantras to simply distract an overwhelmed mind

Once you've selected a mantra that you like, get comfortable, close your eyes, and take a few breaths. Arrive in the moment.

Now, start to repeat the mantra. You can repeat it mentally, whisper it, say it out loud, or even sing it. However you express the mantra, it's a good idea to find a consistent rhythm with your voice and breath, flowing smoothly and feeling your body rise and fall. Meditate on the sound itself. Immerse in it fully, and become aware of the fact of your breath being shaped in your lungs and throat, and how the sound waves are leaving your body and going out into the world. You might like to recite the mantra on the inhale and exhale, or on the exhale only.

One option is to repeat the mantra, then taper it off. So, gradually lower your voice, then for a few repeats, simply move your lips without making sound. Finally, finish by repeating the mantra in your mind only. Imagine that as you open your eyes and carry on with the rest of your day, you are still internally carrying the essence of that mantra, keeping you serene and at peace.

This mantra meditation can be done at night before you go to sleep or in the morning as you prepare to take on your day. But it's also something you can use in the heat of the moment, so to speak. If you become aware of yourself feeling anxious, try to close your eyes, come to your breath and recite your mantra a few times. This can be especially effective if the mantra itself has been "mentally anchored" in the NLP fashion described above. This way you can pair the movement of your lips, the sound of the mantra and the associations of the words with a particular psychological state. Through the mantra, you can access this state whenever you want to.

17. SCAN YOUR BODY

We tend to think of anxiety as a psychological disorder, or something that's "all in your head." It isn't! The stress response has its roots in the ancient fight-or-flight mechanisms that begin in the brain and then manifest in the nervous and endocrine systems. In every organ and tissue of the body, in fact. This is why chronic stress can start to look like headaches, ongoing pain, allergies, digestive trouble ... what began as a temporary state of autonomic arousal has lingered in the body and become illness. There is nothing mystical, then, about saying that many pains and illnesses are simply anxieties trapped in the body.

However, if we learn to scan our bodies and check in with ourselves regularly, we can notice small disruptions to our wellbeing early on before they become full-blown "dise-ease." We can bring awareness to what we're actually feeling, noticing our tiredness, the tightness in the back of our throat, or the pain in our lower back that says, "You've been working too long now without a break!"

Imagine your body works on this hierarchy:

Body > Emotion > Thought

For example, you could be overtired, a little dehydrated, and strung out on coffee (body). This state of arousal in your nervous system is associated with higher cortisol levels, for example, and so it's registered in your conscious awareness as stress, anxiety, or grumpiness (emotion). This emotion then instigates some higher-order thoughts, such as, "I suck at my job" (thought).

We may be used to interfacing with our experience only on this last level, ignoring the fact that the thoughts that we have emerge from how we feel, and how we feel emerges from our physical reality.

If we can become consciously aware of what is going on with us on *all* levels, we can take measures to relax ourselves and undo anxiety at its root. So, instead of dwelling on the question of our job and how much we hate it, we can tune into our emotions first and allow them to point us to the fact that we're overtired and dehydrated. The solution, you find out, has nothing to do with quitting your job—it's simply to give your body what it needs (rest, water) and find equilibrium again.

Doing a body scan is easy and can be done as often as you like, wherever you like. You can use the acronym CALM (or CLAM, if you're feeling funny) to help you remember the four main stress zones of the body to tune into.

C – Chest

A – Arms

L – Legs

M – Mouth

When you check in with these places, you get valuable information about your physical and emotional state. Plus, you get to consciously decide to relax these parts, which then causes your entire body and mind to release anxiety.

Start by finding a comfortable position and closing your eyes. Find your breath and slow down a little. Start with C, your chest. Imagine your consciousness is a scanning light running over every part of your chest, inside and outside. What sensations come to the top of your awareness? Notice everything you can. What is your breathing like? Notice its rate and depth. Notice any muscle tightness, pain, or tension, and where.

After you've checked in, it's time to relax this area. Take a few deep breaths (belly breaths, if you can) and notice how you feel. See if you can melt any tensions you've identified.

Next, move on to A, your arms. This includes the top of your shoulders and all the way down to your fingertips. Is there any movement and tension there? Maybe you notice your palms are sweaty or your fists clenched. To relax this area, squeeze your hands into fists and tense up the entire arm, then slowly release again with your exhale. Do this a few times, feeling the stretch and the release deepen each time.

Next, scan L, your legs. Do the same here, looking for tension and then deliberately relaxing the area. Tense the muscles, then gradually release the tension again. This is called progressive muscle relaxation. Relaxing from the most activated state actually results in a deeper release. Finally end with M, your mouth, which can hold a surprising amount of tension. Notice your jaw, your tongue, your lips. Zoom in on the sensations inside and outside. To relax this area, let everything hang a little looser, let the tension melt away, and if you like, allow your lips to come to a soft and relaxed smile.

As you complete the above exercise, you might notice something: the awareness of physical sensations easily blends into awareness of emotional sensations. That's because our emotions have their basis in the body. For example, the fluttery, nauseous feeling at the center of your chest feels like panic and self-doubt. The hollow wobbly feeling in the pit of your stomach is shame. The tight band of tension around the top of your head is overwhelm. And so on.

As you scan your body, see if it is communicating anything to you. If your chest, arms, etc. could speak, what would they say? What emotions do they each hold? By asking these questions, you develop physiological and emotional awareness at the same time, and you strengthen your mind-body connection. You may even start to see how your anxious thoughts and rumination actually begin in this embodied emotion.

Dr. Lauri Nummenmaa studied seven hundred people and actually mapped out the places in the body where people most consistently experience certain emotions. By asking people to self-report where they experienced certain emotions on a body map, she discovered how consistent the responses were.

For example, anger was most often felt in the hands and head, while disgust centered around the mouth. The fascinating results were published in a 2013 paper in the journal *Proceedings of The National Academy of Sciences*. Dr. Paul Zak of Claremont Graduate University says that the "areas in the brain that process emotions tend to be largely outside of our conscious awareness" and that we can't really know how our body is processing emotions. Nevertheless, we can still increase our awareness of what it is possible to be aware of, and we can still calm and relax ourselves, even if we lack perfect understanding of the underlying mechanisms.

You can learn to use your body to explore your thoughts and emotions. You'll be able to spot emotions emerging in yourself more quickly, and this means you give yourself the choice of how you want to respond—consciously.

You can adapt the body scan to fit your needs. You don't need to use the CALM acronym. You could simply scan yourself from head to toe, or ask your body to show you what it most wants to communicate. One great practice is to finish your scan with perceiving the entire body as a whole all at once. This heightens your mind-body awareness and gives you real insights into your overall emotional state. See how long you can hold on to this heightened awareness as you go about the rest of your day.

18. LAUGHTER MEDITATION

Laughter meditation—is that when you force yourself to laugh? Yes! And it's as cheesy and ridiculous as it sounds.

It's also good fun and surprisingly effective. As a form of meditation, it's easy and straightforward, as there is nothing to achieve and no goal to focus on or anything to visualize. You just laugh, and you do it for no reason at all. Developed by Dr. Madan Kataria, this is definitely an underrated mindfulness practice. The idea is that when you are laughing, your anxious mind cannot run all over the place. You are completely and utterly in the present and in your body—and that's what meditation is all about.

Does it feel strange and awkward to start? Yes. We're used to laughing in response to something. But we *can* laugh whenever we like—and humans are the only animals that can! Laughter lowers stress, improves immune function, and enhances your digestion. And it just feels good. Laughing lowers cortisol levels in the body, too.

A 2011 paper published in *Science Direct* by Ramon Mora-Ripoll found that so-called "simulated laughter" can work as both a preventative for general wellbeing, and as a kind of medicine to treat things like anxiety and depression. The review also discovered that the laughter prescription is one of the few interventions that has virtually no side effects—so you have nothing to lose by trying it!

A 2016 paper by Louie et. al. had similar findings, noting that laughter actually has an analgesic (pain relief) effect. They explore the MCET—the "Motion Creates Emotion Theory"—in other words, if you go through the motions of laughing, you actually create a genuine sense of fun and humor in yourself. So, don't worry too much about "real" or "fake" laughter—your body can't tell the difference, and in fact, fake laughter often turns into real laughter anyway.

So how do you practice laughter meditation?

The best time is in the morning on an empty stomach. Begin by stretching, taking time to loosen up the muscles in your mouth, jaw, and face. Practice smiling. Start small and begin to see how this smile spreads into the other muscles of your face. Start laughing, but don't force anything. Just imagine it flowing out of you.

You're not laughing **at** anything, but rather laughing **with** it. Whatever emerges in your experience, laugh at it. Keep this up for a while. With a little practice, you may find that you're actually able to make yourself have big, full belly laughs—yes, really! When you're done, allow the laughter to fade as gently as it started. Gradually come to stillness again in your body, feeling the warm smile on your face and the good feelings in your body. Find stillness again. Finish the meditation by standing up and having a nice stretch. Let thoughts flutter past you and simply dwell on the sensations in your body. With regular practice, laughter meditation can have powerful effects on your life and banish anxiety.

If you're feeling adventurous, you can seek out a group to practice laughter meditation with. The awkwardness is initially greater, but you may find you reach that mindful state a lot quicker. You will be forced to not take yourself or the activity too seriously. Just access that inner child, be silly, and don't worry about how it all pans out. Meditation, then, can be thought of as play. Completely pointless and a lot of fun. And that's all.

It probably can't hurt to include more humor and laughter in your life more generally. Seek out comedy and funny shows or clips, make jokes and pull pranks, or simply try to see the silly side of life. Laughing at yourself is an incredibly powerful way to melt anxiety knots. Arguing and fighting against stress just makes more stress—but what if you just laugh at it? The next time you're in a big, serious mental tangle and worrying over this or that, try to zoom out and take another perspective. Can you see how silly it all is? How silly *you* are?

19. LOVING-KINDNESS MEDITATION

Let's move on to another very accessible form of meditation that never loses its effectiveness: loving kindness. This kind of meditation (often shortened to LKM) is the perfect way to cultivate compassion in ourselves, and improves not only our relationships with others but with ourselves. It can also work wonders for the stressed-out and anxious mind. During this meditation, we practice focusing kind and benevolent energy toward other people and toward ourselves. It's a technique that is simple . . . but not always easy. Sending and receiving love can be challenging!

A 2018 review in the *Harvard Review of Psychology by Graser and Stangier* collected an impressive amount of scientific evidence for LKM (as well as other types of meditation). According to the researchers, "LKM was effective in treating chronic pain and [. . .] borderline personality disorder. A larger number of nonrandomized studies indicate that [. . .] LKM may be effective in treating a wide range of clinical conditions, including depression, anxiety disorders, chronic pain, and posttraumatic stress disorder."

Other studies have found that LKM can improve marriages, soothe social anxiety, reduce anger, improve empathy, and help with forgiveness (Totzeck et. al. 2020; Zeng et. al. 2015). LKM can also:

- Increase gray matter in the area of the brain associated with emotional regulation (Leung et. al., 2012)
- Boost life satisfaction, and increase feelings of awe, gratitude, pride, and hope (Fredrickson et. al., 2011)
- Make you more likely to help others and be generous (Klimecki et. al., 2013)

Though there are many variations, and you can adjust the approach as you see fit, the general process goes a little something like this:

Step 1: Find some time in your day when you won't be distracted, and sit or lie somewhere comfortable, eyes closed. Find your breath and relax a little.

Step 2: Imagine someone you love dearly. Picture their face. Feel the love and kindness as a glow inside you and dwell on these feelings for a moment. You can visualize this kindness and compassion as a bright light or similar, or you can quietly chant the words, "May you be happy. May you be safe and at peace." Imagine yourself holding this person in a cocoon of light in your heart. However you picture it, the idea is to conjure up strong feelings of love and kindness.

Step 3: Holding on to this warm fuzzy feeling, imagine someone else—someone you like but do not love. Try to project this same loving-kindness onto them. See the humanity in this person. See how they have hopes and dreams and fears. How they were once innocent children. How they, too, hold the spark of the divine within them. "May you be happy. May you be safe and at peace."

Step 4: Move your attention again, this time to someone you're neutral about. Can you feel kindness and compassion for them, too? Can you see how they love as deeply as you do? And that even if you don't know them fully, that deep inside they are a beautiful being who deserves compassion and kindness?

Step 5: Keep shifting your attention. Find someone you dislike a little. This can be difficult, but try to imagine holding them in the same light as you held your loved ones. Even if you don't like them—even if you hate them—can you still find a little well of goodwill for them anyway? Not because they "deserve" it but . . . just because?

Step 6: Finally, take the step that some people find hardest of all: extend your warm glow of loving-kindness to yourself. Drop the desire to label, to judge, to find fault. Just look at yourself in all your flawed and beautiful humanity and imagine bathing yourself in a warm, glowing light of kindness.

Step 7: When you're ready, come out of your meditation, take a few deep breaths, stretch, and continue with your day.

Practice this for a few minutes every day and be prepared to be astonished at how much your life changes. You will find relaxation and calm, yes, but you will also discover other benefits. So many people who battle anxiety are very hard on themselves. But in LKM, we smile kindly on this and accept it. You are just right just as you are. And other people are just right, too. So there is no problem, and nothing to fight against. And so, anxiety can dissolve. Look at others and really try to feel that they are doing their best. Look inward and understand that your anxiety is only trying to help you, and that just because you are not a perfect human being, it doesn't mean you don't deserve understanding and kindness.

If you're the kind of person whose anxiety focuses on other people (social situations, relationships, guilt, etc.), this can be a powerful way to relinquish control. Love and anxiety don't exist together. Fill your heart with warmth and acceptance, and you're far less likely to notice problems or to slip into fearful resistance. What's more, you can find forgiveness—for yourself and others. Why ruminate on what's already been done? Let it go in forgiveness. Not because you agree with it or condone it, but because deep down all you want is peace and happiness for yourself and others. Doesn't that feel so, so much better than anxiety?

That warm glow inside your heart is always there. Practice repeatedly tuning into it, and you'll find it almost impossible to be anxious!

Summary:

- Mindfulness techniques are a proven and effective way to combat anxiety, stress, and overthinking, but you don't have to do formal sitting meditation to get the benefits.
- One easy technique is to take a few minutes to practice deep belly breathing to oxygenate and relax your body.
- Another is to use the 5-4-3-2-1 grounding technique to come back into your body and the present moment by tuning into all five senses. You could finish by seeking out something positive about the situation or yourself.
- Chanting a mantra is another accessible mindfulness technique. Try saying an affirmation aloud or just internally to distract and calm yourself.
- Do a body scan in the morning to check in with how you're feeling and correct any minor tensions before they become strong negative emotions and anxious thoughts. Use the CALM acronym to scan Chest, Arms, Legs, and Mouth, scan from head to toe, or simply ask your body what it wants to communicate to you. Use progressive muscle relaxation to loosen any tension you find.
- Laughter meditation takes a little bravery but can flood you with feel-good hormones and banish stress and anxiety, whether practiced alone or in a group.
- Try loving kindness meditation to calm social anxiety, and learn to be a little kinder and compassionate with yourself.

Chapter 4. The First Step is Seeing It

The thing about "seeing" it in visualization is that you are already an expert at it! When you stress and ruminate and worry, visualization is exactly what you're doing. You are creating distressing mental pictures that then cause an adverse reaction in your body. So, why not use this ability your brain already possesses and put it to better use? In this chapter, we're looking at scientifically proven ways to use the power of your imagination to calm anxiety, gain psychological distance, and learn to exteriorize your experience.

20. GUIDED IMAGERY

Guided imagery is a straightforward stress management tool that helps you relax. You simply imagine, in vivid detail, peaceful settings or situations.

Right now, try to think of a super sour lemon in great detail. Imagine yourself biting into one. Do this for long enough and you'll start to salivate! It's the same with guided imagery. When it comes to stress and relaxation, your brain cannot tell the difference between imagined and real. So when you imagine peaceful things, your body responds physically and releases feel-good hormones. This is why guided imagery has been associated with reduced stress and better relaxation.

A study published in 2014 (Menzies et. al., *Journal of Behavioral Medicine*) took women suffering from fibromyalgia and put them into two groups. One group did guided imagery exercises every day for ten weeks, while the other group didn't. At the end of the ten-week period, the women who did the guided imagery reported significant drops in their pain, stress, fatigue, and depression levels.

Another study (Patricolo et. al., 2017) did something similar, but compared the effects of guided imagery with those of clinical massage. The participants were patients in a progressive care unit. The results? Thirty minutes of guided imagery had the same effect on the participants as fifteen minutes of therapeutic massage. Guided imagery has also been shown to reduce pain, improve sleep quality, relieve fatigue, and improve depression.

Practicing guided imagery is easy, and there are so many ways to do it. You can try it when you wake up, before you sleep, or as part of a yoga practice or meditation session. You can use an audio recording or app to help you, make your own recording, or be creative and guide yourself. Take a look at YouTube or download one of the countless apps now available. The general process goes as follows:

- Sit somewhere quiet and get comfortable. Close your eyes and relax your breathing.
- You could start with any breathing exercise you like or do a little stretching to loosen your muscles.
- Now, in your mind's eye, take the time to imagine a peaceful, relaxing place. Your imagination is the limit: you could visualize an epic and serene mountain range in the snow, a heavenly garden with a palace made of crystal at its center, or a cozy library with a warm crackling fire in the corner. You could also think of a place from your memory.
- Now, don't rush. In as vivid detail as possible, imagine all the elements of this scene using all five senses. The smell of the sea breeze. The sound of children laughing. The sight of sunlight glittering through the tops of the trees... Don't forget to imagine how you feel in this place, too. What are you wearing? What are you doing and thinking?
- How you interact with this scene is up to you. You can walk through a path you create in your imagination, or simply imagine yourself at the center of a tranquil picture and notice what comes and goes. Some people imagine an enormous healing pool with a stone staircase that lowers you step by step into the magical water. Others imagine a stately museum that they browse through room by room.
- As you sink into your visualization, keep your breathing slow and regular and let go of any ideas of what you should be doing. Your only goal is to indulge in the relaxation you are creating for yourself.
- When you're done, take a deep breath, stretch, and open your eyes.

As you can see, there's plenty of leeway for you to make guided imagery your own. It's a good idea, though, to make sure you won't be disturbed (i.e., turn your phone to silent!) and wear comfy clothing. If imagining scenes is difficult at first, don't worry—you will get better with practice. You may find it helpful to first study images and photographs of gorgeous locations. Then close your eyes and imagine you're really there. What else can you see when you explore just outside the frame?

You can use audio recordings and prompts at first, but you may find you're able to go deeper once you take your time and create your own mental image. One great thing to do is create a mental sanctuary that you can repeatedly return to. In a way, this place acts like a "mental anchor" as we explored earlier. Your body and mind come to associate this place with deep relaxation. Every time you "visit," you can add another little detail.

Why not combine mantras with your imagery? This way, even if you don't have time to go into a full visualization session, you can evoke some of the associated emotions just by reciting your mantra. For example, in a stressful moment during the day, you can close your eyes, take a deep breath, and say, "Cool wet grass," to remind you of your inner safe space. It's amazing how suggestible your brain can be, and how quickly you can change your emotional state!

21. METAPHORIZE YOUR ANXIETY

One way to improve your relationship with anxiety is through metaphors. When we use metaphors, we gain psychological distance between us and what's bothering us. We become observers of our feelings rather than slaves to them. Your brain really is an amazing organ, and with a little prompting, you can use it to completely reshape your experience and the relationship you have with your anxiety.

In fact, the idea of having a "relationship with anxiety" is itself a metaphor! It's a metaphor that helps you see anxiety as something that can be understood and collaborated with. Metaphors can help us see new perspectives. Here are a few more useful ones:

Clouds in the sky

The Buddhist conception of anxiety (and all sensation and thought) is that they are like clouds moving across a sky. We are the sky—blue, depthless, eternal. But the weather is always changing. It comes, it goes. Anxiety is like this. It comes and it goes.

When we explore this metaphor, we start to see anxiety not as a problem to solve but as something as harmless and fleeting as passing clouds. Do you get angry at clouds? Do you fight against them or twist yourself into a knot figuring out how to "solve" them? They don't need to be solved. They come, and then they go.

New perspective: Even if right now you are anxious, it doesn't mean you always will be. You can embrace what is. You don't have to fight with it.

Waves in the ocean

Founder of Mindfulness Based Stress Reduction (MBSR) Jon Kabat-Zinn once said, "You can't stop the waves, but you can learn to surf."

New perspective: We can't control anxiety. But we can roll with it. We are able to cope with anything that comes our way.

Trains on a platform

You are the station, and thoughts arrive as trains, each one taking you to a different destination. There are a lot of trains, and the chaos and noise can be overwhelming, but remember: you only have to board one at a time, and you can choose which train you hop on.

New perspective: Just because a thought is there doesn't mean I have to "board" it and follow where it goes. I can watch it come and leave the station without me on it!

A grumpy two-year-old

Your anxiety isn't a fearsome demon set out to torture you for all eternity. It's just an annoying but completely manageable two-year-old who will calm down eventually. You can't ignore a tantrum, but you know that getting upset won't fix anything. Just talk kindly and patiently with the two-year-old and wait for the drama to pass. Forgive the anxiety—it's just afraid and overwhelmed. It's doing its best.

Whenever your brain starts getting carried away with "what if" thoughts, understand that you are occupying a particular perspective. Change that perspective a little and things won't seem as threatening.

You could imagine your anxiety as a tornado (crazy on the inside but relatively calm if you just step out of the center) or a box of worries that you can open at will or store away somewhere safe when you're tired of worrying. You could imagine that you have a soul bank account filled with life units, and every time you worry, you spend one unit of life that you could have spent on something that could make you happy instead.

Whichever metaphor you go with, it should be something that really speaks to you in a meaningful way. When you notice yourself drifting off into a "sea of anxiety," call up the image of waves (or ripples in a pond?). When you notice that critical and negative self-talk dominating your thoughts, imagine a little dial that you can turn to lower the volume so you can hear the rest of life.

Try the "leaves on a stream exercise"

One potent visualization/metaphor exercise is called "leaves on a stream." This is a "cognitive defusion" technique that is used in ACT—Action Commitment Therapy— and is designed to help you get distance from uncomfortable or overwhelming feelings. The shift in perspective is similar to the one we achieve when we metaphorize our anxiety: we realize, "I am having thoughts, but I am not my thoughts."

Here's how to do this simple practice.

- First, sit comfortably somewhere you won't be disturbed, breathing deeply (you know the drill!).
- Next, picture yourself sitting beside a tranquil flowing stream. In this stream are some fallen leaves peacefully floating by . . .
- As a thought pops into your mind, see it there, pick it up, and place it gently onto a passing leaf. Watch it float by out of your field of vision as the stream flows on.
- Do this with ALL your thoughts. Stressful, neutral, blissful. Put them all on the leaves and watch them go.

Now, you're not trying to dispose of thoughts or get rid of them. You're not rushing the stream along or trying to slow it. If you have a thought like, "This stream exercise is dumb," then simply pick that up, too, and put it on a leaf. If you think, "I'm really doing well with this," then yes, you guessed it, put it on a leaf too. Easy. If your mind wanders and you get sidetracked, it's no big deal. Just come back to your task with the leaves and carry on without admonishing yourself or feeling bad.

22. TALK ABOUT YOURSELF IN THIRD PERSON

Why does talking to other people about our worries make us feel better? Even if the problem isn't solved, we still feel some relief. What helps may simply be the fact that talking about our problems is a way to externalize and abstract our worry, putting some distance between it and ourselves. The great thing is, though, that you don't have to literally talk to a friend to experience these benefits. If you can learn to talk about yourself in third person, you still achieve that sense of distance and objectivity.

This is yet another way we can switch perspective and gain some relief from rumination and worry. What happens when you switch your point of view and think of yourself as a friend would think of you? What would happen if you spoke to yourself as if you were speaking to someone you knew (who had your name and all your problems) and who was asking for your help and advice?

A study published in 2017 in *Scientific Reports* by professor of psychology Jason Moser and his colleagues asked these very questions. The researchers found that talking about yourself as though you were someone else can help you relieve strong negative emotions. All you have to do is stop using "I" statements and instead use "he," "she," or "you." So, instead of saying, "I'm having a panic attack," you say, "She's having a panic attack," or, "Anna is having a panic attack."

It doesn't seem like that big of a deal, but Moser's research shows that when people do this, they self-report lower levels of anxiety. Again, we see the power of psychological distance. "By using your own name, and possibly also second-person pronouns, it creates this little separation from the self. It makes you think about your feelings and thoughts like you're looking at somebody else's experience," says Moser.

One experiment went like this. Participants looked at stock images and videos from upsetting news stories, then were asked to think about what they saw, first using the first-person point of view ("I was saddened") and then using third person ("Jay thought this was sad").

Simply by using their own names to talk about themselves, the participants showed more activity in the parts of the brain associated with emotional regulation. The emotion is still there, of course. It's just not as *close*. What's more, using third person takes no more effort than using first person, so it's a great tool to use on the spot when you're feeling overwhelmed.

Imagine you've just heard some very stressful news—a family member has had a serious car accident and is in the hospital, and you've had a panicky phone call from your mother. Your head suddenly explodes into dozens of different thoughts, and you're instantly overwhelmed. You know you should probably ask your boss if you can take some time off work so you can head over to the ER and do what you can, but you notice yourself quickly getting strung out as you start to panic, too. "What if I'm so stressed that *I* have a car accident on the way over? What if I get there too late and everyone is disappointed in me? What if my boss gets unhappy about me taking time off? What am I going to do?!"

Instead, ask yourself, "What is Michael going to do?" Can you instantly see how this takes so much of the panic out of the equation? It's as though you are looking at a movie of yourself from the outside in. Suddenly the stakes aren't as high. You can see a solution or a way forward.

Psychology professor Ethan Kross, who is also director at the Emotion and Self Control Lab, conducted a similar experiment. He asked participants to think about upsetting memories from the past, but to do so using third-person language. While they did this, their brain activity was examined using fMRI. They showed reduced activity in the parts of the brain we know are connected to the experience of pain. In other words, Kross found evidence that talking about painful memories in the third person reduces how painful they feel.

"What's really exciting here is that [. . .] third-person self-talk may constitute a relatively effortless form of emotion regulation. If this ends up being true—we won't know until more research is done—there are lots of important implications these findings have for our basic understanding of how self-control works, and for how to help people control their emotions in daily life," Kross said.

We don't have to wait for further research to be done, however, to get some benefit from making small tweaks to our language. Of course, you don't have to speak like this permanently. Rather, use the third-person trick to defuse especially stressful moments and take the edge off. You only need to do it long enough to gain some distance. Just momentarily take on a different perspective and see if that releases some of the tension. From there, you can take action or choose to let your worry go.

23. ROLE-PLAYING

You're probably familiar with role-playing in general, but did you know that role-playing is a useful tool when it comes to managing anxiety? You can use role-play to rehearse and prepare for difficult conversations or situations. When you role-play, you are exploring potential ways of behaving, finding new approaches and perspectives, and accessing new insights—all while staying in control. Role-playing can also be combined with many of the other approaches we've looked at—like naming how you feel, gaining distance by using third-person language, and being more self-aware.

How can we use role-play to help with stress and tension? First, identify a situation that's causing some anxiety for you. Let's say you're ruminating over a difficult conversation you need to have with a family member. Now, instead of endlessly turning the problem over in your head and causing stress, try to make the issue *concrete*—play out the possible conversation and see what happens. Maybe you enlist the help of a trusted friend or even a therapist. You sit together and try to make the situation feel as real as possible.

Assign the roles you'll each play. For example, if you wanted to clarify your thoughts and squash nervousness, you could play yourself and they could play the family member. Then you could practice the conversation. If you reverse this order, however, you might see different sides to the story and gain fresh insight and empathy into how the family member might be feeling.

Act out the conversation. Notice any anxiety or nerves. Notice how you feel afterward. Notice if anything changes after you start talking and once the conversation is finished. Is there some aspect of the issue you hadn't considered before? Even though role-playing this way can feel awkward to start with, it's actually a brilliant way to turbo-charge your communication skills.

There are many ways to use role-playing when it comes to overthinking and rumination:

- You could rehearse a job interview
- You could practice staying calm and focused during conversations where there may be some conflict to resolve—for example, during a meeting with an angry client
- You could rehearse a "performance," whether that's literally on a stage or a presentation at work, a wedding speech or a first date. Being prepared in advance will help you feel confident in yourself
- You could use role-playing to help you better understand a social situation, testing out possible outcomes and seeing how you'll react. Role-playing can boost empathy and help you get into other people's heads
- You could use role-play to desensitize yourself to fears and phobias. For example, those with social anxiety can practice small talk and introducing themselves, even "rewinding" and trying different tactics to get a feel for it in a safe and low-stakes way

Often, anxiety grows in the face of the unknown. But when you role-play, you are actively grappling with that unknown. You take your fears and worries and put them outside your head where you can work on them productively. You can take the stress-inducing "what if" statements and literally try them out.

When you're anxious, your brain believes that something is more dangerous and threatening than it is. But with role-play, you can prove to yourself that the situation is actually manageable. Scared of monsters under the bed? Well, go with a friend and see for yourself if there's anything there!

One way to approach role-playing is to **start with a fear or threat**. What scares or overwhelms you? Maybe you say "germs" or "busy social situations."

Next, think of your current behavior and attitude, then **imagine a new behavior** or mindset that you'd like to practice. For example, you'd like to be more comfortable and relaxed around meeting new people at parties.

Now, think of ways to **recreate this "threatening" situation**. With a therapist or friend (pick one who is good at acting!), run through some potentially stressful situations. Maybe you most hate those first few moments when you meet someone new and you're struggling to think of what to say. So, practice that over and over. Have the other person pretend to be a stranger and meet them, trying out this new behavior you want to learn.

Don't worry about making mistakes—in fact, messing things up and seeing that it's not the end of the world is all part of it! Think of it as teaching yourself that the threat is not a threat after all.
Gradually **dial up the intensity**. Once you're feeling confident in small talk from a cold start, see what it's like to talk to someone who is actively rude or uninterested. You may find that with enough practice, you actually start enjoying yourself. If you can start to see it all as a game, you know that the role-playing is working!

Naturally, not every anxiety or worry is going to translate into a role-play exercise. And let's be honest, many of us won't have someone we can practice with. But that doesn't mean you can't still benefit from this approach! Simply try *mentally rehearsing* a certain situation. Walk your brain step by step through a threatening scenario and practice what you say, what you feel, what you do, and what you think.

If you like, you can mix things up, too. Try to mentally rehearse the roles of other people in a scenario and see if that perspective shift shines new light on the problem. Or get abstract and role-play with your anxiety itself. Imagine it's sitting in a chair in front of you and literally talk to it. "Anxiety, what are you trying to achieve here? What are you worried about?" Make friends and try to come to a compromise. Sounds cheesy, but when you take the role of your own ultra-wise mentor/therapist, you'd be surprised at what you're capable of!

24. HAVE AN ALTER EGO

Kids who were instructed to imagine that they were Batman ended up having greater perseverance in a difficult task than kids who didn't. That's the finding of a fascinating 2016 study conducted by White et. al. at the University of Minnesota. Coining this phenomenon "the Batman effect," the researchers noted that merely pretending you are someone who is brave, capable, and strong can actually make you perform better.

The idea is that if you can take on the perspective of someone who is stronger and more proficient than yourself, then you literally allow yourself to reflect on a challenge in an entirely different way. Again, we see the power of creating psychological distance. If you can imagine how a person other than you would respond in a situation, you give yourself access to that same response.

In the study, the researchers asked kids who were four to six years old to do a task for ten minutes. They were also offered the chance to break up this task with an appealing video game. The kids who were told to simulate a strong role model actually ended up working harder and longer on the task than other kids. In this experiment, the other groups were told to take a third-person perspective ("Johnny is trying to figure out this puzzle") or an ordinary first-person perspective.

The study showed us that a mental role model could help children with self-discipline, focus, and perseverance. But it can also help adults emulate other characteristics they are trying to develop. Many famous musicians and performers have such an alter ego: even if they have stage fright and low self-confidence, their alter ego doesn't. When on stage, they do what their alter ego would do. Beyonce is said to use her alter ego (called "Sasha") to help her be what she wants to be on stage.

If we think of anxiety as a pattern of thought and behavior, we can think of alter egos as a way to "try on" a completely different pattern. It's difficult to step out of your own character at times, but it's easy to imagine another character. Think about a person who is relaxed, confident, and easy going. Imagine what a strong, self-assured, and in-control person thinks, says, and does. They may be a real person, a fictional character, or an imaginary person of your own creation.

The next time you're feeling anxious or overwhelmed, set your own ego aside for a moment and look at the situation from your alter ego's perspective. Do you remember the "What Would Jesus Do?" bangles that were popular in the 90s? The same principle applies. Granted, you might not always feel up to being as brave or relaxed as your alter ego, but the point is to at least entertain that perspective. The more you identify with that alter ego, the more you close the gap between how you are now and how you'd like to be.

Let's recap some simple steps to unlocking the "Batman effect" for yourself:

1. Think of something in yourself you'd like to work on—for example, your pessimistic self-talk or tendency to catastrophize.
2. Now, invert this. What does the opposite look like? You might decide it's a person who consistently and cheerfully assumes the best and always sees the silver lining.
3. Now construct an alter ego who possesses this characteristic in buckets. They could have other characteristics, too, or you might like to have a different alter ego for each characteristic. You could flesh them out by giving them a name,

an appearance, and so on. Have fun with it. Maybe you're socially anxious and your confident and popular alter ego is called "Catherine the Great."
4. The next time you're facing any challenge or obstacle, ask what your alter ego would do. What would they feel in this situation? Really dwell in their perspective. Then do what they'd do.

Here's how that might look. Let's say you are someone who constantly overthinks things. You decide you'd like to tackle your tendency to stew over minor details and make yourself stressed. You turn this tendency upside down and imagine an alter ego who is happy-go-lucky, calm, confident, and doesn't take things too seriously. This alter ego is a blend of someone you once knew and admired, a fictional character you read about in a book, and someone entirely made up. You call this person Eddie (because he's a bit like Eddie Murphy) and flesh out how he looks and acts. He's always smiling, and he likes to go with the flow, have fun, and see what happens.

One day you're planning a vacation and you notice your overthinking, stressed-out self appearing. You stop and think, *what would Eddie do?* Actually, Eddie would laugh at all this planning. Why so serious? Half the fun is going and figuring out what you want to do on the fly, right? Live life. Be a little spontaneous. Through Eddie's eyes, your nine-page-long Excel itinerary looks a little silly. You laugh at yourself, and when you next think about your upcoming vacation, you speak in his voice as you tell yourself, "I don't know what we're doing when we get there . . . but it'll be fun finding out!"

Summary:

- The imagination is a powerful thing and can be put to use to help combat anxiety and quell overthinking. Guided imagery, for example, is a great way to imagine a peaceful scenario in enough detail that our body responds by relaxing.
- Another effective stress management technique is to use metaphors to help you alter your relationship to anxiety and think of it in a different way. You could imagine that stress is like clouds passing by in the sky, passing trains, or a restless toddler.
- You can also gain this psychological distance by talking about yourself and your anxiety in the third person (for example, "David is worried about this" when talking about yourself).
- Role-play exercises are another way to use the power of visualizing. Literally act out and rehearse anxiety-provoking scenarios with a friend or therapist, or try to practice situations in your mind to de-sensitize you and help you feel more prepared and confident.
- Finally, create an alter ego for yourself who possesses the opposite of some stressful characteristics you want to be free of. Flesh out this alter ego and allow yourself to take on their perspective as your own when you're faced with a challenging or stressful situation.

Chapter 5. Reframe and Shift

In our final chapter, we're taking a closer look at a few key shifts in attitude that can drastically alter your perspective and help you think differently about your anxiety. These are less well-known techniques, but they are nevertheless effective ways to turn anxiety on its head and see it from a completely different angle. Think of anxiety as nothing more than a "spin" on reality—you can just as easily change the narrative in another direction that makes you feel happier, more relaxed, and more confident in yourself. Let's look at how.

25. ACCEPT YOUR ANXIETY

Robert Frost, a poet, once wrote, "The only way out is through."

He could have been writing about anxiety!

If you suffer from social anxieties, overthinking, or excessive stress and worry, your mindset may be something like: "This is wrong, and I need to get rid of it." Maybe we imagine a silver bullet or some kind of overnight insight that will fix us forever. And given how difficult it can be to live with anxiety, it's not very satisfying to be told to just "accept" it.

But a big part of how anxiety works is that it is a reinforcing chain reaction. Let's say you become aware of something that doesn't feel quite right. You focus in on it, you start to imagine worse things, you notice yourself focusing on those worse things, and then before you know it, you're spiraling out of control. However, if we approach ourselves and our anxiety with judgment and resistance, we end up adding even more links to this chain reaction. The irony is that desperately trying to escape problems is just another way to focus on them . . . it's a way we give ourselves *another* problem!

The real way out of anxiety is not to push or pull, not to succumb to it or run screaming from it. It's simply to sit calmly with how you actually feel.

People can mistakenly think that acceptance means we agree with what's happening, or that we like it. We might think that acceptance means we take no responsibility for getting better. This isn't true. Acceptance just means we plainly acknowledge the fact of what is, *without struggle*. It's this absence of struggle that gives us the freedom we want.

And we can have that feeling of freedom even though we still occasionally suffer from anxiety!

An attitude of acceptance tells us that:

- It's not the end of the world to feel anxious
- It's human to feel that way, and many other people do
- There's nothing to be ashamed of
- We are not weak, crazy, or failures because we are stressed or having a hard time
- Thoughts are just thoughts
- It's normal and perfectly okay to feel anxious or worried sometimes
- It is not possible to be completely free of anxiety—but it is possible to learn to live a happy life with a certain degree of anxiety

This last one is important. Sometimes, if we expect that our treatment or self-improvement goals are met to perfection, it can inspire us to give up when we feel we've failed to meet these ideals. But our goal should not be perfection, absolute control, and zero percent anxiety. Our goal is simply to be more accepting, tolerant, and compassionate about who we are, good and bad.

That's why the best way to manage anxiety is not to push against it, run away, fight it, judge it, or avoid it . . . but to simply accept it. The more we fight our thoughts, the stronger they become—especially when those thoughts are anxious in nature. But when you let them pass, they calmly fade away.

Anxiety can be thought of as your brain's mistaken attempt to maintain control. Overthinking feels like problem-solving, but it isn't. To fully accept your anxiety is to let go of this illusion of control and give up churning things over in your head in a way that has no effect on your world except to make you unhappy.

One great way to start practicing more acceptance is to closely watch our self-talk. Watch closely for emotionally loaded, extreme black-and-white thinking, such as beliefs about "always," "never," or "everybody." If you say to yourself, "I have to get this right or else," then stop and consider whether you really *have to*. Is it really, truly a nonnegotiable that you get it right? Will the whole world end if you don't get it right?

A big one is, "I can't handle this." This is basically an instruction to your brain, saying: it's an emergency, you're in a dangerous situation, and you can do nothing about it. Pretty anxiety-provoking, right? It's also very, very seldomly true. Tone it down and change the thought to, "This will be challenging, but I can get through it," or, "Just because I'm feeling anxious now doesn't mean that things won't work out."

The trick here, as you can see, is not to convince yourself that the danger isn't there and that you don't feel anxious. You do! But what happens when you look at that anxiety and say to it, "Fine, no big deal. I see you. It's okay that you're here." Sometimes we can't do much to get rid of our anxious feelings, but we can change the way we interpret that anxiety. This is what acceptance is. You had a panic attack last night? Okay. It happens. People sometimes get anxiety attacks, and you got one last night. Everything is okay now, though. Even if it does happen again, you'll manage it."

If you can do this, you'll realize that fighting anxious feelings is actually half of your anxiety in the first place! If you had a painful spasm in one of your muscles, you wouldn't try to fix it with brute force, right? That would just make the problem worse. In the same way, let yourself off the hook and let go of being anxious about anxiety.

Here's a quick exercise the next time you're feeling anxious: talk to your amygdala. This part of your brain evolved for good reason. The fear response is a gift that keeps us safe and alive. It's a *good* thing that the amygdala can move quicker than our rational brain because in life-or-death moments, every split second counts.

However, the amygdala is just a part of your body. And it can be wrong! We can stop, take a breath, and ask our higher brain to weigh in. We can challenge our thought processes, become aware of what we're doing, and consciously choose what we want to do. The next time you're feeling stressed and overwhelmed, say in your mind, "Thank you, amygdala, for bringing my attention to this. Thanks for trying to keep me safe. My higher brain can take it from here, though!"

It's not that our knee-jerk fight-or-flight response is *wrong* or that we are to blame for being triggered into a cycle of overthinking and rumination. It's simply a misfire. Seeing your reactions this way takes the angst out of them. Anxiety, then, is a bit like having an allergic reaction or getting indigestion—it's uncomfortable, yes, but not the end of the world and not something you have to go to war with. It's not dangerous. It's not shameful. You haven't done anything wrong.

If you can literally visualize yourself thanking your amygdala and your stress response, then giving it permission to stand down, then you take the power away from that anxiety. You realize that just because your amygdala is going crazy, it doesn't mean you have to respond or that you are under its control.

26. TELL YOURSELF YOU'RE JUST EXCITED

As you can see, perspective is everything. Anxiety and stress are facts of life, but so much of how they feel comes down to how we *frame* that anxiety and stress. In other words, instead of trying to tackle anxiety, start by telling yourself that you are not actually experiencing anxiety at all.

Let's take a look at this word "anxious." When you diagnose your state of mind with this word, the next steps are clear—you want to mitigate the anxiety, fix it, escape it, accept it, or deal with it somehow. But let's take a step back and consider whether our appraisal of "anxiety" is even accurate.

Physiologically, anxiety is actually arousal—our autonomic nervous system is activated, and we are on high alert. But in truth, there is nothing especially wrong with this state of mind—unless we convince ourselves there is. After all, physiological arousal also happens when we're stimulated, excited, thrilled, or inspired. This is why some people can look at jumping out of an airplane as a catastrophically scary event, while others may see it as exhilarating. The body response is the same—only the narrative about what those sensations mean changes.

One way to deal with anxiety is to try to relax ourselves. That's a good strategy. But another strategy is to ask, "Hang on a second, is the way I'm feeling really so bad?" A study by Dr. Alison Wood Brooks found that eighty-five percent of questionnaire participants said they thought the best thing to do with anxiety was to relax. But as we all know, "just relax" is easier said than done! What if instead you said, "I'm not anxious, I'm just excited"? You don't have to change anything.

When you reframe, you're already where you need to be.

Maybe it's a *good* thing that you feel a little stressed being outside your comfort zone—it shows you're growing. For example, if you feel anxious that you have "imposter syndrome," you could reframe the experience. Isn't feeling a little anxious part of the learning process? If it seems like too much of a leap to say you're excited, say, "I'm looking forward to being excited," or, "Well, this is interesting!" Just a subtle switch from fear and resistance to curiosity can make all the difference.

Dr. Brooks also did some fascinating experiments. She surprised study participants with some moderately anxiety-inducing tasks—one of which was to sing a song ("Don't Stop Believin'" by Journey, if you're interested). Participants were told to say either, "I'm anxious," or, "I'm excited." The group who said they were excited actually felt more excited and sang better as measured by a machine that records pitch and volume. The same thing happened when other participants were tasked with giving a speech to a camera. The "excited" group was measured objectively as more persuasive and confident.

Here's the interesting part: in each case, both groups showed the same amount of anxiety. Their heart rates were the same; their cortisol levels were the same. But by simply using this word "excited," they put themselves in an **opportunity** mindset rather than a **threat** mindset. And so they felt better and performed better.

It might not feel very natural to claim how enthusiastic you are about everything, but just try it. You will get better with a little practice. And as with so many other reframing and perspective-switching exercises, you don't have to one hundred percent believe what you're saying, either. You may benefit simply from *not* saying that you're anxious.

So, there are three main ways to deal with anxiety:
1. Emotional suppression
2. Emotional regulation or acceptance
3. Emotional reappraisal

A 2009 study in *Behavior Research and Therapy* by Hoffman and colleagues has suggested that reappraisal and acceptance are more effective than trying to suppress anxiety. In their research, they asked 202 participants in three groups to give an impromptu filmed speech. The first group was the reappraisal group, the second the suppression group, and the third the acceptance group, according to how they were told to approach their anxiety. The suppression group actually ended up increasing their heart rates and worsening their anxiety.

"However," the researchers concluded, "the acceptance and suppression groups did not differ in their subjective anxiety response. These results suggest that both reappraising and accepting anxiety is more effective for moderating the physiological arousal than suppressing anxiety. However, **reappraising is more effective for moderating the subjective feeling of anxiety** than attempts to suppress or accept it."

To practice this kind of reframing in your own life, you need only make a conscious effort to remove words like "stressed," "worried," anxious," and so on from your vocabulary. Instead, talk about opportunities, chances, excitement, enthusiasm, interest, or even just novelty. You'll see just how easy it is to convince your body that the butterflies in your stomach are a pleasant sensation!

27. WRITE TO YOUR FUTURE SELF

One creative way to gain perspective on your anxiety is "future journaling" or writing notes to your future self. Anxiety tends to narrow perspective. We can be horrible judges of reality when we're hyper focused on some perceived problem. But when we write a letter to our future selves, we broaden our vision.

Imagine you're stressing about the renovation of your new home, worried about money, and feeling overwhelmed by everything you need to do. Let's say you sit down and write a letter to ninety-year-old you. What do you say? Try this exercise when you're feeling swamped in a problem, and you'll be amazed at just how clarifying it is. What will ultimately matter when you're that old, looking back on your life? Will you really care about having done everything perfectly, or will your memories be about how you worked hard to create a family home that you could fill with love?

It's funny how a little distance can help dissolve all the nonsense of life and help us see our deepest values more clearly. You can future journal to yourself in two weeks or in twenty years. You can confide in and share worries with your older, wiser self, and even imagine what that self would tell you in return. Almost always, your older self *wouldn't* say, "I think you're not anxious enough—you should worry more"!

When you future journal, let your thoughts wander a little.

What does the ideal resolution to the current challenge look like?

Why does this challenge bother you so much?

What's really important here ... and what isn't?

What will happen here if things don't go to plan?

How would you look back on this current situation, being older and wiser?

That's not all, though. After you've written the letter, come back to it later. Did the thing you were so anxious about come to pass? And if it did, was your reaction what you thought it would be? Was it as bad as you predicted?

When you're in the grip of anxiety, you can start to take your own fears and assumptions as gospel. But when you get a broader view across time, you realize, with some relief, that you're often just plain wrong. What you thought was a big deal in May turns out to be forgotten completely in June. What you thought you wanted turned out not to be the thing you needed, and so on. So, the next time you're in a panic about something, you can pause and remember that your assessment just might be inaccurate.

In a study published in the *Journal of Experimental Psychology*, Dr. Kitty Klein and colleagues asked seventy-one students to do three twenty-minute expressive writing exercises over a period of two weeks. *"The results suggest that the simple act of writing about stressful events can have a positive impact on academic performance—although for how long remains unknown,"* concluded the authors. When we combine this expressive writing with a long-range view into the future, we gain a few insights:

- *How we feel today is not how we'll feel tomorrow*
- *We are not always accurate in our predictions about the future*
- *Though transitions and challenges can be difficult, we have coped before and will cope again*

Future journaling is something you can incorporate into a regular journal-writing habit, or you can try it out specifically when you're having a hard time. Keep track of goals by writing a letter to a future self after the time you expect to achieve that goal. Have you achieved what you wanted? If not, what does that look like? Are you happy? What did you do next? What did you learn, and how did you overcome your challenges?

You can just ask your future self these questions without needing to answer them. Simply allow the questions to clarify and condense your own position in the present. If you like, you can combine this exercise with a visualization session—try to imagine your future self. Alternatively, talk to your future self mentally and do a role-play. What would you learn if you interviewed your future self about the current problem you're facing?

You could use these letters to rehearse different outcomes and see how you feel about them. Imagine that everything goes "wrong" and that what you're worried about comes to pass. What does that actually look like for your future self? Is it that bad? Most problems shrink down to nothing when you consider whether you'll actually care about them in a year's time.

If you're on the cusp of making a decision, slow down and consult with your future self. What would they think of your choice? Try to be reasonable and rational. Don't leap into anything new until you've taken the longer view. One fun thing to do is to write yourself an email and schedule to have it delivered to you on a set date in the future. Or write yourself a letter on every birthday to read in one year's time. The act of seeing where you were a year ago and forecasting where you'll be a year from now is a powerful and grounding practice.

Finally, a variation on this exercise is to write a letter to a future anxious self when you're currently feeling strong and happy. Write from your calm, content point of view. What would you like to tell your future stressed-out self? When you're in the grips of stress and anxiety, it's so hard to pull yourself out of it, but if you can get a glimpse of yourself in a happier state of mind, you remind yourself that not only is it possible to feel that way, but that it's likely! "Dear stressed future self, I know things look pretty rough right now, but you actually have a great life with a lot to be thankful for. You know how it is; you struggle for a few days, but you always find your way through . . ." Think of it as a greeting card from better days—"wish you were here!"

28. LEARN HOW TO SAY "I DON'T"

This trick is for all those people whose anxiety and stress comes from being a people-pleaser or not knowing how to say no. Sometimes, the best way to manage stress is to set up stronger boundaries so that we don't take on more than we can handle. Saying *no* can be hard for some people, but with a simple switch in perspective, we can see that it's really about saying *yes* to what really matters to you—your priorities.

Everyone finds turning people down a little awkward, but if this is a weak point for you, thankfully there are some scientifically proven ways to best say no. First things first, change your perspective:

Saying no is a healthy, normal thing to do. You don't have endless resources or time, and so you have to prioritize certain things over others. Saying no helps you shape your life according to your values, and you are not required to say yes out of guilt or obligation to others. In fact, saying yes to everything not only creates stress for you, but it's seldom the favor to others we think it is!

Well, now that that's out of the way, let's consider the most effective method for saying no. In a research study published in the *Journal of Consumer Research*, 120 participants were divided into two groups, one group saying, "I can't," when turning down a request, and the other saying, "I don't." For example, turning down a tempting treat of ice cream could be done with "I can't eat ice cream," or, "I don't eat ice cream."

Afterward, the participants answered some unrelated questions. They then thought the study was over, but it wasn't. As they were leaving, each participant was offered a chocolate bar or healthy granola bar. The results? Those who were told to say "I can't" earlier ate the unhealthy chocolate bar sixty-one percent of the time. Those who said "I don't" only ate the unhealthy chocolate bar thirty-six percent of the time!

The same researchers designed another similar study, inviting thirty women to a "wellness" seminar and dividing them into three groups. After being asked about their long-term health goals, one group was told to "just say no" to temptations, the second group was told to use "I can't" language, and the third to say, "I don't." Only three out of ten of the "just say no" group were able to persist with their goal throughout the ten-day seminar. The "I can't" group only managed one woman out of ten who stuck to her goal. And the "I don't" group fared best of all, with an impressive eight out of ten women achieving what they set out to.

Granted, this study focused on self-discipline and goal setting, but the principles also apply to establishing and maintaining boundaries. This is because "I don't" language is all about control and empowerment. We tell ourselves that we're the kind of people who follow certain values. It's an inborn trait rather than something imposed on us from the outside (doesn't "I can't" just make you think of someone passively following a rule someone else set for them?).

I don't is a choice freely made and immovable.

I can't is an external limitation, an excuse—and it invites resistance!

Take a look:

"Hey, can you look after my nine obnoxious bulldogs this weekend at short notice?"

"Oh, I'm sorry, I can't! I'm, uh, having guests over that weekend."

"Oh, no problem, they won't be any trouble. Your guests will love them!"

Compare this to:

"Hey, can you look after my nine obnoxious bulldogs this weekend at short notice?"

"Oh, I'm sorry, but no. I don't have dogs in my house, I'm afraid!"

"Oh, well, that's a shame."

When you say no the right way, it's not in order to get the other person to really believe it; it's to make sure that *you* really believe it and communicate that sureness clearly. It's a skill to say no and really mean it. Keep your no:

1. Short
2. Firm
3. Polite

If they ask again, simply say no again without feeling like you have to do something else to appease them or apologize for not acquiescing. Don't jump in to solve a problem or beat yourself up for not being more accommodating. Just say no (you don't even have to give a reason) and smile politely.

If you feel like you've been caught off guard with a request, a great tip is to say, "Let me just think about that and I'll get back to you soon." This buys you time to think clearly through your wants and needs and your practical limitations. Do you really want to do it? Plan your response (try a role-play or rehearsal!) and then be assertive but polite if you say no.

It always pays to be polite, but do so in a way that doesn't leave you open to "negotiation." If you say things like, "I wish I could, but I can't," you are inviting the same request later. Finally, don't forget that you can give a modified yes.

"Could you finish this report this evening before you go home?"

"No, that's going to be a big rush, I'm afraid. I can complete it for you tomorrow afternoon if you're willing to wait?"

Time, resource, and energy management is the same as stress management. It may feel awkward at first to be more assertive, but remember that a polite no is actually an act of respect—for yourself and for the other person.

29. HAVE NO OPINION

Let's end our book with a simple but effective attitude to hold when it comes to the stress and anxiety of life. In the words of famous Stoic philosopher Marcus Aurelius, "You always own the option of having no opinion. There is never any need to get worked up or to trouble your soul about things you can't control. These things are not asking to be judged by you. Leave them alone."

In a world where seemingly everyone has to have an opinion about everything (usually, a forceful opinion), it can be a welcome relief to remember that opinions are actually optional. You don't *need* to go in and make a pronouncement or judgment about every little thing that comes your way. It's simple but easy to forget: having an "opinion" about something that we cannot change and are not responsible for is a perfect way to invite dissatisfaction and anxiety into our lives. But we can always choose to leave them alone.

You don't have to be a fixer.
You don't have to decide who is right or wrong.
You don't have to agree or disagree.
You don't have to engage at all, in fact.

So often, this kind of engagement comes with anxiety, especially if we are getting tangled up in things that are not really our business. For example, you scroll through social media and discover a post that you can tell has been designed to polarize people. There's a goodie, there's a baddie, and you're being invited to harshly condemn or mock the baddie. How many times have you taken the bait and gotten worked up about this kind of thing?

Suddenly, people and issues and ideas that you hadn't heard of a moment before fill your brain, and you immediately jump in to decide what you think about it. In fact, you may even consider it some kind of duty to pick which side you fall on and why. It may feel like getting outraged is the righteous, noble thing to do. This knee-jerk reaction can be so swift that you never even stop to consider if you *want* to get involved with it in the first place.

Let's consider another example. You've messed up at work and you're feeling completely stressed out about how you're going to save face and how you're going to make it up to people. You ruminate endlessly about it. It's as though your brain wants to answer the question: "Just how bad are you?" Sometimes you get defensive and feel like blaming other people; other times you're filled with embarrassment about what you've done and feel really bad.

But who says you have to play this game at all? Is it really necessary to find out who's to blame and just how much they are to blame in order for you to carry on? You can take your steps to address the situation without getting emotionally involved at all.

The Stoics were fans of serenity and the emotional regulation that comes with letting go of what really isn't in your control. Does having an opinion improve your life? If you're honest, the most likely answer is "no." And considering that "opinions" often come with a dose of confusion, anxiety, stress, and obligation, why not just drop them? There are a million problems out there in the world, and always will be. But none of them are asking you to have an opinion of them. What's more, you having an opinion is not necessary for you to be happy, to be effective, or to act toward your goals. What freedom!

There's another way we can interpret Aurelius' quote: we can always delay our opinion if we must have one. In the face of uncertainty or confusion, we can learn to comfortably say, "I don't know," or "I'll make a decision . . . but just not yet." Stress and anxiety go hand in hand with rushing. But when it comes to the most important things in life, you don't have to rush. Be okay with letting the moment be unclear, unknowable, or in process. You always have that option.

Summary:

- We are always at liberty to reframe our anxiety and look at things in different ways. One way to do this is to consciously practice acceptance of how we feel rather than always trying to escape it, fix it, or judge it. This doesn't mean we agree with it or don't want to be better; it just means we relinquish the struggle.
- Simply by saying, "I'm excited," instead of, "I'm anxious," opens a different perspective and helps us interpret the same physiological arousal as less threatening, helping us perform better.
- Try writing to your future self to gain deep perspective and remind yourself of what ultimately matters. Ask for advice from a wiser, older version of yourself, or write a note from your calm self to your stressed self, offering advice.
- Stress management is often time management and knowing how to say no to too many commitments. Be short, firm, and polite and say, "I don't," instead of, "I can't," if you want people to respect that boundary.

- Finally, take Aurelius' advice and remember that you always have the option to have no opinion. You don't have to judge, decide, agree, or take sides. And if you must, realize that you can always postpone your judgment.

Summary Guide

CHAPTER 1. YOUR ANXIETY MANAGEMENT TOOLKIT

- Whatever form stress and anxiety take in your life, it's worth having some psychological tools to help you manage it mindfully. Build more self-awareness by learning to label your emotions and noting how they feel on your body in the moment. We can also build self-awareness by keeping a regular thought diary, or by taking psychometric tests.
- We don't have to accept our anxious thoughts as gospel. The Socratic questioning method asks us to look for evidence, become curious, and deliberately seek out alternative interpretations. We can likewise test our false beliefs by reappraising our assessment of the situation and the "threat" we see.
- Making a mind map gives us perspective and clarity on the chaos that may be in our minds. Start with a single word or phrase and do a "brain dump," then look for patterns and themes, asking what you can control and what you cannot. One of the best cures for anxiety is to ask what you can realistically **do** about your situation.
- The ABC model helps us understand the antecedents, beliefs, and consequences of our stress reaction, and allows us to re-engineer our perspective and behave differently.
- One option is to simply distract yourself by giving your brain an engaging "mind game."

CHAPTER 2. AN ANXIETY-FREE LIFESTYLE

- Easy, everyday lifestyle changes can make a big difference with anxiety and overthinking. An obvious area to examine is whether you're having too much caffeine. Try to limit yourself to four hundred milligrams daily.
- Everyone worries, so at least do it strategically by scheduling worry time. Keep a worry journal so that instead of fighting worry, you postpone and contain it, tackling it on your own terms.
- Practice gratitude daily to gently shift your perspective to focus on everything that is going well in your world. Use a journal or write thank-you notes to people who have shown you kindness.
- Mental anchoring is a technique that, once established, can be used as often as you like to help ground and calm you. Choose an anchor, choose a desired state, then

connect the two during visualization so that revisiting the anchor brings you back to that state of mind.
- Have a consistent morning routine where you focus on good food, nature, healthy habits, and quiet contemplative time where you set your intention for the day. Make sure you're hydrated, since dehydration can elevate cortisol levels.
- Finally, choose a hobby that can act as a pleasant distraction—but make sure you're choosing something you genuinely enjoy.

CHAPTER 3. ENTER YOUR MIND

- Mindfulness techniques are a proven and effective way to combat anxiety, stress, and overthinking, but you don't have to do formal sitting meditation to get the benefits.
- One easy technique is to take a few minutes to practice deep belly breathing to oxygenate and relax your body.
- Another is to use the 5-4-3-2-1 grounding technique to come back into your body and the present moment by tuning into all five senses. You could finish by seeking out something positive about the situation or yourself.
- Chanting a mantra is another accessible mindfulness technique. Try saying an affirmation aloud or just internally to distract and calm yourself.
- Do a body scan in the morning to check in with how you're feeling and correct any minor tensions before they become strong negative emotions and anxious thoughts. Use the CALM acronym to scan Chest, Arms, Legs, and Mouth, scan from head to toe, or simply ask your body what it wants to communicate to you. Use progressive muscle relaxation to loosen any tension you find.
- Laughter meditation takes a little bravery but can flood you with feel-good hormones and banish stress and anxiety, whether practiced alone or in a group.
- Try loving kindness meditation to calm social anxiety, and learn to be a little kinder and compassionate with yourself.

CHAPTER 4. THE FIRST STEP IS SEEING IT

- The imagination is a powerful thing and can be put to use to help combat anxiety and quell overthinking. Guided imagery, for example, is a great way to imagine a peaceful scenario in enough detail that our body responds by relaxing.
- Another effective stress management technique is to use metaphors to help you alter your relationship to anxiety and think of it in a different way. You could

- imagine that stress is like clouds passing by in the sky, passing trains, or a restless toddler.
- You can also gain this psychological distance by talking about yourself and your anxiety in the third person (for example, "David is worried about this" when talking about yourself).
- Role-play exercises are another way to use the power of visualizing. Literally act out and rehearse anxiety-provoking scenarios with a friend or therapist, or try to practice situations in your mind to de-sensitize you and help you feel more prepared and confident.
- Finally, create an alter ego for yourself who possesses the opposite of some stressful characteristics you want to be free of. Flesh out this alter ego and allow yourself to take on their perspective as your own when you're faced with a challenging or stressful situation.

CHAPTER 5. REFRAME AND SHIFT

- We are always at liberty to reframe our anxiety and look at things in different ways. One way to do this is to consciously practice acceptance of how we feel rather than always trying to escape it, fix it, or judge it. This doesn't mean we agree with it or don't want to be better; it just means we relinquish the struggle.
- Simply by saying, "I'm excited," instead of, "I'm anxious," opens a different perspective and helps us interpret the same physiological arousal as less threatening, helping us perform better.
- Try writing to your future self to gain deep perspective and remind yourself of what ultimately matters. Ask for advice from a wiser, older version of yourself, or write a note from your calm self to your stressed self, offering advice.
- Stress management is often time management and knowing how to say no to too many commitments. Be short, firm, and polite and say, "I don't," instead of, "I can't," if you want people to respect that boundary.
- Finally, take Aurelius' advice and remember that you always have the option to have no opinion. You don't have to judge, decide, agree, or take sides. And if you must, realize that you can always postpone your judgment.

Book 3: Transform Your Self-Talk: *How to Talk to Yourself for Confidence, Belief, and Calm*

Table of Contents

TRANSFORM YOUR SELF-TALK: THE ART OF TALKING TO YOURSELF FOR CONFIDENCE, BELIEF, AND CALM

CHAPTER 1. THAT VOICE INSIDE YOUR HEAD
THE SCIENCE OF SELF-TALK
SELF-TALK AS AN AMPLIFIER
EENIE, MEENIE, MINIE, MOE

CHAPTER 2. GOOD VERSUS EVIL
POSITIVE VERSUS NEGATIVE SELF-TALK
A SIMPLE COST-BENEFIT ANALYSIS
MEET YOUR INNER CRITIC
FIVE LEVELS OF SELF-TALK

CHAPTER 3. ALL YOU NEED TO DO IS LISTEN
THE KEY TO SELF-AWARENESS
ASSESSMENT TOOLS AND TIPS

CHAPTER 4. REPLACE, TRANSFORM, EVOLVE
THREE-STEP COGNITIVE BEHAVIORAL THERAPY
STEP 1: OBSERVE
STEP 2: CHALLENGE
STEP 3: REPLACE

CHAPTER 5: MORE THAN WORDS
EVERYDAY REINFORCEMENT
A SELF-EMPOWERMENT HABIT
THE CULMINATION OF REWRITING YOUR SELF-TALK

Summary Guide

Chapter 1. That Voice Inside Your Head

It's been there so long sometimes you barely even notice it—that little "voice" inside that quietly narrates, judges, encourages, explains or interprets the world around you. Though you may recognize the concept of an inner voice from self-help literature, the fact is there's nothing abstract or mysterious about this inner chatter. "Self-talk" actually has a surprising body of scientific evidence behind it, informing a fascinating set of theories that seek to understand exactly what's happening when we "talk to ourselves."

In this book we'll take a closer look at what self-talk actually is, the various theories that have been proposed over the years to explain the phenomenon, and the facts we've amassed so far about both its psychology and physiology.

We'll discover the different types of self-talk, investigate why it happens, explore what's normal and what's not, and most importantly, we'll see that self-talk can be changed for the better. As Bruce Lee famously said, "As you think, so shall you become." Using a series of scientifically supported techniques to identify and improve your self-talk, you can take more conscious control of your thinking and perceptions, boosting confidence, self-mastery and resilience in a challenging world.

Self-talk is something we do every day, and this is partially why it's so hard for us to change. We don't even realize we are doing it.

You wake up in the morning and the second you open your eyes the stream of thoughts starts flowing: "What day is it? Oh right, Tuesday. I mustn't forget that appointment later this afternoon. God, I have such a bad memory, why am I such an idiot all the time? I bet I'll forget it. Typical. I'm always doing things like that. Oh look, it seems like it'll be a sunny day today. That reminds me, I have to get my mole scan done at some point... but what if it's cancer? But it's not going to be. I mean, it *might* be. That would be just my luck. Great-Aunt Matilda had skin cancer. I think? If I die of cancer who will look after my kids? That would literally be the worst thing I could think of... but what's the point in getting it checked out? Doctors are all useless... That reminds me..."

You may not do all this every day, but you likely do *some* of this *some* days.

Self-talk is that stream-of-conscious, ongoing internal dialogue that runs inside our minds, affecting every aspect of our lives from our moods, to our behavior, to our self-confidence, to our appraisal of risk and reward. It's the constant conversation we have with ourselves. It can be neutral and mostly observational ("oh right, it's Tuesday"), or filled with criticism, pessimism, doom and gloom ("I shouldn't try that, I'm not good enough"). Often, all of the above become inseparable from the objective truth of a matter.

Our inner self-talk is the built-in narrator that runs alongside our lives, playing over everyday activities and in the background of every action or decision we make. This narration colors the entire tone of our lived experience, telling us how to interpret both good and bad experiences, and how to understand ourselves and our place in the world. It amounts to a narrative we tell ourselves, and this narrative is solidified well before we become adults.

Importantly, self-talk can be unconscious or conscious, negative or positive, beneficial to our lives or working entirely against our best interests. With some awareness and effort, negative and self-defeating inner talk can be identified and changed, so that the voice in your head supports rather than undermines you.

There are three primary types of self-talk.

The most obvious type is negative self-talk, and the thought-stream above is a prime example. These pessimistic interpretations, judgments, accusations, complaints, and catastrophic predictions leave us feeling awful. Some people in some circumstances might find negative self-talk motivational, but this comprises only a small percentage of negative self-talk ("They said I can't do this? I'll prove them wrong!" versus "I'm not good enough to do it, so I just won't try."). This is your inner self-critic who always sees the glass as half-empty. He can be useful and warn us about certain dangers, but again, that only takes place a rather small percentage of the time.

On the other hand, true motivational self-talk, or positive self-talk, is that which actively encourages and supports us as we navigate life's challenges, aim for our goals or cope with difficulties. This can be an affirmation-style phrase that you consciously use to correct biased thinking, or it can be simply smiling at yourself in the mirror before an interview and saying, "I'm going to be great! I can do this and I certainly deserve it!"

Neutral self-talk is the bulk of the internal conversation, and consists of simple observations and comments, while instructional self-talk is the kind of dialogue we have with ourselves to help us through certain tasks, sports or performance, for example: "keep looking straight ahead," "easy does it," and "OK, try again but this time focus on the ball…" But even these statements can take a positive or negative tone if not carefully managed.

For the purposes of our book, we'll be looking primarily at negative and positive/motivational self-talk—and how to turn the former into the latter.

The Science of Self-Talk

In 1911, neurologists Dr. Gordon Morgan Holmes and Dr. Henry Head published a series of papers exploring the connection between the body and the brain. They related a story of Victorian women who, at the time, would have worn large, fashionable feather hats and would sometimes duck to walk through a doorway even when they weren't wearing the hats.

Why? The idea is that a person's mind holds a mental picture of what their body looks like, and acts accordingly. Dr. Branch Coslett of the University of Pennsylvania found, over a century later in 2013, that women with anorexia did something similar—they angled their bodies through doorways as though to squeeze through even when they clearly had enough room. Their *mental image* of themselves didn't match their *actual* selves.

What these seemingly simple observations tell us is something rather important: that we all have a mental representation of ourselves that may or may not align with reality. We do need this internal representation (or else we'd bump into things a lot more often!), but some studies suggest that to our brains, imagining certain actions is no different neurologically to actually doing them.

It's not merely a mysterious suggestion that "thoughts create your reality;" there is a mounting body of evidence suggesting that the way you see yourself has a profound effect on your perceptions, your mental health, your behavior, and even things like your experience of pain and illness. Self-talk is the soundtrack that constantly informs us of these departures from objective reality, for better or worse.

Better stated, self-talk is one of the mechanisms we use to establish and maintain this inner representation of ourselves. Using narratives and certain kinds of language, we employ considerable brain power to literally tell ourselves who we are—and it goes way beyond giving yourself a pep talk in the mirror or saying an affirmation.

For a quick demonstration on the power of self-talk and just how specific it can be, professor Ethan Kross at the University of Michigan published research in 2014 that showed using "I" pronouns in self-talk caused more stress and precluded feelings of self-love when compared to using your own name or "you." Have you ever spoken to yourself in the second person (e.g. "John, you've done it again!" or "You're just tired right now")? The linguistic distance created by this small shift is enough to remove you somewhat from your actions, allowing you to be kinder to yourself and give yourself more objective support.

This small change in self-talk alone seems to help people act more rationally and self-regulate more effectively. We all know how much easier it can be to be compassionate towards others than ourselves—this shift in self-talk allows us to almost treat ourselves from the outside, looking in. It's almost unfathomable for such a transformation to come from something so small, but that is indeed the basis of this book—just how damaging our normal and frequent words to ourselves are, and how much we can seize upon our potential with small changes.

For another quick demonstration of this impact, psychologist David Sarwer asks his patients with eating disorders to stand in front of a mirror and use more neutral, non-judgmental language to talk about what they see. Instead of saying "My stomach is revolting and fat, and my legs are disgusting," they practice saying "My stomach is round. My legs are pale, soft, and bigger at the top."

The idea is that you change your life not by changing your life, but by first changing *your inner representation of your life*. Just as an anorexic will never feel good about their bodies no matter what they look like, it's no use tackling external phenomenon when the problem might lie with your inner perceptions. Just as we construct mental models of what our physical body looks like so that we can interact in the world, we do the same on a psychological, emotional, relational and even spiritual levels. It turns out Bruce Lee was right—the underlying message is what's important, and not necessarily attending to the symptoms of something deeper.

Dr. Shad Helmstetter is an independent researcher who studied and observed the Amway multi-level marketing business model as an outsider for many years. He was interested in what we all secretly say to ourselves; in their case, what convinced people to join and buy into such an organization. He found that the way we talk to ourselves has profound effects on our self-perception, which in turn goes on to affect our behavior, choices, opinions, identity, relationships and more. This mechanism alone may explain why some people reach success while others seem to perpetually self-jeopardize.

Rather than believing that success is something meant for others, something that we have to be born with or even just pure luck, Dr. Helmstetter tried to show that the basic architecture of success was all in the head. The brain, he says, begins to believe whatever is repeated most often; if you consistently program yourself with self-talk that is positive and supportive, with time you create a real, physical reality that matches up with this representation of yourself. Whether it's in the area of business, relationships, family, learning, navigating life's challenges or all of these, our lives reflect the self-talk we adopt.

And actually, there is quite a bit of neuroscience to support this idea. Indeed, an entire area of brain study, including habits, muscle memory, schemas, automatic actions, and heuristics, is involved. *Neuroplasticity* is the key—i.e. the characteristic of the brain that means it can always change, physiologically and psychologically. Neuroplasticity is how any type of habit is formed. It may be helpful to think of each repetition as wearing a small groove in the brain's pathways. The more repetitions of any given thought or behavior, the deeper the groove gets, and the more ingrained it becomes within us.

This means that whatever story you're currently telling yourself, you can always stop and tell a new one. But it also means that the current story will be tough to shake.

There is a *physical* consequence to the thoughts we hold and the stories we tell—those with more negative thinking have actually been shown to have less neuronal development in certain areas of the brain than those who think positively, who develop more in the left pre-frontal cortex of the brain. This is a big deal. It means that "positive thinking" is not merely some whimsical nonsense or a comforting delusion—it's a way of actually, literally, and physically remodeling your brain to suit your own purposes.

Besides the neuroplasticity angle of self-talk, there are two additional major theories.

The first is basically that there are many discrete "I" viewpoints within one person, and that these viewpoints engage one another in internal conversation; i.e., self-talk is essentially an inner dialogue between different parts of yourself. This is called the Dialogical Self Theory (DST). The other theory suggests that ordinary language and inner self-talk are basically the same thing, and are both relational. There is a two-way relationship between words and their meanings, and this relationship comes from within us and from the society we live in. This is called the Relational Frame Theory (RFT).

The Dialogical Self Theory

The "I" in self-talk can be many different people—a child, a parent, a worker, a partner, an adversary, etc. Each of these identities has different feelings, desires, needs, and fears, and sometimes they conflict with one another. The "I" that is a diligent employee may conflict with the "I" that is a loving parent (for example, missing time with your child because you often work overtime at a job you also love), and the resulting inner dialogue is one that can help us resolve the tension or else keep us feeling trapped and unhappy.

Have you ever heard a judgmental inner voice only to realize it's not really your own, but the voice of an internalized parent, boss or partner? This happens because the perspectives of others can become part of our own dialogical selves. Dialogical Self Theory may be a useful theory to work with if you frequently find your self-talk arguing against itself, or you often feel guilty, unsure of who you are, conflicted, and so on. By asking how your various perspectives interact with each other, you can begin to find cooperation between them.

The Relational Frame Theory (RFT)

Language, self-talk and emotion are all constantly engaging with one another. Self-talk and language in general share one interesting characteristic in common: they are relational. This means that we respond to a stimulus in terms of another stimulus: things are like or unlike other things, or they relate to them in hierarchical, special or comparative terms. In other words, language constantly refers back to itself.

Self-talk is also relational in this way, and all the symbols it uses are interconnected to one another every time we ruminate, overthink, self-criticize or indeed self-praise. The benefits of language largely depend on *how* we use it. We can use language to dream up all sorts of novel and even impossible concepts, but we are always deeply affected by the language we use. It follows then that we should be aware of and willing to rework the relational frames we employ in our self-talk.

Both theories are attractive and go a long way to explaining the phenomena that modern cognitive psychology research is investigating to this day. For our purposes, however, the most important takeaway is that self-talk is not a fixed fact of life, but can be changed no matter the mechanism through which it presents. These theories are focused on the "why," and we are focused on the "how to change and improve" in this book.

Self-Talk as an Amplifier

Talking aloud to oneself conjures up certain images—perhaps a mad scientist furiously muttering to himself as he works. You've probably heard the old wives' tale that "talking to yourself" means you're crazy, and many people are reluctant to admit it or feel embarrassed if caught talking aloud to themselves. Do you loudly chastise yourself for making a mistake, give yourself a little pep talk in the bathroom mirror before a first date, or mentally say things like, "Okay, think carefully, where did you leave it? Don't panic!"?

Rest assured this is all perfectly normal. When you think about it, isn't this exactly what *thinking* is? Most of us are engaged in an almost nonstop stream of self-talk and talk to ourselves so often that we've actually become unaware of ourselves doing it. Inner talk is one thing, but people can worry that talking *out loud* to themselves is somehow different, and spells trouble.

Actually, it's a habit that is astoundingly common, and can even help us process things better. For example, speaking thoughts aloud slows them down and heightens focused awareness. By activating our language centers, we concretize and formalize our thoughts into something we can work with more tangibly—and this often has the effect of calming us down. Self-talk has the capacity to amplify whatever you want, but it comes down to whether you can harness this power.

Talking to yourself engages your meta-cognition and higher order processing, and gives you a chance to process emotions. In fact, grasping the fundamentals of language and self-talk may be the very thing that helps us develop self-control as children, according to developmental psychologist Jean Piaget.

An interesting 2001 study by Gruber and Cramon found that monkeys use different parts of their brain to do a visual matching task than they do an auditory matching task, but humans actually use both areas of the brain for both activities. However, the study also showed that humans can behave more like monkeys in this respect if they prevent self-talk, for example by saying mindless words like "blah blah blah" during the task. This study shows that self-talk has direct effects on our self-control of our behavior—or rather, it has the potential to aid us in broad and fundamental ways.

A study by Alexander Kirkham at Bangor University showed that talking out loud enhances self-control when doing a task, more so than merely saying things quietly in your own mind. Concentration skills and overall performance were improved in those who spoke aloud as they completed a task. So, the next time you talk aloud to yourself, be grateful for the hard work your brain might be doing for you!

Occupational therapist Dr. Julia Harper explains, however, that just because self-talk is common and normal, that doesn't necessarily mean it's always *beneficial*. The way we talk to ourselves makes all the difference. It may seem fairly obvious, but the "good" kind of self-talk is all about neutral and helpful statements, using positive and supportive language, which frames things in a way that is more likely to inspire your success. In other words, the content and emotional tone of what you say matters most.

Random and distracting thoughts running in every direction, mindless mental chatter, and an inability to focus on relevant information can in fact be bad for our mental health. An out-of-control, wandering mind may have us unconsciously linking ideas and making nonsensical associations that can lead to inappropriate responses or incoherence. But note that it's not self-talk per se that is the problem, but whether we are able to use self-talk properly and appropriately to serve our goals.

When used with discernment, self-talk has plenty of benefits. A 2012 study in the *Quarterly Journal of Experimental Psychology* by Lupyan and Swingley showed that people more quickly found lost objects when they repeated out loud the name of the object to themselves as they searched. Neuroscientist Dr. Don Vaughn also explains that talking out loud while studying boosts retention, and self-talk can act as a kind of "spoken journal" to help you work through difficult emotions. Self-talk is a way for the brain to organize its thoughts, solidify memories, regulate emotions and plan future behavior. Talking aloud is no different from silent self-talk, but merely an extension of it.

Ultimately, self-talk is something that is not only normal, but potentially very useful, if done consciously. We'll discuss becoming more aware of and mindful of inner talk later in the book, but for now, whenever you talk to yourself, commit to actually listening as well! Pause and take a moment to process. Ask yourself questions and give yourself support or encouragement.

Talking out loud to yourself is not a sign of mental illness, but could actually be evidence of high cognitive function, memory, and conscious control of your intellectual faculties. That being said, anxious and uncontrollable mental chatter that runs away with itself is not likely to have the same effect.

If you're up in the early hours of the morning ruminating and getting carried away with anxious thoughts, you may find that assigning your brain a task like reading could stop unhealthy self-talk and get you relaxed again. Likewise, self-talk, aloud or silent, is not a problem when directed to yourself, but may be a cause for concern if addressed to hallucinations or people who aren't really there.

Eenie, Meenie, Minie, Moe

As we've seen in the previous section, not all self-talk is created equal. There are many variations, and some types are more helpful than others. If you've been wondering exactly what counts as self-talk, consider that all of the following can be considered self-talk:

- Making positive or negative statements to yourself ("This will fail" or "You got this!")
- Conscious or unconscious silent inner speech that may follow a dialogue ("You can't have left the keys at the store because you had them when you arrived home. But what if you left the door unlocked and just came in? Well, I never leave the door unlocked, I must have had my keys with me...")
- Out loud self-talk (Saying "you idiot!" when you make a mistake, or rehearsing your shopping list to yourself in the car)
- Out of control and anxious rumination, such as the racing thoughts that come with depression or panic attacks.

Research into the different kinds of self-talk has led to diverse findings in all kinds of areas, including education, sports psychology, neural development and even personality. As we saw earlier, the quality of one's self-talk can have either positive or negative effects, but some of the more recent research has found that self-talk:

- Helps with emotional regulation (such as in the research conducted by Mischel et al., 1996 and Carver and Scheier, 1998).

- Helps with self-distancing if using "you" statements or your own name rather than "I" pronouns (as we saw with Kross in a previous section). This gives you the room to take a more neutral and compassionate perspective on yourself.
- Helps you give self-instruction and self-motivation (see Hatzigeorgiadis et al., 2011). This is common in sports where coaches recommend verbally saying aloud, "You're doing great! Just take it easy, that's it…"
- Improves your sense of self-awareness, bolstering a more accurate self-evaluation and encouraging more mindful reflection on how your brain is working, and how that in turn affects both your emotions and your behavior (see research done by White et al., 2015 and Morin, 2018).
- Strengthens and fortifies certain cognitive processes (Langland-Hassan and Vicente, 2018), including perspective-taking and monitoring language development and speech production.
- Helps with regulating the emotions and coping with painful or difficult experiences (Orvell et al., 2019 and Kross et al., 2014, 2017), encouraging mental toughness and emotional resilience.

If that seems like a lot of benefits, then you're beginning to understand why this area of research has garnered so much attention!

Some researchers have used the STS, or Self-Talk Scale, to identify four main types of self-talk. These include self-criticism after negative events, self-praise and reinforcement after positive events, self-management and the attempt to decide what to do and how, and social-assessment, which is self-talk that refers to social interactions in the past, present or future.

Each of these four types likely overlaps, with a mix of different effects and functions which heavily depend on the context, the person doing the self-talk and its intensity and duration.

Though different theorists, coaches and thinkers will refer to slightly different definitions and models of self-talk, the key point to bear in mind is that self-talk varies greatly. It can be helpful or unhelpful, conscious or unconscious, cruel or compassionate, sensible or deranged, inspiring or completely self-sabotaging.

Our goal with this book is to use some of these theories as a springboard to gain a better understanding of our own self-talk. This can be done with conscious awareness, calm compassion, and a little curiosity. You might notice that you have a running narrative going on in your head whenever you speak to others, or that you sometimes adopt a very harsh and overly critical attitude to yourself when you believe you've failed. For instance, a small selection of the types of negative self-talk we might want to become aware of and avoid:

- Overreaction: "Everything is terrible."
- Personalization: "Why is this happening to me?", "It's my fault."
- Absolute language: "I'm a bad person."
- Assumption: "He thinks I'm not good enough!"
- Expectation: "This isn't how it's supposed to be!"

- Comparison: "Why can't I be like her?"
- Regret: "If I hadn't done that…"

Self-talk can be a one-off statement or a deeply held core belief that you return to again and again, not being even slightly aware of the alternatives. People battling depression or low self-esteem may have a relentless repeat of the same self-talk playing in their mind 24/7. Others may end up putting a lot of their self-talk down on ink and paper, or find that their "inner critic" is actually the voice of someone else they've taken on as their own.

Whatever your self-talk is, you can consciously pause and watch it happen, and decide deliberately whether the stories you tell truly align with the goals you want to reach in life. Every time you talk to yourself, you are potentially cementing limiting and harmful habits and keeping yourself in a place you don't want to be.

On the other hand, according to Dr. Helmstetter, we can choose to engage in the more beneficial and affirming forms of self-talk:

- *Habit-changing self-talk* is that which deliberately seeks to break away from old habits rather than strengthen them. For example, pausing every time you think "I'm stupid" to consciously change your wording to "I'm learning." This self-talk is establishing a new habit—one of self-esteem and kindness.
- *Attitude-changing self-talk* aims to build up your positive self-belief and esteem, for example, "I'm trying my best and I'm doing great."
- *Motivational self-talk* goes a step further and takes the form of affirmations and self-encouragement as we attempt something scary or new.
- *Situational self-talk* is about taking a different perspective on situations in life, such as changing frameworks to deal with adversity, accidents or problems as they arise. For example, "How am I going to smooth things over here?" or "How can I look at this problem differently?"

In this chapter, we've looked at what self-talk is, the different types, and how it can help or harm, as well as some common theories used to understand the phenomenon. And you're hopefully convinced that there is nothing strange about occasionally muttering to yourself under your breath!

In the following chapters, we'll further flesh out some of these concepts, so you feel able to not only understand your own inner talk, but gain conscious mastery over it. You might naturally be wondering how to start changing your negative self-talk into a more positive internal dialogue. But to do that, we first need to fully understand the difference.

Takeaways

- Have you ever noticed a voice inside your head that is constantly chattering about something or the other right from the moment you wake up? You might have grown so accustomed to it that you barely notice it anymore, but it's definitely there, and it's either hurting or helping you. No perspective is truly neutral. This voice, a part of your stream of consciousness, is an inner

monologue that runs alongside your life, observing and commenting on its various happenings. It tells you who you are, and how you should feel about your identity and the events that occur in your life.
- There are three main types of inner voices or self-talk. The first is positive self-talk, which acts as a continuous reaffirmation of the good things about you and your life. This type of inner voice bolsters our confidence and elevates happiness levels. However, on the other end lies negative self-talk. This voice is always critical and saying degrading things to us about who we are, what we do, etc. If left uncontrolled, it can lead to several mental health issues. The third type is neutral self-talk, which simply consists of unbiased observations as we walk through life—although this almost always has a positive or negative subtext.
- Our inner voice, regardless of type, represents the inner representation we have of ourselves. Often, this is not consistent with reality. The way we think we are and what we actually are can be miles apart, but reality seldom matters if we're convinced that things are a certain way. This leads to why having healthy self-talk is so important. It influences our thoughts, perceptions, and the way we view ourselves, all of which have physiological correlations that affect how we feel and behave. The basis behind this is neuroplasticity, as the more you repeat something, the more it changes your brain's structure and becomes your reality.
- If you're wondering what exactly counts as self-talk, it includes positive or negative statements we say to ourselves, our ruminations, racing thoughts, and the conversations we have with ourselves. Regulating this self-talk can have many positive effects that are essential to our well-being, such as improving sports performances, reducing stress, promoting better self-esteem, and helping us cope with the ups and downs of life. Monitoring self-talk is the key to changing your emotions, behavior, perspective, and life potential.

Chapter 2. Good Versus Evil

Positive self-talk is everything that helps us regulate our emotions, work through memories or complicated experiences, maintain awareness of ourselves and our world, and encourage ourselves as we deal with problems or challenging situations. It is the set of messages we constantly repeat in our heads over and over that help us see the optimism, joy, and hope in any given situation. This is the angel perched on our left shoulder, while the right shoulder has, well, the devil.

Positive self-talk *sounds* simple, but the fact is that so many people consistently engage in negative self-talk despite desperately wanting to do better. We end up internalizing negative and irrational messages about who we are, the way we act, our abilities, etc., from external sources. Recognizing self-talk as it's happening is simple but not easy—because we are so used to our constant internal chatter, we may forget we're even doing it. Heck, you are doing it right now when reading through a process called *subvocalization*.

Rather than being aware of the fact that we are running a constant internal narration, we assume that we are simply perceiving life as it is, i.e. that the story we are telling ourselves is true, objective fact. This is especially the case when our self-talk coincides with our fears or implicit beliefs about who we really are. However, with some attention and effort, we can use our self-talk to reaffirm positivity in a way that keeps anxiety and negativity at bay while allowing us to accomplish goals that we previously considered beyond our capabilities.

Positive Versus Negative Self-Talk

Positive self-talk doesn't mean you indulge in over-the-top and insincere self-flattery, and it isn't vain or unrealistic. Brazenly telling yourself, "It's going to happen this time, I just know it" as you buy a lottery ticket might be considered by some to be positive thinking, but it's not a particularly helpful line of thinking, not least because it won't change your chances of winning!

When people engage in cognitive behavioral therapy (more on this in a later chapter) they are essentially attempting to undo negative self-talk, and replace it not with flowery platitudes but with more neutral, rational statements that more closely align with reality. We are our own worst critics, and that can often lead us to ignore genuine positives in a way that becomes detrimental to our mental well-being.

Though most people struggle with overly negative rather than overly positive thinking, what you really want is to aim for thinking that a) most closely lines up with the real world around you and b) actually helps you achieve the goals that are important to you.

So, when we talk about "positive" self-talk, we can also imagine it means balanced, self-aware, healthy, and useful self-talk. We want to avoid distorting reality or behaving in ways that undermine our goals—whether that's in overly positive or overly negative ways. If the reality is negative, we want to find a way to accept and feel better about it, and if it's positive, we want to believe in it and have confidence.

We now know there is no value in endlessly bolstering self-esteem with excessive praise. Far healthier is a balanced, robust perspective that has a respectful relationship with reality, including its dark sides!

Consider the following self-talk phrases:

Thought A: "I'm a hideous fat blob and I'm ugly. I can't bear for anyone to look at me."

Thought B: "I'm beautiful and perfect in every way!"

Thought C: "I'm OK with how I look. I could probably lose a few pounds, but I have some attractive features too and besides, there's so much more to me than how I look."

Thought D: "Your BMI is slightly into the overweight category, but only by a few pounds, and your overall health is excellent."

Which of these thoughts is the "right" one? Which is positive and which negative? You'll notice that the actual appearance of this person is beside the point. Which thought is more likely to lead to a resilient sense of self-esteem, well-being and beneficial actions toward meaningful goals?

Thought A is negative, overly emotional and likely to lead to apathy and self-hate (whether it's "true" or not!), whereas Thought B is "positive" but not in the least likely to encourage honest self-appraisal of areas that need improvement. Thoughts C and D are more neutral, though D is mostly negative until the very end, by which time you're more likely to focus on the bad than what is good. It's Thought C that strikes a balance between "true" and compassionate. It recognizes room for improvement ("I could lose a few pounds"), but stays positive overall.

This is what we mean by positive self-talk. Rumination (i.e. endlessly turning over worst-case scenarios in your head, all-or-nothing statements, overly emotional judgments, criticisms, anxious overthinking and "what if?" thoughts than you can't seem to switch off…) is neither objective nor encouraging. This, along with statements that criticize or undermine, is what we mean by negative self-talk. And the subsequent impact it has on self-image, perspective, and self-worth is significant.

So, generating positive self-talk doesn't merely involve turning a negative self-talk statement into its equally unrealistic opposite. Real self-esteem doesn't rely on falsely boosting the ego—this exaggeration is only more of the same and will never feel truly satisfying. Rather, it's the calm and stable awareness that comes with knowing *you* are in control of your mind, you can be aware of and respectful of your feelings, and you have irreducible value and worth as a human being, no matter what.

In many ways, trying to convert negative to positive can come with perils—we risk reinforcing limiting perspectives and further digging ourselves into a hole. For example, if a person struggled with their weight (as in the above examples) they might decide to substitute more positive self-talk that claimed, "You are overweight and some people like that more, which makes you superior to other skinny and malnourished-looking people, and proves that you're kinder and more intelligent than those other superficial people…"

It's not positive thinking to be baselessly proud of legitimate flaws and mistakes, to compare yourself to others, or to put others down. You also might have noticed that "everyone hates me" and "everyone loves me" share the same weakness—they put the locus of worth *outside* of the person, rather than inside, making for a self-esteem that is fragile and inauthentic.

Let's look at some other examples.

Negative:
This is too hard and I can't do it.
Success should come quickly and with no effort.

Positive:
I'm proud of how hard I've worked. I don't have to be the best in the world, but I really tried, and I learnt a lot in the process.

Negative:
Nobody is interested in dating a loser like me.
Women are so shallow these days.

Positive:
Dating can be tough sometimes, but I'm using the opportunity to learn about myself and grow where I can.

Negative:
There's no hope of changing things so I may as well give up now.
Life is unfair, what's new?

Positive:

I can't tell what the future holds, but I know I will always do my best to live according to my own principles.

A lot of your inner talk may appear to be rather neutral—i.e. when you're instructing yourself on how to do something or making an observation about the environment. But the self-talk we're interested in is all those statements that seem to address us directly, and go toward building that inner representation of ourselves and how we relate to the external world.

It can be difficult to give examples of good and bad self-talk because self-talk is always going to be unique to every person and their context. There are some general sentiments and attitudes, however, that lead to self-talk statements that most of us can probably find useful in our lives.

If you're unsure about what constitutes positive self-talk, you may consider the following positive statements and try them on for size in your own life. If they feel overly foreign, outlandishly positive, or even unthinkable, it's probably pretty clear that you aren't used to thinking of yourself in a positive manner.

At this early stage, it might be useful to notice which statements you feel most resistant to, or which seem most at odds with your own worldview.

- This isn't what I wanted to happen, but I've definitely learnt some valuable lessons.
- This is just a thought, and a thought can change.
- I can always choose how I respond to adversity.
- I can always choose what stories I tell about myself.
- Though this is challenging, I can always keep trying, and every challenge is an opportunity to learn something new.
- I don't have to do everything perfectly all the time.
- I accept that I sometimes feel down and unhappy, because I accept myself.
- I am proud of all that I have achieved and overcome so far.
- I'm a person worthy of respect and compassion and I have value, no matter what.
- I will try hard not to worry about things I can't control.
- My opinion, my boundaries, my goals and my preferences all matter.
- No matter where I am now, I can learn, grow and change.
- There may be some things I can't do, but I can try, experiment and adapt.

You may notice something about the above sentiments: they are all *internal*, and can be held no matter what external circumstances you find yourself in, good or bad. The truth is that the world can be difficult and confusing at times, and we don't have endless control over everything that happens to us.

But we do have control over what we consciously create in our own minds, and we can always choose the story that best allows us to feel good and achieve what's important to us. No matter what form it takes, positive self-talk reinforces the belief that on a fundamental level, "I am enough."

Negative self-talk, on the other hand, only undermines your goals, potential, talents, value and abilities. These are the thoughts that lead to inaction and apathy, to hiding away from life, to depression and anxiety, fragile thinking, giving up, blaming others or avoidance. Negative self-talk is perhaps even more varied and unique to the person thinking it, but it, too, has some common elements that you'll see cropping up again and again:

- I'm not worth making the effort for, I'm not worth compassion or understanding, I'm not worth fighting for or protecting, I'm not worth any investment of time or energy.
- I can't do this, or anything. I'm useless/stupid and I'm not capable of improving.
- I could try and make an effort, but there's no real point, because nothing I do makes any difference anyway.
- I'll be rejected if I try, people will laugh at me and judge me, and people don't like me as I am.
- Other people are smarter, better looking, more successful, kinder and just better than I am. When compared to others, I'm inferior.
- I won't bother hoping for anything or starting something new because I know I won't finish it, and I don't have a hope of achieving my goals.
- I'm a failure. I have to be perfect or I shouldn't even bother. I can't make any mistakes or I'm a bad person.
- What I think doesn't matter in the grand scheme of things.
- I can't really trust life or myself.
- People are bad and always will be.
- I have to compete with everyone around me and there is never enough to go around.

Phew! It's easy to see how negative self-talk is a one-way ticket to depression and low self-esteem. Let's hope that you didn't find those sentiments too familiar or frequent in your life. Underneath many of these different thoughts and feelings is one core belief: "I am not enough."

Much of our negative self-talk stems from a fundamental disbelief in our own value. We believe that we are fundamentally useless, and need to prove to others how good we are in order to be considered worthy. We take failure personally, criticize ourselves harshly and self-sabotage everything good or promising in our lives because deep down, it doesn't fit with the story we've spent so much time telling ourselves: "I am not enough."

A Simple Cost-Benefit Analysis

Motivational speaker Tony Robbins has said, "Change happens when the pain of staying the same is greater than the pain of change." When we truly understand the cost of engaging in negative self-talk and compare it to the potential gains of adopting positive self-talk, the choice to change is an obvious one.

Benefits of positive self-talk

So far, we've been considering the most obvious benefit of positive self-talk: it makes us feel good. Supportive, compassionate, and encouraging self-talk understandably strengthens self-esteem. Though we often seek validation from others, positive self-talk allows us to motivate ourselves. But there are more benefits, the main one being a reduction of stress levels.

A 2004 research paper by Iwanaga, Yokoyama and Seiwa suggests that those with more positive self-talk habits typically have better coping mechanisms when faced with stressful life scenarios or challenges. It makes sense. If you can gently re-frame a problem, you give yourself a fresh perspective that allows you to see new solutions and opportunities, while reducing the stress of feeling disempowered.

A 2008 study by Lyubormisky found that optimistic people with healthy self-esteem simply do better in life, whether it's performance at school, recovery from injury or achieving general life goals. In other words, positive thinking is a self-fulfilling prophesy. When you believe and behave as if you are fit for the task of life, you are more likely to approach events with exactly the attitude most conducive to success.

In a 2012 paper titled *Optimism: An enduring resource for romantic relationships* by Assad, Donnellan, and Conger, the researchers discovered that couples who were optimistic cooperated more and had generally better relationship outcomes. This also makes sense: people who are confident, proactive, and compassionate are always going to make better partners!

Positive self-talk has been associated with a wide range of outcomes including better performance in sport, healing body dysmorphia and eating disorders, and more effective education. Most importantly, healthy self-talk can alleviate mental health issues like depression, PTSD, stress, anxiety, poor self-esteem, and aggression (see Leung and Poon, 2000; Owens and Chard, 2001; Kendall and Treadwell, 2007).

The benefits of positive self-talk are so wide-ranging because the neurotransmitters associated with such thoughts (for example serotonin, dopamine and GABA) affect every part of the body. This is another aspect of neuroplasticity we reserved for this chapter. Most of us think of emotions as abstract, airy things, but they have a *physiological reality* in our bodies, regulating our feelings of well-being, motivation, energy levels, interest in life and ability to relax and feel good about ourselves.

The system goes both ways: neurotransmitters affect how we think and feel, but thoughts and feelings in turn can affect neurotransmitter levels—which then go on to have an effect on every bodily system. Thoughts are first converted into electrochemical signals in the brain, which is then stimulated to release hormones and neurotransmitters that travel throughout the body, affecting the structure and function of every tissue and organ.

How Negative Self-Talk Sabotages Your Life

Positive self-talk can leave you feeling calmer, more proactive, and more confident about your life, but the flipside is that negative self-talk does exactly the opposite. It's easy to imagine that being talked down to and insulted throughout the day (which is exactly what negative self-talk is!) would leave you feeling bad emotionally. It turns out there are real, neurological reasons why.

When you engage in negative self-talk, you encourage your body to release chemicals called catecholamines from your adrenal glands, for example dopamine and norepinephrine. Your body responds to the "threat" of this self-talk as though it were any other danger, even producing cortisol that permeates through the entire body.

Cortisol has lasting effects on the body. It compromises the immune system and decreases the volume of the left pre-frontal cortex—the part of your brain associated with positive emotions. Thinking about yourself negatively affects your body, not just your feelings. Even worse, a self-fulfilling feedback loop is established, wherein the more negatively we think, the easier it is to keep on thinking negatively, and so on. The basic upshot is that you are in a constant state of stress and alarm, and each thought will build upon the previous one. It's only a matter of time until you explode like Mount Vesuvius.

The stress that comes with negative self-talk affects every single part of the body. You may tell yourself "I'm a failure" and then feel stressed and anxious. This causes a physiological response throughout your nervous system, which in chronic cases can affect your brain, leading you to keep thinking negatively... It's a vicious cycle.

Most of us tend to think of negative self-talk, low confidence and so on as merely emotional or psychological phenomena, and not something "real" like cancer or a broken leg. But nothing could be further from the truth. Negative self-talk actively undermines your physical health. This is because you *are* your body. Your body and brain (and all the thoughts in it) are not two different things!

You may notice unexplained gastrointestinal trouble like a stomach in knots, bloating or discomfort. Ulcers are most commonly associated with stress. Heart attacks, of course, happen to young and healthy people because they are in so much distress.

You also may feel completely exhausted and wiped out for seemingly no reason. Constant negative self-talk can wear you down over time, leaving your motivation for life at a low ebb. Some people find that negative self-talk impacts sleep (all that three a.m. catastrophizing!), and all this combined can certainly make it harder to focus and concentrate.

Negative self-talk leaves us feeling pessimistic, hopeless, irritable, and apathetic—and it's all due to our system being chronically bathed in stress hormones. Negative self-talk is associated with many of the symptoms we think of as accompanying generally poor mental health: changes in appetite, getting sick often, random aches and pains, and low mood. This is all without mentioning just how disempowered you might feel when bombarded with constant negative self-talk, and how you might never reach your dreams or goals because, well, you've told yourself they're "impossible."

And it all starts with something decidedly *nonphysical*: your thoughts. Unfortunately, we all suffer from something called the negativity bias. This bias refers to the phenomenon wherein we tend to focus on and emphasize negative stimuli far more than we do positive stimuli. This is because our brains require more neural processing to interpret negative stimuli, causing it to have a longer-lasting effect on both our minds and bodies. Though the bias has its roots in the evolutionary advantages it provided—avoiding negative experiences protected our ancestors from danger—it can make negative thoughts that much more challenging to cope with. In a way, we're hard-wired to be negative, and it is this very impulse that we need to learn to overcome.

None of us would fare very well if we had a team of "reverse cheerleaders" following us around all day, yelling insults, criticizing our every move, and telling us how awful we looked every time we walked past a mirror. And yet, many of us *are* experiencing this very reality every day, only it is self-inflicted and invisible.

Meet Your Inner Critic

If positive self-talk is so great and negative self-talk so harmful, why do so many of us engage in negative self-talk?

What's the source of this devastating little voice inside?

Some people have called it the "inner critic," and it's that internal voice which criticizes, demeans, belittles or judges us, often with little respect for what is actually true. This voice shapes our identity, sense of worth and our belief in what's possible. You'll know the inner critic is speaking when its weapon of choice against you seems to be shame, guilt or fear.

It can be enlightening to think about where and why we first acquired this inner narrative voice. It's certainly not a choice. Your life experiences, the way you've been parented, social expectations, cultural norms and all the details of your unique context may set up this voice inside you.

The inner critic itself has been theorized to come from the internalized voices of others who at some point really did criticize or undermine you. If you are frequently told "you're useless," it's no surprise that you would soon come to tell yourself the same thing, long after the words were first uttered. If you grow up in a culture or family environment that stresses competition, a scarcity mindset, or shame, then you may live as though this is a normal way to think and feel.

For those with chronic self-doubt, low self-worth or even beliefs that border on the delusional (such as a beauty pageant winner insisting she's hideous, or the woman with "imposter syndrome" who believes she has achieved nothing even though she's a successful CEO), it can be helpful to ask about the origin of this voice.

Is the little voice really *yours*? Many people are surprised to notice that their inner critic sounds suspiciously like their parents, previous teachers, or other critical voices.

Just as negative self-talk can cause depression, it can also be a symptom of depression and other mood disorders. Being highly self-critical can accompany a host of health conditions, mental and physical. But in a way, it doesn't matter all that much *why* you think as you do, only that you do. It can be incredibly healing to see that your inner voice doesn't even strictly belong to you. This voice is a combination of your conscious and subconscious thoughts, along with the host of external influences that we encounter in our daily lives.

If you see that your self-talk is not based in reality and is actively causing you harm while shutting out many good things in life, you can work toward making changes, no matter the cause or source of your self-talk.

If your self-talk is a little engine or machine that churns to produce statements, beliefs and feelings, then self-esteem is the fuel that it runs on.

Your brain is a powerful tool, but it can only process what it's given: feed it with low-esteem (i.e., fuel it with the fundamental belief that "I am not enough") and all its output will be negative and self-denying. Feed it with healthy self-esteem (i.e., fuel it with the fundamental belief that "I am enough") and its output will be life-affirming, goal oriented, and optimistic.

Your beliefs inform your thinking, which then cements those original beliefs and inspires your behavior, which then produces results that feed back into your original beliefs. And so the cycle continues, and soon you believe "this is how I am" when in fact all you have been doing is telling yourself a very convincing story for a very long time.

But what is this fuel for optimism, self-esteem? We've alluded to it in earlier sections, mentioning how self-esteem is *not* idealistic optimism, vanity, narcissism, denial of the facts of life or wishful thinking.

Self-esteem is essentially our own self-concept, or the sense of who we are in the world. It's all about how we perceive ourselves, and how we feel about who we think we are. Positive and strong self-esteem means we experience ourselves as good, worthy and lovable people whom others view in good terms. Negative or weak self-esteem has us feeling like people who are unloved, wrong, broken, stupid, unworthy or just *bad*.

Our self-esteem comes from many sources—past experiences, our own personal development, our goals and expectations, our relationships to others, our culture, family history, gender, belief system, age and more. It can be stable or change with time, and takes dips and boosts with life's seasons.

We all have the ability to feel as though we are largely satisfied with ourselves, flaws and all. Having good self-esteem comes down to believing that you have innate worth and many good qualities. It's "having a good reputation with yourself" and generally liking and respecting yourself, with a moderate expectation that others may do the same.

If we dig a little, we see that negative self-talk is actually just a symptom of our inner beliefs about ourselves, i.e. our self-esteem. But that begs the question: what causes low self-esteem?

There's plenty of evidence to suggest that our experiences with our primary caregivers as children shapes our perception of our self-worth and consequently, determines the tone and content of much of our self-talk. We may develop low self-esteem because of:

- Disapproving/critical authority figures who caused feelings of shame ("you'll never amount to anything").
- Caregivers who were neglectful or too preoccupied with their own lives to pay you attention when you most needed to be acknowledged and praised. This can leave you feeling unimportant, invisible, unknown, and not worth noticing.
- Caregivers who fought with each other. Young children can internalize the feeling that they are to blame.
- Bullying at home or school, and feeling as though you weren't important enough to be protected. Can create feelings of being abandoned, lost, or victimized.
- Overly coddling or supportive parents. They may have made you feel like their support was unwarranted and exaggerated, causing deep shame about who you "really" are.
- Receiving no support through academic challenges, making you feel stupid or defective.
- Sexual, physical, or emotional abuse can make a child believe their will is not worth as much as others', that they are worthless, or even to blame for what happened to them.
- Cultural or religious beliefs that emphasize shame and judgement for who you are—this can include unrealistic images and ideology from the media.
- Low confidence may even have a genetic component; we may each be born with different levels of serotonin and oxytocin (hormones associated with happiness and well-being) and this affects our temperament, which in turn affects our behavior. Some people have personalities that are more cautious, watchful or inhibited, which is not necessarily a bad thing, but may preclude high confidence.
- Life experiences can prime us for poor self-esteem, for example harassment, trauma, or discrimination.
- Low self-esteem can, as we saw above, also be a side effect of other mental health issues such as anxiety and depression.

- Certain childhood traumas can have us internalizing the blame for things that aren't our fault, and converting it into a deep feeling of shame that we carry into adulthood.

Not everyone who experiences the above will develop poor self-esteem, and not everyone with poor self-esteem has necessarily experienced these things. Most importantly, though understanding childhood causes of low self-esteem can be insightful, it doesn't mean we are bound to our past. We can always change. Understanding why we feel as we do, we can start taking steps to build a healthier, more realistic internal picture of who we are.

The parenting you received is not the only possible source of low self-worth. Many of us engage in daily habits that actively erode our self-esteem and lead to negative self-talk, without us even realizing it.

It seems obvious, but not taking care of yourself physically makes it so much harder to care for yourself mentally. Poor health habits can be damaging in many ways—denying and neglecting our own care sends a message that we are not worth more.

Similarly, spending too much time alone can lead to rumination that isn't balanced by the input of socializing or other activities. Several studies have found that prolonged isolation increases stress, which acts as a gateway to depression and anxiety, thereby reducing self-esteem. Being socially isolated can also lead to us hesitating to ask for help we really need it, closing ourselves off to sources of affirmation and support in the process. We neglect our own self-care and barely notice that we're "running on empty."

Finally, spending too much time around overly negative people can also invite negative self-talk, especially if those people are critical, judgmental, or cruel to you. Deliberately avoiding discussing or fixing relationship problems is a common but underrated sign of lack of self-care, and only maintains poor self-image and negative self-talk.

Five Levels of Self-Talk

As you can see, self-talk is something that both establishes and maintains our faulty narratives about ourselves. But when we deliberately choose our own self-talk, we can change the process, and use our self-talk to create ourselves in a new image—one that *we* choose.

The process of improving self-talk usually happens by degree—we don't become healthy and balanced overnight. As we slowly gain healthier self-esteem, we are able to generate self-talk of an increasingly higher quality.

Level 1 self-talk is harmful self-talk that reinforces a negative narrative about ourselves. Becoming aware of this kind of inner dialogue and why it's present has been the focus of the book so far. This is the most common level of self-talk, so don't fret if you find yourself at level 1 right now. Most people, unfortunately, may never move past this level. Some relevant examples are:

"I can't do this."

"I wish life were fair but it's not."

"I suck."

Level 2 self-talk is a slight improvement in that it recognizes a need for changes to be made, even though it doesn't offer any actual solutions.

"I really should exercise more."

"I've got to do something about my low mood."

"This can't go on anymore."

Level 3 self-talk takes things a step further into actual practice. However, if we don't act on our thoughts from level 2, it leads us to regress back to level 1. In level 3, we use our self-talk to our desired ends, deciding to help ourselves by actively reprogramming a new image of ourselves. Notice these examples are framed in present tense, which means they are somewhat subject to change and not wholly certain:

"I find things to be grateful for every day."

"I'm calm and focused right now."

"I won't crave unhealthy food."

Level 4 self-talk goes in and replaces all level 1 and 2 self-talk, working comprehensively to shape our new identities with self-respect, self-belief and positivity. This is a level of belief that is not false or forced.

"I'm a positive person."

"I act with resilience and awareness."

Level 5 self-talk is about a more universal affirmation and acceptance of ourselves and everyone else. In fact, it even becomes negative in the sense that it acknowledges negativity and accepts it. This is the broadest view possible, and a wholesale affirmation of life itself.

"I focus on the things I can control."

"I choose my thoughts, my values and my actions."

"I may be overweight but I am content with this."

Glancing at these different levels or kinds of self-talk, you may ask yourself where the bulk of your mental effort and energy goes. Is it into negative statements that don't go anywhere, only make you feel bad? Do you frequently note a problem but never take steps to move on from it? Most of us work on levels 1 and 2 only. However, once we proceed to level 3, the path ahead becomes much simpler because we start reaping the benefits of our healthy practices. As we proceed to level 4, and finally level 5, we start to exercise decisive control over the thoughts that enter and dwell in our minds.

You may be surprised to see just how much of your precious and powerful mental energy is being wasted on causing suffering, when you could use it to actively reprogram yourself and move on from the unconscious programming you received as a child. In a way, positive self-talk is not some difficult and effortful task to master, but rather the shifting of all the ways your brain already maintains your self-concept, day after day.

In the chapters that follow, we'll explore exactly how to make the switch.

Takeaways

- It is easy to mistake positive self-talk for being vain, narcissistic, and shallow, overloading oneself with praise—but this is far from the case. Similarly, ignoring negative self-talk does not mean blinding yourself to your faults. Improving our self-talk is aimed at being more attuned with reality in a way that is conducive to achieving the goals we desire. Often we focus on the negative much more than the positive, and this distorts the reality of a situation. By practicing more positive self-talk, we're trying to get past this bias and see things the way they are so that we can improve accordingly.
- There are many benefits of engaging in more positive self-talk. Several studies have looked into the matter and concluded that those who are more positive perform better at work and sports, are better at getting through challenging life circumstances, and have healthier relationships. Moreover, they also have a better self-image and feel good about themselves since they have a healthy sense of self.
- On the other hand, negative self-talk can be extremely damaging to our well-being. It releases cortisol in our bodies, compromising our immune function and preventing positive emotions from arising. Negative self-talk can also lead to a host of mental health issues such as depression, anxiety, panic disorders, and other undesirable outcomes like apathy, anger, self-pity, etc.
- If you're wondering where our self-talk styles originate from, the answer is a host of factors that include our parenting, socio-cultural norms, our immediate environment, biology, our own biases and beliefs, among others. Many who have experienced strict or uncompromising home environments at a young age, or have routinely had their boundaries violated, come to adopt a low self-esteem, which in turn causes negative self-talk that can be hard to get rid of.
- These factors, along with experiences like bullying and different forms of abuse, also determine our self-esteem levels, which is the main determinant of whether our self-talk is negative or positive. As we understand why exactly our self-talk is the way it is, we can start to change and improve it to suit our needs.
- We end up with five levels of self-talk, each a higher amount of acceptance and self-esteem. Indeed, it starts with purely negative, then moves to aspirational,

to positive, to a new identity, to newfound acceptance of both the negative and positive.

Chapter 3. All You Need to Do Is Listen

To engage in better self-talk, the first step is to identify and correct negative self-talk as it happens. It can sometimes be hard to distinguish between negative self-talk and self-criticism that can actually be conducive to growth. The goal here is to retain the latter while excluding the former so that we can attune ourselves to reality and improve our self-esteem.

Becoming aware of exactly when (and why) we address ourselves as we do is the only hope we have of stepping in and reclaiming our own inner landscape to create the reality we want for ourselves. All you need to do is listen, a much easier task than it seems.

The Key to Self-Awareness

Just because your self-talk is running unconsciously, doesn't mean that it's not having an effect on your life. Why not take conscious control of a process that is happening anyway? *Mindfulness* is a powerful way to gain awareness of our self-talk so we can bring it into the light of consciousness.

Clinical psychologist Dr. Mikaela Hildebrandt explains that there are two ways to relate to our thoughts, memories, opinions and perceptions: we can either stay *inside* this mental world and take it as a given, or we can step *outside* it, realizing that it is in fact our minds producing these thoughts and ideas. This is more or less the skill of metacognition, which is to be able to think about your thinking processes.

Mindfulness can help us shift from the former into the latter, taking a step back from our own mental chatter rather than fully identifying with it. It is the process wherein we consciously bring our attention toward our present experiences and thoughts while reserving all judgment to create genuine awareness of feelings or emotions. Research has shown that mindfulness can improve body image, relieve anxiety and depression, combat addictions, and support healthier lifestyle changes.

When we're mindful, we deliberately put ourselves in a conscious state where we are proactive rather than reactive. With a little mental distance, we can more easily accept the things that are beyond our control, and focus on those things that we can change.

Endlessly ruminating never gets us anywhere (it is staying trapped in level 1 and 2 self-talk) because we don't see our thoughts *as thoughts*. We assume those thoughts to be indicative of reality. Basically, we take our own word for it.

But if we are mindful, we notice ourselves thinking.

This helps us become aware of our thoughts without automatically having a negative or positive reaction to them. It allows us to evaluate and reflect upon those thoughts to see whether they actually have any merit. We can then choose to let go of judgments and criticisms, and even experiment with what it feels like to simply hold uncomfortable or negative sensations as they are, without leaping in with criticisms or doom-and-gloom thinking.

By being mindful, we give ourselves the time and space to untangle all those chaotic (and very damaging) self-talk messages we'd otherwise bombard ourselves with without a second thought. When we take on the perspective of a non-critical observer of our own thoughts, our awareness increases while our negative feelings decrease. We start to see how much of a *choice* it is to engage in tangled thought patterns. Perhaps most importantly, we introduce a space or pause between an initial reaction and a subsequent action.

Though we've spoken about the benefit of positive and healthy self-talk, the fact is that there is a lot to be gained from simply not engaging in negative self-talk. Negative self-talk does most damage when we are not aware of it, and don't acknowledge our own part in maintaining it.

By being mindful, we take the power away from negative self-talk and get enough distance to start imagining ways we could do things differently. If you think mindfulness merely entails you sitting around passively doing nothing, think again. Mindfulness is a powerful tool that helps us control what we focus on. It allows us to shift away from overwhelmingly negative emotions to hone in on something less threatening, like our breathing, sensory perceptions, bodily sensations, etc. Being mindful also cultivates a quality that's essential for all development and growth: curiosity.

When we are curious, we take on a proactive, interested perspective on life that moves us closer to acceptance and further from judgment. With an enquiring mind we can behold all our perceptive experience—good or bad—and simply sit with *what is*, without reacting, denying, clinging or trying to change anything.

When was the last time you watched your own thoughts with gentle curiosity? Can you sit with an open heart, willing to fully know whatever experience emerges? "Staying with" what happens within and without is a step toward not only awareness, but compassion for ourselves, wherever we are.

Mindfulness is the pause and the deep breath that allows us to ask: What is this? Can I let it be? Let it go? Watch it unfold?

Of course, sometimes you need to spring to action, but being mindful beforehand will allow you to develop the discernment needed to know exactly *when* to act, and when to yield. Practicing this way, we calmly step out of the whirlwind and torrent of stories, criticisms, judgments, worries and all the rest, strengthening our ability to self-regulate. What we are learning is mastery of our own attentive awareness, directing it to where *we* want it to go, rather than mindlessly chasing every distracting thought.

It helps us control our mind instead of letting it control us.

If you can deliberately and selectively focus on particular stimuli in your (inner and outer) environment, you are in effect shaping your world and your experience in it. Ask yourself where your attention usually goes—watch as it happens. What is the effect of this attention, and can you change it? This is the heart of mindfulness practice.

With mindfulness, you play with reprogramming your unfolding mind in *real time*, moment by moment. Don't watch yourself like a monitor, however, judging how well you are remaining aware or criticizing your mind for wandering. It's all grist for the mill—simply notice without judgment when your attention turns to negative self-talk. When you are aware, you can see previously unseen things— and allow yourself to change them, if you want. Neuroscientist Norman Farb found in a 2010 paper that meditators differed from non-meditators in their response to unpleasant emotions, showing less "cognitive elaboration" and an ability to more quickly move on. They felt their emotions as much as anyone, only they were not so carried away with them.

You don't need to embark on a strict meditation practice to be more mindful. Simply notice your thoughts. The following is a summary of *the 3-Minute Responsive Breathing Space* from Zindel Segal et al., 2012:

Rest in a comfortable position, either lying down or sitting upright. The exercise consists of three steps, each lasting a minute each. See what emotions arise, and notice how they play out on your body, in your breath, in your mind. Don't rush—just sit with what's there. Notice what catches your attention and choose to stay with it, bringing back your focus if it wanders. Then, narrow your field of attention to just your breathing and block out everything else. Do this for about a minute before expanding your field of attention to include your body and any sensations that you might be feeling.

Like many mindfulness exercises, Segal intended this practice to be a way for one to check in with one's own thoughts and then move on from them by first narrowing, followed by expanding our focus. After a few minutes, reflect on the experience: where did this thought or emotion come from? What does it do to you? Do you want to go deeper into it, or do you want to let it go and put your attention elsewhere?

If it seems complicated, it isn't—but it takes practice and willingness. Throughout your day, pause, take a breath and watch your inner landscape, using the following prompts to guide you:

1. What thoughts, feelings or sensations am I paying attention to?
2. Is my attention in my thoughts, emotions, body, or all three?

3. When did I start attending? How did I start and how is the sensation changing over time?
4. What is the nature of my attention—am I stuck in a loop, curious, focused, daydreamy, fantasizing, or focused in on one tiny detail?

The more you practice mindfulness, the more you'll become aware of your own thinking patterns. Question number 4 above asks about the quality of your conscious awareness, what your attention is resting on, and how. But if you've spent a long time unconscious of your own thinking, these questions can be difficult to answer.

Here are some styles of thinking or common mental patterns that you might notice—see if you recognize any in yourself, in order to get a more concrete grasp on them the next time you encounter them!

- Black and white thinking

This is thinking in extremes with no room for nuance or gray area (or compassion!). For example, "he used to be The One, but now I see he's the worst person in the world" or "I'd better do this perfectly or I might as well give up forever." Watch out for all-or-nothing, zero-sum, high-stakes thinking and words like "always," "never" or "must." Black and white thinking is a common defense mechanism that we typically use when we are unable to grasp the complexities of a particular situation, person, etc. Though this can help us feel less anxious, it inevitably leads us to distorted views of reality.

You might see what happens if you soften these statements to make them more subtle—"He and I don't get on anymore, but we did have some good times together" or "I'll do my best with this and it's not the end of the world if I make a few mistakes."

- Catastrophizing

If you're mentally stuck thinking of worse and worse possible outcomes, you'll know what catastrophizing feels like—and how easy it is to get carried away with it! "If I don't do well in this exam, I'll definitely fail and not only will everyone else think I'm an idiot, I'll fall further and further behind and I'll have to graduate late, and I'll never get a real job, and I'll be broke and unhappy forever, and my parents will be so disappointed and…"

Try telling yourself that bad things might happen, but so what? Can you stay in the moment, right here, where everything is actually just fine? One of the reasons why we feel tempted to catastrophize is that we implicitly believe our worrying over an outcome will actively protect us from experiencing it. However, the opposite is true. It only makes that outcome more likely, and remembering that can help us refrain from engaging in this type of negative self-talk.

- Filtering

Filtering involves excluding all positives while focusing overwhelmingly on negative details, as if you were wearing glasses that filtered out the good and emphasized the bad. You deliver a brilliant speech but trip slightly on your way down from the podium. You forget everything you did right and zoom in on the one thing you did wrong. You have put a negative filter on your experience.

- Overgeneralizing

Related to this is taking one distinct experience and assuming it applies to every other experience. You tripped coming off a podium once and now tell yourself "I always mess up speeches." You get dumped once and decide that every person of the opposite sex hates you as well.

- Mind reading

Your boss doesn't greet you as you walk past her in the canteen. You think, "she probably hates me." You end a first date convinced the other person finds you awful, despite a lack of evidence. Every time we assume we know others' thoughts, motivations or feelings, we risk interjecting our own. Like black and white thinking, mind reading is often a response to uncertainty, which is instinctively mitigated with negative thoughts.

- Emotional Reasoning

As the name suggests, this cognitive distortion involves jumping to certain irrational conclusions based on just your emotions. This happens when we assume that feeling a certain way means that we really must be the thing we feel. So if we fail a test and feel like an idiot or failure, we conclude from this that we actually are those things, even if there isn't any evidence to support it beyond individual outcomes.

Stop and double-check the evidence in front of you. Trust that people say what they mean, and mean what they say. Look to see what core beliefs of your *own* are being reflected back at you.

As you can imagine, all five of these patterns can be combined. For example, someone is asked to babysit their nephew one evening but nervously thinks "I never get this kind of thing right, I'm not good with kids, I'm the worst auntie ever (black and white thinking). I bet they only asked me because they couldn't get their normal babysitter (mind reading). My sister and brother-in-law *always* do this, always put me in these difficult situations (overgeneralization). I bet I totally mess up and the kid sets himself on fire or something (catastrophizing)."

In this example, the woman might have also conveniently forgotten the time she already babysat her nephew with no problems at all—definite filtering!

Assessment Tools and Tips

As you become more and more aware of that voice that appears inside you and exactly what it says, you'll become better at appraising its accuracy. If you're just starting out, you may believe you don't even have self-talk—but look closer and you'll notice it soon enough. Some self-talk is obvious, but often the more insidious type slips under the radar, and needs your conscious awareness to be detected.

Slowing down and deliberately asking yourself what you're thinking can make your self-talk more apparent and tangible in the moment. You could do this by practicing the mindfulness exercise above, or you could notice yourself feeling upset, triggered, or stressed, and decide to write out your thoughts in a journal.

By writing things down, you can see your more transient thoughts on the page, and understand that a lot of what you think of as an irrefutable fact of life really isn't. Journaling, speaking out loud or meditating help you see your *thoughts as thoughts*, so you can step outside your mind for a moment and take control of your beliefs, rather than letting them control you. While writing your thoughts down, the psychologist David Burns recommends making three columns where you first write your negative thoughts, identifying the negative thinking pattern (like the ones mentioned above) that is at play, and coming up with a rational response to your original thoughts as an effective way to make self-talk more positive.

Get into the habit of asking yourself, "Is what I'm thinking really true? Is it a provable fact or merely a belief/worry/rumination/assumption?" More often than not, the answer will be immediately apparent to you.

Don't take your own word for it—look for evidence. You might think "those people over there are laughing at me, they must think I look stupid," but by pausing for a second you soon see that there's zero reason to believe this. If you can see a thought is irrational and causing you upset, you give yourself the chance to drop it. You'll also recognize that your assumption is a result of trying to read minds, a cognitive distortion we've covered above.

You could also seek alternative explanations. The people might be laughing at a joke someone has shared, and they may not have even noticed you. By not going along with your worst and most irrational assumptions, you give yourself the chance to pursue other, healthier trains of thought. You can check this by noticing how you feel once you examine other possibilities.

In time, you can use any instance of self-talk as a helpful clue that points to your negative underlying beliefs about yourself and the world. You could arrive at some of these hidden but powerful beliefs by asking, "if this thought were true, what would it imply about me or the world?"

You may answer this question with, "It would mean I was an inferior/ridiculous/stupid/wrong/bad person"—demonstrating that as we've discussed, the root of harmful self-talk is poor self-esteem or a deeply held core belief in our own lack of worth. In such cases, what might help is assuming the answer (being stupid, wrong, etc.) to be true, and asking yourself, "Would it be the end of the world if it was true?" and "If it's true, what can I do to change that?" Realizing that something isn't as bad as we initially thought makes us doubt the truth of the claim itself, helping us discard negative and unhelpful thoughts in the process.

By becoming aware of and examining our self-talk, our thoughts will lead us to the underlying beliefs from which they spring. Crucially, we can start to dismantle them—the next time we see the belief rear its head, we can ask ourselves if we'd like to entertain it or let it fade away in favor of a healthier, more objective one.

In time, you can start to notice your own unique patterns, and work consistently to reprogram old beliefs with ones that better serve you. You begin the work of choosing your attitude, rather than having your beliefs operate silently against you in the background of your awareness.

Ask yourself the following questions to guide you closer to your own unique patterns of self-talk:

- Am I using black-and-white terms?
- Am I expecting perfection?
- Am I jumping to conclusions?
- Am I exaggerating anything or blowing anything out of proportion?
- Am I only focusing on the negative side?
- Am I being irrational or illogical in my conclusions?
- Am I taking things personally when I shouldn't?
- What feelings are beneath my current thoughts?
- What does this thought say about my deep beliefs?
- Ultimately, are these thoughts having a helpful or hurtful effect on me?

Awareness is half the battle won. But the other half is learning to consistently challenge negative core beliefs as you unearth them, so they can be replaced. When you're starting out, you may be tempted to cling even more tightly to a negative belief. You may not be willing to accept alternatives, or you may believe that you have more evidence for a negative belief than you really do.

You need to systematically (and compassionately) challenge yourself. Think of it as a debate with yourself, and try coming up with points that undermine the narrative in your mind. Eventually, this will become habitual when you experience negative self-talk.

You might find that *some* of your thoughts are actually true, or at least partly true. Others will be wildly exaggerated or completely false. But when you're upset, how do you know which is which?

Properly appraising your self-talk is not very different from constructing a convincing and logical argument. Imagine yourself trying to poke holes in irrational narratives like a lawyer or scientist would, looking for hard evidence and dismissing unfounded assumptions.

There are a few tips and techniques to help you do this:

Imagine how someone else may think about this same situation. Picture a close friend, confidante, or admired mentor and how they would approach the same idea. You could also imagine saying your thought out loud to someone you love—this will very quickly show you if a thought is needlessly unkind!

Anchor in reality. Ask yourself, "How do I know this will happen? Is there really any evidence this thought is true? What else could happen instead, and how likely is it? What are the actual facts here?" Notice if you're assuming you already have the answer when you don't, or are attempting to predict the future when it's not possible. Become curious about what's happened before and its relationship to the current moment. Look at how sure you feel about certain self-talk statements and ask whether your perspective is founded. Grounding in reality means taking a step back and distinguishing between fact and fantasy. It may sometimes be helpful to simply say, "I haven't got enough information to make a judgment just yet" instead of assuming the worst.

Look at the thought itself and ask whether it's doing you any good to hold it. How does it make you feel, and do you want to feel that way? Is the thought helpful in any way?

De-catastrophize your thinking. Ask what's the worst that can happen, and whether it's really all that bad. Let's say people *are* laughing at you—does it really matter all that much? Is it the end of the world? Most things we worry about won't matter in a month, let alone a year. Ask yourself whether the thing you're ruminating about will last forever, to gain perspective. Try to remember that good things might happen too—have you included them in your ruminations?

Consider alternatives, and entertain the possibility that things could go better than expected. You might decide you need to find more information—often, anxiety and low self-esteem worsen in uncertainty, but disappear when you have more objective and empowering information at hand. Try to open your thinking to allow in other thoughts, explanations, appraisals, and predictions. Put on the brain of someone else and look at the issue again. If all else fails, you can often halt negative self-talk in its tracks simply by recognizing you're doing it and committing to stepping away from the problem until you feel calmer and ready to tackle the situation again.

Of course, this isn't always possible. We're all human and thus prone to making terrible mistakes that really can be every bit as bad as we think them to be. In such cases, it is important to not beat ourselves up. Instead, we must look to learn and improve from our missteps in the future. With the right attitude, even the worst negatives can be turned into something positive. By regulating our self-talk, we can ensure that our mistakes don't become a damning indictment of who we are, and how we view ourselves.

Assessing your self-talk entirely in your mind can become taxing and convoluted given the sheer number of thoughts we experience at any given moment. To make things easier, there are several activities you can choose from to help you evaluate and improve your self-talk.

First, you can try the paper clip technique: in the morning, put a handful of paper clips in your right-hand pocket and, whenever you become aware of yourself engaging in negative self-talk, switch one of the paper clips over to the left-hand pocket. At the end of the day, you'll have a record of how frequent your negative self-talk really is. This is a great technique if you've already identified a common pattern and want to keep track of it, but it's not enough to reveal the content of your self-talk.

If you'd like a more detailed log of your self-talk, keep a journal where you jot down the thoughts every time you notice one pop up. Include the date, whether the thought was positive or negative, what events triggered it, and the thought itself. You may also choose to rate individual thoughts based on how rational they really are. When you see yourself realizing that many of them aren't, and that you yourself see them as irrational, they will inevitably bother you less. You can also include any core beliefs you can connect them to, and a gentle alternative thought. Journaling self-talk allows you to more clearly spot patterns, but does take more time to do.

Choose a journaling technique that works for you and your lifestyle. You might try using a short journaling technique wherein you only rate your self-talk on a scale at various points in the day, giving you quantitative data over time about how the tone of your self-talk is changing. This can be helpful if you're using another dedicated practice to improve self-talk, but would like to track the results and improvement over the long term.

Another clever technique is to not wait until you naturally experience negative self-talk, but deliberately try to summon it through visualization and mental imagery. Close your eyes, vividly imagine a challenging scenario and walk yourself through it, watching to see the thoughts that spring to mind as you do. This is also a great way to rehearse alternatives, working through the same situation again but with a different set of thoughts, noticing how you feel.

Finally, you might decide rather than keeping track of your self-talk, to more directly monitor your overall self-concept and self-esteem. After all, this is the layer at which we hope to make the most profound changes—a healthy sense of self is always the goal of improving self-talk.

How do you know whether your self-esteem has actually improved?

The most obvious way is to go by how you feel, and you may with time notice that your self-talk is shifting to better reflect a sense of self-respect and value. If you'd like a more quantitative measure, however, there are many tests and psychological inventories designed to put an exact figure on various aspects of your self-concept.

These tests all have different theoretical underpinnings but will give you a handy way of tracking progress over time. Many of them are short and can be found online.

The Personal Self-Concept Questionnaire (PSQ) created by Goñi, Madariaga, Axpe & Goñi (2011) measures things like autonomy, self-fulfillment, and emotional self-concept. You will need to rate your agreement with a series of 22 statements on a scale of 1 to 5, to get a total score.

Saraswat's Self-Concept Questionnaire (SCQ) is older (published 1984) but still popular, and measures self-concept over six areas: physical, social, temperamental, educational, moral and intellectual. Counselor Susan Harrill's Self-Esteem Inventory is more specifically aimed at measuring self-esteem using 25 statements that you respond to with a rating between 0 and 4.

These scales (and there are many, many others available—a quick Google search will return dozens of options) will give you a rough idea of where you stand. It's important to use the same one if you intend to compare measurements over time. If a full-on psych assessment seems unnecessary, try other activities to get a snapshot of your self-esteem as it stands.

Make art, doodle, mind map, or journal to answer the question "who am I?" and cover your likes, dislikes, strengths, weaknesses, values and so on. Reflect on compliments you've received, on your self-talk and your goals with it, your progresses and challenges. Generally, it's advisable to measure your self-esteem through the things that are intrinsic to you, rather than external factors such as your wealth, appearance, your career, etc. All of these are subject to change with time and circumstances, but the best indicator of healthy self-esteem is that it remains constant through thick and thin.

Re-read previous negative self-talk statements and see if they still resonate, notice if you're more comfortable receiving compliments, or take note if you feel better about yourself in general. This will give you a more qualitative look at how healthy your self-concept is.

Takeaways

- The first step to recognizing and correcting your inner voice is to become aware of it. A powerful way to do this is through practicing mindfulness. Mindfulness is the activity wherein you train your mind to become aware of your present emotions, sensations, or experience and accept them without clouding them with any judgment.
- There are many different mindfulness activities you can follow. One of them is called the three-minute breathing space and it proceeds in three steps, as follows. First, simply take in all your thoughts and observe them without attempting to control their flow. Then, narrow your focus away from them and simply concentrate on your breathing for a minute. Lastly, expand your focus to include your body and physical sensations. Activities like these help you recognize your thoughts and move on from them without overthinking.
- As you practice mindfulness, you will become aware of some negative thinking patterns that we commonly engage in. One of them is called black

and white thinking, where we mislead ourselves into looking at the world in strictly binary terms. Another is catastrophizing, which involves drawing exaggerated conclusions from comparatively minor incidents. Patterns like these distort our thinking and obscure the nature of reality.
- Journaling is a powerful tool for not only recognizing negative thought patterns, but also challenging them to come up with more rational and thought-out alternatives. Writing your thoughts makes them seem more tangible, and allows you to evaluate them better than when it's all in your head.
- However, if journaling doesn't sound suitable to you, there are other ways to assess your self-talk. Reflect on your negative thoughts and core beliefs as they come to you and compassionately, but systematically challenge them. Play the role of a lawyer and look for logical holes. Try to identify the thinking patterns that are distorting your self-talk, and work on replacing them with healthier thoughts.

Chapter 4. Replace, Transform, Evolve

This is the chapter where all our self-awareness, focused intention, and consistent effort culminate in changes to our self-concept that can concretely improve every area of life.

Cognitive Behavior Therapy (CBT) is an effective framework for organizing attempts to reprogram your self-talk, thought by thought. It's typically practiced with a psychotherapist or counselor, but the principles are accessible and can be applied on your own—in fact, some of the exercises in the previous sections have been informal examples of CBT exercises.

CBT can address a whole range of life problems, but is particularly suited for understanding and changing underlying core beliefs in a systematic way. CBT techniques help you identify and take control of certain mental processes, cope with stress and adversity, resolve conflicts, and deal with grief, illness, trauma and more. When practiced regularly, CBT can also induce changes in brain chemistry that were once thought possible only through medication. As such, improvements that result from CBT are highly likely to be long lasting, since they can fundamentally alter the way our minds function.

While the risks associated with CBT are minimal, it's worth being prepared to face some potentially uncomfortable feelings, or confront difficult beliefs and fears. Most importantly, CBT won't magically make life's problems go away. Rather, it will teach you to better cope with them, and to face challenges with empowered autonomy and the self-confidence needed to cope and thrive.

CBT doesn't always work (and it's OK if it doesn't!), but you can improve your chances of success by:

- Opting to work with a counselor or at least sharing your journey with someone you trust.
- Being willing to be open and honest with yourself—embarrassment and denial will only get in the way.
- Being dedicated. We may be convinced that our own case is hopeless and beyond repair, but CBT takes time and consistent effort to work. Bear in mind that there are no miraculous overnight results, and half-hearted attempts here and there are unlikely to have lasting effects.

Three-Step Cognitive Behavioral Therapy

CBT is evidence-based and well-suited to tackling the inner dialogue that accompanies worry, anxiety, regret, shame, grief, guilt, blame and low self-esteem. Life is filled with challenges, adversities, and unexpected events. These can either be viewed as painful and unfair, or manageable and growth-inspiring—all depending on the mindset we cultivate with our self-talk.

CBT is not about "thinking positively" but thinking more clearly, realistically, and neutrally—without cognitive distortions. In CBT, our thoughts, feelings, and behavior are all interconnected, i.e. if we can change our thoughts, we can change our feelings and consequently how we act (and vice versa).

We've covered some cognitive distortions already—catastrophizing, black and white thinking, etc.—and have begun recognizing the language of negative self-talk in ourselves. Observing your thinking and becoming aware of previously automatic thoughts and distortions is step 1.

Step 2 is learning to gently and consistently challenge these thoughts and their underlying core beliefs, testing just how accurate they are. We considered this in the previous chapter where we asked ourselves questions, tested our assumptions, and encouraged ourselves to seek alternatives.

Step 3 is doing the work of replacing these distorted thoughts and beliefs with ones that are healthier, more accurate, and more likely to lead to a balanced and optimistic life. Before we move on to this very important step, however, we need to look a little closer at the language of negative self-talk, and how to spot triggers and warning signs so that we can step in and stop cognitive distortions *before* they take flight in our minds.

Step 1: Observe

Self-talk is made of words. That's all it is.

It's literally like a film script that you run internally. But words can be edited, deleted, rewritten. In previous sections, we've focused on fact vs. fiction, and the importance of comparing our thoughts against objective reality as much as possible. This is a way of fine-tuning the *content* of our thoughts, but there's also the question of the style, grammar, vocabulary and tone of the language we use when we talk to ourselves.

You've utterly failed, you big fat idiot.

You didn't pass the quiz that time.

Both of these statements can refer to the same event, and in a way are factually equivalent—i.e. "didn't pass" is the same as "failed." However, it's obvious that they carry very different emotional nuances, and will have very different effects on the person thinking them.

Automatic, negative self-talk has a certain flavor that you can recognize with practice. It's usually short, spontaneous and emotionally loaded with strong words, or has a rambling, looping quality. It's filled with overgeneralizing language like *always, never, nobody, should, nothing, must, completely*, or language filled with guilt, self-flagellation and judgment.

Watch for language that spirals or feeds on itself or steadily mounts in intensity. Look out for thoughts that you accept as true immediately in the moment without a second thought. Automatic thoughts are usually strongly infused with feelings of fear, anger or shame, and will appear in language that suggests this—at the very least, you'll know it's negative self-talk simply because you feel awful when you listen to it!

Step 2: Challenge

If you catch yourself in negative self-talk—congratulations. Even better, however, would be to avoid it altogether, or stop it before it happens using your knowledge of what usually triggers these thoughts for you. Negative thoughts are easier to recognize and handle when they are still small.

As a technique, "thought stopping" appeared in the late 1950s in the sport psychology world, and was used to cut short self-defeating and anxious thoughts that got in the way of performance. An excellent overview can be found in Zinsser, Bunker and Williams' 2010 book, *Cognitive Techniques for Building Confidence and Enhancing Performance*. The idea is to use a behavioral or mental cue to snap out of a negative self-talk spiral.

For those suffering from mental health issues like panic disorders, it can be especially hard to distract yourself once a negative thought appears in your mind. This technique acts as a tool to help become aware of and then replace these thoughts in a way similar to practicing mindfulness.

Pinching yourself, imagining a red light or saying "stop" out loud can all act as cues to bring your conscious awareness to the moment and away from negative self-talk.

It's essentially the art of beneficial distraction, and even more effective when you then quickly redirect your attention to a preferable subject (a more realistic thought, perhaps?) It's an assertive stance you are taking against that inner dialogue that you know only carries you to places you don't want to go.

The technique can potentially backfire if you end up constantly monitoring yourself to look for failures you can pounce on—the trick is to bring mindfulness to the process, not punishment or judgment. If you try this technique for a while and find it actually worsens the problem, ease up, be more compassionate, or simply attempt a different technique. Thought stopping may help for more superficial rumination, but not for deeper anxieties that may respond better to slow, deliberate engagement.

If you'd like to try the technique, however, here's how to begin:

Write down a list of all the most distressing, recurring, distracting and unwanted thoughts you wish to stop paying attention to. Try to rank them from most to least distressing. Include anything from "one day my boss is going to figure out how inept I am and fire me" to "this lump probably means cancer."

Next, do some prep work by practicing—sit alone in a private room and spend some time visualizing any situation in life where the most distressing thought might conceivably intrude. For a while, go into the thought and focus on it, feeling out its contours. Then, as abruptly as you can, stop the thought.

Stand up quickly, say "stop!" out loud, snap your eyes open, make a loud clapping noise or click your fingers. Empty your mind and try to hold that emptiness for thirty seconds or so. If the thought tries to intrude again, repeat "stop" as often as necessary.

What you are trying to do is gain practice at stopping rumination mid-thought. In time you can be less drastic with your interruption, and eventually internalize the "stop" so you only say it quietly to yourself. You don't necessarily need to use the word *stop*—you could also visualize your thoughts as traffic that stops dutifully at a red light. Try saying out loud "I'm having a thought about XYZ right now" to remind yourself that it's just a thought, and to gain distance.

Whatever you do, simply remind yourself that thoughts are just words—just a script that you can stop in its tracks and rewrite. The hard work is to recognize the thought, but once you do, realize it has no hold on you unless you pay attention to it. Make a habit of using certain phrases to interrupt unwanted thoughts, divert your attention and affirm your *choice* to follow certain thoughts and drop others:

Don't go there

Let it be

Let it go

It's in the past

Leave it alone

Focus

Don't pay attention

Slow down

This, too, will pass

It doesn't matter

Breathe

You've got this***

Using this thought stopping technique may make some people uncomfortable—aren't you just ignoring your problems?

It's worth remembering that thought stopping is best used for those thoughts that you know are intrusive, unwanted, and genuinely unhelpful. These are the thoughts that you have already identified as irrational, untrue, or exaggerated, and you know that entertaining them will only lead to stress and worry.

Your goal is to tolerate and manage anxiety, rather than turn a blind eye to it. Similarly, having thought stopping in your mental toolkit doesn't mean you are unable to hear your own intuition or engage when a situation warrants genuine concern. Thought stopping is merely a mental fuse that lets you halt catastrophic rumination before you get too carried away with it.

For some people, the thought-stopping technique outlined above may feel a little punitive and may not work for them. Thankfully, there are plenty of other techniques underpinned by the same principles. You could try scattered counting, for example. Counting to ten is a common anger management technique, but it's easy enough to become automatic, allowing your brain to carry on ruminating even as you count. Rather, jump around with random numbers to engage your thoughts more, e.g. "43, 12, 5, 88, 356, 90, 5…"

In the same way, a mantra or spoken word can interrupt runaway thoughts—choose a more complicated nonsense phrase or something in another language to prevent yourself from doing it too automatically. Alternatively, you can select affirmations based on your specific triggers or perceived negative qualities. Though they can take time to work, the reason so many find them effective is that our brains eventually come to think of them as true. These affirmations can be specific quotes from religious texts, or statements like "I believe in myself" and "I am in charge of my thoughts." These can be recited both mentally and out loud, but with conviction. Repeating lines you don't really believe will be pointless, so choose your affirmations wisely.

You could try self-soothing with encouraging positive self-talk, such as "don't worry, you can handle this" or "you're doing great!" Play a song you like or listen to a podcast to engage your auditory channels and pull attention away from anxious overthinking.

A distracting cue can also be physical in nature—physically move yourself into a different position, get up and do a few jumping jacks or go for a quick jog outside to break out of thought loops. You can also switch to more bodily/somatic awareness by simply focusing on your breath, and practicing a technique called muscle isolation.

Sit or lie comfortably, close your eyes, and then work your way through all your muscles, starting from the ones in your toes. Squeeze them as tightly as you can for five seconds and then release and relax completely. Then focus on the muscles in your feet and legs, moving up until you reach the muscles in your face and scalp. Not only will this help immensely to release physical tension, but it will distract your overactive mind and bring it more fully into the present moment.

Muscle isolation can be an excellent warmup to a more formal sitting meditation practice, or a great way to end a mindfulness session. Combine it with gentle soothing music or head outside where you can feel the sun and breeze on your skin.

Another classic CBT technique is to decide that instead of stopping or running away from scary and overwhelming thoughts, you'll simply stare them down and ask what's the worst that could happen. Look squarely at your ruminations and say, *so what?* It's rarely as bad as you think, and seldom something you truly cannot handle. Research has found that even those who lose their limbs or eyesight—suffering tragedies anyone would consider horrifying—soon return to a median level of happiness because of how powerful our modes of adaptation are. As such, no matter what it is you're worried over, you're very likely to be able to survive it just fine even if the event were to occur.

You might like to visualize yourself actually encountering the worst-case scenario with grace and poise, tackling the problem and seeing that it isn't in fact the end of the world, even if the worst does come to pass. This alone can take the steam out of your most catastrophic ruminations.

Step 3: Replace

Some thoughts are so useless and untrue that they can be discarded immediately, or stopped using any of the techniques described above. With practice, you'll be able to recognize totally harmful thoughts (like, "I'm probably going to die" or "everyone hates me") and release them immediately.

Some ideas and thoughts, however, are a little more subtle and are more appropriately rewritten rather than discarded entirely. These thoughts are often those that we believe have a grain of truth to them. Here, it's necessary to practice a degree of conscious discernment to determine what kind of life script will serve you best. Again, this is a step that can only be done *after* you've gained a good awareness of the kinds of self-talk you engage in—otherwise you risk having these techniques exacerbate rather than solve the problem.

Exercise 1: Think it through

This exercise takes some time and effort. The first step is to note down your self-talk using any of the methods already discussed (for example, by using a bullet journal, writing down your core beliefs or periodically taking a self-esteem inventory). Then, after a week, try to look for particular themes or patterns.

What kind of self-talk is it (for example catastrophizing or mindreading)?

What events, thoughts, feelings, people, or situations triggered the self-talk?

What common threads can you identify?

What was the effect or result of these thoughts?

What do they say about your core beliefs?

Reflect on what you see. Get some distance on your thoughts. This way, we're more likely to evaluate them truthfully, as opposed to in the moment when our feelings might cloud our judgement. Notice if your self-talk has actually held you back in life or made you feel bad. Ask yourself, how would it feel to have positive self-talk instead? What might your life look like and what could you achieve if you didn't limit yourself in this way?

In thinking through things carefully, the more positive alternative is likely to appear to you. For example, you may see that you constantly exaggerate physical symptoms and then get stuck in doom-and-gloom thought loops about what might happen if you fall ill. Seeing all this objectively noted on paper, seeing how it negatively impacts your life in many ways, and seeing how utterly irrational it is, you slowly begin to loosen the self-talk's hold on you.

By completing this exercise, you can begin to see the more accurate and realistic options available to you. Better yet, when you try them out and monitor yourself for a week, you may be surprised to learn just how much wasted mental energy and anguish you can avoid by consciously and deliberately dropping negative self-talk.

Exercise 2: Change channels

The previous exercise is a gentle way of supporting yourself as you naturally find your way to healthier cognitive alternatives. But you might need something a little more direct, especially for those core beliefs that are more persistent.

You can do this exercise alone or add it onto the Think it Through exercise above, and it's essentially what you would do with a CBT therapist. Write down a negative thought as it pops up. Now, deliberately reword the sentence in front of you until it is more neutral and objective.

- Remove all-or-nothing language like *never, everybody, none,* etc.
- Remove emotive and harsh language like *idiot, hate, fail, disgusting,* etc. Replace the word "difficult" or "impossible" with "challenging" and use "annoyed" instead of "angry." Use language that is more time-limited, for

example "I'm feeling sad today" rather than "I'm sad," which implies a permanent state of affairs.

- Make the tone more neutral and compassionate.
- Instead of saying "can't" try saying "don't." Own your preferences and the place you're currently in. Rather than saying "I can't do it" simply say "I don't do it" or even "I don't want to do it." This doesn't shut off the possibility of doing it later; it's just a statement of fact, whereas "I can't" sets a hard limit.
- Similarly, avoid hedging language like "I'll try" or "maybe" or "I guess I could…" Speak directly and state what you'll do.
- Remove any outright falsehoods or attempts to mindread or predict the future.
- Phrase things gently and compassionately, as though you were speaking to a loved one or even a person in a professional context.
- You might like to add some positive phrases like the ones already covered earlier (e.g. *you've got this*).
- Remove assumptions and unsupported conclusions. You might try replacing these statements simply with "I don't have enough information yet," which is far more neutral and accurate.
- If you can, rephrase statements as questions. Instead of saying something is impossible, ask *how* it could be possible.
- Likewise, see if you can switch focus entirely and reframe things to the positive: instead of identifying limitations and problems, pinpoint resources, options, alternatives, and possibilities.
- Put the words in the mouth of a trusted mentor and loved one and see how they fit—what would they say instead? How would they phrase things?

Here are some examples:

Negative: "I embarrassed myself in front of all those people and they'll never ask me to do a presentation ever again."

Positive: "That didn't go as I planned but it's OK. I did my best and learnt a lot, and will prepare better for next time. It's not the end of the world if I receive some constructive feedback from my bosses."

Negative: "Who would want to have a relationship with an old, unattractive person like me? There's no point dating, nobody would look twice."

Positive: "I have no evidence that trying to meet someone new would be impossible. I deserve a loving relationship, so I'm going to put myself out there. Whatever happens, I can love and respect myself."

Negative: "It's hopeless starting a business in this economy, you'll only fail."

Positive: "I have faith in myself and a lot to offer. There are always options, and I'm going to do my best and keep a positive attitude."

After you've changed a statement, deliberately make an effort to redirect your attention toward this new version instead of more negative statements. You can combine this with thought stopping, halting the negative thought and then redirecting to your reworded script instead. Practice makes perfect, i.e. the more you tell your brain something, the more it believes it's true!

Exercise 3: Testing for accuracy

Some self-talk has been going on so long that it's become embedded in layer upon layer of assumptions, even becoming part of our identity and worldview. These beliefs take time to dismantle! Learning to get to the root of a statement's objective accuracy sounds easy, but it's definitely a skill that takes time and effort to master.

- Is your self-talk fact or opinion?
- Where does this idea really come from?
- What is the evidence and what assumptions have you made?
- Can you think of any counterexamples to disprove this idea?

Testing for accuracy can be as simple as noticing yourself say "nobody thinks my art is any good" and changing it to "I haven't shown many people my work, but I do remember that nice compliment I got once." Even the smallest positive that is demonstrably and objectively true can act as a counterweight to a whole universe of negative thinking that actually has no proof to support it at all.

Remember, you don't have to go to the other extreme—the goal of positive self-talk is not to become a narcissist who is incapable of accurately seeing their own faults. Rather, you are seeking moderation, balance, and a realistic and healthy viewpoint. You'll be surprised by how unremarkable "healthy" self-talk sounds in comparison to what you're used to!

You can use these re-scripting techniques in the moment you have a negative thought, or you can do it more systematically, for example at the end of a day when you sit down with a journal and reflect. You might include some mindfulness and guided meditation, too.

To commit to shifting to your more positive self-talk phrases, pin new phrases and affirmations to a wall or visible place. Start the morning by reading through them or regularly take five-minute breaks throughout the day to check in with yourself, breathe, and recalibrate, using these statements as cues.

All of these techniques can be used in combination. For example, someone might keep a self-talk diary for two weeks where they note down the thoughts that emerge as well as the triggers, results, and accompanying emotions that go with these thoughts.

They soon see a pattern: that much of their self-talk can be boiled down to the core belief "I'm not as good as everyone else" and that the low self-esteem behind this belief expresses itself in mindreading ruminations. For example, "They said they liked my shoes but I'm sure they think they're hideous and were just lying to make me feel better…"

Reflecting on this, the person decides that self-defeating attitudes like this one have only served to undermine them all through life, and that they are ready to embrace a more realistic, compassionate outlook toward themselves. They note down a range of thoughts that pop into their head throughout the day and then systematically ask whether they're all that true.

Is it *really* true that you are a failure? Maybe it's more accurate to say that you didn't do as well as you thought you would on one particular task, but that your overall performance is great. Is it *really* true that other people are sitting whispering amongst themselves about how awful you are? Far more likely is that people barely notice you and your missteps, because they are far too busy dealing with their own!

By gradually testing the truth of the self-talk we are increasingly aware of, we realize how many other options there are. We can try to rewrite some of the most commonly occurring thoughts and themes, with improved alternatives:

"They don't like me" turns into "They don't know me, but there's no reason for them not to like me."

"I'm falling behind in life" becomes "I'm doing the best I can and I'm on my own path. I don't have to compete with anyone."

"Everyone else is so much more talented compared to me" is reworded into "I admire the skills of others, but that doesn't mean I don't have good points of my own. Besides, I'm willing to learn."

These rewritten statements can be pulled out or recalled when the person spots themselves falling into a detrimental thinking spiral again. They can use the "stop" technique to halt negative self-talk in its tracks, then redirect. They can build in moments of meditation and self-reflection throughout the day, regularly using positive statements like, "you're just fine" and "don't go down that path" when negative self-talk rears its head. Here is one potential internal monologue:

"You're such a loser, you're doing all this stupid positive self-talk stuff and you know it'll never work, that's for other people, but you'll just mess it up. Besides, it's not negative self-talk, it's the truth—you really are a loser… STOP. Take a deep breath. Remember, these are just thoughts, not reality. I recognize this pattern. This is my inner critic and I've already decided I don't care what they say. You're doing great. Breathe. Now look at the situation again and make a conscious decision about your inner script. You're *not* a loser, you're working hard on your self-esteem and that's admirable. It will work with time. *It probably won't.* STOP. I already know what lies down that path, and I'm not biting. I'm going outside for a run…"

If the above stream of consciousness seems a little extreme to you, consider this: your mind is *always* running a script very much like the one above, but it may be conscious or unconscious. If it's unconscious, it will run along unawares, quietly affecting every aspect of your life. But if you can make it conscious, you can change it, and reap the benefits. It's your choice.

Though we've uncovered several different techniques and approaches to help you unravel unhelpful self-talk and gradually replace it with healthier core beliefs and supportive inner dialogue, the process is likely to be a lot more ad hoc in real life.

What's important is that your approach works for *you*. Try a few things and give them time to work, but don't be afraid of tweaking these methods to your own ends, combining them or trying something completely different.

Other helpful tips to keep in mind as you master the art of re-scripting your inner mental world:

- Do re-scripting work when you're calm and feeling optimistic, and not when you're stuck in the middle of a mental storm or feeling upset.
- Keep at it—it's better to do a little and often than expect that one session will solve everything forever!
- Run through your new script even if you don't quite believe it at first—with repetition, your brain will soon start to literally rewire itself.
- Don't be afraid to make changes to your script—you might not get it right the first time. Remember, it doesn't have to be over-the-top enthusiastic and unrealistically positive. It just has to be neutral and relatively unbiased.
- It's up to you to evaluate your script as you go. How does the new self-talk feel? What effects does it have on your mood, your self-concept, and your behavior?
- Don't beat yourself up if occasionally you end up ranting, complaining or going down a stress rabbit hole—it's perfectly normal to be grumpy or pessimistic at times. Likewise, a little stress or criticism isn't the end of the world. Just keep things in perspective and try whenever possible to return to awareness of your thoughts *as thoughts*.

The language of positive self-talk flows naturally from a healthy self-concept. But if you're trying to undo the damage of a poor self-esteem, you may find yourself upgrading your negative self-talk in the hopes that it positively influences your self-concept.

There's no fixed script about what exactly to say when you talk to yourself, but speaking from the right frame of mind (i.e. from a position of self-respect and compassion) will get you most of the way. Nobody can tell you precisely the right words to use in your own mental dialogue. Your life context is unique, and every new situation will require you to respond spontaneously and authentically.

Using a pre-written script is a great first step—a little like mental training wheels as you find your confidence. But in time it should be easier to generate your own impromptu positive self-talk, in real time, and it will feel more and more genuine with practice. The end goal is not simply to rehearse a script, but to automatically and sincerely talk to yourself in a positive way.

Until that time, however, here's a brief self-talk checklist to make sure you're on the right track.

Positive self-talk should ideally be:

- Framed in present tense
- Simple and straightforward (statements that lead to endless cycles of rumination are likely to be negative self-talk whereas good, wholesome, affirmative self-talk is typically direct and uncomplicated)
- Honest, which means it must include potential room for improvement or shortcomings wherever relevant
- Personal and meaningful to you
- Able to make you feel better
- Practical and realistic
- Optimistic and hopeful—neutral is great, but if you're talking to yourself, why not be your own best friend and offer some supportive and encouraging words while you're at it?

Takeaways

- This chapter explores cognitive behavioral therapy (CBT) and other related techniques that can help us improve our self-talk. The whole aim of changing self-talk more or less falls under the process of CBT.
- CBT is a popular and effective therapeutic framework that emphasizes our thoughts as the key component of our feelings and behavior. The underlying principle of its techniques is that our thoughts influence how we feel, which in turn determines the way we behave. This creates a feedback loop that ultimately influences our thoughts, and the way to improve is to get out of this vicious cycle. We must replace our negative thoughts with more positive ones, with the condition that the latter be realistic and not merely vain self-affirmations that have no backing or truth to them. The general process for our purposes is to observe, challenge, and replace negative thoughts and self-talk.
- One effective method to reduce negative self-talk is an activity called thought stopping. This involves distracting yourself from troublesome thoughts using some behavioral or mental cues, such as thinking or saying "Stop!", pinching yourself, etc. Though this technique can backfire in some cases, it has been observed to be effective in curtailing superficial but unproductive rumination.
- Besides using cues, other ways to stop negative self-talk include listening to music or podcasts that you like. This distracts you by engaging your auditory faculties. You can also use scattered counting— counting random numbers instead of proceeding linearly like in 1,2,3, and so on. The idea is to catch yourself in the process and distance yourself from unhelpful thoughts.

- If thought stopping doesn't work, you can also practice thought replacing. Here, you take a negative thought and strip it of all the components that make it unpleasant, replacing them with more positive alternatives. One way to do this is to simply think your thoughts through and assess how valid they are. If you find them to be irrational, substitute ones that make more sense to you and promote healthier emotions.

- Alternatively, you can write particular thoughts down to edit and rewrite them. Eliminate extreme words like only, never, absolutely, etc., along with any harsh descriptors like idiot, loser, ugly, and others. Also replace outright lies, unfounded assumptions, and other logical faults to improve your self-talk.

Chapter 5: More Than Words

Let's remind ourselves *why* we bothered to change our negative self-talk to healthier, more affirming self-talk.

The words inside our head are just words—but they have powerful, tangible effects on the world we live in because those words directly impact our behavior and the actions we take, every day. When these words are negative, they lead to anxiety, depression, self-pity, inaction, and all sorts of undesirable outcomes. However, when they're positive, they can carry you through even the darkest of times and help you emerge even stronger.

As you practice better awareness of your own self-talk and learn to rewrite the scripts that are holding you back, you will naturally start to notice that you may behave differently, make different choices, say different words out loud to others, and take different actions.

Self-talk is internal, but it's also the way we interface with our external reality. Bearing this in mind, our final chapter will focus on all the ways we can use external factors to support and encourage our positive self-talk. The relationship is reciprocal: good self-talk leads to healthy choices and behaviors, which themselves re-affirm good self-talk.

Our focus so far has been on the words we say quietly and internally to ourselves, but plenty of other elements affect our self-talk. The kinds of friends we have, the situations we put ourselves in, the media we expose ourselves to, our environment, our daily habits—all of these feed information into our self-talk engine and make it harder or easier to maintain self-esteem and compassion. While we can't control all these external factors, what we can control is how we perceive and respond to them and the influence they wield over us.

Everyday Reinforcement

Mindlessly saying a mantra into a mirror each morning when you don't really believe it is unlikely to have much effect. But by this point in the book, you've hopefully zoomed in on those alternative thoughts and core beliefs that directly challenge the negative self-talk that is unique to you and your life.

Starting each morning with a deliberately positive session of self-talk sets the tone and intention for the rest of the day. It's making a commitment to yourself to frame the rest of the day positively, with you set up as your own best friend and supporter.

The words you speak to yourself inside your head have a way of extending themselves outside your head and becoming real. You'll unconsciously use the same language out loud or when talking to others, which will in turn affect how they respond to you. Start the day on a life-affirming, hopeful footing and you'll not only find it's easier to be compassionate with yourself, but with others, too.

Negative thoughts lead to negative words and actions, and negativity toward other people that is likely to be reflected back to you. It seems like such a simple thing, but it makes all the difference in the world.

Do you begin your day with gratitude and optimism, speaking kindly to those around you and giving yourself the pep talk you need to get through the day's challenges? Or do you complain about everything that went wrong, assume the worst of those around you, find fault in everything and predict disaster at every turn?

It's all a choice. And good choices have a habit of breeding more good choices. This book is about the little words we say to ourselves in our minds, but it's about so much more than that—it's about our attitude to life itself, our entire mindset, our perspective on all our important relationships, and the engine that drives all the major decisions of our life.

So, a cheesy mantra said without conviction is not enough! That said, affirmations and positive scripts can be an immensely powerful way to retrain a mind stuck in negative self-talk. Our mind doesn't innately know right from wrong; it believes what we feed into it. That's why positive affirmations work. Use your words for good.

Regularly get some distance from yourself and your thoughts through meditation, journaling, or literally telling yourself "this is just a thought." Give your inner critic a name, so you can say, "Oh it's just Gertrude again, I can ignore her!" The important lesson here is that your thoughts aren't you, they're simply words that may or may not be true. Practice thought stopping or visualize putting useless self-talk in a box where it can't distract you. Then actively replace these thoughts with ones you've consciously chosen as supportive and more realistic—i.e. mantras, affirmations or scripts.

These can seem a little glib and silly on the surface, but they really work. It doesn't really help to just copy inspiring messages you hear from others, as nice as they may be. You need to choose words that personally resonate and speak directly to your unique core messages.

A good mantra can capture the essence of the attitude you want to emulate. Successful people often use mantras as positive personal mottos that they regularly rely on to boost their confidence and help them navigate adversity.

For example:

"You've survived worse before!" (Halts catastrophic thinking—you tell yourself that even the worst outcome is something you are strong enough to deal with.)

"You'll figure it out." (Shifts you into a more practical, objective frame of mind and away from rumination.)

"What matters most right now?" (Gets you out of obsessive thought loops and onto your values and goals.)

"I choose my own experience." (Empowers you to take charge of your ability to consciously rewrite your own script.)

"I am of value and I have purpose in this world." (Affirms that you are a human being with real worth who deserves care and respect, no matter what.)

"Will this matter in six months?" (Puts things in perspective!)

"The past is the past. What can I do now?" (Switches your focus to where it matters—action in the present moment.)

"There are always options." (Takes you out of black-and-white, doom-and-gloom thinking and into the realm of possibilities.)

"You're doing your best. Well done." (Self-affirmation that doesn't depend on outcome—acknowledges the hard work you're doing.)

"You rock!" (A little cheesy, but cuts to the chase—you have worth and are a valuable, lovable person. *No matter what.*)

"I'm unique in the world and nobody is like me." (Reminds you not to make comparisons.)

"Which path do you want to go down?" (We all have choices. This reminds you that you can always pour your energy and attention into what matters.)

"Today, I choose peace, gratitude and love, for myself and others." (Reasserts your values as an antidote to negativity, and asserts your power to control your own inner reality.)

"It's not how many times you fall down, it's how many times you get up." (Refocuses your attention on learning, and not getting bogged down in "failure.")

When something doesn't go right or you're struggling, pulling out a mantra or affirmation is like giving yourself a leg up, or having your own built-in guru who is on your side, cheering you on. It can definitely feel cheesy, but why not put some of these affirmations somewhere prominent where you can see them every day? Remember, the more something is repeated, the more your brain believes it's real.

A mantra or affirmation is a great way to cement positive self-talk and a healthy self-esteem, but there are other ways to support yourself, too. It would be a shame to nurture your self-esteem only to have it cancelled out by unsupportive or hostile people or situations around you.

As you practice affirming your own self-worth and working on your self-talk, you might more clearly notice the negative people in your life. You don't need to cut someone out of your life completely just because they had a bad day or ranted a little too much at your last meeting. Rather, it's about carefully noticing whether some people *consistently* affect your self-concept and self-talk in a negative way.

The attitudes of people around you can greatly influence your own. Though good friends support one another through challenges, pay attention if you have friends or family members who seem to steadily complain without taking any action, bring others down, are abusive, or simply have an air of negativity around them that makes everyone feel bad.

It can be hard to reduce your contact with such people, and it's not something to be done lightly. However, if you can see a regular and ongoing pattern of negativity that threatens your own efforts to maintain hope and optimism, it's time to set up a boundary. Limit time spent together or cut it out entirely, if possible. Your attitude to negative people who try to bring you down is not much different from your attitude to negative self-talk: recognize it for what it is and proactively move away from it.

Finally, keep a close eye on the media you consume. Do you spend ages online reading anxiety-inducing news articles? Do you waste hours on social media that only leaves you feeling worthless and out of the loop? Do you deliberately seek out information to confirm negative core beliefs?

Think of the media and the internet in general as a person—what kind of relationship do you have? It may be time to choose more balanced, healthy media to consume or step away from social media completely if you notice it eating away at your self-esteem. Can you find sources of information that inspire and encourage you rather than leave you feeling bad?

A Self-Empowerment Habit

The more you practice positive self-talk and cultivate a healthy self-esteem, the more and more your attitude will seep out into the world at large, affecting every part of your life. You may start to realize that healthy self-talk is just one small aspect of a healthy lifestyle; it's not just about supporting your mental health, but your entire well-being.

It's the little daily habits that accumulate and build a robust sense of confidence over time. It's the consistent effort and commitment to choosing the life you want that makes the difference. Self-talk is the ultimate habit in that it is something you're engaged with throughout the day, every day, for your entire life. But other habits can also weigh in on your overall self-concept and well-being.

Gratitude

The last thing your inner critic wants to do is appreciate the little things in life, or notice how lovely the sunset looks right now. Gratitude seems like a small thing, but it can be an incredibly powerful antidote to complaining, chronic anxiety, and dissatisfaction with the way things are—the essence of most negative self-talk.

The effects are backed up by science—a 2013 paper in *Psychology Today* showed that young people who kept gratitude journals experienced more energy, determination, attention, and feelings of enthusiasm than those who didn't. Gratitude changes the brain's focus, boosting serotonin and dopamine levels, and helping us feel more resilient in the face of challenges.

A gratitude journal is a place where you can consciously write down the things you are grateful for—a great cup of coffee in the morning, your pet doing something cute, sunshine on your skin, a beautiful song, a hug from a friend. Big or small, note it down so your brain has something tangible to focus on. Aim for three to five things a day—and you can always find a few things to be grateful for, no matter how tiny!

Closely related to this habit of gratitude is the habit of avoiding comparison. Like complaining, comparing yourself to others only robs your life of joy and keeps you focused on the negative. When you compare yourself to someone else, you deliberately ignore all the unique, wonderful things that make you *you,* while emphasizing perceived weakness and deficits that might not even be real.

Concentrating on what you don't have is a game that goes nowhere. You might see someone else's life and be envious of their financial situation, their relationships or families, their health and appearance, their talent and achievements, and so on.

But this is usually a distortion—you don't get to see inside that person's head to *their* self-talk, and you probably don't see their challenges, their fears, failures, shortcomings or anxieties. What others present to the world is typically the "highlights reel"—all the best parts of their lives.

What you don't see is what they're ashamed or unsure about; the hidden debt, the unhappy marriages, the mental health issues, and even the low self-esteem. You may be surprised to know that the person you admire and envy feels no better about themselves than you do, and actively wishes they were someone else!

Is there someone in the world who is objectively doing better than you? Of course. Does it matter? No.

There are also very many people doing worse, and when you think about it, how can you really measure this "better" or "worse" anyway? The truth is that everyone's life is very, very different, and most people are doing their very best with the gifts and limitations they have. Ultimately, someone else's life doesn't imply a single thing about you and your own life.

Try to adopt an attitude of compassion and kindness for everyone, even those annoying people who seem so perfect! Everyone is facing an uphill internal battle that we may not be aware of, and it's always advisable to be a positive influence on those around us. Practice taking joy in others' accomplishments, compliment them and be happy for them, knowing that it will never undermine your own value. They're not "better" than you, but they may well have knowledge, attributes and skills that you can learn from. Take inspiration from them and let them inspire you to work hard toward what you care about.

At the same time, understand that everybody is on a unique path. Comparison is not only unhelpful, it's also impossible. Life is not a race or a competition.

If you regularly find yourself comparing your life to others', ask what's really important, *to you*, and how you can bring those things to life. It's not your business what other people do, but it is your business what you do—focus as much as you can on your own self-determined values, goals and strengths, and you will never feel threatened by anyone else doing the same.

The Culmination of Rewriting Your Self-Talk

In this book, we've covered a number of different activities, approaches, techniques and methods to not only recognizing and understanding our self-talk, but actively rewriting the script and creating a better self-esteem. We've talked about the power of meditation, journaling, exercise, reframing and switching perspectives, thought-stopping techniques, relaxation methods, de-scripting and more.

But ultimately, all these activities point to one underlying aspect behind all these approaches: cultivating self-compassion.

What's the difference between someone who has naturally high self-esteem and who regularly engages in positive self-talk, and someone who doesn't? It's not that they've mastered any particular technique. Rather, *it's that they love and respect themselves, and conduct both their inner and outer worlds to reflect that deep belief.*

While the concept of high self-esteem was the focus of psychological research in the '80s and '90s, today more and more attention is being paid to self-compassion, and how it helps us reach our full potential beyond the old theories of high confidence. While the temporary boost that comes from comparing ourselves to others or putting others down can feel good, lasting feelings of self-worth derive from somewhere deeper.

In the past, parents were encouraged to tell their children they could be anything they wanted, and that they were special and different. But is that really true? And do we *need* to be special or different to deserve care, respect and consideration?

Praise and affirmation are great—but we need a sense of self that goes beyond this; we need to be able to remain solidly within our compassionate self-concept *despite* adversity, criticism, failure or weaknesses. Anyone can feel great when complimented, but do you have a sense of self strong enough to remain sure of your value even if nobody else sees it, and you aren't praised?

The solution is not to evaluate yourself and give yourself a high rating, *but not to evaluate yourself at all.* No labels. No judgment, good or bad.

Just acceptance of ourselves, exactly as we are, right now.

Many people unconsciously hold back on being kind to themselves, because they believe that they haven't earnt it, or that being too nice to themselves will make them lazy or selfish. Isn't that crazy, when you really stop to think about it?

What we could aim for is neither self-criticism ("you're hideous"), nor trying to prop ourselves up with false self-esteem ("you're way better looking than him"), but finding that calm, rational space in the middle where we love and accept however we are in this moment ("I look how I look. I accept that. I deserve love in any case").

Self-compassion is deeper and more lasting than high confidence because it is not dependent on fleeting external factors. If I attach my self-worth to being wealthy, or fit, or clever, it means my self-worth will disappear if I lose my money, fall ill or encounter someone more intelligent than I am. In other words, only internal, self-determined worth is true worth.

Self-compassion is not just something that sounds nice—it's backed up by solid research as a way to achieve greater well-being, contentment, emotional regulation (less anxiety and depression) and resilience. A 2008 paper by Neff and Vonk in the *Journal of Personality* showed that self-esteem and self-compassion are fundamentally different—and that self-compassion may surpass self-esteem in many ways. Perhaps best of all, being kind to ourselves makes it easier for us to be accepting of others, connecting mindfully with our common humanity.

Practice gentleness, understanding and kindness that doesn't depend on anything at all—simply give them to yourself and others for free, just like that. No ego needed. With self-compassion you don't take things personally, and seem to avoid some of the common pitfalls of overly high self-esteem—for example narcissism, feeling disappointed by neutral feedback, feeling like a failure because you're average, or having a sense of self that yoyos along with life's ups and downs.

Self-compassion says that *you are a human being and have intrinsic worth* that has nothing to do with who approves of you, your actions, failures, fears, or anything else. It's unconditional. This means you're OK with who you are, warts and all, and embrace even your imperfections, rather than claim there aren't any or work intently to get rid of them.

Self-compassion says, "Relax. Forget about asking whether you're good enough. You're alive and you're OK, exactly as you are." Open your heart, let things be as they are, and you'll find it much, much easier to drop the habit of beating yourself up.

An unexpected benefit of self-compassion is that it seems to remind us of a more universal sense of our interconnectivity, of our shared experience as human beings. It invites us to connect with something bigger than our tumultuous egos. With self-compassion, we paradoxically recognize the joy there is in serving others, and we develop a rich worldview that prioritizes the truly important things in life.

Actually being kind to yourself is harder than it seems at first—for some people, almost impossible. We might find that being hard on ourselves has been so effective at pushing us to do better that we're afraid to lose our motivation by allowing ourselves to relax. But there's a good way to bootstrap yourself into more self-compassion: imagine talking to yourself as you literally would to one of your dearest friends. This is because even those with the harshest self-talk can often summon up incredible depths of care and kindness for those they love—the trick is just to transfer it to themselves!

How do you treat a friend who is feeling down, scared, nervous, or who has just made a mistake? You probably don't tell them they're a complete idiot and that nobody loves them! So why do you do it to yourself?

The first thing to do is drop the idea that self-compassion means you're being indulgent. The truth is that kindness, understanding, and empathy almost certainly make you a better employee, spouse, friend, and person in general. Once you realize that your inner critic isn't actually making you a better person but instead undermining you, you are free to give yourself the support that will actually improve your life.

Imagine a toddler who bursts into tears because they are frustrated they can't tie their shoelaces. You wouldn't laugh at them, tell them they were useless or get angry that they were unhappy. You'd be patient, explain that they'd learn eventually, and that you still loved them no matter what. Do the same for yourself, especially when *you're* in the middle of a tantrum and feel like you're failing!

Use this approach every time you hear the voice of judgment and criticism emerging within you. Don't berate yourself for oversleeping; instead notice that you're not getting enough rest and choose to care enough about yourself to go to bed earlier that night.

Don't agree with the rude person who insulted you on the bus—put a boundary up and tell yourself, "It's them, not me," then forget about it. Don't psyche yourself out with self-doubt as you write your resume, but look over your own shoulder and give yourself some encouragement: "I know this is hard but you're great. You're doing good work."

When negative thoughts pop up, recognize that it's just the inner critic speaking, like a monster under the bed. If it has something useful to say, listen, but don't entertain any idea that damages your well-being or isn't true. Would you allow a random stranger to waltz up to a loved one on the street and tell them, "You're worthless, and you don't deserve to be here"? Have the same reaction for yourself—even if you're the one who's being mean to you!

A great exercise is to write out a "job description" for your inner critic. What is their main function in your life, really, and how do they go about doing that work? Do you let them? Is your inner critic keeping you safe or are they limiting you? Are they supporting you or breaking you down? What effect do they have on your life? Are their words motivational or do they do the opposite of inspire?

Looking at your inner critic as a separate entity who is only doing their job gives you some distance and perspective on negative self-talk when it appears. How will you play manager to this employee? Just like it's a mosquito's job to occasionally bite you, you will sometimes encounter negativity in your life. But that doesn't mean you have to accept it!

Takeaways

- Previously we discussed how to rewrite our internal monologue, but in this chapter we focused on all the external factors that contribute to having healthier and more positive self-talk. There are everyday practices we can do to contribute to a more positive self-image, or just snap us into sharper awareness of our beliefs and narratives.
- Starting your morning with a dose of deliberately positive self-talk sets a pleasant tone for the rest of your day. While it may feel silly to feign positivity in the beginning, this technique really does work. The more we repeat something to ourselves, the likelier we are to start believing it (remember neuroplasticity?). By repeating positive statements that represent our

desired goals throughout the day, we can easily boost our confidence and self-esteem in the face of adversity.

- Having said that, we are bound to struggle in remaining positive if those around us continue to be negative and judgmental. As we practice positive self-talk, we're more likely to notice the negativities of our friends and families. In such cases, we must set good boundaries to limit our interactions with negative people in our lives, and even refrain from it altogether if required.

- Many of our habits, when cultivated properly, can help reinforce positive self-talk in our lives. For example, learning to be grateful is a great way to increase our overall happiness. Maintain a gratitude journal and update it daily with three to five things you were grateful for on that day as a way to count your blessings. Other productive habits include avoiding comparisons with others, being kind in your interactions, and avoiding overly critical thought patterns.

- Another healthy habit we must develop is practicing self-compassion. This merely involves treating ourselves with more kindness and generosity. Too often, we are our own worst critics, but being compassionate to yourself is a tried and tested method for improving your self-esteem, happiness, and overall health. One easy way to do this is to talk to yourself as you would to a dear friend. We are generally much more accepting of our friends' mistakes than our own, and we must extend the same courtesy to ourselves.

Summary Guide

I would be highly, greatly, amazingly grateful and appreciative if you felt like taking just 30 seconds and leaving me a review on Amazon! Reviews are incredibly important to an author's livelihood, and they are shockingly hard to come by. Strange, right?

Anyway, the more reviews my books get, the more I am actually able to continue my first love of writing. If you felt any way about this book, please leave me a review and let me know that I'm on the right track.

[CLICK HERE TO REVIEW](#)

CHAPTER 1. THAT VOICE INSIDE YOUR HEAD

- Have you ever noticed a voice inside your head that is constantly chattering about something or the other right from the moment you wake up? You might have grown so accustomed to it that you barely notice it anymore, but it's definitely there, and it's either hurting or helping you. No perspective is truly neutral. This voice, a part of your stream of consciousness, is an inner monologue that runs alongside your life, observing and commenting on its various happenings. It tells you who you are, and how you should feel about your identity and the events that occur in your life.
- There are three main types of inner voices or self-talk. The first is positive self-talk, which acts as a continuous reaffirmation of the good things about you and your life. This type of inner voice bolsters our confidence and elevates happiness levels. However, on the other end lies negative self-talk. This voice is always critical and saying degrading things to us about who we are, what we do, etc. If left uncontrolled, it can lead to several mental health issues. The third type is neutral self-talk, which simply consists of unbiased observations as we walk through life—although this almost always has a positive or negative subtext.
- Our inner voice, regardless of type, represents the inner representation we have of ourselves. Often, this is not consistent with reality. The way we think we are and what we actually are can be miles apart, but reality seldom matters if we're convinced that things are a certain way. This leads to why having healthy self-talk is so important. It influences our thoughts, perceptions, and the way we view ourselves, all of which have physiological correlations that affect how we feel and behave. The basis behind this is neuroplasticity, as the more you repeat something, the more it changes your brain's structure and becomes your reality.
- If you're wondering what exactly counts as self-talk, it includes positive or negative statements we say to ourselves, our ruminations, racing thoughts,

and the conversations we have with ourselves. Regulating this self-talk can have many positive effects that are essential to our well-being, such as improving sports performances, reducing stress, promoting better self-esteem, and helping us cope with the ups and downs of life. Monitoring self-talk is the key to changing your emotions, behavior, perspective, and life potential.

CHAPTER 2. GOOD VERSUS EVIL

- It is easy to mistake positive self-talk for being vain, narcissistic, and shallow, overloading oneself with praise—but this is far from the case. Similarly, ignoring negative self-talk does not mean blinding yourself to your faults. Improving our self-talk is aimed at being more attuned with reality in a way that is conducive to achieving the goals we desire. Often we focus on the negative much more than the positive, and this distorts the reality of a situation. By practicing more positive self-talk, we're trying to get past this bias and see things the way they are so that we can improve accordingly.
- There are many benefits of engaging in more positive self-talk. Several studies have looked into the matter and concluded that those who are more positive perform better at work and sports, are better at getting through challenging life circumstances, and have healthier relationships. Moreover, they also have a better self-image and feel good about themselves since they have a healthy sense of self.
- On the other hand, negative self-talk can be extremely damaging to our well-being. It releases cortisol in our bodies, compromising our immune function and preventing positive emotions from arising. Negative self-talk can also lead to a host of mental health issues such as depression, anxiety, panic disorders, and other undesirable outcomes like apathy, anger, self-pity, etc.
- If you're wondering where our self-talk styles originate from, the answer is a host of factors that include our parenting, socio-cultural norms, our immediate environment, biology, our own biases and beliefs, among others. Many who have experienced strict or uncompromising home environments at a young age, or have routinely had their boundaries violated, come to adopt a low self-esteem, which in turn causes negative self-talk that can be hard to get rid of.
- These factors, along with experiences like bullying and different forms of abuse, also determine our self-esteem levels, which is the main determinant of whether our self-talk is negative or positive. As we understand why exactly our self-talk is the way it is, we can start to change and improve it to suit our needs.
- We end up with five levels of self-talk, each a higher amount of acceptance and self-esteem. Indeed, it starts with purely negative, then moves to aspirational,

to positive, to a new identity, to newfound acceptance of both the negative and positive.

CHAPTER 3. ALL YOU NEED TO DO IS LISTEN

- The first step to recognizing and correcting your inner voice is to become aware of it. A powerful way to do this is through practicing mindfulness. Mindfulness is the activity wherein you train your mind to become aware of your present emotions, sensations, or experience and accept them without clouding them with any judgment.
- There are many different mindfulness activities you can follow. One of them is called the three-minute breathing space and it proceeds in three steps, as follows. First, simply take in all your thoughts and observe them without attempting to control their flow. Then, narrow your focus away from them and simply concentrate on your breathing for a minute. Lastly, expand your focus to include your body and physical sensations. Activities like these help you recognize your thoughts and move on from them without overthinking.
- As you practice mindfulness, you will become aware of some negative thinking patterns that we commonly engage in. One of them is called black and white thinking, where we mislead ourselves into looking at the world in strictly binary terms. Another is catastrophizing, which involves drawing exaggerated conclusions from comparatively minor incidents. Patterns like these distort our thinking and obscure the nature of reality.
- Journaling is a powerful tool for not only recognizing negative thought patterns, but also challenging them to come up with more rational and thought-out alternatives. Writing your thoughts makes them seem more tangible, and allows you to evaluate them better than when it's all in your head.
- However, if journaling doesn't sound suitable to you, there are other ways to assess your self-talk. Reflect on your negative thoughts and core beliefs as they come to you and compassionately, but systematically challenge them. Play the role of a lawyer and look for logical holes. Try to identify the thinking patterns that are distorting your self-talk, and work on replacing them with healthier thoughts.

CHAPTER 4. REPLACE, TRANSFORM, EVOLVE

- This chapter explores cognitive behavioral therapy (CBT) and other related techniques that can help us improve our self-talk. The whole aim of changing self-talk more or less falls under the process of CBT.
- CBT is a popular and effective therapeutic framework that emphasizes our thoughts as the key component of our feelings and behavior. The underlying

principle of its techniques is that our thoughts influence how we feel, which in turn determines the way we behave. This creates a feedback loop that ultimately influences our thoughts, and the way to improve is to get out of this vicious cycle. We must replace our negative thoughts with more positive ones, with the condition that the latter be realistic and not merely vain self-affirmations that have no backing or truth to them. The general process for our purposes is to observe, challenge, and replace negative thoughts and self-talk.

- One effective method to reduce negative self-talk is an activity called thought stopping. This involves distracting yourself from troublesome thoughts using some behavioral or mental cues, such as thinking or saying "Stop!", pinching yourself, etc. Though this technique can backfire in some cases, it has been observed to be effective in curtailing superficial but unproductive rumination.
- Besides using cues, other ways to stop negative self-talk include listening to music or podcasts that you like. This distracts you by engaging your auditory faculties. You can also use scattered counting— counting random numbers instead of proceeding linearly like in 1,2,3, and so on. The idea is to catch yourself in the process and distance yourself from unhelpful thoughts.
- If thought stopping doesn't work, you can also practice thought replacing. Here, you take a negative thought and strip it of all the components that make it unpleasant, replacing them with more positive alternatives. One way to do this is to simply think your thoughts through and assess how valid they are. If you find them to be irrational, substitute ones that make more sense to you and promote healthier emotions.

- Alternatively, you can write particular thoughts down to edit and rewrite them. Eliminate extreme words like only, never, absolutely, etc., along with any harsh descriptors like idiot, loser, ugly, and others. Also replace outright lies, unfounded assumptions, and other logical faults to improve your self-talk.

CHAPTER 5: MORE THAN WORDS

- Previously we discussed how to rewrite our internal monologue, but in this chapter we focused on all the external factors that contribute to having healthier and more positive self-talk. There are everyday practices we can do to contribute to a more positive self-image, or just snap us into sharper awareness of our beliefs and narratives.
- Starting your morning with a dose of deliberately positive self-talk sets a pleasant tone for the rest of your day. While it may feel silly to feign positivity in the beginning, this technique really does work. The more we repeat something to ourselves, the likelier we are to start believing it (remember neuroplasticity?). By repeating positive statements that represent our desired goals throughout the day, we can easily boost our confidence and self-esteem in the face of adversity.

- Having said that, we are bound to struggle in remaining positive if those around us continue to be negative and judgmental. As we practice positive self-talk, we're more likely to notice the negativities of our friends and families. In such cases, we must set good boundaries to limit our interactions with negative people in our lives, and even refrain from it altogether if required.
- Many of our habits, when cultivated properly, can help reinforce positive self-talk in our lives. For example, learning to be grateful is a great way to increase our overall happiness. Maintain a gratitude journal and update it daily with three to five things you were grateful for on that day as a way to count your blessings. Other productive habits include avoiding comparisons with others, being kind in your interactions, and avoiding overly critical thought patterns.
- Another healthy habit we must develop is practicing self-compassion. This merely involves treating ourselves with more kindness and generosity. Too often, we are our own worst critics, but being compassionate to yourself is a tried and tested method for improving your self-esteem, happiness, and overall health. One easy way to do this is to talk to yourself as you would to a dear friend. We are generally much more accepting of our friends' mistakes than our own, and we must extend the same courtesy to ourselves.

Book 4: Anti-Anxious:
How to Control Your Thoughts, Stop Overthinking, and Transform Your Mental Habits

Table of Contents

ANTI-ANXIOUS: *HOW TO CONTROL YOUR THOUGHTS, STOP OVERTHINKING, AND TRANSFORM YOUR MENTAL HABITS* BY NICK TRENTON

TABLE OF CONTENTS

CHAPTER 1: REFRAME YOUR INTERNAL DIALOGUE AND TAKE CONTROL OF YOUR SELF-TALK

PROBLEM 1: THE ALL-OR-NOTHING DISEASE
PROBLEM 2: "OUT OF POWER" LANGUAGE
WHAT TO DO ABOUT IT
HOW TO IDENTIFY YOUR COGNITIVE DISTORTIONS

CHAPTER 2: ANALYZE THYSELF: THE ABC METHOD AND THOUGHT JOURNALS

STEP 1: HOW TO KEEP A THOUGHT JOURNAL
STEP 2: RETHINK... AND REDO
DECENTER, SHIFT PERSPECTIVE, AND CREATE DISTANCE
HOW TO TAKE A STEP BACK
A WORD ON THE MOST USELESS HABIT IN THE WORLD
TRY A COGNITIVE DEFUSION EXERCISE

CHAPTER 3: MASTER THE ART OF DISTRESS TOLERANCE AND SELF-SOOTHING

HOW TO SELF-SOOTHE
TIPP SKILLS
WHAT RADICAL ACCEPTANCE REALLY MEANS
THE ACCEPTS SKILL
BRAIN DUMPING, MENTAL NOTING, AND SCHEDULED WORRY TIME

CHAPTER 4: UPGRADE YOUR PSYCHOLOGICAL TOOLKIT WITH STOIC *AMOR FATI* PHILOSOPHY

BEYOND RADICAL ACCEPTANCE: AMOR FATI
NEGATIVE VISUALIZATION
WHAT IS YOUR ORIENTATION: SOLUTION OR PROBLEM ORIENTATION? THOUGHT OR ACTION?

CHAPTER 5: AVOID THE TRAP OF TOXIC POSITIVITY AND FEEL YOUR FEELINGS

THE POSITIVE IS POWERFUL, BUT . . .
GOOD VERSUS WHOLE
LETTING GO OF TOXIC POSITIVITY
ONE UNDERAPPRECIATED WAY TO GENUINELY FEEL BETTER
EMOTIONAL REGULATION
THE LIFE CYCLE OF AN EMOTION

CHAPTER 6: BUT WHERE DOES NEGATIVE THINKING REALLY COME FROM?

YOUR NEGATIVITY MAY BE "HARDWIRED"
COUNTERING THE BIAS FOR THE NEGATIVE
RETHINK TOXIC RELATIONSHIPS—INCLUDING THE ONE YOU HAVE WITH YOURSELF

SUMMARY GUIDE

Chapter 1: Reframe Your Internal Dialogue and Take Control of Your Self-Talk

If you've picked up this book, there's a good chance that you've noticed that your own internal thought processes are . . . not what they could be. Pervasive negative thinking is the kind of problem that initially seems to fly under the radar. A person with a predisposition to interpret everything in a negative light can convince themselves for a long time that they are completely neutral and objective observers, and the negativity simply lies in what they're observing. That there seems to be an awful lot of negativity "out there" only dimly arouses their suspicion!

Pervasive negative thinking is like having a poisoned pot in your kitchen, so that everything you cook in that pot becomes poisoned, too. You think you have one problem: *Everything* you eat seems to make you sick! But in fact, you have another, perhaps more serious problem—you continue to use the poisoned pot.

If you regularly find yourself saying things like, "Everything is awful," then you can be pretty sure that you have a poisoned pot in your mental kitchen. So much personal development and self-help material out there is designed to help you fix the problems that your mind has told you are there:

How do I stop being so lazy and unmotivated?

How do I get over being so fat and out of shape?

How do I stop being such a loser?

But you can see the problem. The solution you really need is to be curious about the mindset that allows you to think that you are a fat, lazy loser in the first place!

You already know that the way you think influences how you see yourself, the world, and everyone around you. But it goes even further than this. **How you think doesn't just influence your life, it *is* your life**. If the mind is the means by which we tell our story, interpret those stories, and ascribe meaning to our experiences, then the mind is more or less in charge of all of it.

The way we think determines what we believe is possible, how we solve problems, what we can expect in the future, and how to plan for it, and therefore how we act.

The way we think tells us why our experiences happened and what they mean, and therefore our value in that story, i.e., our self-worth.

The way we think highlights certain events as all-important and allows us to forget others so that we reinforce not what is most real, but what most fits our assumptions.

The way we think even decides what enters our conscious awareness in the first place and determines which parts of the big, wide world we never even realize are right there...

So, if your thinking is heavily skewed to the negative, you have a serious problem. Humankind has long recognized the possibility of having so warped and distorted a mental filter that the person is assumed to have lost touch with reality entirely. We know that people in severe depressive episodes or those with psychosis or paranoia have not just made a misinterpretation of reality—they cannot see it at all. And yet, how many "normal" people are walking around with a head full of thoughts that are just as unconnected to reality?

If a paranoid schizophrenic says, "I'm queen of the moon and I need to find my way back there before the mole people catch me," we can easily recognize the claim for what it is—nonsense. But if a friend tells you, "I can't come with you to the speed dating thing tonight; that kind of thing just doesn't work for me. Plus, I'm too old," then you might not only take their word for it, you may even start to behave as though it's one hundred percent true! But if you look closely, this second claim has no more evidence to support it than the first. What's more, the second claim can wreak havoc just as surely as the first one can—perhaps, it can cause even more damage.

As you embark on the approaches and techniques covered in the rest of this book, you'll be trying to do something you may not have done before: **think about how you think. This is called metacognition**. Trying to change negative thinking is a peculiar task because we are attempting to change our minds... using our minds. If we bring negativity to the process, we only amplify the problem of negative self-talk rather than address it at its root. Therefore, as you read, try to bear a few things in mind:

- **You will need to think in ways you haven't thought before**. This means that the exercises will *necessarily* feel unfamiliar, awkward, uncomfortable, or even wrong. This isn't a problem or a sign that you should stop. It's only proof that you're stepping outside of your comfort zone. Always remember why they call it a comfort zone—it's comfortable. But that's about all it is! You probably agree with the advice that says, "Don't believe everything you read." In the same way, try not to "believe everything you think."
- **You are not broken or unique in your tendency to think negatively**. In fact, the preference for focusing on the negative has been hardwired into your brain over thousands of years of evolution (more on this in our final chapter). So, you don't need to feel ashamed, and you certainly don't need to feel negative about how negative you feel! Rather than dwelling on the "root

cause" or beating yourself up for not being better sooner, just get on with the business of living the life you actually do want to lead.

- **From this moment on, you will no longer take your own word for it**. In other words, you will make a deal with yourself that from now on, you will understand thoughts for what they are: *thoughts*. Not reality, not truth, not fate or destiny. Just thoughts. Just electrochemical activity in your brain. Be careful, though. This doesn't mean you should become a total skeptic. Don't accept everything that pops into your brain, but at the same time don't dismiss it either—rather, withhold judgment entirely. Be neutral. First, don't react.
- **Finally, at no point in the chapters that follow are you required to be relentlessly "optimistic."** Changing the way you think is not about self-deception, denial, or believing comfortable lies. To say it another way, being a negative thinker is not the same as being more intelligent, more realistic, or more pragmatic. And really, it's about the *quality* of your thinking processes, not the *content*. Some of those relentlessly "positive" people out there have more cognitive distortions than anyone else!

We will explore each of the ideas above in more detail as we go along, but for now, it's enough to simply be aware of one thing: Our ability to genuinely change our thought patterns is not some superhuman ability reserved for just a few people. It rests on two things:

1. honest awareness, and
2. a willingness to take conscious and inspired action.

That's all. Just those two things. That means that no matter how negative your thought patterns currently are, and no matter how trapped and frustrated you currently feel, it IS possible to change. In fact, by beginning this book, you have already made the first small step in the right direction. Well done!

Problem 1: The All-or-Nothing Disease

Your brain is great at what it does. Its job is to make the world navigable for you—it creates shortcuts, rules ("heuristics"), and predictions so that you can make sense of the events unfolding around you. Your ancestors survived precisely because they were able to do this and, putting it bluntly, make sweeping generalizations and apply stereotypes. And you do it too.

Let's say one day you try Nepalese cuisine and find it absolutely disgusting. You make a conclusion: "I don't like Nepalese food." This conclusion prevents you from repeating the unpleasant experience, and, at least from a neurological perspective, you can be said to have *learned* and expanded your experience of the world. However, there's one inconvenient problem: Your conclusion isn't *true*.

Our mental shortcuts, assumptions, biases and stereotypes are great at saving time and effort but are not one hundred percent accurate one hundred percent of the time. When we take a single experience and extrapolate our conclusions to apply to other experiences we haven't actually had yet, we gain a sense of control and mastery over the situation... but at the risk of losing accuracy and nuance. Our world becomes more manageable, but that's because it becomes smaller. So, the truth may be that you only dislike around sixty percent of the most common Nepalese dishes, but you've rounded this up to "all Nepalese food" and carried on with life, none the wiser that you've oversimplified reality in this way.

Whenever you use the following words, **oversimplifying reality** is exactly what you're doing:

Never

Always

All

None

Forever

Never

To counter all-too-common black-or-white thinking, people are told to drop these words from their vocabulary. This is a good start, but **it's not the words you need to be on guard for, but the sentiment behind them**. *Any time we overextrapolate from one experience to other experiences we haven't had*, we are making an error.

Thinking in extremes is a problem because it's inaccurate, yes, but the bigger problem is that you are living as though it is true. And this goes far beyond what words you use or don't use.

For example, Jenna finds socializing difficult and is having trouble making friends in a new city. After a few weeks of trying unsuccessfully to join Meetup groups or connect with people at her gym or church, she says the following to a friend back in her hometown: "You know how it is. It's harder to make friends in your thirties, especially if you don't have kids. People just don't have time to socialize. Everyone stays in their own little clique and it's impossible to get to know them." Jenna's friend agrees instantly. Wouldn't you?

The trouble is, although Jenna hasn't used the words "never," "all," or "always," she is still extrapolating to an enormous degree:

Step 1: My current experience is XYZ.

Step 2: Therefore, XYZ is the way it is for *all* people, in *all* times, and will forever be.

Jenna could have said, "I'm having a little difficulty these first few weeks trying to meet people," or "I haven't really connected with anyone at the gym yet." Instead, she concocts a broad theory about all people everywhere. In fact, she makes a pronouncement so grand and all-encompassing that it seems to speak to the human condition as a whole. *People just don't make friends in their thirties.* Can you see how she makes this statement as though it were as naturally obvious and true as the law of gravity?

It **isn't** a natural law. But what Jenna has done is created a world in which it is. Then she lives in that world. She behaves as though it were true. Without even knowing it, she begins to lessen the effort she makes to meet people. She goes through all the motions, but at the back of her mind is this little theory of human nature that she has created, which says, "People aren't *really* interested; you cannot join their little clique, as hard as you try." So, she tries, but not really, and it doesn't go anywhere. People don't respond to her lukewarm efforts, and this reflects her own ambivalence.

Et voila—Jenna finds herself living in a world that looks suspiciously like how she said it would look. This is the natural result of thinking in extremes, using all-or-nothing language, and making grand theories off the back of one or two personal experiences: a self-fulfilling prophecy. When we talk about the world as though it's either black or white, all or nothing, perfect or abysmal . . . then that is precisely the way it becomes.

One final point you might not have considered: other people are usually more than happy to go along with whatever conclusions you've made about life or yourself, and *help you make that true*. Imagine that a friend of Jenna's has been listening to her complain about how difficult it is to meet people in your thirties. One day, Jenna's friend finds an interesting article in the paper about how isolated childfree women can feel. The friend actually doesn't agree with the article, nor care, but she thinks, "You know who will like this? Jenna." She shares the article with Jenna, who reads it and becomes even further entrenched in her narrative, which is quickly cementing itself in her mind.

Can you see what's happened? Jenna's friend, trying to be helpful, is rushing in to confirm and reiterate the (faulty) belief she knows Jenna already has. It is as though Jenna is slowly creating a "filter bubble" around herself, and reality's "search algorithms" keep supplying her with the kind of content she keeps seeking out! Consider that people in your world are doing this too, consciously or unconsciously, all the time. This is the power of a thought pattern—it can be so effective at creating reality that it can even extend to other people. Your environment cannot help but respond to your thought processes—what beliefs is it amplifying?

Problem 2: "Out of Power" Language

Let's stay with Jenna's example, in particular her claim that, "Everyone stays in their own little clique and it's impossible to get to know them." You have probably heard people say things like this before—or maybe you say them yourself! Things like this:

"Look, I'll give it a try, but you know how these things go."
"It's always such drama trying to get a straight answer out of these people . . ."
"Well, I've come down with the flu, so the whole week's a write-off."

Let's be honest. We live in a world that can be incredibly difficult and trying. There's a lot going on out there, and with a twenty-four-hour news cycle hellbent on reminding everyone of the near-constant catastrophes unfolding all around us, it's no surprise that most people's default setting is a mild (or not-so-mild) pessimism.

But words have power. When you speak, you are not only saying, "This is how the world is," to those around you, you are saying it *yourself*. "This is the way I am."

When Jenna says, "Everyone stays in their own little clique and it's impossible to get to know them," she is actually saying a lot more. She is saying:

The situation cannot be changed, i.e., it's hopeless.
She doesn't have any real control over how it plays out, or any agency to change the outcome.
This is true not just for some people, but for all people, including those she hasn't met yet.
Life is largely determined by other people's choices, not her own.
The entire friends-making endeavor is, at its core, a negative experience.

Pretty heavy, huh? Jenna takes all this and carries it with her to every single Meetup and get-together. It impacts her ability to perceive whether people are being kind and friendly to her or not. It changes the way she responds to rejection—or imagined rejection. It alters how she thinks of other people (self-absorbed, kind of mean) and herself (an outsider, passive). In fact, Jenna echoes this very sentiment to someone new she meets at gym one day. "Oh my gosh, it's so nice to finally meet someone *cool*! People in this town can be a little uptight, don't you find?"

Very subtly, she tells the other person exactly what her world is like. Without knowing it, and perhaps without the other person knowing it either, that feeling of hopelessness, negativity, and passivity is quietly shaping her world, and not in good ways. Jenna wants to communicate, "I'm having a hard time meeting people at the moment," and instead communicates, "People don't meet my standards. I'm subtly judging them for not including me." If you were the person in the gym, which attitude would *you* find more attractive and appealing?

Any time we use **"out of power" language, i.e., language that is passive, self-victimizing, doubtful, angry, unconfident, fearful, excuse-making, or pessimistic, we send out powerful messages to ourselves and others. And these messages come back to us**—we can see our attitude reflected to us in the way we feel about ourselves, the way people respond to us, and the way our life is unfolding in general. If all we see and experience is negative, there's a good chance that *we* are the likely common denominator (remember the poisoned pot?).

Habits of speech reflect thought patterns, but in time, they become our choices and actions, and these change and shape our world so that it literally conforms to the thoughts we have about it. This is powerful stuff. Like a sculptor who creates a statue with each scrape of the chisel, you are bit by bit creating your own reality with every word, thought, and action. Luckily for us, though, destructive habits can be identified and replaced.

Try it yourself right now.

It's easy to see the principle in hypothetical Jenna's life—but what does it look like in *yours*? There's a good chance you don't even know. The most damaging and stubborn thought patterns are those that we're not aware of. That means our first task is to become aware of them! You can't look inside your head. But what you can do is monitor your language and infer the contents of your head.

Your **verbal habits** will tell you everything you need to know. <u>For the next twenty-four hours, commit to (neutrally!) observing the language you use to talk to and about yourself.</u> Like a scientist, just gather data for twenty-four hours and refrain from interpreting or judging it. Notice the words you use, the way you frame things, and the things you *don't* say. Notice the images you use, the subject and object, and, yes, the content, too. Note any assumptions and guesses. What patterns keep appearing?

What to Do about It

Earlier we said that the only things you need to combat negative thinking (or any bad habit) is honest awareness and the willingness to take action—in that order. We will consider many ways to approach both these tasks in later chapters. But for now, see if you can note down in a journal the various verbal habits you've noticed in yourself. Once you do, you can start to gently take action in a different direction.

Everything that is passive is reframed to emphasize your agency and conscious choice. Everything that is imprecise or inaccurate is made specific and realistic. Everything that radiates an energy of hopelessness is replaced with an attitude of mastery, self-command, and purpose. Here's how.

1. "Reframe forward"

It's a question of focus. You could talk about what you can't, won't, or don't do, but why not focus instead on what you *can*? You could choose to talk about what isn't working or what you don't like, but why not choose to talk instead about what you love, what excites you, or what you want to create and build?

"I'm an introvert. I hate big crowds," becomes, "I really love one-on-one conversations."

The first is closed, static, and negative; the second is open, alive, and dynamic.

2. Embrace shades of gray

To combat overextrapolating and the all-or-nothing disease, get comfortable with nuance, ambiguity, and degree. Be willing to accept that you are seldom in a position, existentially, to make any all-encompassing statements about the nature of reality.

Instead, just be curious and open-ended. This will allow you to take a peek into the "other side" and see what's there . . .

"All the good men are taken," becomes, "I wonder where all the single guys hang out?" "If a woman hasn't gotten married by forty, it's a red flag, beware!" becomes, "I wonder what kind of person she is and what she cares about."

    3.   Talk to yourself like you talk to a loved one

Negative self-talk can naturally lead to low self-confidence. Your inner critic is simply the voice of negativity directed at *you* as a person. It's no different from physical self-harm, though. Most of us wouldn't dream of insulting our friends, family, or colleagues, yet we readily do it to ourselves daily. It's one thing to pause and consider if the thought you've just had is accurate, useful, or true. But sometimes, the harm of a thought lies in its *tone*.

Check yourself by **asking if you'd say the same thing to someone you love or even just care about. No? Then don't say it to yourself.** It's not about *what* you say but *how* you say it. If it's rude to deliberately hurt another person's feelings, it's just as bad to hurt your own. Another alternative is to imagine that you're speaking to a little child, or the five-year-old version of yourself. If it seems totally cruel to say to a young, innocent child, then isn't it also cruel to say to yourself?

"You're a nasty fat pig and nobody will love you unless you sort it out already," becomes, "you are overweight, but you're still loved and you deserve support and kindness while you try your best to be better. And you're making real progress every day. Well done!"

Note that framing things in kind, gentle terms doesn't mean lying or ignoring the truth. Many people are suspicious of reframing their thoughts with more kindness because in the past, they have associated "kindness" with "fakeness." It isn't! Rather, it means talking about the truth *with love*.

So, once you've gathered twenty-four hours of data and gained a glimpse into your unique style of talking to yourself, pick a single idea or theme from that data and try to apply the above three approaches. For example:

Recurrent thought: *I hate this job, but I'm stuck doing it if I want to keep paying this stupid mortgage!*

Alternative thought: *It's true that this job isn't a breeze all the time, but I choose to do it because it allows me to pay for a home I love. I'm talented and hardworking, though, so I can always choose to do something else.*

This alternative is "reframed forward" (all about conscious choice and agency: you are not stuck; you love your home), phrased in less absolute terms (the job is difficult, but only some of the time) and with more kindness (focusing on strengths and possibilities). Now you try it!

How to Identify Your Cognitive Distortions

So far, we've spoken of "negative thinking" as though it's all one solid, indistinguishable mass. In the novel *Anna Karenina*, Tolstoy begins with the line: "Happy families are all alike; each unhappy family is unhappy in its own way." It's arguably the same with thought patterns—positivity tends to manifest in a uform way, whereas there seem to be about a million ways for thoughts to be "negative"!

In the last chapter, you monitored your thought processes for just one day and worked on reframing a single thought or idea that stood out to you. In this chapter, we'll continue on this path and take a closer look at some of the kinds of negativity we're likely to encounter when we pay attention to our "thought traffic." In other words, if negativity is a distortion of reality, then this distortion can manifest in several different forms. Learn to identify these forms, and you'll become better at spotting distortions rather than being taken in by them.

A cognitive distortion is an incorrect belief, perception, or thought.

Of course, nobody is perfect and infallible, and we're all wrong sometimes, but *persistently* distorted cognition is a problem—and it's about a lot more than simply being "right" or "wrong." Where do these distortions come from? For the time being, assume that every mental twist and warp served a purpose at one time. Typically, distortions help us overcome trauma or loss in the past—however, if they continue long after the threat has passed, they tend to undermine rather than protect us.

Crucially, it does not really matter where these distortions come from. Trying to analyze *why* you think the way you do is a little like being shot with an arrow and then sitting down, in agony, wondering which direction the arrow came from and who shot it and why. There's no need! Just pull the arrow out, and you will instantly feel better. This is why, in this book, we won't spend too much time delving into the past, because, after all, that's not where the trouble is. What matters is how you think here and now. Why a belief started is less important than how you're *sustaining* it right now.

We've already explored one major and very common distortion: **all-or-nothing thinking**. This is when we overextrapolate and break the complex world down into two either/or polar extremes and force ourselves to pick one of them (a decision we don't notice that we *ourselves* have insisted on). This kind of distortion is characterized (but not *always*—ha!) by absolutist terms like *always*, *never*, *everyone*, *none*, etc.

"If you don't agree with me, then you're part of the problem."

"If I don't get into college, my life is ruined."

Or, for that matter: "Either I think positively, or I think negatively."

Let's look at some more distortions you may uncover as you gain awareness.

Mental Filtering
This is basically like having a sieve in your head that only allows you to perceive and engage with certain data, while whatever doesn't "fit" is allowed to pass right through

as though it doesn't exist. Once you're done filtering, the only things left in the sieve are those things that align with the preconceived worldview you started with.

Consider the example of Carrie, who has a severely distorted idea of what she looks like (sadly, all too common in a world that stands to gain by her insecurities). Carrie goes out shopping for clothing one day and enters the changing rooms of several different stores. Three of the four mirrors reflect a fairly flattering image, while the final place she visits is a store with extremely poor light.

Carrie gets home after the shopping trip and says, "Well, that was a waste of time! I don't know why I thought I'd find anything that looks half decent on me . . ." She completely forgets about the three flattering changing rooms and only remembers the one where she *didn't* look good. Her mental sieve is shaped in such a way as to catch and collect all those experiences that align with the conclusion she has already come to about herself—she is unattractive—and completely disregards anything that challenges this conclusion.

In Carrie's world, it's as though those flattering reflections never even existed. If a friend points this out, she might reply, "Yeah, sure, but those mirrors artificially make people look better so you buy their clothes!" In other words, Carrie's distortion is this: Only the negative is true or to be focused on; the positive is insignificant or an illusion. This is connected to another distortion that's called "disqualifying the positive." Here, we may be aware of data that doesn't fit the preconceived idea, but we make up some story about why that data doesn't matter.

"Oh, it was just a lucky break/beginner's luck."

"The ten times I've succeeded so far were just a fluke; this most recent time that I failed was the real deal. That was all me."

"People don't mean it. They're being polite/kind/their opinions don't count."

If Carrie's friend says, "You forgot about all those lovely dresses we tried on earlier and how nice you looked in them!" Carrie might say, "Well, you would say that because you're sweet and you're my friend." In fact, Carrie might go as far as to find something negative *in* the positive, secretly thinking, "I bet she pities me and is just trying to make me feel better by pretending I look better than I do. It must be even worse than I thought!"

Later in this book, we'll look at how Carrie's tendency, although extreme, is actually a fairly common phenomenon called "negativity bias," which has evolutionary roots.

Personalization

Mental shortcuts and biases exist because the brain is trying to explain to itself *why* something happens, and to make sense of events. Call it an existential self-centeredness, but human beings can sometimes imagine that random things have more to do with them personally than they actually do. In the realm of negative thinking, this can look like assuming that anything negative must be somehow your fault or reflect poorly on you.

While filtering can make you zoom in on the negative or imagine that it's there when it isn't, personalization is where **you perceive a genuine negative but incorrectly ascribe its cause or source as yourself**. It's as though you say, "There's a bad thing over there, and I'm a bad thing over here . . . so we must belong together somehow."

One day, Carrie goes to a friend's wedding and is obsessing all morning about whether the outfit she has chosen looks okay. When she gets to the event, the friend is hurried and busy and says in a lighthearted way, "Well, we haven't had any disasters yet, but let's just say not everybody seems to know what *semi-formal* means these days, if you know what I mean . . ."

Carrie immediately thinks that this comment is aimed at her and that her friend is implying that she isn't dressed properly. In other words, she has correctly noticed the stress and fluster of her friend, but has incorrectly ascribed the cause to herself, passing it again through the same filter, which only ever allows one conclusion: You look awful. Similarly, when Carrie's boyfriend cheats on her later that year, she doesn't skip a beat before concluding that he has done so because the other woman was better looking.

(In case you're wondering, the personalization bias can go the other way, where we find ourselves taking credit for things that have nothing to do with us, but this is usually less common! The most common and subtle way to personalize neutral stimuli is simply to assume that we're the center of the universe, and to find ways to refer every external event back to ourselves. We tend to do this in a way that confirms our other existing biases. So, for example, someone might tell Carrie they're feeling depressed, and Carrie might assume, "They probably hate the way they look.")

Jumping to Conclusions and Mind-Reading
Closely related to the above distortion is the tendency to **make assumptions about other people's intentions and motivations, in the absence of any evidence**. Carrie automatically assumes that she is the only one at the wedding that the friend could possibly be referring to, and also assumes that her own mental filter exists in her boyfriend's head, too, who couldn't think anything else but, "Carrie is unattractive." **Mindreading is unconsciously filling in the blanks and assuming that others' thought processes must broadly be in alignment with our own.** This is easy to do when you consider how infrequently we stop to actually communicate and check what people really are thinking!

In fact, rather than thinking about the situation from many perspectives, Carrie weaves an elaborate tale in her head about his cheating: He finds her unattractive and always has, and as soon as someone better looking came along, he went for her . . . and who can blame him? In assuming that his cheating is purely to do with her, Carrie is not just personalizing but mindreading. Without having a stitch of evidence, she "knows" that he thinks this. Her distortion blinds her to a more likely interpretation: Her boyfriend cheated because he's a dishonest and disloyal person. Or he's immature and made a foolish mistake. Or, just maybe, he himself has no idea why he acted as he did . . .

Catastrophizing

Also known as magnification or minimization, depending on which direction your distortion wants to go! Basically, this is **the tendency to exaggerate**. Carrie never says she's *plain* or *average looking* but full-on *hideous*. She's not just unattractive, but the most unattractive person who ever lived. And the fact that she's hideous also implies the worst possible outcome, namely that nobody will ever love her and that she's doomed to an ugly, lonely life where small children burst into tears upon seeing her in the street.

Minimization can be just as distorting as magnification, though. Carrie could spend an hour getting ready one morning, doing her hair, fixing her makeup, and dressing in beautiful clothing, only to announce at the end of it, "It makes zero difference; I still look the same."

Negative thinkers tend to exaggerate the size of a threat while, at the same time, downplaying their own resilience, their resources, their strength, and their ability to cope with that threat, real or imagined. The negative gets amplified and carried to extremes, while the glimmer of hope is reduced to nothing.

Carrie sits alone one evening and imagines that her life is over. The negativity around her appearance has become so all-encompassing that it takes on the feeling of a catastrophe. It doesn't matter that she has a fascinating job, lots of caring friends, a happy family, and countless talents and interests. The perceived faults in her appearance are magnified so much that they eclipse all these things and reduce them to insignificance while she sits to the side, completely powerless to stop any of it.

"Shoulds" and Labels

Here's where it gets interesting for Carrie. When she starts becoming more aware of her own thought patterns and habitual negativity, she realizes that much of her perception comes from comparing herself against an idea of what she *should* look like. Her hair is wavy and fluffy—but it should be straight and silky. She is on the taller side, but she *should* be more petite. Her eyes are black when they *should* be blue or green or at least hazel.

Now, this book is not about to ask where Carrie got all these expectations from (although most of us can probably guess). Instead, it's about the fact that comparison against some real or imaginary standard is so often the source of negativity. Many of us are perfectly happy with our lot . . . right up until we start to see how we measure up against everyone else. Only then do we feel a lack.

Closely related to this is the idea of labels. We can think of labels as a whole collection of "shoulds" that have coalesced into one. The label "beautiful woman" is then a checklist of shoulds. A beautiful woman must be X, she must be Y, and she must be Z. This is not reality, however, but an arbitrary rule we create about reality . . . and then we suffer because we don't align with that rule. If you doubt this, consider how all the women with straight hair would love to have curls, and all the women with curly hair would love for it to be straight!

If Carrie's example seems superficial to you, then consider something a little more serious. Imagine that Carrie's friends are all intelligent, successful, and independent young women who are more than aware of the burden of beauty standards and the effect they have on mental health. One day, she opens up and says that she has always hated her appearance and wishes more than anything that she could look like those beautiful women she sees in social media.

How do these friends respond? They dismiss it. "You should love yourself! You shouldn't pay attention to that garbage, and anyway, physical appearances don't matter. People should value one another for what's on the inside." Sounds nice. But it's also a kind of cognitive distortion. Clearly, appearances *do* matter. Instead of making Carrie feel better, this is the kind of thing that's likely to make her feel worse—not only is she now unhappy about her appearance because she *should* look prettier, she's now also unhappy about her own unhappiness because she *should* be confident and self-accepting enough not to care . . .

Comparing against some assumed normal or correct standard is a little like arguing with reality. Sometimes, we put ourselves in the role of CEO of the universe, there to unilaterally decide what happens and when, putting labels on things according to our own (flawed) understanding. So we say things like, "A beautiful woman is supposed to be dainty and small," or, "A confident woman shouldn't have those kinds of insecurities." *Says who?* When you say "should," then what usually follows is a judgment—usually not in your favor!

As you can see, a really juicy cognitive distortion doesn't limit itself—it can be all of the above and more! Carrie's distortions are a complex cocktail of a range of different biases and assumptions. But each of them is working in the same way, reinforcing a negative worldview and completely destroying the chance of arriving at a more realistic, healthy one.

But consider this: What would happen if Carrie's mind wasn't working so hard to undermine her at every turn? What if instead, its powers of critical thinking, conscious awareness, and intelligent choice let her live a completely different kind of life? Once you've identified your cognitive distortions and seen all the many ways they can show up in your stream of self-talk, then you're going to naturally start wondering . . . what does life look like *without* all these distortions?

How to Challenge Your Inner Critic

You don't need a formal introduction to your inner critic—you are well acquainted and have probably heard from it several times already today! This is the "voice" inside that criticizes, judges, and condemns. Your anti-cheerleader.

"You're doing it wrong."
"That's nowhere near good enough."

"Everyone's talking about you."
"You may as well just give up."
"Who do you think you are?"

We've looked at a few ways to reframe your perspective, embrace shades of gray, and adjust how you speak to yourself so it's closer to how you'd speak to a loved one. But a funny thing happens once you start paying attention to your inner critic—it starts to feel like it's *everywhere*! Now what?

Step 1: See thoughts as thoughts

This is the most important step. When your inner critic says, "This is hopeless," you hear it, but you can say to yourself, "My inner critic is telling me that it's hopeless." Big difference. Your negative self-talk is not reality. Simply remind yourself of this and you've drastically reduced its power over you. Your thoughts are just thoughts. They come; they go.

Step 2: Gain distance

Make it really obvious to your brain that these are thoughts and that they are separate from reality and from who you really are at your core. Give your inner critic a name. Maybe imagine that it's literally an annoying little bug standing in the corner, trying to get a rise out of you. There's an enormous shift in perspective when you go from, "Everything is hopeless and terrible," to, "Look at that, here's the Depression Fairy again coming to visit. Hey, Mildred, how are you doing?"

Step 3: Be compassionate

One temptation is to rail against the inner critic when you find it. You might want to argue viciously against it or perhaps feel shame that it's there at all. Resist this temptation. Instead, treat the inner critic with civility, attention, and kindness. Imagine yourself pulling up a chair at the table and feeding your inner critic a meal just the same as you would your inner defender. When we are compassionate, we normalize negativity and take away its sting. "You're feeling sad right now. That's okay. You do feel sad sometimes, but you've also had lots of joyful experiences, too."

Step 4: Do nothing

Yes, really! This one is easy—refuse to act while guided by your inner critic. It can be a passenger in the car, but it certainly doesn't get to drive! We can't always help how we feel, but we *can* make conscious choices about how we act and what we say. Own that power. Refuse to act from your inner critic—act instead from that part of you that is aware, healthy, and realistic. "Yes, Mildred, I know you want to pick a fight right now, but instead, we're going for a walk!"

What Positive Self-Talk Actually Looks Like

Positive self-talk is not just the absence of negative distortions. It has its own quality and character, and you'll know what these are by the way you feel when you talk to yourself in this way: calm, hopeful, curious, grateful, stable, confident.

Positive self-talk doesn't mean we are constantly giving ourselves an over-the-top pep talk about how utterly fabulous we are—this is, after all, just another distortion. Rather, there is a kind of **dignified willingness to face reality as it is, and the confidence that comes with owning your free will and acting in ways that align with your values.**

So, when something unexpected and unpleasant crops up, you think, "Huh, look at that! This is going to be challenging, but I wonder how I can get around it? I'm not sure yet, but I'll find a way." When something new and promising pops up, you look it square in the eye and say, "Wow, I never thought about this before—let's follow it and see what happens!"

Positive thinking is not just *content*—it's *feeling*. As you get into the habit of pausing to notice what's in your head, don't just look at the concepts; look at your attitude and emotional state. This will also help you avoid the common pitfall of "toxic positivity"—approaching your positive self-talk from a place of anxiety, self-hate, and avoidance!

In your comfort zone is the way you've tended to always think, and outside of it is the way you could think—a potentially better way. Separating the two is a line, which at some point, if you want to evolve, you have to cross. If you've been a negative thinker for a long time, your automatic response to everything we've explored so far might be, "Sounds fine, but that will never work for me," or, "That's too simple; the real world is a lot more complicated!"

The thing is, before we go any further, be aware that at some point, **you have to take a leap of faith and cross that line—even if you don't have evidence yet that it will work.** All the positive affirmations and mindfulness exercises in the world will do nothing if you're making the unconscious decision to never cross that line.

<u>Before we move to the next chapter, challenge yourself to one final exercise.</u>

For the next twenty-four hours, *act as if* you are a person who thinks positively all the time. It doesn't matter if you believe it or not yet, just try it out and, for twenty-four hours only, let go of any doubts and suspicions. Bring a sense of humor to it, if you want to. Then, at the end of the twenty-four hours, pay attention to how you feel.

Once you can actually **feel for yourself**, in your own experience, the power of positive thinking, you will no longer be engaging with the techniques and exercises on a purely superficial level. You will no longer be satisfied with staying on this side of the line, only peeking over to the other side without ever taking the leap.

Summary

- How you think creates your life; negativity poisons everything in your world.
- Changing negativity requires a degree of metacognition (thinking about thinking) and a leap of faith to do something that hasn't been done before. Anyone can change their thought patterns; it requires only honest awareness and a willingness to take conscious and inspired action.
- Our mental shortcuts, assumptions, biases, and stereotypes are great at saving time and effort, but are not one hundred percent accurate one hundred percent of the time. The "all-or-nothing" disease is when we overextrapolate from one experience to other experiences we haven't had; we are making an error.
- Words have power, and our speech reflects our thought patterns. "Out of power" language is passive, self-victimizing, doubtful, angry, unconfident, fearful, excuse-making, or pessimistic, and can create a self-fulfilling prophesy.
- Become aware of your internal verbal habits. Then focus on what can be done, embrace nuance and shades of gray, and speak to yourself like you would a loved one.
- A cognitive distortion is a persistently incorrect belief, perception, or thought—for example, mental filtering, personalization, jumping to conclusions, mind-reading, catastrophizing, and using "should" statements and labels.
- Positive thinking is not just the absence of distortions, but thinking that helps you feel calm, hopeful, curious, grateful, stable, and confident.
- To challenge your inner critic, commit to not allowing your thoughts to dominate you. Gain psychological distance by labeling the thoughts as thoughts, not reality, and have self-compassion.
- Change happens outside your comfort zone, so realize that at some point, you'll need to take the leap and try something new.

Chapter 2: Analyze Thyself: the ABC Method and Thought Journals

We've explored the idea of reframing thoughts, and began to identify cognitive distortions as well as gently challenge them as they emerge. It's important that we have these fundamental paradigm shifts in place *first*; otherwise, we will merely be working **within** our negative mindset, not working **on** our negative mindset. As Einstein famously said, "We can't solve problems by using the same kind of thinking we used when we created them."

In this chapter, we'll look more closely at a concrete technique for **slowing right down and rewriting the very programming that our negative thinking runs on.**

But first, let's look at the insights gathered by the founder of cognitive behavioral therapy (CBT), Albert Ellis. In his work, he couldn't help but notice that different people seemed to respond very differently to similar events. Why? The events themselves didn't explain the difference—it must be the thoughts, feelings, and beliefs of the people who were *interpreting* these events. Over the years, Ellis came to the same conclusion that Shakespeare arguably did in *Hamlet* when he said, **"There is nothing either good or bad, but thinking makes it so."**

Thoughts, feelings, and actions are all connected and work together to create your response to external events. The ABC method, inspired by this understanding, helps us tease apart the different elements:

A is for activating event. This is neutral in the sense that it only takes on meaning and value according to our response to it.

B is for beliefs. How we respond internally to the event.

C is for consequence.

Importantly, the outcome (consequence) is not a direct result of the event, but of our *interpretation* of the event. The event is always neutral. You can see where this is going: If we want to change our lives, we shouldn't start with A, the external events, but B, how we think about the events these events come from.

The way that each of us responds to Event A is wholly a matter of conditioned response and association. To put it simply, we've *learned* to respond to activating events in very particular ways. Again, these associations are neutral. It's the resulting consequences that make the difference. If we find that our conditioned responses are continually undermining our effectiveness and wellbeing, then we can take action to adjust things—noting, of course, that the adjustment has to happen with the relationship between A and B, and not at C, which is really just a symptom of our conditioning and not the problem itself.

In CBT, the goal is to make adaptive changes, so two new letters are added:

D is for disputation. This is where we challenge the ideas in B.

E is for new effect. Something different to replace the old C.

Let's look at an example. Dan has always loved motorcycles and owns several. One fateful day, he is out riding at night and has an accident: He collides with a car, severely injuring the mother and daughter inside, totaling his favorite bike and leaving him with spinal damage that means that he will not ride a bike again for years—if ever. That's one big, gnarly activating event!

Believe it or not, Ellis would say that this event, tragic as it appears, is neutral and has no meaning by itself. But Dan is right there and responding instantly: He is completely destroyed with guilt and remorse. He calls it a tragedy. His world is so shaken by the event that he considers it a pivotal moment—before the accident, he was happy, carefree, and innocent. After it, he was a condemned man, miserable, doomed to carry the remorse of the damage he'd caused—not to mention the physical pain from his own significant injuries.

Dan refuses to forgive himself. Despite being forgiven by the mother and the daughter in the car, and despite everyone around him telling him that it was an accident and not his fault, Dan is eaten up with shame and the deep wish to turn back time. He falls into a depression and, perhaps unconsciously, starts to punish himself. He withdraws socially and stops taking care of himself. A pattern of self-defeating, negative thinking seeps into his world.

Here's how the ABC method applies to Dan:

A – The activating event is the accident.

B – There are many beliefs here, but the big one is, "I am guilty. I'm a bad, bad person."

C – The consequences are obvious. Dan spirals into depression and self-loathing, unable to forgive himself or move on.

Now, the ABC part of the model is a roadmap to help explain the relationship between thoughts, feelings, and behavior. But it's only when Dan seeks therapy with a CBT psychologist that he is asked to add on the other two letters and work through this dynamic so it can be transformed.

Filled with grief and distress, Dan enters therapy and wants to talk about the details of the gruesome accident. The therapist listens, but he is not interested so much in the details of the story as he is in the meaning underneath them—he listens for the *beliefs* that inform the way Dan talks about his experience. Dan uses plenty of cognitive distortions (catastrophizing, "should" statements, and a heaping dose of personalization), but the therapist doesn't engage with these—instead, he becomes curious about the core beliefs that these distortions are serving.

They work together, and Dan becomes aware of the story he is telling himself about the event. Simply realizing he is telling a story in the first place allows him to gain some distance and perspective (more on this in the next section). The therapist starts to gently challenge Dan—**is there possibly a different way of looking at the whole thing?** Seeing clearly how the current story is damaging his life, Dan agrees he has nothing to lose and that he will try out a different perspective:

"It was a sad and regrettable accident, but I did not do it on purpose. It's true that I am responsible for the pain caused, but I never intended to hurt anyone, and that means that I am *not* a bad person, but just a person who made a mistake. Carrying shame and guilt doesn't serve anyone, including me. It's okay that I have found this difficult, but I can also give myself permission to move on now and live my life again."

So, is that the "right" story? Maybe. Dan could also tell another one:

"The day of the accident was the worst day of my life. But despite all the pain, I am grateful it happened because it taught me something precious: to never take anything for granted, to live while I can, and to appreciate every moment I have. That means going out there and living life in the best way I possibly can so that when it's my time to die, I know I've lived well and will not be filled with regret."

Completely different story. In fact, there are probably an infinite number of stories to tell about this event. None of them are right or wrong. However, all of them will lead to particular consequences. Are those consequences in line with a happy, healthy life that we want to create for ourselves? *That's* how we tell if a story is one we want to adopt.

Often, CBT is simply presented as a way to make simple and superficial tweaks to single sentences—for example, instead of saying, "This is hard; I can't do it," you say, "This is challenging, but I'll try my best." Make no mistake, this sort of alteration *is* incredibly helpful. It's just that, in real life, you've probably noticed that your problems tend to take the form of stories rather than simple, discrete statements.

You can use the principles of CBT in your own life. By using a "thought journal," you can carefully work through the three elements (event, belief, and consequence) and start to replace destructive or unhelpful beliefs with better ones. Before we look at that, though, here's a note on what "better" looks like when it comes to thoughts.

No, they don't have to be relentlessly "positive." But a good replacement will be:

- **Accurate** – it is a close reflection of external reality
- **Helpful** – it actually assists you in achieving what you want in your life

- **Congruent** – it aligns with who you are and the values and principles you hold dear. It goes without saying, but the thoughts you use to replace unhelpful ones shouldn't be simply copied and pasted from someone else's life—they have to genuinely mean something to *you*.

Being your own CBT therapist is a little like applying the Find and Replace function on Microsoft Word. There are two parts. First, observe and identify your thoughts. Second, rewrite these beliefs and allow the change in perception to filter through to your actions and behaviors in the external world. Then, take note of the results, adjust, and repeat!

One warning: try to remember that you are not psychoanalyzing yourself. If Dan started to unpick his childhood and unravel his relationship with his mother and came to some lofty and complicated ideas about how the motorcycle is really a phallic symbol representing his masculine id, and how the accident was really a manifestation of his repressed rage and an unconscious ploy to castrate his father, who was simultaneously cruel but masochistic . . . then this is just another story. A weird one.

At best it's a distraction from real improvement; at worst it might more deeply embed certain harmful beliefs into Dan's mind. Remember that your task is not forensic and is not based in the past. You are not required to construct an interesting-sounding theory about why things have happened as they have. Instead, just keep focused on the response you are having to neutral stimuli.

What are the consequences? What can you change to arrive at consequences you like more? That's all there is to it.

Step 1: How to Keep a Thought Journal

This is not a conventional journal in the sense that you simply sit down and write whatever comes to you. While doing so has some therapeutic value, you'll want to be a little more focused and deliberate when keeping a thought journal. You're trying to understand:

What are the main events that have occurred in my life?

What are the beliefs I hold about these events?

What are the emotions that result from thinking this way?

How do I act and behave because I hold this belief?

A thought journal can be used in a non-directed way if you merely want to gain some self-knowledge, but it's best used when there is a particular problem you're working through. Sit down when you won't be disturbed, and give yourself five or ten minutes to just explore how you think and feel. Put it all down on paper—it doesn't have to be perfect or make sense. Hold it all loosely and don't try to interpret anything just yet. After the time is up, you may choose to take a little break before looking at it again.

When you look again, you may notice some patterns and themes emerging. Maybe you go back through the text and pull these out with a highlighter. Or maybe you allow the main ideas and thoughts to coalesce into a few sentences. You'll probably notice a few cognitive distortions in the mix!

As you're writing or re-reading, don't try to avoid painful or uncomfortable themes—in fact, lean into those, as they will most reliably lead you to your core beliefs about the event that's underway. Try also to avoid making any pronouncements just yet—don't let that inner critic weigh in with judgments and diagnoses. Give yourself permission just to honestly express everything—yes, even that thing you're trying hard not to think about! In the beginning, it's just about curiosity.

Let's look at an example: Carl's boss has alerted him to an industry conference that he'd be willing to pay for—if Carl can come up with a good presentation. Carl's anxiety instantly goes through the roof. He sits down to journal it out, slowing his thought processes so he can get a handle on them.

As best he can, he tries to write down a neutral, objective account of events: He's been asked to do a presentation. He's never done one before. What beliefs does he hold? He just writes them down before he can second-guess himself: *I'm not good enough. My boss thinks I'm more able than I am. I hate public speaking. This is going to be humiliating . . .* What emotions does he feel? There are the obvious ones: fear, panic, self-loathing. But he also identifies another feeling—it's almost like tiredness, like the anticipation of being overwhelmed.

He looks more closely at this feeling, and it reveals another, quite hidden belief he has: If I succeed at this, then I'll have to keep on doing it, and I'm not sure I want to. Seeing this, he realizes he's felt this way before: that if he succeeds, then people will come to expect that from him, holding him to higher standards, and his life will suddenly get harder and more demanding. Because he thinks and feels this way, his behavior suddenly makes more sense to him: He feels avoidant and noncommittal and says yes to the conference, but only out of a sense of duty.

Teasing all these feelings apart is not just an academic exercise—finding out his *exact* thought patterns around this issue will allow Carl to make the best of the next step. After all, if you saw the problem as low self-belief, it would suggest a different solution than if you saw the problem as a lack of alignment with values, or even burnout. Take some time with your own issue, and don't rush it. There may be several layers to your ingrained thought patterns!

Step 2: Rethink . . . and Redo

Once you've identified the key thought patterns and core beliefs hiding inside your current situation, it's time to **get curious about alternative ways of looking at things**. Once you've done that, then the next step becomes obvious, too: You **think of ways to implement those new beliefs via action**.

It might be helpful to summarize things neatly by creating a table of two columns. One column is the negative thought pattern you currently hold, and the other column is where you brainstorm new beliefs and interpretations. The key point about this exercise, though, is that *intellectually* understanding what a better alternative would look like does not mean that you instantly replace it. Chances are, your negative thought patterns have been there for a while—it will take time to experience a genuine and lasting shift to something different, so be patient and realistic.

In Carl's case, he narrows down his beliefs on this issue to a few key thoughts:

I am only allowed to do the work I'm good at.

I can't let people down, even if living up to their expectations makes me really unhappy.

If an opportunity comes along, you have to take it because you never know if you'll get another one.

Carl recognizes that versions of these beliefs have popped up all throughout his life. He brainstorms a few realistic alternatives that he feels he can live with:

Just because I do well at something, it doesn't mean that I'm committed to doing it forever.

People's expectations of me are their own business, and I am not "letting anyone down" by doing what is right for me.

I can face any new opportunity with curiosity and gratitude, but I can also take the time to decide whether it aligns with my goals.

However, writing something new in the second column is the very least you can do. You have to imagine really drilling this new way of thinking into your mind—it has to become *real* for you. There are many ways of doing this, but passively waiting for your mind to catch up is not likely to work. This is where action can help. Imagine that everything you write in the second column is purely hypothetical—that is, until you take action to make it real.

Here are a few ideas:

- **Take action that supplies you with evidence that supports your new belief.** Your brain is intelligent—it doesn't want to believe something without proof. So, in Carl's example, his unhelpful thought is, "I am obligated to deliver on every expectation people have of me." He can put it to the test. In a small way, he can refuse to let someone else's expectations determine the action he will take. Or, for a bigger step, he can tell his boss he is attending a conference—but a different one that is more aligned with his interests and expertise. When the boss is okay with this and the world doesn't actually end, Carl can make a mental note—maybe his beliefs are not as accurate as he thought. Then he can take another small step. Gradually, he is accumulating evidence for his new belief: "*People's expectations of me are their own business, and I am not 'letting anyone down' by doing what is right for me.*"
- **Create and strengthen a new filter.** Your old mental filter worked hard to only notice those things that confirmed your core belief. Every day, pause to deliberately ask yourself to look at things in a way that aligns with your new

belief. For example, the old thought "I get depressed in winter" will give way to the new one "There are many things about winter that I still enjoy" if you try to find five things you love about each winter day when you wake up. In Carl's case, he can gradually start to build a filter that reframes people's expectations of him not as demands, but as genuinely interesting *opportunities and possibilities*—ones he is always at liberty to appraise as he sees fit. And when people communicate their expectations and hopes for him, he can filter this so their excitement is interpreted as care and kindness. He can slowly learn to respond to this good intention, rather than getting stressed that it means that he suddenly has to perform or else.

- **Practice self-compassion**. Remember that cognitive distortions are not only about *content*, but about *feeling*. You might find that your thought processes are fairly rational and realistic, but the problem is that they're just too harsh! For example, the thought, "Most of my life is behind me," may be literally true . . . but it's kind of unflattering. Here, taking action may simply mean being brave enough to face what's uncomfortable with humor and kindness. "Well, you can't go on an epic journey without putting a few miles on the clock!" Be polite and courteous to yourself. A little tact goes a long way. Try a handy trick for quickly cultivating self-acceptance: Put the words ". . . and I love that" at the end of something you're framing as a problem. "I failed my driver's test . . . and I love that." It's not a magic wand, but isn't it interesting how it shifts your perspective? Maybe it's not the end of the world that you're flawed or struggling in the way you are. At least consider the possibility.

  In Carl's case, a little compassion could remind him that he is entitled to seek out work he values and to be a little easier on himself. He may find out, in fact, that his boss actually has no big expectation of how the conference will go and was only making a suggestion—all of the pressure was coming from Carl alone.

- **Change statements to questions**. Your core beliefs are just that—beliefs, not facts. If you find in the first column the thought, "Nobody wants to hire someone with my skills." Change it to, "*Is* anyone hiring someone with my skills?" Literally go and check! Sounds too simple, but we often allow assumptions to act like facts in our lives. Be curious. Don't say how the door is closed—ask about any other doors around you that *are* open. In fact, while you're at it, ask about secret escape routes hidden under the floor you're standing on! Carl could simply come out and ask his boss, "If I really do well at this conference, do you envision asking me to make more presentations in the future?" Imagine all the stress that Carl could avoid if the boss says, "Not at all. I just thought you might enjoy it."

- **Go into learning mode**. A great trick is to ask yourself "how?" Instead of saying, "I can't do this," say, "How can I do this?" If something isn't working, don't focus on that fact—ask what *does* work. If you have the belief, "I'll always be bad with money," then combat it with a very concrete, realistic question: "How can I start to improve my financial literacy?" This way, you're not getting hung up on the fact of a challenge or obstacle, you're just skipping right over it and refusing to dwell—instead, asking what happens next. One very powerful question to ask, no matter what you're struggling with, is, "What kind of person do I have to be right now to cope with this well?"

For Carl, a great way to get out of his particular thought pattern is to ask, "What do I expect of myself? If I don't like making presentations, then what do I like doing? How can I do more of that at work?"

Decenter, Shift Perspective, and Create Distance

Meet Chris. It's Monday morning, and just as Chris gets into his car to make the daily commute to work, he notices a red light flashing on the dashboard. He swears under his breath and drives to work anyway, trying to ignore the warning bell, but with a sinking feeling in his gut that this means a big nasty bill that he won't be able to avoid. He gets to work after sitting in traffic for a while and is immediately met with a message that a client has submitted a complaint about him. His boss wants to chat. At the same moment, he realizes that he's forgotten his wallet at home and hasn't brought any lunch with him.

When a colleague peeks her head around the door and asks if he's okay, he says, not really joking, "Just kill me now please." She asks what the problem is, and he says, "I don't know, *life*?" The colleague mentions that she wanted to ask him a few questions about a funding request he submitted last week, and he quips, "Oh yeah? What's wrong with it? Let me guess, I've made a mistake and have to spend ninety years in prison for fraud? Or wait, I've got it. They've done the calculations and *I* actually owe *them* money, right?"

The colleague mutters something and scuttles off. Chris sits fuming in his office and all at once feels like crying. He hates himself for it, but whenever an unexpected expense comes up, he finds himself panicking. He remembers how his mom and dad struggled financially and battled to keep their beat-up old car running, once or twice having to forfeit the heating bill or that week's groceries to pay for an unexpected repair.

Here's something that many people seldom think about: **Pessimism, negativity, and gloomy nihilism are all coping mechanisms**. It might not look like it, but these responses signal that at some point, you came to the conclusion that your best bet was not to expect too much from life and instead be ready to assume the worst. This kind of negative attitude is a coping mechanism . . . but it's certainly not a good one. That's because it disempowers you and tends to more firmly entrench the things that are oppressing you, rather than enable you to rise above them.

When you begin to shift your thinking to a more positive direction, you may be taking away the only coping mechanism that is protecting you from experiencing a whole world of pain, hurt, disappointment, anger, and fear. Luckily, though, we don't have to live in the world without coping mechanisms—we can choose better, healthier ones.

Sh*t Happens . . . Even if You Think Positively

There is a perhaps unconscious assumption that if only you learn to master the fine art of positive thinking, your life will somehow be much, much easier. This may be true, but only in the sense that with positive thinking, **you become more resilient and better able to cope**—positive thinking, it should be said, doesn't magically make your life completely free of adversity. It doesn't remove challenging events but gives you a different way of responding to them.

Most of us are able to maintain a sunny disposition for a while (i.e., as long as nothing goes too wrong!), but we falter when we encounter our old wounds and traumas, the unfairness of life, a painful loss, or a moment of genuine confusion and chaos. The irony is that these moments are when we need positive thinking the most.

In the previous chapters, we looked at fixing our relationship with our own minds and making sure that we weren't deliberately undermining ourselves with destructive and distorted thought patterns. But, as any good pessimist would point out, they are negative for a *reason*! Those reasons are seemingly infinite: unexpected car repairs, complaints and conflicts, silly misunderstandings, and accidents . . .

We cannot avoid a degree of friction in life. And we certainly can do nothing about things that have already happened in the past. But how can we cope with it in a calmer and more measured way? What does a healthy coping mechanism look like? Let's bear in mind that sh*t happens even if you think positively. The trick is to accept this fact and find a good way to manage it.

How to Take a Step Back

Think about Chris's colleague in the example above. She comes in, chats with him for a moment, and then quickly decides to retreat. Why? Probably because she can tell what a foul mood he's in! She knows there's no use engaging when he's so grumpy, so she doesn't. She physically removes herself from the room. We're considering the colleague only because she is able to do something that Chris, in that moment, cannot: gain distance. She can observe the behavior as it unfolds and realize that it's temporary. But Chris is stuck right in it, completely at its mercy.

When you gain psychological distance, what you are doing is taking a deep breath, stepping back from the situation, and becoming a temporary observer rather than a wholly enmeshed and identified participant.

With psychological distance, you are able to step out of the narrow tunnel of your immediate experience and look at the bigger picture. Had Chris been able to do this, he might have said to himself or his colleague, "Look, I'm having a difficult morning and I'm stressing a little about money. It's okay and it will pass, but before I do anything further, I just want to wait until I've calmed down a bit."

Here are a few other techniques that Chris could have tried.

Create Spatial Distance

Literally separate yourself from the problem—go outside and take a walk if the place you're in is overwhelming, or write worrying thoughts in a journal and make a ritual of setting this journal in a locked drawer in another room—i.e., where it's far away from you. Perhaps Chris imagines physical space—he meditates for a few moments where he visualizes himself in a peaceful faraway garden where he can gather his thoughts for a moment.

Create Temporal Distance
We can take a step away from difficult experiences not just in space, but in time. Think about how this situation will look to you in one, two, or ten years' time. Can you think of a similar challenging situation that happened in the past? How do you feel about it now that some time has passed? Did any of your fears come true? How did you cope? Have you actually evolved and learned new ways of coping since then?

Chris zooms out—way out—and visualizes himself on his death bed. He feels calmer as he realizes that life was indeed filled with annoying crises that came and went, but that they mean absolutely nothing in the grand scheme!

The next time you're struggling with something, gain distance by imagining your future self in ten years' time. Then, as your future self, answer the following questions:

- What do you think about the current issue?
- What is your stress rating of the issue compared to the stress rating your current self is experiencing (on a scale of 1 to 10)?
- What do you know that your current self doesn't know?

Another way to do this exercise is to think to the past and a stressful event that happened then. Ask yourself these questions:

- How distressed were you (on a scale from 1 to 10)? At what rating did the feeling peak?
- How long did the feeling last?
- When and how did it stop?

Play with Role-Switching
What would other people do in your shoes? Think of someone you respect and admire, and imagine the problem through their eyes. This helps separate you from your own blind spots and tender points. Chris has a lot of traumatic memories from his childhood, but he always loved and revered his father. He thinks about how his dad was tough and no-nonsense about practical problems and would say, "To hell with it! I'll learn to fix it myself." This inspires Chris because it reminds him of his own resourcefulness.

Another possibility is to imagine your Higher Self, whatever that looks like to you. Some people may like to imagine a deity, a guardian angel, or a supernatural being who provides sagely guidance. If an all-knowing, wise, and loving entity looked with interest at your current problem, what would they advise you to do? If that doesn't feel authentic to you, imagine a personal hero or role model and how they'd respond—even if they're fictional!

Focus on Concrete Action
When Chris is having his Monday morning meltdown, he isn't thinking clearly, to put it bluntly. His distress and anxiety is like an amorphous cloud that engulfs him, and his mind jumps from one catastrophic and negative thought to another, with certain

themes quickly taking on epic proportions. He is not thinking about how to book his car in at the service station, but dwelling bitterly on deep psychological fears of poverty and the feelings of failure and humiliation that brings, of his relationship with his father, of how he feels like he's on a rat wheel and the rat wheel is always just about to break . . .

This "head storm" is simply his brain in overdrive. It's normal to look for patterns, elaborate on themes, make predictions, come to conclusions, or ask *why*. But a distressed brain can do this in an out-of-control fashion, becoming completely untethered from reality. How do you tether it back again? By finding and anchoring to the concrete world.

Ask yourself: what can you **do**? Don't imagine the next three weeks or the next ten steps. Just think of the very next concrete action you could take. Chris takes a deep breath and answers this question: He needs to get his car examined at a garage so he knows what the problem is and can get some quotes for repairs. Next step, then, is to make some calls. That's all. It's not his job to think about the *outcome*—just about the next step in the *process*.

Make a detailed and dispassionate list. Acknowledge your emotions as they come up, but politely ask them to sit aside for the moment while you tackle the issue at hand with calm, neutral objectivity. **When you catch your mind wandering, grab a hold of the thought and ask plainly: "Can I do anything about this?"** If the answer is yes, stop ruminating and do that thing. If the answer is no, stop ruminating—since ruminating won't help. Either way, you don't need to ruminate!

When Chris catches the thought, "This morning is just a disaster," he stops and asks if that thought is actionable. Nope. It has no shape. It's just a vaguely threatening cloud that doesn't go anywhere. When the thought, *You just never get a chance to get ahead in this life* crosses his mind, he definitely ignores it. Following it will lead him nowhere.

When he thinks, "I bet fixing that damn car will cost me a fortune," he pauses, then decides to turn it into a question. *Will* it cost him a fortune? He doesn't actually know. He makes a list of three service garages to call and commits to getting a quote from each of them. If it really will cost him a fortune, well, at least he knows this for sure now and can make his next move. In the event the quotes are actually very low, though, he has spared himself a huge amount of useless anxiety.

In fact, as Chris goes about dealing with his morning from hell, he realizes that this is precisely the quality he most admired in his dad—the ability to just get on and do what needs to be done without too much whining, angst, or handwringing. He takes a moment to experience what this new perspective actually feels like. How the problem is still there, but somehow *he* is different in relation to that problem. Chris calls three places, and they agree to send him quotes within the hour. But he discovers that even though nothing much has changed for his situation, he feels much better simply for having taken a positive, proactive step.

If your negative thinking is running out of control, immediately ask it to focus on one *small*, *concrete detail* right here in the *present*. Forget about grand narratives that will only lead to the distortion of overgeneralization. **One amazing way to get distance and shift perspectives, then, is to get out of your own head and into the concrete, physical world of action.** Sometimes, nothing can dissolve useless rumination, negative thoughts, and pessimism as quickly!

A Word on the Most Useless Habit in the World

When a captive parrot is extremely stressed or unhappy, it can sometimes start to pull its own feathers out. To the dismay of its owner, it will sit and yank out its own feathers one by one so that it has raw, bald patches all over its neck and chest, and a dirty cage filling up with feathers and down. Granted, parrots do this for a range of complicated reasons, but human beings have a tendency to do something similar—a kind of mental feather plucking.

The habit in question is **complaining**. Every time you complain, it is as useless and destructive as a parrot plucking one of their own beautiful, healthy feathers and throwing it to the ground. It serves no purpose, it solves no problem, and all it achieves is to make the parrot look awful. Most of us think of complaining as relatively harmless, but the ease with which we can make little complaints here and there is precisely what makes the problem so insidious.

Consider Christina, another one of Chris's hypothetical colleagues at work. Nothing in particular happens to her that Monday morning, but that doesn't stop her from releasing a steady stream of background complaints throughout the day.

"Ugh! They're out of decaf again. This place is a joke."

"I think I have a headache coming on."

"Have you seen the price of gas lately!?"

"I wish it were Friday."

"So we got the decorators in, but *of course* they messed it up, and now we have to get someone in to fix their work . . ."

"I'm so tired."

"Gah! This thing's broken again. I just can't handle it."

"That woman at the café was so rude, seriously. Would it have killed her to smile?"

And on and on and on . . .

Any single one of the above statements might not seem like much on their own, but when *every* sentiment seems to be a mild complaint, the effect is a little like a bald spot on a parrot. Christina isn't having the crisis Chris is, but she is just as surely creating a negative world for herself with her thought patterns.

Complaining is powerful. It is the opposite of gratitude. It is also incompatible with conscious, inspired action.

Complaining is identifying a problem without seeking a solution, or passively whining so that others will solve it for you. It's a subtle way to deny our own responsibility for an issue, or to quietly place blame. It is one hundred percent "out of power" language and can lead to a creeping attitude of victimization.

When we complain, we amplify negativity while doing nothing to actually address it. At its worst, complainers make a nuisance of themselves, and their dissatisfaction can almost be weaponized against others, as though they were constantly saying, "Wah! I'm unhappy, and I'm going to make things unpleasant until someone does something about it!" Basically, complaining is like a low-level, background temper tantrum!

If you recognize a little of yourself in Christina, don't worry—we all complain sometimes. There is nothing wrong with being irritated, tired, sad, or confused. **What matters is what we consciously choose to do about it**. Ask yourself the same question Chris does. Can I do anything about this? Complaining, like pessimism, is a kind of coping mechanism (but a rotten one!). You may discover that it's actually far easier to cope when you remind yourself of a simple fact: If you don't like something, you have the power to change it.

How Is Your Media Hygiene?

Before we move on, let's briefly consider another equally useless habit that may have snuck into your life without you realizing the damage it causes day to day. Remember Christina's list of complaints above? Take a look at the following:

Four-year-old's savage murder "the worst thing I've seen in my life," says commissioner.

Russia destroys Ukrainian hospitals in missile attack.

Weather experts now predict even more extreme weather events for 2024.

Germany's Greens in freefall amid corruption allegations.

The housing crisis is breaking people's brains.

Everything's terrible; slit wrists now.

Okay, so maybe that last one is made up, but you get the idea. If complaining is identifying a problem without also identifying a solution—even just a potential solution—then the doom and gloom that floods into our nervous systems from the media is like turbocharged complaining. It's obvious why: Most of us can do very, very little about the awful things we read about in the news or on social media.

That means that when you mindlessly and endlessly "doomscroll" on your phone, while taking no action, you are essentially amplifying all those bad feelings, while at the same time making yourself feel more and more hopeless (by the way, two key signs of depression—hopelessness and helplessness—are a natural result of exposing yourself to certain kinds of media. It's not a mistake that it makes you feel so apathetic; it's by design).

You don't have to live in a cave or pretend that there aren't problems in the world. But like Chris and Christina, it's worth remembering that you do have the power (perhaps it's even a responsibility) to maintain a certain distance from especially negative material out there in the world. Become mindful of the kind of content you consume.

What effect does it have on your emotions?

What kind of beliefs and thoughts do they encourage?

How do you behave when you think and feel the way you do after taking in such content?

Most of us understand the need to maintain physical hygiene, to protect ourselves from toxins and germs, to avoid UV rays, and to run away from people wielding knives in dark alleys . And yet, we may deliberately choose to waste hours of every day soaking up content in the media that terrifies, saddens, angers, or alienates us. In other words, we have poor media hygiene. The environment can support or hinder us; it can impact the way we feel and the beliefs we hold. If you don't like the way that your media intake is making you think or feel, then you know the solution: Create distance!

Try a Cognitive Defusion Exercise

In reading the stories above about people like Chris or Dan, you can be forgiven for thinking that when it comes to your own life, things are seldom so simple or clear cut. It can often seem like all these ideas make sense . . . but only long after you've already gotten trapped in negative thinking or even had a full-blown episode or panic attack. Whatever term we use to describe this phenomenon when it happens, we have to acknowledge that sometimes, our negative thoughts get the upper hand on us, and we feel ourselves sinking.

The advantage Dan has is that he can use the ABC framework at his own pace, over many weeks and months with a therapist he trusts. When Chris wakes up to a hellishly bad day, he can gain a little distance and, if he gains control over the negativity spiral, feel better the next day. **But what about when you're *right in the middle of some very negative thoughts and you can't get out?*** One obvious characteristic of really negative thinking is that it warps our ability to see everything, including the problem as it's unfolding. We stop being able to imagine a way out, and start to think that things have always been this bad and will continue to be forever.

Action Commitment Therapy (ACT) is a psychological approach that has a word for this exact feeling of being flooded with negativity: **fusion**.

When we are fused with thoughts, we are so close to them that we cannot think, feel, or act outside of them. The thought consumes us. It *is* us. It's a little like watching a movie and being so engrossed in the unfolding story that you forget you are watching a movie at all (and incidentally, that you can always just walk out!). In the same way, when we are fused, we forget that we are having thoughts at all. And so we are at their mercy, assuming that our current and transient experience of reality is permanent, unalterable, and completely out of our control.

When we discussed Dan and how distance and perspective gave him enough breathing room to gently challenge and replace his negative thoughts, we were also talking about fusion. However, when we are *really* fused with negative thoughts and ideas, it can often take a lot more than a day or a few perspective shifts to help us change gear.

Your brain is not a machine that perfectly regards reality, but a machine that creates a picture *of* reality, or a story *about* reality. When we are fused with negative thoughts, however, we have told ourselves such a convincing story that we believe it fully and cannot escape.

Ellen's Story and Finding the "Big You"
Ellen's world is a dark, dark place. She has felt broadly miserable about life and herself for as long as she can remember. From the outside, Ellen looks like an ordinary person, and she has friends and family who love her. On the inside, though, Ellen's mind is like a tailor-made torture chamber designed just for her. She doesn't just feel and believe that she is worthless and that life is completely not worth living; she *knows* it's the case.

It is, in fact, the only thing she is ever really sure about. She has gone to therapists of all kinds, tried medication, spoken to friends, read the self-help books, and even once or twice gone to retreats and workshops. But nothing really shifts Ellen's deep, lasting conviction that life is misery, and that to be alive is basically to suffer. Constantly. Yes, she is what people call "depressed." If Ellen's life was a movie, it would be a gritty and miserable black-and-white drama that ends with everyone dying in the apocalypse.

Ellen's thoughts and feelings have been stuck in this mode for so long that they have cemented themselves into core beliefs that form the very foundation on which the rest of her world is built. No matter what happens, Ellen's mental filter makes sure that the only conclusion she can ever reach is, "Life is awful." And Ellen is completely, one hundred percent *fused to this thought*. They are stuck together like glue.

So, when she sits in the therapist's chair, she doesn't ask for coping strategies or help understanding why she can't stop being so negative. Instead, she asks, "Why is life so miserable?"

When she confides in a close friend who is trying to understand how to help her, Ellen can only say, "How can you help me? There's nothing you can do. There's nothing anyone can do—that's why I'm so unhappy in the first place."

When her husband tells her that's she's beautiful and that he loves her, all she can say is, "Well, it must be nice to be so delusional!"

You can see the problem. Not only is Ellen wearing some very black-tinted glasses, she is **completely unaware that she is**. So even when she attempts to solve the problem, she is solving the wrong one. Her position goes deeper than Chris's or Dan's because not only is she at the mercy of some very powerful negative thoughts, she isn't even able to recognize that this (and not the state of the world around her) is the source of her misery.

How on earth does someone like Ellen escape her dark thoughts—in other words, how does she defuse?

Again, it's a question of a mindset shift, i.e., learning to look at the problem on a completely different level. Earlier, we mentioned one way to gain distance from the inner critic: giving it a name and treating it as though it literally was someone separate from you and someone you could send away (remember Mildred?).

Here, we will try to imagine that the Mind (capital M!) in its entirety is a separate entity. This means that you can step back from it and look at it from afar. This poses the question, what is doing the looking? Aren't you your mind? The answer is a resounding NO!

Not only is it a good idea to imagine that your Mind is something separate from you and that you can watch, it's a good idea to connect to that You (capital Y!) that is doing the watching.

"There goes boring old Mildred again, my old friend the inner critic, coming up with a million reasons to tell **me** why I can't do something. Get out of here, Mildred!"

The me in the above statement is You—the big You.

This may seem like a weird philosophical point to labor, but it's important because by doing this (separating your Mind from You), you are giving yourself a powerful **lever** to get out of any trap that your Mind puts you in.

Let's imagine how this might work for Ellen. Let's say she's having an especially dark time and is feeling completely overwhelmed by the negativity she sees around her in the world. All she can see is that the world is a dark, chaotic place filled with greedy, crazy people who seem hellbent on hurting one another (you've probably had a similar thought at some point or other, right?). Her brain is like a hurricane of negativity, so she sits down with a journal to try to release some of it onto the page.

She writes,

I just don't see the point of it all. I work so hard, and it's basically for nothing. Why bother trying? I could go out there and start a new project and get all hopeful and blah blah blah, but someone will only come and smash it all down. That's not to say I'd even get to finish anything in the first place, because I'm too tired. How many things have I started and never finished? I don't have the time, and honestly, there isn't really a thing I'm good at—not in this world. Maybe if I were a cut-throat psychopath or something, but I'm not. So I just don't care anymore.

Phew! A negativity hurricane, indeed. But let's look closer. On the advice of her therapist, Ellen tries something different. She puts everything down on paper, then looks at the notebook. She takes her pen and draws a big box around all the words. In a different-color pen, she writes above it in bigger letters: THIS IS WHAT MY MIND IS TELLING ME. Because Ellen's quite creative, she cleverly turns the box into a speech bubble, which is coming from the mouth of a little grumpy face in the corner of the page.

And just like that, there are *two* voices. Ellen's and this little grumpy face on the page. Now, Ellen might do this exercise and *still* side with the negative thoughts. The difference is that this time, she's done so knowing that this point of view is *not* the only game in town. She is aware now that she has chosen it; in other words, she starts to see her negative perspective not as reality, but as a negative perspective.

Ellen does this for a few days, and after a while, a lightbulb goes off: She looks at all the negativity on the page (that's outside her head and somewhere out there where she can see it) and thinks, "Wow. *That's* what I carry in my head all the time. That's messed up."

Does Ellen cure herself overnight of her negative thinking? No. It took her a lifetime to learn. But the next time she has one of her darker days and she sits with her journal again, she notices all those same thoughts again, just as before. Except now, she's not quite so tied to them. She watches herself have them. The change is subtle, but after some time, something happens. She thinks to herself one day, *I'm feeling depressed* instead of *life sucks*.

The great thing about a lever is that it can work to shift an enormous load even if you can only fit the narrow end of the wedge in at first. Once Ellen gets the smallest inkling **she is not her thoughts, she is just having thoughts**, that realization grows and grows. One day, Ellen picks up her journal again and flips through pages and pages of negative thoughts she has put down over the weeks and months. She asks herself a question: Is this really what I want? She is no longer wondering why life is so bad for her; she is wondering whether the thought that life is bad is actually helping her in any way.

The end of this story is not that Ellen permanently vanquishes depression from her life forever—it hardly ever works out that way. But she does something far more impressive, if you think about it. *Ellen learns to think outside of her own mind.* She starts to look at the thoughts in her head not as absolute truth but as arbitrary tools—some of them are useful, some aren't. Some build her up and give her courage and fill her life with meaning, and some make her feel despairing and trapped. Some are rational and some aren't. Some inspire action, and others convince you that action is even possible.

For those who battle with depression, the biggest trap is to think, "I'm unhappy because life is so unbearable," but it really might be the other way around: because you are fused with the thought that life is unbearable, you feel unhappy as a consequence.

Make Your Beliefs Earn Their Keep
A thought is just a thought.

It's not automatically the "truth."

You don't have to act on it.

You don't have to agree with it.

You don't have to respond to it at all.

It doesn't have to *mean* anything about the situation at hand, or you as a person.

It's not good or bad.

It's just a thought.

Once you realize a thought is just a thought, then you are able to let it do what thoughts do best: pass. Here is a question: If a bus suddenly pulled up in front of you right now, would you automatically board it and allow it to take you away? Well, you'd probably want to know where it was going first. That's how you should think about thoughts.

Where does this thought take me? Do I want to go there?

If not, don't board the bus. Let it go on its way and don't attach to it or fuse with it. It's not your bus. It has nothing to do with you. If it *does* take you where you want to go, then get on board—and forget about all the other buses. In fact, get behind the wheel and steer that bus yourself to the destination of your choice. Stay on the bus as long as it helps you get where you need to go, and when it doesn't, find another vehicle or another route there. The bus system is there, after all, to serve *you*. It's there to help you navigate your city and get around. Thoughts are the same. They're there for you. And not everything that pops into your head deserves your full attention and buy-in. In fact, the vast majority of them don't!

This turns the relationship between You and your Mind on its head. Instead of your Mind calling the shots. You are the one in charge. You make your thoughts earn their keep. Unless they are accurate, productive, supportive, congruent with your values, practically useful, or, at the very least, pleasant, then you have no use for them. So you can let them go.

Ellen did this when she looked at the steaming pile of negativity she was holding on to and realized it did precisely *nothing* for her. It wasn't on her side. It wasn't helping. You don't have to be in as bad a state of Ellen, though, to do the same. Try the following:

1. Ask yourself what you value most in life, or what you are trying to achieve. Maybe it's something big like the love of your family, personal growth, or your faith. Maybe at the moment, all you can think of is something immediate like "some peace and quiet" or "a less crummy job." Even in the most negative mindsets, we all want *something*. Hold that thought in your mind.
2. Now, like Ellen did, become aware of the negative thoughts that are coming up for you.
3. Take a close look at this thought. Tell yourself, "I am having this thought." Pause and let it sink in that this is your Mind talking, and it's just a thought. If you like, give it another label, too. Call it by its name: criticism, doubt, curiosity, fear, observation, resistance, etc. Get acquainted with what kind of thought it is. Create some distance by using third person, if you like, "Ellen is having a self-hating thought."

4. Now, don't worry about whether the thought is "true" or not; instead, ask if it matches up with what you identified in Step 1 as something you want or value. **Is this thought going to take you closer to or further away from that thing?**
5. If the thought takes you closer, then great. If it doesn't, or if it's neutral, you now have a *choice*. Will you actively choose something that goes against what you already know you want? Or will you let it pass by? You also get to choose whether you'd like to spend your time and your brainpower on a thought that *will* help you get what you want. (Yes! Thoughts can be your servants and work for you!)
6. Do this as often as you like. Thoughts are a bit like buses—there's always another one on its way . . .

Ellen does it like this:

Though she's not happy about much in her life, she does love her husband, and she does care about her pets and her nieces and nephews. Even in her negative state of mind, she can identify that she wants her husband to be happy, and that she wants to spend time with her nieces and nephews and be a responsible pet owner.

One Saturday morning, she's lounging in bed and feeling despondent. The thought pops into her mind: "You're a waste of space, slobbing around in bed all day while other people are living their lives!" She immediately stops this thought in its tracks and examines it. She even says aloud to herself, "Hello, Depression, I see that you're speaking right now." She realizes she's having a negative thought. Now, in this precious empty space after this realization, she understands that she has a choice. She can decide what to do next.

She thinks about her husband, her nieces and nephews, her dogs. Does thinking that she's a waste of space make her a better wife? Does it help her get closer to her nieces and nephews? Does it help her take care of her pets? No. At best, it does nothing; at worst, it gets in the way. If she gets on that bus, she will soon start thinking other thoughts, too. That she is worthless, that she may as well not be here, and so on. In that moment, even though she still feels despondent, she decides to let the thought go. She can't cancel it out or pretend she didn't have it. But she decides she won't *continue* to have it. In a few minutes, she experiments with changing the thought. She could say, "How lucky am I to have a nice cozy moment in bed on such a peaceful Saturday morning?" She notices how it feels to hold on to this thought, instead.

It's Never a War

You'll notice that Ellen doesn't kick the negative thought to the curb and yell at it. She doesn't go head to head and wrestle it into submission. She just *doesn't* hold on to it. That's a big difference.

Before we conclude this chapter, it's worth mentioning how defusion is not about fighting off a negative thought. That's because resisting a negative thought is just another way to fuse with it. If we are fearfully or angrily resisting a thought, we are just as much at its mercy as if we were closely identifying with it.

When you become aware of a thought, just keep it at that level—awareness. Try avoid taking the extra step of adding on your own judgment or interpretation of that thought. Try not to criticize a thought, condemn yourself for having it, or even be pleased because it's a "good" thought. Just be aware. You *will* appraise the thought, but only in terms of its usefulness, i.e., whether it really serves any purpose in your life.

If you do notice that judgment, resistance, or clinging coming up, that's fine too. It's just one more thing to notice! Maybe you think, "I could kill him," but instantly think, "You shouldn't be so angry." There's no point judging the second thought, either, and feeling bad because you felt bad about feeling bad! Just stop, ask what is working and what isn't, and let the thoughts go. Remind yourself that thoughts can't hurt you or anyone. They only mean something when you decide they do.

Psychiatrist and much-loved author of the inspirational book *Man's Search for Meaning*, Viktor Frankl, once said, "Between stimulus and response there is a space, and in that space lies our growth and our freedom." You don't have to have everything figured out, or magically turn your thought process around until you're thinking the "right" way. If all you can manage is to pause and realize that you are thinking in the first place, then you have already done so much. Hold on to that pause.

Remind yourself of your conscious choice. You don't even have to make a decision yet; just be aware it's there. You might find that you actually like not having to respond or choose . . . isn't it nice to just let negative thoughts do what they want and burn themselves out and dissipate all on their own, without you having to get worked up about them in the least?

Summary

- To rewrite our negative thought patterns, we "can't solve problems by using the same kind of thinking we used when we created them."
- We can use the ABCDE acronym (activating event, belief, consequence, disputation, and new event) and explore the stories we're telling in a thought journal. We can decide whether a new alternative is a good one according to its accuracy, helpfulness, and congruence with our values.
- Once you've identified your current thoughts, ask if there's a different way to think about things, and how you can bring that idea to life with concrete action. Seek out evidence for a new belief, practice self-compassion, and go into learning mode, asking questions instead of making statements.
- Negativity can be relieved by shifting perspectives and creating psychological distance. Remember that pessimism, negativity, and gloomy nihilism are all coping mechanisms and once served a purpose. But right now, we can choose to cope with adversity in different, healthier ways (and there always will be adversity!)
- Create spatial, temporal, and psychological distance from distressing thoughts, ask what others might do in our situation (role-switching), and turn your mind to concrete action instead of asking why. Focus on a small, concrete detail in the

present and ask what you can **do**. Avoid identifying problems without seeking solutions—i.e., complaining! Be mindful of your media use and minimize negative content that is draining you.
- When we are stuck in intense emotions, we can try the ACT technique of defusion. Imagine that your Mind is something separate from you and that you can watch it.
- Remember that you are not your thoughts; you are just having thoughts. Make your thoughts earn their keep!

Chapter 3: Master the Art of Distress Tolerance and Self-Soothing

Perhaps you read about Ellen's tales of woe and thought, "Fair enough... but some of us have *real* problems we're dealing with." This is a good observation—sometimes, people think negatively... because they're simply responding to something negative in their environment.

Few of us will get through life without experiencing an emotional crisis, a big loss, an upheaval, or an accident at some point or another. It's one thing to learn to master your thought processes so that you're not creating unnecessary suffering for yourself—but it's another when you're faced with a legitimately negative circumstance that cannot be avoided. What then?

In this chapter, we'll talk about distress tolerance and how to cultivate it. This is a set of skills that most people don't really think about until they're in a crisis situation and need them urgently. But many of the same principles of defusing, perspective-switching, reframing, and challenging your cognitive distortions can be used when we're facing a situation that makes us feel out of control. Call it a toolkit of crisis survival skills!

The tools we'll describe below can be used when

- you're in extreme pain—emotionally or physically,
- there's a formidable temptation that you have to resist,
- you're dealing with a temporary but very challenging situation that can't be avoided,
- it's an emergency and you have to be productive and focused... even though you're completely overwhelmed,
- there's a conflict and you need to put aside raw emotions to communicate effectively,
- you're absolutely terrified but need to act wisely anyway.

A crisis can put a major dent in anyone's sense of emotional mastery and control. **When the chips are down, it's easy to slip back into old patterns of behavior or default to clumsy, destructive, or unconscious ways of coping.** Trouble is, though these habits may feel momentarily soothing, they ultimately create more problems and set up negative feedback loops that keep amplifying themselves.

Alex has hurt his back at his job. He's received some worker's comp, but he's basically off duty until he gets better. He's at home alone (his partner works all day), the doctors and physiotherapists don't feel like they're helping, and there's no end in sight. His boss has been kind enough, but Alex knows it's only a matter of time before they need to let him go. His back is getting worse, not better, and Alex is unsure how they'll fund the enormously expensive surgery if he needs it, or what they'll do for money once his savings and insurance money are gone.

In other words, Alex is in a crisis. He's in pain and can't be prescribed any more painkillers since they're addictive. But on some days, the pain is so intense, Alex doesn't know what to do with himself. He can't move. He's depressed, anxious, bored, lonely, scared, and exhausted. And every day, he faces excruciating pain that doesn't let up. What can he do?

Alex's "solution" is threefold: He soothes himself with comfort eating and junk food, he sits immobile on the sofa for hours-long marathon gaming sessions, and he starts abusing alcohol. These things don't help exactly, but they make everything a little more bearable. They also make everything worse. Within a few months, Alex is not only depressed, anxious, bored, lonely, scared, and exhausted, he's also gaining weight, usually drunk or hungover, and staying up until 3 a.m. every night and sleeping past noon the next day.

Nobody would say that Alex doesn't have a legitimate "reason" to feel negative. Nobody could say that he is to blame, and most would agree that the way he is dealing with the crisis is understandable, even if not ideal. However, the irony is that Alex's methods for dealing with distress have become their own form of distress. Alex cannot help that he injured his back; however, he doesn't have the skills needed to survive the crisis, and in a way, this is a bigger problem.

The coping mechanisms he's chosen are **false coping mechanisms** because, ultimately, they create more of the problem, exacerbate suffering, and keep him trapped where he is. The more he drinks, the less emotionally available he is for his partner, and the worse they communicate. This means that the coping mechanism of drinking robs him of an important source of potential support: a loving relationship.

The more junk food he eats, the worse his overall health. This means that "comfort" eating is actually impeding his body's ability to heal quickly. The extra pounds that make it even more difficult to complete the exercises the physiotherapist prescribed make him feel anything but "comfort"! The late-night gaming is just as addictive. It's a welcome distraction, but it also makes him angry and combative, and since he's ruined his natural sleep cycles, his anxiety and depression get worse, not better.

In a crisis, the challenge of staying calm, positive, rational, and accepting may seem like a Herculean task. It may seem almost impossible. Let's be honest, it's not something you *want* to do. But the point of Alex's story is to show that living the life that false coping mechanisms create is actually much, much harder! We don't tolerate distress because we enjoy it and have to learn to grin and bear it. We tolerate distress because it is *less hard work and less suffering* than allowing ourselves to be swallowed by it.

How to Self-Soothe

In life, pain is inevitable. But we have a choice in how we respond to it.

Self-soothing is a way to acknowledge and accept pain that is inevitable—*without making it any bigger than it should be.*

When you rail against pain and loss and injustice, you are actually prolonging and expanding that negativity. You are placing all of your focused attention on that pain and amplifying it. There's nothing wrong with this response—in fact, your ancient ancestors evolved this hyper-focus on pain because it forced them to go into problem-solving mode and quickly remove or escape from the threat in order to survive.

If someone has done something to hurt you, one way to cope could be to hyperfocus on their guilt and get caught in a loop blaming them again and again. This feels good . . . for a short while, at least. It's good to use the opportunity to adjust your boundaries, change your process, reassess a relationship, or just forgive and move on. Once you've genuinely done this, though, there is no reason to keep dwelling on the fact of the other person's guilt (i.e., hold a grudge) since that's really just a way of telling yourself over and over, "I'm powerless. I'm hurt. It's not fair . . ." Not unlike pressing on a bruise so it can't heal properly!

But there are some types of pain that *cannot* be escaped. For these types of pain, struggling and resisting can only *add* to the portion of pain you have to suffer through. The person who complains that it is raining has one additional problem compared to the person who knows it is but chooses to just carry on with life instead of focusing on the fact.

Self-soothing is not the same as distraction or avoidance or having a little rant about how unfair life is. Rather, it's about being kind enough to yourself that you refuse to add any more to the suffering you're experiencing, whether it's a suffering on the scale Alex is experiencing or something more trivial like a rainy day. If you genuinely cannot do anything to remove a pain (and we will look in a later chapter at an excellent way to figure this out for yourself), then the only rational next step is to do what you can to bear it.

Grounding is a great way to self-soothe. When you anchor into your senses, you are pulling your conscious mind away from anxieties, ruminations, regrets, and fears that are based in the past and present, and asking it to rest gently in the present instead. The irony is that we create a lot of drama for ourselves trying to run away from a painful moment in the present we think is too much to handle. But if we did stay with it for a while, we'd see that it wasn't as bad as we thought it was.

Your five senses are your gateway to the present. Pause, breathe, and become aware. Take five minutes to find something to dwell on for each sense—without judgment or any agenda at all. For Alex, when his back pain reaches distracting levels, instead of defaulting to addictive behaviors, he pauses, takes a deep breath, and makes a conscious choice *not to run away*.

He looks closely at the texture of the sofa cushion and the almost infinite shades of blue he can discern in the weave of the fabric. He listens to the faint buzz of the refrigerator in the next room that he hadn't noticed before. He smells the reassuring and faint aroma of laundry softener in the blanket on his lap. He touches the blanket; there are places where his own rough skin catches against it. He can sense the lingering taste of coffee still on his tongue from his morning cup . . .

After a few minutes, Alex isn't magically not in pain anymore. But, what seemed completely overwhelming and engulfing a moment before doesn't seem so big anymore. He has done something different—instead of fleeing pain, he has anchored into the present and ridden it out.

TIPP Skills

Anyone can see that Alex isn't helping himself by eating garbage, being sedentary, and wasting hours staring at screens. It's obvious that maltreating the physical body this way can only cause psychological, social, cognitive, emotional, and even spiritual damage. But we seldom appreciate the fact that this relationship goes the other way, too: If we soothe and regulate the physical body first, we can calm down the central nervous system and improve our psychological state.

TIPP stands for

Temperature
Intense Exercise
Paced Breathing
Paired Muscle Relaxation

These four things can immediately calm down an aggravated limbic system and lower your overall arousal. Physical arousal influences and informs psychological arousal.

Try cold water. Splashing the face with cool water actually activates what is called the "mammalian dive response," which is an ancient adaptation that results in slower heart rate, slower breath rate, and an overall calmed nervous system. Have a quick, cold shower, rub an ice cube on your neck or wrists, or dip your feet in cool lake or seawater, if you can. Cold temperatures affect your body's metabolism, limbic system, and homeostatic balance, with the overall effect of making you feel calmer. Even fanning your face to create a little cooling breeze can help you, quite literally, cool off. **Get moving.** Intense exercise likewise has a balancing and regulating effect on the body. A burst of intense physical activity releases adrenaline and creates momentary euphoria. Hard exercise is a healthy distraction that floods your body with oxygenated blood, and the increased heart rate reinvigorates every tissue and organ of the body. Do anything that gets you panting for air, makes you sweat, or brings some color to your cheeks! Nothing helps a tangled up, distressed mind as much as taking inspired action. And what could be more active than . . . well, being active?

If you don't feel like a jog, do something else to get your heart rate up. Get stuck into decluttering and deep cleaning your house, chop wood, play with a child, dance, or even punch a pillow if you're feeling angry or overwhelmed. All of it counts, so long as you are getting back into your breathing, moving body, and out of your head (it goes without saying that this step needs to be adapted if the pain you're trying to tolerate is purely physical. Even if you're hurt or ill, however, you'll feel better and more in control if you breathe deeply, stretch, and gently push yourself to your physical limit, whatever it happens to be).

Pace your breathing. Your breathing and your emotional state are closely connected. If you are breathing slowly, deeply, and rhythmically, you simply cannot be in a panicked or overwhelmed state. Just try it! Inhale slowly for a count of two or three, pause, then exhale with control for a count of two or three. As you do so, imagine your blood pressure and heart rate dropping.

Remind yourself that as you breathe, you feel. If your breathing is shallow and constricted, then your emotions will be similarly tight and tense. If your breathing is irregular, so, too, will your thoughts be. Remember that the relationship goes both ways—how you breathe impacts how you feel, but how you feel impacts how you breathe. Changing either one will change the other.

Use PMR—paired muscle relaxation. Choose a pair of muscles (for example, the tops of both thighs or the muscles in each big toe) and tighten them as hard as you can as you inhale. Hold it, then very slowly and with control release the tension as you exhale. It is difficult to be emotionally tense and agitated if your muscles are relaxed.

Tensing muscles before relaxing leads to a deeper calm. Repeat a few times and then move on to another paired muscle till you have worked through your entire body. This is an excellent mind-body connector that allows you to slow down, go quiet, and release. It can be paired with paced breathing and is especially useful in bed at night to help you get to sleep.

You don't have to run through your entire body if you don't have time, however. Just choose a muscle, focus, breathe deeply, and ground yourself in the sensation. Try to imagine that your brain can only ever be in one of two places—out there in the past or the future or in no man's land, thinking up hypotheticals, or it can be in the here and now. If you bring it firmly into the here and now (where your body is), you automatically pull it away from anxious or unhelpful thoughts. You get closer to your real, lived, embodied experience, while creating that magical distance between you and your thoughts.

There is one huge advantage to using TIPP: your mind is not required! You can notice negative thoughts, temptations, upset emotions, and anxious loops. Yet you don't have to deal with them at all, but engage on the level of your body alone. So many of the more psychological self-soothing techniques don't work because they're attempted with a body that is aroused. If you try to have a rational argument with yourself about why you shouldn't panic, for example, it won't really sink in if your heart is racing, your muscles are tense, and your blood pressure is through the roof. You need to relax first and *then* engage at the level of thoughts, feelings, and rational arguments.

The TIPP technique is excellent for creating calm in the immediate moment. Once you lower your overall limbic system arousal, you likely can start to think more clearly, and deliberately choose more helpful coping mechanisms. For the longer term, keep thinking of your body and how if you support it, it will support you:

- Eat well. Cut out processed foods and make plants and quality protein the backbone of every meal. Avoid the physiological stress of fasting, and give yourself nice, smooth blood sugar levels by eating small balanced meals more regularly.
- Avoid dehydration by drinking plenty of water and tea throughout the day.
- Maintain a regular sleep pattern—the number of hours is not as important as the consistency of the routine. Keep the same sleep and wake times every day.
- Stay away from stimulants—that includes coffee and sugar. You don't have to abstain, just be mindful and keep an eye on staying balanced and even, rather than chasing extremes.
- Try yoga or other deep stretching techniques. You'll regulate your breathing, strengthen the mind-body connection, get your blood and lymph system flowing, oxygenate your tissues, and keep supple.

For Alex, his situation improves when he starts incorporating a specific habit into his routine. Though he can't stand for long periods, he does a morning workout where he uses his arms and adapts exercises so he can do them lying down. Once he is hot and sweaty, he cools off in a cold shower and finishes off with a brisk rub with a towel. He finds that no matter how much of a bad mood he started with, he always feels a little more alive and in control when he starts mornings this way.

He is also learning that when the physical pain gets too intense, he can distract himself by grounding and using breathing exercises. He is also finding that paired muscle relaxation at night before bed helps stop a racing mind and lets him get better quality sleep. These things are not miraculous, but they allow Alex to lower his arousal levels so that he is more receptive to other strategies like the above—thought restructuring, reframing, and so on. The pain is still there, and the problem is still a problem, but his response to it is now adaptive and masterful.

What Radical Acceptance Really Means

Most of us have an incorrect understanding of what the word "acceptance" means. We resist accepting things that feel bad because we think that it means we agree with them, that we want them to continue, or that we are passively condoning what we know is wrong. We think that if we accept something, it means we are somehow making it more likely that it will keep continuing. If somebody walks up to us in the street and tries to hand us their bag of trash, then of course we don't have to "accept" it.

But radical acceptance is not about accepting in the ordinary sense of the word. For some more fundamental aspects of reality, we are *not* being offered the choice or asked, "Do you want this?" We are not asked if we like it or agree with it. In fact, our agreement seems utterly irrelevant to whether we get it or not! Some parts of reality are up for debate, and others aren't. We can choose to live a healthy life and to be safe and avoid catching germs. But we cannot choose whether or not we die. We can choose how we respond to crises and emergencies, but not whether those events happen in the first place. For the parts of reality that are not up for debate, we need **radical acceptance, which is basically the decision to stop fighting reality**.

When we take action against something we don't like but can change, then we have a chance of changing it.

When we take action against something we don't like but *cannot* change, it stays exactly as it is, and we only become bitter, resentful, or exhausted.

You can accept reality without liking it. You can accept reality without liking it and still live a meaningful life. You can make choices and take action on some things even if you don't get to decide on others. Life can be hard but manageable.

In fact, acceptance can sometimes be the one thing that makes a bad situation pass more quickly. Imagine a woman in labor. At the first sensations of pain, she is terrified and thinks, "I can't do this. I don't want to do this. I hate this." What happens is that, because her mind is completely unaccepting, her body follows suit and tenses up completely, trying to push back against that pain.

But because she is tense and resistant, the labor becomes more difficult. Her muscles don't relax enough, so the process becomes more difficult and more painful. She gets even more terrified, tenses up further, and soon there is a full-blown crisis. Her lack of acceptance has, in effect, prolonged and amplified the pain. If she had instead accepted the pain, she would have relaxed, and the birth would have been easier. What happens physiologically during birth can also be said to happen psychologically and mentally whenever we encounter something we think we don't want, don't like, can't accept. The irony is that when we fight pain, it is often *extra* painful, and we only set ourselves up to get the exact opposite of what we want.

Easier said than done, of course! Let's imagine that Alex is making strides, but after a few months, the doctors tell him they will need to operate. They also tell him that the procedure carries a roughly fifteen percent chance of resulting in total paralysis from the waist down. Ouch. This fact is like a brick wall he smashes into. Alex researches, gets second opinions, and gathers what data he can, but in the end, he still faces an immovable fact: He needs an operation that has a moderate risk of permanently paralyzing him. If he doesn't operate, his life will become unbearable and he may damage his spinal column even further. Alex thinks, "This shouldn't be happening. I can't deal with this. This is not fair. I can't face it."

How can Alex accept this horrible "choice" he has? How could he, heaven forbid, possibly accept being paralyzed, should that be the outcome? You may not be facing a reality quite so stark as Alex's, but the process he uses to find acceptance is exactly the same one you can use when you find yourself "arguing with reality":

Step 1: Acknowledge that you are in fact fighting against reality. Really take a moment to let it sink in that you are pushing against an object that cannot move. Did you notice the word "should" in Alex's thought? Notice your struggle. Notice what it feels like in your body—tension, queasiness, etc.

Step 2: Tell yourself that it cannot be changed. This is harder than it seems. Just like complaining is focusing on a problem without the active effort to change it, wrestling with reality is a negative reaction that does precisely zero to change the facts.

Step 3: Be honest about the reality you face. If you must accept it, know what you're accepting. The truth is always easier to bear when you can see all sides of it! Look at cause and effect. Become curious about the details.

Step 4: Imagine how you would behave if you did accept these facts. What steps would you take (or not take)? How would you cope? What would you choose?

Step 5: Embrace and honor how you feel. Just because you are accepting your reality, it doesn't mean that you suddenly don't feel how you feel. Completely acknowledge any feelings of anger, regret, sadness, or disappointment.

Step 6: Remind yourself of what matters. Life is still worth living even though you are in pain at this moment. Remember the things you value, the principles that guide you, and the dreams you're hoping to achieve. It may be that you have to postpone or resize these dreams. That's okay. Re-negotiate your future and start to be curious about the meaning you can make from your experience.

The ACCEPTS Skill

This acronym stands for:

A – Activities
C – Contribute
C – Comparisons
E – Emotions, i.e., trying on emotions the opposite to the ones you have
P – Push away or shelve the problem
T – Thoughts, i.e., keeping your mind busy on other tasks and not on crisis-related thoughts and feelings
S – Sensations, i.e., grounding in the five senses as described above

For Alex, this might look like:

A – Stays busy with exercises, hobbies, DIY at home, cooking, and pushing himself to do walks when he can
C – Volunteering with a mental health crisis helpline, which he can do from home and which brings him some satisfaction that he can help others
C – *Helpful* comparisons—he realizes that as bad as his injury is, it could have been worse, and that he was in many ways lucky to have received the support he did
E – When he feels absolute despair, he tries to laugh at himself and have a sense of humor about the situation
P – Overwhelmed at the decision he has to make (operate or don't operate?), he chooses to just rest and process for a while, shelving the decision until he's calmer
T – Keeps his mind busy writing shopping lists, making detailed budgets, solving riddles, or planning for a DIY project in detail
S – Does a grounding exercise every time he can feel his thoughts spiraling into negativity again

As you can see, even in a situation that feels totally hopeless, you always have a choice, and there is a lot you can do even when it feels like there isn't! At the same time, **distress tolerance is a set of skills to help you survive and cope—it is not a long-term strategy for living your best life.** It's there as a crutch to help you deal with distress without making things worse. But it's not enough on its own. Sooner or later, Alex has to decide whether to get the operation or not.

If you're ever overcome with negative feelings, know that you always have the tools to calm yourself down physically, self-soothe, accept what is happening, and find ways to cope with the most intense emotions as you ride them out. These tools won't solve the problem—but they will help you make it through the worst of it in one piece until you're ready to look at solutions when you're feeling stronger and clearer.

Brain Dumping, Mental Noting, and Scheduled Worry Time

Chris had trouble navigating annoying and irritating life obstacles.

Carrie had to challenge the distorted mental filters she was using to look at herself.

Dan battled to reframe the story of guilt and shame he was living inside.

Ellen struggled to step outside of her depression and low mood.

And Alex had to learn to cope with the very real limitations of physical pain.

Each of these people had to deal with very different problems, but ultimately, each of them worked through their own version of negative thinking and how to find a way out of it. There is one manifestation of negativity that we haven't yet considered, though, and that's anxiety. This chapter is for you if you find your negativity taking the shape of worry, rumination, overthinking, and stress.

In the spirit of radical acceptance and not fighting against our mind or against reality, we'll begin with **a basic CBT principle when dealing with anxiety: We are not attempting to force ourselves not to worry**. It's just like being told "don't think of a pink elephant." Merely saying it makes you think of a pink elephant! So, first things first: getting anxious about your anxiety and worrying about your worry is not going to get you anywhere.

Instead, tap into the capital letter You and remind yourself that you have a choice. In the technique of "worry postponement," we essentially tell ourselves, "Okay, Mind, you have full permission to worry. I'm not stopping you. All I'm going to do is decide *when* you get to do it and for how long." In fact, tell yourself that your intention is to **worry more efficiently**. So, for example, you decide that instead of worrying right this instant, you're going to deliberately worry later tonight at 6 p.m. for twenty minutes.

Scheduling your negativity and worry may seem like an odd thing to do, but it works. This is because

1. You're learning to be aware that you are in fact worrying. (Again, it's about gaining distance—it's not, "Money's tight!" but, "I'm having a stressful thought about money right now.")
2. You avoid getting tangled up in that worry but also avoid going to war with it, resisting it, or denying it.
3. You take control. Just because a thought pops up and says, "Look at me!" it doesn't mean you have to obey.
4. You gain a deeper sense of how worry actually plays out in your life—how it comes and goes, rises and falls, and in time, how utterly useless it usually is . . .
5. You put yourself in a proactive state of mind where you stop worrying and start *strategizing*.

Anxiety is exactly the kind of mental activity that, if not engaged with, will eventually dissipate. You can probably think of a few things you were really worried about a day or a week or ten years ago, and which barely even register with you now. Why? Simply because some time has passed.

When you schedule your worry to take place some other time, you may notice how often you actually forget about it when the allotted worry time rolls around. Or, when the time comes and you have free rein to worry to your heart's content, you realize that the issue just doesn't seem that important anymore. Sometimes, when you arrive at your future worry appointment, you discover that you don't even *want* to worry anymore, that you are feeling way more calm and able to deal with any negativity that remains, or that the negativity has already resolved by itself.

Here's how worry postponement might look in practice.

Be Mindful
You're noticing a recurrent them here, right? It all starts with simply being aware that you are having anxious thoughts and worries in the first place. Just perceive and observe; don't judge. Try not to be too hard on yourself if you notice a worry spiral that seems to be getting out of hand. Try to practice a little radical acceptance.

"I'm feeling extremely worried and anxious at the moment."

"I am feeling so on edge. My stomach's in knots."

"I keep having the thought *what if* and am having trouble stopping it."

Postpone
Even if you have to do it out loud, give yourself permission to worry; only, the worry has to be deferred to a time of your choosing. Make sure that the time you choose is at least a couple hours away (to give your mental state time to change) but not so far off that you unconsciously feel like it won't really happen. Write down

- the day, date, and time,
- the duration for the worry,
- what you will worry about.

For example, let's say you're worrying about an upcoming performance review at work. You notice your anxious overthinking: "*Maybe it'll be really embarrassing. What am I going to do if they keep talking about the incident in March? It may be that they've already discussed it amongst themselves already. Maybe everyone has discussed it, and they're getting ready to fire me at this very moment. What if I cry or get angry during the meeting? What if I say something I regret . . . ?*"

You stop and become mindful and realize that your anxious thoughts are getting carried away. You say out loud, "That's okay, but we're not worrying right now." In a notebook, you scribble down "11 a.m. Tuesday, ten minutes worry time, concerns about upcoming performance review." Then you close the notebook. You've made an agreement with yourself, and so you don't have to keep worrying.

Follow Through

Naturally, your mind will soon start up again with worries. "Do you think you should maybe prepare a few clever rebuttals for if they want to talk about what happened in March? Just in case?" You notice this, and you don't argue with it. You also don't act or respond in any way. "No, Mind, we aren't doing this now—we're worrying tomorrow at 11 a.m., remember?"

Actively remind yourself that the big important issue your brain is trying to draw your attention to will certainly get the attention it deserves . . . in due course. Tell yourself that you're allowed to focus on the present moment's tasks because the worry is actually taken care of for now. All the time from now until 11 a.m. tomorrow is now "free." When the thought pops up, confidently tell it, "Oh, don't worry, I've already dealt with you!"

What about when 11 a.m. comes around? Well, do as you said you would and sit down and worry for ten minutes. But really worry! Don't let your mind wander to *other* worries—just the one you said you'd tackle. You may as well really go for it because once the ten minutes are up, you're not going to think about it anymore. Notice what happens when you do this. You might

1. no longer care about this problem,
2. feel better able to cope with it or manage it,
3. realize an action you can take to fix it,
4. still be at square one with no solution in sight.

Almost always, the outcome will be 1, 2, or 3. Occasionally, though, you will chew over something, and it will still be bothering you. Try your best to ask if there is one small thing you can do, there and then, to improve the situation. Then schedule that in, and promptly forget about it. If you catch yourself worrying further—then repeat the process. Postpone that worry till another time. At the very least, you are limiting your exposure to a difficult situation that you cannot do anything about.

You might start to notice that you keep worrying about something that either a) never comes, or b) does come and isn't as bad as you thought it would be, or even c) it does come, it *is* that bad, and it doesn't matter because you were able to cope with it.

One variation of this practice is to externalize worries while you're postponing them. So whatever pops into your mind, imagine that you're redirecting it to the page and writing it down there. The rule is, once it's written down in the worry book, it does not need to be in your head anymore. The worry book is like a repository. All through the day, collect little nagging fears and concerns as they crop up and put them aside to mull over later, on your own terms.

After a while of doing this, ask yourself a few questions:

Are there any recurrent themes?

How often does the thing you fear actually come to pass?
Is there any difference in outcome when you do worry versus when you don't?

A final variation is called "brain dumping," and it's exactly what it sounds like. When it's your scheduled time to worry, go all out and put EVERYTHING down on the page. You can rant, you can rave, you can say what you like and let it all out. For five whole minutes (try not to go too much longer than this!), you have no limits and can experience the full cathartic power of worrying as hard as you can worry.

Imagine that your brain is like a room in a house that has just become too cluttered with junk. When you do a brain dump, you're basically throwing all this clutter out. The power lies in acknowledging the thoughts and putting them outside of yourself. A big reason we worry is because our brain thinks it's being useful. It wants to keep drawing our attention to something that may be threatening or a problem in the future, but if you put it down on paper, this sends a strong message to your unconscious mind: "I've noted this. It's being dealt with. I won't forget. You can stop reminding me now!"

What should you include in your brain dump? Whatever you need to. Scribble down stream-of-consciousness ideas, thoughts, feelings, and fears. Put down things you're worried about forgetting on your to-do list. Regrets, concerns, complaints—anything you like.

What you do with your brain dump from there is up to you—the wonderful thing is that once it's out on paper, you can do something about it. Here are a few options:

- Burn, crumple, or throw away the paper if what you've expressed is just useless or destructive material. Breathe a sigh of relief.
- Process what you've written. Pick one thing that's bugging you and consciously decide to take a step to address it. Just one thing, though—you can't tackle it all!
- Go through the material, identify negative and self-defeating beliefs, and gently rewrite them. Turn them into affirmations that you begin the following day with. The ABC method described above can be a great technique to incorporate here.
- If it makes sense to you, pray about or meditate on some of the things that are weighing on your heart but you're stuck with. Ask a higher power to help you carry the burden, or do a visualization exercise where you release yourself from having to worry about it anymore.

Turning Anxiety into Mindfulness
People who struggle with anxiety are actually blessed with a secret superpower. If they harness it, they are able to tap into an enormous potential for heightened conscious awareness. Every intrusive and anxious thought can be like a "meditation bell" calling you to awareness and bringing you back into the moment. How?

Try "mental noting." It's easy.

1. Become aware and observe yourself having thoughts. No judgment.
2. Note the experience and label it. "I'm thinking."
3. Keep going. Repeat until the thought dissipates or you move on.

Every time you have a thought, any thought at all, you can stop and remember to become aware of yourself. In some Buddhist temples and monasteries, a mediation bell rings periodically so that wherever people are and whatever they are doing at that moment, they can stop and reconnect to the present again. You can do the same with your own thoughts and self-talk. Every time you hear an anxious thought, treat it as a bell that has rung to remind you to come back to the present.

Of course, you won't be able to maintain awareness one hundred percent of the time, but if you can grab hold of an anxious thought and note it for what it is, then you can transform *any* thought into an opportunity to be mindful.

This technique is inspired by many different mediation techniques and is designed to quell distractions and calm down what the Buddhists call "monkey mind"—that inner chat that thoughtlessly leaps from one thing to another. Mental noting might not seem like much, but if you pepper your day with little moments of metacognition in this way, be prepared for big, big changes in the long run. Practice this often enough and you will find it much more difficult to become "fused" with negative thoughts. You simply maintain too much distance to ever get too tangled up.

Just remember three key elements when you practice mental noting:

Your **intention** should be to maintain awareness of the present moment.
Your **attention** should be on everything that is happening in the present only.
Your **attitude** should be non-directional, non-judgmental, and kind.

The classical approach during mediation is to say, for example, "There is hearing," or, "Hearing has happened," when you notice a dog barking outside. You might be really Zen and simply note, "Hearing." You don't allow yourself to run off and follow the hearing so that you are soon thinking, "That's the neighbor's dog," or, "I wish it would shut up." You simply note and label what your brain is doing, then move on.

In the case of anxiety, you do something similar to stop yourself from getting "distracted" by thoughts that seem urgent and important but really aren't. So if you're sitting at your desk, trying to work, and you notice a thought pop into your mind ("The performance review is going to be so awkward!"), you stop in your tracks, note the thought, label it, and move on without engaging. "Ruminating," you say, and pass it by.

Another way to bring in the principles of mindfulness to a brain that's hooked on anxiety is called "mundane task focusing." If you're one of the many people who dislike meditation or simply don't find room in their lives to practice it, don't worry—the Buddhists and meditators do not have the monopoly on mindfulness!

All that's required to calm an anxious mind is to remain in the moment. Anxieties and worries live *elsewhere*—they're in the past or the future. If you anchor right here and right now, though, your world slows down and becomes calmer and way more manageable.

1. Pick a mundane and everyday task that doesn't require too much brainpower—for example, washing dishes.
2. Do the task but do it very intentionally. Pay ultra-close attention to what you are doing. Focus on the bubbles of the soap. The temperature of the water. The rhythmic movement of your hands, and the weight of each dish as you hold it (as you can see, this is a form of grounding).
3. When your mind wanders, pull it back to the task at hand. Commit every last ounce of your attention to the task unfolding before you, nothing more.

You can find immense relief from overthinking and worry by doing completely ordinary everyday tasks, like walking to the post office or filling the car with fuel.

Summary

- We need distress tolerance skills to help us cope with extremely trying or painful moments, or emergency situations. When we're distressed, it's easy to slip back into old patterns of behavior or default to clumsy, destructive, or unconscious ways of coping—these are false coping mechanisms.
- Self-soothing is a way to acknowledge and accept pain that is inevitable—without making it any bigger than it should be. It is not distraction or avoidance, but about anchoring in the present using your five senses—a technique called grounding.
- TIPP stands for temperature, intense exercise, paced breathing, and paired muscle relaxation, all of which can help lower physiological arousal. Try cold water, vigorous movement, or breathing exercises to calm the limbic system.
- Practice radical acceptance, which doesn't mean we like what is happening, only that we have agreed to not fight with reality. Acknowledge how you feel and the reality of the situation and remind yourself of what matters.
- The ACCEPTS acronym (Activities, Contribute, Comparisons, Emotions, Push away, Thoughts, and Sensations) can help you better tolerate momentary distress—although not for the longer term.
- With anxiety, our goal is not to force ourselves not to worry, but to worry more efficiently. Scheduling worry time puts you in proactive control and helps you gain distance.
- Notice the anxiety, write down the time you'll postpone to—with the duration and content—then follow through as agreed.
- Mental noting and focused mundane tasks can help you turn anxious moments into opportunities for mindfulness.

Chapter 4: Upgrade Your Psychological Toolkit with Stoic *Amor Fati* Philosophy

Long before the first psychiatrists and psychologists began to make their models of human suffering, the ancient Stoics had a fully developed understanding of the human condition and a philosophy of living they believed to be the most balanced and rational. The fact that so many modern people still find solace and strength in these ancient principles is a testament to how useful they really are.

The Stoics were masters at "living in the present." They saw clearly that the answer to negative thinking and especially anxiety and worry was to come back to the only place you actually have any control: the present. The past matters, but it should be studied and learned from—then forgotten. The future also matters, but we should not obsess uselessly over it; instead, we should use what we have right now to make plans to prepare for the worst and set in motion projects that will serve us best. Beyond that, the future, too, should be forgotten—after all, it will arrive in due course one way or another!

Beyond Radical Acceptance: Amor Fati

One way of rethinking your relationship to the past is to adopt the Stoic attitude of *amor fati*. This translates roughly to "love of one's fate" and is a sentiment that is sadly not common in modern hearts and minds. With this attitude, one does not merely tolerate one's fate but embraces it—loves it. **Whatever happens in life—and that includes all the painful, confusing, and difficult parts—is welcomed and appreciated as something beautiful and, in its way, necessary.**

In his book *Enchiridion*, Epictetus advises us, "Do not seek for things to happen the way you want them to; rather, wish that what happens happens the way it happens: then you will be happy." In other words, learn to want what is, and you cease to fight against anything. He tells us in a later work *The Art of Living*, that "prudent people look beyond the incident itself and seek to form the habit of putting it to good use."

In his famous work *Meditations*, much-loved Stoic philosopher Marcus Aurelius says, "Universe, whatever is consonant with you is consonant with me; if something is timely for you, it's neither too early nor too late for me. Nature, everything is fruit to me that your seasons bring; everything comes from you, everything is contained in you, everything returns to you." Can you feel the enormous sense of *relief* in that passage?

These philosophers suggest that we quietly bear our misfortunes and be strong, but they are taking it somewhat further—our misfortunes, with the attitude of *amor fati*, are in fact not things to bear and endure and tolerate, but things to embrace. If reality itself has seen fit to make certain things occur, who are you to argue? In fact, why should you do anything other than be *glad* that events have unfolded in the way they have?

This way of thinking takes some time to digest since it is so radically different from the typical sense of regret, dissatisfaction, and resistance most of us are taught to eliminate when it comes to our lives. Though the original principles came from Stoic philosophers like Seneca and Aurelius, it was also the philosopher Friedrich Nietzsche who revived the theme in his book *Ecce Homo*, saying, "My formula for greatness in a human being is *amor fati*: that one wants nothing to be different, not forward, not backward, not in all eternity. Not merely bear what is necessary, still less conceal it—all idealism is mendacity in the face of what is necessary—but *love* it."

This is a profound paradigm shift. What do you think your life would be like if you genuinely wanted "nothing to be different" and embraced every event—past, present, and future—as something marvelous? This sentiment goes beyond accepting what is (and the Buddhist philosophers would certainly understand this point)—it is about being decidedly enamored with *all* the shapes and contours of one's own life.

Nietzsche continues in his book *The Gay Science*,

"I want to learn more and more to see as beautiful what is necessary in things; then I shall be one of those who makes things beautiful. *Amor fati*: let that be my love henceforth! I do not want to wage war against what is ugly, I do not want to accuse; I do not even want to accuse those who accuse. *Looking away* shall be my only negation. And all in all and on the whole: someday I wish to be only a Yes-sayer."

Here, Nietzsche hints at the enormous potential that the *amor fati* attitude can bring about. If we not only accept but love what is our fate, we give ourselves the opportunity to find, create, or amplify any possible beauty, meaning, and power in those events. We can transfigure and transform them. We go from being reactive strugglers against reality, always saying "no" to those who have gratitude, curiosity, and positivity built into everything they do, so that there is nothing that they cannot say "yes" to.

If all of this sounds overly abstract, don't worry. There are very simple ways to cultivate *amor fati* in your own life, right now.

Tip 1: Define the event as objectively as possible

Remember that a thing is only good or bad because of the perspective you're taking on it. What is a tragedy for one is a blessing for another—and completely neutral for a third. Try to look at events without the veil of your own resistance, judgment, or opinion spread on top of it. To do this, write down an account of the event in the plainest, most neutral terms you can imagine, as if you were an uninvolved third party watching from afar. Do not put any interpretations, emotions, or opinions into the mix. When you read this back to yourself, you will see how much more manageable it is.

Remember the following old Buddhist proverb:

> *A farmer and his son had a beloved horse who helped the family earn a living. One day, the horse ran away, and their neighbors exclaimed, "Your horse ran away. What terrible luck!" The farmer replied, "Maybe so, maybe not."*

> *A few days later, the horse returned home, leading a few wild horses back to the farm as well. The neighbors shouted out, "Your horse has returned and brought several horses home with him. What great luck!" The farmer replied, "Maybe so, maybe not."*

> *Later that week, the farmer's son was trying to break one of the horses, and she threw him to the ground, breaking his leg. The neighbors cried, "Your son broke his leg. What terrible luck!" The farmer replied, "Maybe so, maybe not."*

> *A few weeks later, soldiers from the national army marched through town, recruiting all boys for the army. They did not take the farmer's son because he had a broken leg. The neighbors shouted, "Your boy is spared. What tremendous luck!" To which the farmer replied, "Maybe so, maybe not. We'll see."*

Tip 2: Have a mantra

Jocko Willink is an ex-Navy SEAL and an author, and his mantra for all difficult or unpleasant situations is simple: "Good." He says,

> *"When things are going bad: Don't get all bummed out, don't get startled, don't get frustrated. No. Just look at the issue and say: "Good." Now, I don't mean to say something trite; I'm not trying to sound like Mr. Smiley Positive Guy. That guy ignores the hard truth. That guy thinks a positive attitude will solve problems. It won't. But neither will dwelling on the problem. No. Accept reality, but focus on the solution. Take that issue, take that setback, take that problem, and turn it into something good."*

Whatever mantra you choose, say it out loud to yourself when you catch yourself feeling decidedly not in love with your fate.

"Okay."

"Thank you."

"So it is."

"Yes."

"I welcome it."

Tip 3: Focus on action, focus on solutions

It would be a big mistake to assume that loving one's fate is the same as being a passive, defeated fatalist. In fact, the opposite is true; only when you fully and completely embrace what is can you properly engage with your full range of choice, agency, and power. We should love what is—but that doesn't mean we forfeit our chance to have a say, take action, and attempt to influence that reality.

When we love a challenge, we transform it into an opportunity.

When we love our flaws and weaknesses, we start to see that they open doors to our evolution and growth.

When we love our enemies, we can begin to see them as teachers.

When we love our tragedies, accidents, and losses, they begin to feel to us like gifts.

Take a look at the problem you've described and ask about your scope to change it. Think of what you can do, break that task down into smaller chunks, and then commit to taking the very next step, right now if possible.

If we only ever resist adversity, say "no" to reality, and fight against it, all those potential gifts, opportunities, lessons, and insights are lost. When you really think about it, is it such a wonderful thing to always get what we think we want? Do we *really* want to live in a world where we are never challenged, never uncomfortable, never surprised or humbled?

Negative Visualization

The Stoics called this technique *premeditatio malorum.* Modern motivational speakers and self-help gurus warn against entertaining the worst possible outcomes or dwelling on negativity, but for the Stoics, this activity actually had some value.

The idea is that you **occasionally spend a short amount of time imagining in detail the negative things that could happen in life**. By doing so, you generate a renewed appreciation for all the things you do have. It's like you recalibrate, remembering what's important and putting your current concerns and worries into perspective as you find more gratitude for what is already working well for you. More than this, though, negative visualization is intended to put you back in control and take the sting out of worries and anxieties. When we insist on avoiding any negative premonitions at all, we don't give ourselves the chance to plan and prepare for them, and in a way, we give them more power over us.

In his 45 BC text *Tusculan Disputations*, Cicero explains, "I am ready to borrow of the Cyrenaics those arms against the accidents and events of life by means of which, by long premeditation, they break the force of all approaching evils. And at the same time I think that those very evils themselves arise more from opinion than nature, for if they were real, no forecast could make them lighter."

In his letters to Lucilius, Seneca echoes this sentiment by saying, "He robs present ills of their power who has perceived their coming beforehand." Elsewhere, he writes,

> *"I will conduct you to peace of mind by another route: if you would put off all worry, assume that what you fear may happen will certainly happen. Whatever the evil may be, measure it in your own mind, and estimate the amount of your fear. You will soon understand that what you fear is either not great or not of long duration."*

But this technique is not just for use when times are tough, but when things are going well, too. In *Epistles* 18.6, he says,

> *"It is in times of security that the spirit should be preparing itself to deal with difficult times; while fortune is bestowing favors on it then is the time for it to be strengthened against her rebuffs. In the midst of peace, the soldier carries out maneuvers, throws up earthworks against a non-existent enemy and tires himself out with unnecessary toil in order to be equal to it when it is necessary. If you want a man to keep his head when the crisis comes, you must give him some training before it comes.*

In other words, if we wish to be mentally tough and resilient, we need to train ourselves to endure possibly negative outcomes, just as an athlete trains themselves to be strong in the face of physical adversity. Granted, the Stoic mindset can seem a little alien at times, and their advice may sound strange to modern ears. Exactly how can you apply negative visualization in your own life—and how is it different from simply catastrophizing?

Think of the aim of the exercises as three-fold. When you practice negative visualization, you are:

Increasing gratitude for what you have right now.

Desensitizing yourself to adversity and increasing your tolerance and resilience to it.

Allowing yourself to prepare for negative outcomes.

To hit all three aspects, here's an exercise to try.

1. Start by writing down one to three things that are very valuable to you, whether they're material things like a house or a laptop, or something abstract like a relationship, good health, talents, or time. This can also work well if you pick something that is currently causing you trouble.

2. Once or twice a week, sit down somewhere quiet to meditate for five minutes on what your life would be like *without* these things. How would you feel? Explore the scenario in detail, pulling no punches.

3. Then, dig deep and imagine what mental, physical, and emotional resources you could draw on to deal with such a loss. In what ways might you be able to survive?

4. Finally, end the exercise by thinking of a few ways you could minimize the loss of such a thing, should it ever happen for real. After you contemplate loss in this way, is there something in your present behavior that needs to change? End your meditation session with a quiet moment, letting your fresh insights sink in and welcoming a sense of tranquility.

Let's consider an example. Eve is having a difficult time with her job. It's not the best fit for her and is causing a lot of day-to-day stress that frequently makes her consider quitting for something less intense. She begins to practice negative visualization twice a week, and one day, she picks "my job" as something to meditate on. She has been in the habit of thinking negatively about this job for months now, but for five minutes, she does the opposite and considers what would happen if she suddenly lost this job tomorrow.

She explores the feelings that come up. There's relief, yes, but she also realizes that the sudden lack of salary would be terrifying, and that she'd have to hunt for a new job—also an awful prospect. She pictures herself walking around her flat with little to do during the day, and imagines how she'd have to tighten her belt with spending until she secured another position. She can also see, though, how she'd cope—she knows that with effort, persistence, and drawing on her various networks, she *could* find a new job, one way or another.

When she comes out of her meditation, she has a new, subtler perspective on the issue. Though the problems are all still there, she is able to actually be grateful for the job, warts and all, and sees that her position is not so bad as she thought it was. She decides to take action. She *will* quit her job, but she will do so strategically. She commits to getting her resume up to scratch and start looking for possible positions, all without leaving the comfort of her current job just yet. The next day, all the same work stresses and irritations are there, just as they were before, but Eve is less bothered by them, more assured about her own ability to manage any outcome, *and* actively shaping a future outcome she'd most prefer.

Stoicism and CBT Combined—the "What-If" Technique

A useful CBT technique is inspired loosely by the spirit of Stoic negative visualization and is an interesting approach to use in the face of negative thinking, anxieties, and worries. The process is simple but powerful:

Step 1: Write down a future event or potential outcome that is causing you some anxiety.

Step 2: Then ask yourself the following questions:

"What if this were actually true?"

"What is the worst that could happen . . . and is that really so bad?"

Write down the answers to this question—including any negative thoughts and worries that it inspires.

Step 3: In response to these new fears, ask the same questions again. Repeat the process on *those* answers, and so on. Keep going until you arrive at a core fear and realize that it would not in fact be the end of the world.

For example:

Step 1:

"I'm worried I'm never going to meet anyone."

Step 2:

"What if this were actually true? What is the worst that could happen?" Answer: "If I never met anyone, I'd have to live the rest of my life alone without a partner. I'd never find anyone to love."

Step 3:

"You'd never have anyone, you'd be alone, etc. What if all of this were actually true?" Answer: "I'd be devastated! It would mean that I was totally unloved. I'd miss out on a big part of life."

Step 3 again:

"You'd be devastated, unloved, and missing out on a big part of life . . . so what if that were really true? Would it really be that bad?" Answer: "Well, it wouldn't be the absolute *worst* thing that could ever happen. But it would be pretty bad. I'd have to go to events on my own, live alone in a house . . ."

"Living alone in a house . . . is that really that bad?" Answer: "Well, I guess it's not the end of the world."

Often, when we're trying to make ourselves feel better, we may inadvertently run away from, deny, or avoid our fears instead of facing them head on so that we can see that they are not actually as serious as we've told ourselves they are. Take a look at the worst thing you can imagine—is it really that bad? *Really?* With this technique, we stop running and turn around to face our fear instead. What is the actual shape and size of this fear? Is it the end of the world even if it is as bad as you guessed?

Hidden in the core of many anxious beliefs is a deeper belief that "I can't cope" or "I can't bear it." But this is usually not true. People can and do cope with all sorts of things! It's not what you prefer, and it's not what you want. But it's doable. It can be managed. If you subtly change the way you think about it, it can even be reframed as something of value. Do this exercise and you'll realize that "living all alone in a house" is actually a secret fantasy of many coupled people. They might do the very same exercise as you but begin with the terrible fear they can't cope with: "I never get to be on my own or have my own space . . ."

When this technique is combined with *amor fati* and a little negative visualization, the "problem" can take on all sorts of interesting new dimensions. You start to open up to all the ways that you actually *love* living alone on your own terms and that, in its own way, never finding anyone to love is simply one more thing that gives color and flavor to your unique and beautiful life. Some of the world's most fascinating, accomplished, and self-actualized people never partnered up. Not *despite* their lack of life partner, but in many cases, *because* of it.

Consider what would have happened if you instead refused to entertain any negative premonitions about this fear. If you instead said to yourself, "I refuse to be anxious about this; I *will* meet someone one day," and spent your time on guided visualizations where you picture yourself meeting your soul mate. What then? Well, you might meet someone. But what if you don't? Your "positive visualization" has then left you with enormous expectations and very few resources to deal with their disappointment. By not engaging it, the fear becomes bigger. Besides, the person with a fear of being alone who is temporarily in a relationship has not genuinely addressed that fear—just *masked* it. The moment they find themselves alone again, they will find the fear is still there, just as it always was.

So the question is, who has the most mastery over their fear—someone who quickly finds a way to run away from it, or someone who can look squarely at it and not be afraid anymore?

"Remember that You Must Die"
Speaking of fears, let's dive into what is arguably humankind's biggest one: death. *Memento mori* is Latin for: "remember that you will die." How would you live your life if you knew that at the end of this week, it would all be over for you? Well, you'd probably be unwilling to waste a single moment and would take extra special care to live well—whatever that means for you.

You wouldn't get hung up on the opinions of people you don't care about.

You wouldn't struggle through difficult books because everyone else thought they were good.

You wouldn't tolerate bad behavior from those around you.

You wouldn't continue in a pointless job that didn't make use of your talents.

Here's the truth, though: this little thought experiment is not an experiment at all. **You really will die**. No, not at the end of the week (if you're lucky . . . although, what proportion of people who are reading these words right now won't be so lucky?). But eventually. Sooner than you think, most likely.

The intention with remembering this is not to make you depressed or defeated. Quite the opposite. It's to invigorate you; to inspire you to grasp, with fearsome gratitude, the miracle of your life right now; and to remind yourself that once this life is over, it's over. If we have dreams and desires, the time to make them happen is now. If we have fears and vices controlling us, the time to unshackle ourselves from them is now. Because, one day in the future, it is an absolute guarantee that we will no longer have the time to do either.

Tomorrow, when you wake up, remind yourself that you are alive. When you go to bed, remind yourself that you do not have infinite nights like these, and one day, you will lie down for the last time. In the novel *All the Light We Cannot See*, author Anthony Doerr says, "Open your eyes and see what you can with them before they close forever." If time is limited, don't you want to find a way to make all your worries, adversities, and problems *mean* something? If time is limited, don't you want to live in such a way as to squeeze every last drop out of the pleasures you have been gifted?

What is Your Orientation: Solution or Problem Orientation? Thought or Action?

Imagine a group of four friends is traveling together, but as they assemble at the airport, they realize that one of them has forgotten his passport at home. In the time it would take him to go back home, fetch it, and return, the plane will have already left. The group erupts into anxious chatter.

Friend 1: "I can't believe I've done this! I'm such a moron. I'm so sorry! I had no idea, really. I've never done something like this before. Oh man, what are we going to do? This is awful."

Friend 2: "It's okay. It's not your fault. You probably were just rushed when you packed this morning. Do you remember where you might have left it?"

Friend 3: "We're not going to make it. We can't go home now; he'll make us all late. No way he can come with us now. It's impossible. We'll be late."

Friend 4: "I've had a look online and there's a flight leaving two hours after this one. It'll cost 150 dollars to switch flights, but we still have time to do that. We three can go ahead and meet you on the other side?"

Each of us has a unique way of looking at life—and it goes beyond "negative" or "positive." Some of us focus on problems (like Friend 1 and Friend 3), others on how the problem came to be and its details (Friend 2), and still others focus on solutions (like Friend 4). In the above example, though, all four friends are facing the *same* issue—it is their response to it that makes all the difference.

Problem-focused thinking zooms in on what's wrong.

Solution-focused thinking zooms in on what *could* be right.

In our example, Friend 1 and Friend 3 are only looking at the fact of the problem. And the result is that they complain, express negativity, or blame one another. They hold on to the negativity feeling associated with the situation . . . and keep on holding on to it! They exclaim again and again how stupid it was to leave a passport at home, how bad it would be if they missed the flight, how unfortunate the whole thing is . . .

But Friend 4 is not looking at all this. They're looking at **solutions** and **actions**. What can be done?

Let's be clear: In this example, both interpretations are possible. There's no doubt that this *is* a frustrating and terrible situation to be in. Friend 4, however, isn't oblivious to these things—they're just not focused on them. Likewise, it's not that Friend 1 or Friend 2 can't agree that there's probably a solution to their problem—they're choosing in this moment not to focus on it.

You can probably see that the big difference between being problem-focused and solution-focused is acceptance of reality. Friend 4 has essentially said to themselves, "Yes, the whole thing is annoying . . . but we can't change that now, and dwelling on it won't bring us closer to fixing the problem."

Once you start becoming aware of problem-focus, you will suddenly see it *everywhere*. This attitude is sadly too common, with many people unconsciously defending their negativity by saying, "I'm just being realistic." Here lies a real danger: being firmly problem-focused while incorrectly assuming that you are solutions-focused. You believe, in other words, that your negativity and dwelling on the problem *is* how the problem gets solved.

Be Honest with Yourself

Do you have a problem-oriented attitude? Most people who do don't *think* they do. Radical honesty is a must. Have you ever said, "Why is this happening to me?" or complained about how unfair something is? Do you ever go on at length about what you *wish* was the case (but clearly isn't)? Do you even consider yourself uniquely unlucky or that there is something about you in particular that elicits a bad outcome from the universe at large? Chances are, you are predominantly problem-focused.

Problem-focus (or "out of power" language as discussed above) is passive, reactive, and negative by definition. It often shows itself in a few characteristic ways:

1. Asking "why?" of a problem
2. Complaining
3. Assuming a victim role
4. Blaming others
5. Self-pity
6. Framing things in terms of "fairness"

For example, you get on the scale one morning and discover that you've gained ten pounds over Christmas. Big problem. With a problem-focus, you think, "Why is life so unfair? Why is everything that makes you fat so delicious?! It's all that garbage everyone pushes you to eat over Christmas . . . with my bad metabolism, I never stood a chance. And now I look awful in my clothes . . . I just can't believe it . . ."

Can you hear the refusal to accept reality in the above? Do you also notice that there isn't really an answer to the question, "Why is life so unfair?" It's a bad question. In fact, it's not a question at all, but a complaint, and it makes several poor assumptions—mainly that life *is* unfair. If the unfairness of life is your starting position, you are framing yourself as a poorly treated victim and concluding that there is nothing to be done about it . . . except whine. This immediately shuts you off from your own agency and from a very obvious fact: You can lose the weight if you try.

However, having a solutions-focus is not about magically seeing a million ways to fix a problem—it's more the frame of mind that believes that *there is a solution* in the first place. Being solutions-oriented doesn't mean you instantly become a formidable problem-solver, barging through life's obstacles with ease. It simply means you are open enough to ask, "What can I do here?" and to follow through on that.

By the same token, being problem-focused is not always a bad thing. Problem-focused people are good at analyzing situations and seeing exactly where a breakdown has occurred, and why. However, unless they eventually move into solutions-focus, they will continue to dwell on the problem indefinitely and never give themselves the chance to convert their insight into action and to change things. Being too solutions-focused may mean that you lack nuanced understanding of the problem, and race in to fix things that you don't really grasp, just because you can't bear facing the discomfort of the problem for too long.

So, it's a question of balance:

Thinking about a problem is useful, but it needs to be combined with concrete **action**.

Noticing, understanding, and analyzing the **problem** is a valuable thing to do, but only if it's combined with a focus on the **solution**, too.

For an extremely problem-focused person, everything they look at is a problem, and even if they're offered a solution, they can instantly identify what's wrong with it. (Have you ever played a game of "yes, but..." with someone who was determined not to have you solve their problems for them?)

On the other hand, for an extremely solutions-focused person, everything looks like a solution—including things that really aren't. What's worse is that they may be so keen on finding a quick fix that they skip over the part where they analyze and understand the problem they're supposed to be fixing. You've probably met someone like this before—there is a constant and almost frantic hopping from one promising idea to the next without stopping to understand the problem better first.

Because this is a book about the question of negative thinking and how to overcome self-sabotaging thought patterns, there's a good chance you struggle more with being overly problems-focused rather than too solutions-focused. So for now, we'll ignore that possibility and look at how to be less problem-focused.

What is your attitude to problems? Do you instantly throw your hands up and get angry or defeated, wondering why life has dealt you this blow? Do you get so focused on negative feelings that you become obsessed with them, unable to see beyond them? Do you go into victim mode and unconsciously hope that someone else will come and rescue you somehow?

These are difficult questions, and the way we individually face problems is a complex topic. We may have learned this behavior as children when our core beliefs about ourselves and our capacities were laid down. We may have had formative experiences that taught us not to expect too much or to have little faith in our own problem-solving abilities. More broadly, we may simply have the attitude that life is bad and difficult and unfair, so when a problem occurs, our response is more or less, "So what else is new?"

For now, one important theme is to remember that **negativity is a perspective**. It's not truth, but a particular view on the truth. And this view is one that is chosen . . . which means a different point of view can be chosen! The next time you feel yourself facing a problem, try the following Stoic-inspired exercise to help you acknowledge the problem without letting yourself get distracted from the task of finding a solution—if there is one.

Keep It Simple with the Two-Column Exercise

The Stoics believed that those things in life that cannot be changed must be borne with dignity and fortitude, but that it is also our duty to do our best to work at those things we *can* change. Resilience and strength, but never resignation and passivity. You might have seen this sentiment echoed in the Serenity Prayer, which goes,

"Grant me the serenity to accept the things I cannot change, the courage to change the things I can, and the wisdom to know the difference."

We can apply this to our own lives every time we face a problem by using a two-column technique. It's simple to do. Take a piece of paper and draw a line down the middle to create two columns. Label one "things I can change" and the other "things I cannot change." Now, spend a few moments thinking about the issue that is bothering you and (honestly!) assign its various aspects to one column or the other.

If you like, you might choose to do a kind of "brain dump" beforehand just to tease out all the elements of your problem. This is also an excellent practice to combine with any CBT techniques, or exercises where you're fleshing out your core beliefs.

Once you have thoroughly dissected the problem this way, it's time to start processing. Recall the skills of radical acceptance and *amor fati*—you will need this attitude when dealing with things in the "cannot change" column. Unless you apply a degree of acceptance and embrace what is, you risk getting trapped in a problem-focused loop, complaining, blaming, or acting the victim.

For things you *can* change, you will need a solutions-focused approach, and to switch your mode into action. For things in this column, ask yourself the following questions:

What can I practically do to address this problem?

What do I need to prepare or plan for?

What is the first step I need to take?

What do I need to learn?

Who do I need to ask for help?

How can I remove the current obstacle standing in my way?

How can I break the bigger task into smaller ones so that I can act right now?

You may discover that you prefer to have *three* columns: one for what you cannot control, one for what you can, and a third column for things that you have partial control over. The rest of the process is similar: Ask yourself what can be done and then commit to taking actions toward that goal. That portion that is not in your control can be let go, while you can carefully extract the portion that you can do something about—even if it's just a small thing.

Let's return to our earlier example of discovering that you've gained weight over Christmas and aren't too happy about it. Your two-column list may look like this:

Things I can't change

The fact that I have gained ten pounds

What I did and what I ate in the past

Things I can change

What I eat and what I do now and in the future

How I talk about the problem and how I talk about myself

As you look at the second list, the next actions to take are obvious: commit to eating better, exercising, and refusing to blame anything or anyone else for choices you made in the past. For the things you can't change, well, it's worth spending the time to acknowledge that yes, you have gained weight and yes, it's probably your own fault—but don't dwell on it. Negativity is "useful" only in the sense that it creates insight that drives us to evolve. Learn what lesson you can, then move on. You serve nobody by beating yourself up or getting obsessed with guilt, shame, blame, or regret.

A variation on this exercise is even quicker. Identify what it is that you want, and then ask yourself, **"Is what I'm doing, thinking, or feeling bringing me closer to that?"**

If you're overweight and unhappy about it, then you probably want to lose weight. Notice yourself blaming Christmas, complaining about your metabolism, or focusing on how bad you feel in your clothes . . . and ask if any of it brings you closer to losing weight and being happier with yourself. No? Then it's useless. Have the serenity to just let it all go. Instead, become curious about the kind of things you'd feel, do, and think if you were someone who was losing weight right now . . . then do that. Yes, it will take courage.

In the end, it's not that being solution-focused in always superior to being problem-focused. Rather, as the Stoics understood, it's about the *wisdom* of knowing when to apply one and not the other, and in what proportion.

Summary

- The ancient Stoics were masters of living in the present.
- One way of rethinking your relationship to the past is to adopt the Stoic attitude of *amor fati*. This translates roughly to "love of one's fate." Whatever happens is embraced, wanting "nothing to be different." To practice it, look at events as

neutrally as possible and then respond to them with a simple mantra like "good." By focusing on action and solutions, we are able to transform adversity.
- Negative visualization is where we occasionally spend a short amount of time imagining in detail the negative things that could happen in life. This renews appreciation and gratitude for what matters, allows us to prepare for the future, and creates psychological resilience.
- With the "what-if" technique, we write down a fear and ask, "What if this were true?" and explore the worst that could happen, showing ourselves that it is tolerable and not so bad after all. Likewise, remember *Memento mori*, Latin for, "remember that you will die" to help remind you of what matters.
- Problem-focused thinking zooms in on what's wrong. Solution-focused thinking zooms in on what *could* be right and looks to taking action to change the situation. Thinking needs to be balanced with action. Focus on the problem needs to be balanced with focus on the solution.
- Remember the Serenity Prayer and try the two-column exercise to help you identify what you can change and what you can't. Accept what you can't, act where you can.
- Ask what you want and value, then ask yourself, "Is what I'm doing, thinking, or feeling bringing me closer to that?"

Chapter 5: Avoid the Trap of Toxic Positivity and Feel your Feelings

Craig is someone who has really turned his life around. In his early twenties, he suffered terribly from depression, anxiety, and low self-esteem. But that was before he joined a community yoga class and felt so much better that very same day. Within a few years, he was reading countless fascinating New Age self-help books, taking classes on the law of attraction manifestation, and had become a vegetarian. He grasped what he felt was an unavoidable truth: *As you think, so shall you become.*

To Craig, the universe was pure consciousness and love—if you could match that frequency of trusting and generative positivity, then you would always align with the good that was flowing all around you at all times. If you're negative, though, the universe will mirror that negativity straight back at you. In time, Craig starts to understand all the adversity that he'd experienced as a manifestation of his own lack of self-love and his own doubt in universal abundance.

And thinking this way worked for him. Until it didn't. When his sister died, Craig was completely bowled over by an unmanageable mass of negative feelings that caught him off guard. He told himself that there are no mistakes in life, that she was somewhere better, that it was all okay, and that there was no need to mourn since energy never disappears—it only changes form... And yet, he still felt devastated. He hid these feelings of devastation, even from himself. He couldn't admit that part of his new conversion to the light meant obsessively guarding against any experience of the dark.

He put on a brave face, and when people asked how he was doing, he responded with speeches about the transcendental nature of mortality and the Tibetan Book of the Dead and how he was ecstatic to receive this lesson in non-attachment. In response to the mourning of his other family members, he remained aloof and occasionally sent them "inspiring" quotes that actually upset them. One day, he makes his mother cry when he not-so-subtly suggests that her continued upset is evidence of her poor spiritual development, and that she should meditate more instead of moping around. It sounds cruel, but it's only a natural conclusion of the very same philosophy that had helped Craig up till that point.

Craig's only crime was that he sincerely wanted to be *good*. Only good. He saw himself as strong and wise and happy. Who wouldn't want the same? And when he instead felt weak and foolish and desperately sad, he didn't know what to do with those feelings. When he spoke to his fellow New Age friends, and even when he consulted a local counselor, they only gave him pithy Zen koans or said, "Everything happens for a reason," or, "Try to remember the good times," unconsciously affirming this fear that negativity was unacceptable, and to indulge it to any degree meant that you were a bad person. For Craig, "bad" meant unenlightened, unevolved, and unintelligent. Things he really didn't want to be.

One day, a few months after the death of his sister, Craig is at rock bottom again. How did this happen? What about all that positive personal growth and development? What about all that positivity and enthusiasm—where did it go? He goes online to all the social media accounts that once gave him so much motivation and inspiration (did you know that Instagram has over fourteen million posts with the hashtag goodvibesonly?), and he only feels worse.

He again falls into a depression, not because he is mourning his sister's death, but because he sees his own mourning as something to be ashamed of. Everything feels worthless, imperfect, wretched. Craig looks at himself with hatred and thinks that he would be able to pull himself out of this misery if only he were more enlightened, more aware, more spiritually wise. But the truth is, Craig is in this mess **because** he sought out all these things in the first place—at the expense of acknowledging his authentic experience.

The Positive IS Powerful, But . . .

Toxic positivity is an overgeneralization of a positive and optimistic attitude. In a way, it's a cognitive bias because it refuses to acknowledge states of mind, events, thoughts, or feelings that are deemed "negative."

Positivity is a wonderful thing. This book would not exist unless there was some belief in positivity's power. Some would say that the most successful among us are not the pessimists or the realists, but those who encounter life with a *slight* glass-half-full approach. However, if you've encountered the "positive vibes only" brand of positivity in the self-help world, you've probably wondered whether this overly rosy view of the world is really the best approach to take.

Toxic positivity is actually pretty negative if you peek under the hood—**it's about denial, minimization, and invalidation . . . of your own experience. So, it's not positivity itself that is toxic, but our insisting that our genuine and real experience be something else.** Toxic positivity has us wearing masks, silencing our real feelings, and extending this invalidating attitude to others, too. As we see in Craig's case, the results are often the exact opposite of what we want.

The truth is, human beings are *complex wholes*. They contain both good and bad. Carl Jung once said, "I'd rather be whole than good." As the originator of the idea of the human shadow, Jung was fascinated by the psychic material we ignored, repressed, and disowned—where did it go? In Carl's case, the disidentified emotions just went underground until all that depression burst out and caused him to fall into a deep sadness.

There are lots of reasons we deny the "negative" parts of ourselves:

- We don't want others to think we're boring or unpleasant downers
- We don't want to cause others pain
- We don't want to admit that we are confused, mistaken, or flawed—i.e., our egos!
- We don't want to admit that we are frightened, weak, or vulnerable in any way
- We are worried that once we acknowledge negativity, it will flood us and we'll lose control

According to renowned shame author Brene Brown, these negative feelings are cultivated in silence, secrecy, and judgment. In Craig's case, his "positive thinking" came with a set of unspoken rules:

Silence: Don't admit that you are feeling distraught, even to yourself, and don't talk about it.

Secrecy: Hide the facts of this experience from everyone so it becomes your private torment

Judgment: Criticize yourself harshly for feeling this way

Craig cultivated a particular image of himself that he takes pride in. But secretly, he tells himself, "If they only knew what a total toxic and negative mess I really am, and if they really knew what a phony fake I am, they'd reject me for sure." Have you told yourself something similar? That you couldn't ever really reveal your true feelings to others for fear of the repercussions? *Understand that this is a judgment you have already made of yourself.*

The costs of denying our *full* experience (both positive and negative) are high. We live inauthentically and lose touch with what we really want, think, and feel—i.e., with who we really are! We feel isolated from others. Because we cannot open up in genuine vulnerability and truth with them, we never really connect, and so we feel even more alone in our shame.

What's more, we carry that attitude to others. We tell others to, "Think happy thoughts!" and what they actually hear is, "You can only be around me if you are also pretending to be this fake, eternally happy person." After all, if you can't bear your own negative feelings, how could anyone trust you to handle theirs with any care and tact? We end up attracting more inauthenticity. Our world gets increasingly more curated and controlled and *looks* happy, but feels emptier and emptier.

In the preceding chapters, we've worked hard to identify and root out distorted, unhealthy, and self-defeating thoughts and beliefs. But that doesn't mean you should replace all these with their polar opposites, glibly believing instead that everything is awesome, you can do absolutely anything you put your mind to, and that a fully actualized person is just brimming with joy and enthusiasm twenty-four-seven. Let's not allow the pendulum to swing too far in the other direction!

Good Versus Whole

Make your goal to be a person who **accepts** their complete, full selves, both dark and light.

It takes maturity to embrace what is, even though that may be imperfect, flawed, uncomfortable, or confusing. No human being is one hundred percent invulnerable. "Negativity" is built into the fabric of life itself—without it, we would never understand gratitude, we would never learn what we valued, we would never be challenged to improve, and we would never face the natural consequences of our behavior and the fact that not all choices are good for us. We are mortal. We can be hurt, we can make mistakes, and we can even be the "bad guys" sometimes.

To acknowledge all this is NOT to be negative any more than to deny it means we are positive.

The following sentiments are common whenever toxic positivity is in full swing. Notice if you use these phrases on yourself or with others, and gently challenge yourself to find room in there for your *real, full experience* instead:

"Stay positive!"—"How are you feeling, exactly? What is your experience like right now? I'm listening without judgment."

"Failure is not an option."—"Failure is learning. It's a part of life."

"It'll all be okay."—"What is happening for you right now?"

"Every cloud has a silver lining/Everything happens for a reason."—"Sometimes, bad things happen. What do you need to feel supported?"

"You got this!"—"I'm here for you no matter what. You deserve kindness and support even if you're having difficulty."

"Good vibes only."—"Ancient Roman Playwright Terence puts it best: '*Homo sum, humani nihil a me alienum put,*' which means: 'I am human, and I think nothing human is alien to me.' In other words, all vibes are allowed because they are part of the rich, three-dimensional fabric of human experience."

Keep reminding yourself that toxic positivity does not have any benefits. It does not make life easier to bear, it does not guarantee more favorable outcomes, and it does not give you a kind of cheat code that allows you to bypass all the messy and uncomfortable parts of life. In fact, if anything, it makes the hard parts of life more difficult to bear. What we shove out of conscious awareness doesn't disappear. It only festers somewhere else, where it doesn't get the benefit of our compassionate awareness to help process it. Thus, the negativity that we don't acknowledge never has the chance to teach us or enrich our lives in any way—what is "positive" about that?

Step 1: Make friends with discomfort

Toxic positivity is, at least at first, the easy way out. Facing your discomfort head on takes courage and honesty. If you notice yourself leaping in to reassure, dismiss, invalidate, or soothe a negative feeling, stop and notice what you're doing. Try to instead "sit with" your unpleasant emotion. Don't try to destroy, fix, dissolve, or triumph over it . . . but don't succumb to it, either. Just sit alongside it. Put a name to your feeling and leave it at that. Watch your mind try to run around everywhere to escape it, and bring it back to the present and to the truth of reality.

"I'm sad. I feel a deep, deep sadness about my sister passing away. I'm so confused and hurt." Then don't judge, interpret, or rush to fix what comes up. Just let that emotion be what it is.

Step 2: Be patient

Toxic positivity can feel like a quick fix and an instant relief. But working through your emotions takes time. Don't rush and be overly keen for a happy resolution, or barge ahead wanting to skip over the difficult bits so you can get to the happy ending where you've learned your lesson and can move on. Seeds sprout when they're ready, wounds heal as best as they can, and emotions come and go, but on their own schedule. Take it as your duty to give them comfortable passage—don't hold on to them but don't be too eager to rush them on, either.

"I'm sad right now. I don't know how I'll feel tomorrow. I know this won't last forever, but I'm willing to let it last as long as it needs to."

Step 3: Distinguish between productive and unproductive negativity

Finding a balance between positive and negative is not complicated. If there is a negative side to positivity, then there is a positive side to negativity. You can navigate your way through them both by framing it all in terms of productivity or usefulness:

<u>Productive negativity</u> – pure, authentic emotion that does not contain judgment, shame, or resistance to that emotion. Negativity that promotes insight, learning, resilience, or inspired action.

<u>Unproductive negativity</u> – the secondary negativity that emerges around an authentic emotion and serves to prolong and exacerbate it without any benefit. Negativity that limits options, inhibits action, and leads to passivity, despair, and loss of agency.

Let's go back to Craig and his example. When he looks at his second big bout of "depression," he can ask whether it's unproductive or productive. He may see that there are actually two emotions—one is sadness, and the other is a mix of shame, anger, and irritation *about* that sadness. The secondary emotions don't seem to go anywhere—in fact, they only seem to make him feel worse. But he also notices that when he focuses on the primary emotion—the initial sadness—it hurts, but if he doesn't heap judgment and shame onto it, it doesn't feel as bad as he thought it would.

In fact, once he fully acknowledges how he actually feels, he notices with surprise that he doesn't feel that way for long. His sadness, once acknowledged, actually spurs him on to feel new, different things. After a few weeks of "sitting with" how he genuinely feels, something else stirs in him: He wants to act. He feels compelled to do something meaningful in his sister's memory—something he wouldn't have dreamed of if he was still pretending that everything was okay!

Like so many people who learn to let go of toxic positivity, Craig understands that the remedy for depression is not happiness, but *authentic sadness*. Toxic positivity doesn't help, but neither does stagnant depression and despair. Instead, Craig finds a way out through the middle: by accepting what is so that it can be processed and released.

Step 4: Reconnect to your values and shift to problem-solving

Emotions exist for our benefit. They are there for a reason and have evolved to keep us safe, help us to connect, and allow us to live a life of meaning. Emotions—*all* emotions, even the awful, inconvenient, or embarrassing ones—can teach us something if we are willing to listen. It is not necessary in life to suffer needlessly just for the sake of it. Rather, you are a human being who is tasked with finding meaning and purpose in your experiences. If you can invoke your values and principles, you can imbue your suffering with meaning—and transform it into something beautiful.

As you accept and sit with uncomfortable emotions, try to look for the hidden blessing. Not in a "everything happens for a reason!" way, but in a way where you graciously make the best of everything that comes your way. Compare experiences against your values. For example, if you value independence and autonomy, allow a frightening cancer scare to teach you the value of interdependence and the power of asking for help. On the other hand, you might find that negative experiences with someone who keeps violating your boundaries confirm for you values that you never knew you had before—the principles of dignity and self-worth.

The trick is that you cannot be inspired and taught by negative emotions until you *feel them fully*. You cannot skip over the painful part and rush to the blessing in disguise part—the blessing is only revealed **by** enduring the negative emotion in the first place. Craig, for example, values intellectual mastery, truth, and spiritual development. But if he acknowledges his real emotions, they may teach him that, ironically, the best way to move forward sometimes is to go backward, and the best way to grow is to be willing to let go of your ego's idea of what life should be like.

Identify your personal values and the principles you hold most dear. And then let them inspire you to take action and solve problems. If you are going through a difficult time, remind yourself of what makes life meaningful for you. Then take action that incorporates the way you feel but brings you closer to what matters. For example, you may face the fact of deep regrets you have about your past. But you remind yourself that you **value** who you are today—and that person is who they are because of those past experiences. You take **action** and forgive yourself, vowing also not to act today in ways that you might regret tomorrow.

Think of negative emotions as a pathway into more deeply understanding your values—and bringing them to life in action. Ask yourself, **"How does a person who values what I value behave when they experience what I'm experiencing?"**

One Underappreciated Way to Genuinely Feel Better

Toxic positivity is not really about feeling good feelings—it's more about the *desire* to feel good feelings, or even the expectation and entitlement to those positive feelings. It's this unrealistic expectation that makes encountering real life even more unpleasant than it would ordinarily be! If we have a vision of what life should look like (do you catch the distorted thinking?), then we are at risk of labeling even normal or neutral events as "negative" when they aren't—they just don't match up to some artificial image of what we think positivity looks like. So, we may wake up one day to a completely normal and ordinary life, but because we are not super energetic and enthusiastic, our work doesn't light a fire in us, and we don't happen to be madly in love with our partners that day—we think something is wrong.

In a way, toxic positivity has an unfortunate side effect: it makes us ungrateful. We may be permanently dissatisfied if we compare our lives to an unrealistic vision of the glittering and eternal contentment we feel we're supposed to have. If you genuinely want to feel happier, though (right now, not when all your pesky problems are solved and you are finally perfect), then try to focus with gratitude on what you have.

It sounds too simple to work, but it does. Start every morning with a list of five things that you are grateful for in your life right now. Sometimes, we already have wonderful and positive lives—we've just become desensitized to our blessings and begun to take it all for granted. Right now, can you think of five things that are perfectly "ordinary" in your life that are, in fact, wonderful gifts?

Emotional Regulation

As we become better at recognizing negative and distorted thinking, and as we learn to guard against fake, unrealistic "positive thinking," we find that we are developing a skill that goes far beyond positive and negative: **emotional regulation.**

When we are capable of emotional regulation, we become conscious and capable masters of our own ever-unfolding emotional experience. We can reuse to engage in destructive or distorted thinking, while at the same time know when to tolerate and "hold" negative emotions, asking ourselves what good we can extract from them. We are likewise aware when we are feeling calm, content, joyful, hopeful—and welcome that too, being fully aware of how to cultivate and enjoy those emotions when they happen.

Consider the emotion of anger.

Is anger a "positive" or "negative" emotion? Well, it really depends.

If you're at work and dealing with an irritable customer, you cannot freely express your anger or let it get the better of you. Instead, you have to notice the anger, choose not to succumb to it, and act as professionally as you can.

However, if someone in your personal life insults you and attempts to violate a boundary, you would feel anger, too. In this case, though, expressing some of this anger may be exactly the right thing—since it clearly communicates your limits, asserts your dignity, and lets the other person know to back off!

Anger is a normal and natural emotion to have in both situations. However, in the first, it's much less useful to express it than in the second. In both these cases, there is a higher awareness that is taking control and asking, "What am I feeling? Why? What is the cause of this emotion, and what will be the effect of me acting on it? What do I want to achieve here? How can I help this emotion move on?"

This is the voice of emotional self-regulation. It is not merely a case of "upregulating the good feelings and down-regulating the bad ones," but rather a meat-emotion that allows you to be aware of and take charge of your emotional state—and then take action in a way that makes sense for you in any given context.

So, what makes an emotion "positive" or "negative" is a mix of

1. our own goals
2. our context
3. the values and principles we're living by

If we are not in control of ourselves, not aware, and not acting with a mind to our goals and values, then even if we feel "positive" emotions, we can't really be said to have mastered self-regulation.

First things first—emotional regulation is NOT the same as repression, toxic positivity, or ignoring how you really feel. Rather, it's about consciously choosing

- which emotions we pay attention to and encourage
- when we have them
- how we express them externally
- how we experience them internally

Note that there is no option to "choose whether I feel emotions or not." We all do! Emotions are a fact of life. But we do get a lot of say over when, where, and how we express them. We choose all the above in relation to our **goals and values**. For example:

On receiving a terrible birthday gift, "I choose not to express disappointment right now because I value my friendship with this person and don't want to hurt their feelings."

Before heading into an important job interview, "I choose to drastically dial up my feelings of confidence and enthusiasm so I can impress my interviewer because my goal is to get hired."

During some alone time with your journal on a Sunday morning, "I choose to explore and express my sadness right now because I want to process and release these feelings and grow as a person."

Goals and values provide a framework. Together with our awareness, they help us decide on the **intensity**, **quality**, and **duration** of our emotional response. So, we saw that Craig was in the grips of toxic positivity and was being emotionally inauthentic with himself and others. But what would it have looked like for him to demonstrate emotional regulation instead?

Intensity – Craig could have faced his sadness but altered how much of it to show to himself and others depending on the situation. He could have allowed himself to be completely vulnerable and expressive during therapy, moderately open with his friends, and honest but more guarded with his work colleagues.

Quality – "Sadness" is a pretty big emotion that contains lots of subtler shades and nuances, which Craig could play up or down depending on the situation. With his New Age yoga friends, he could express the bittersweet and wistful sides of mourning, but with his mother, engage more on the level of death being an incomprehensible injustice. With his therapist, he can focus on the raw, unapologetic feeling of grief and explore childhood memories of his sister. With a colleague, he can express a more formal sentiment. And so on. All these expressions are "real"—it's just that Craig is choosing for his own purposes to focus on each of them in different moments.

Duration – Craig can also put himself in charge of how long he engages his emotions. In conversation with a close friend, for example, he might allow himself to reveal plenty of vulnerable emotions, but he consciously chooses not to let this expression go on and on. Instead, after a few minutes, he steps out of the limelight and allows his friend to talk, too.

If it seems a little weird to have so much control over your emotions, consider the fact that emotions themselves are often short-lived and context-dependent anyway. Remember that emotions are there for a reason and serve a function—there is nothing wrong with consciously stepping in and *choosing* what that function should be! Likewise, all emotions are brought into being through and with our cognitive evaluation and the activation of our core beliefs. This happens whether we realize it or not—so why not choose the core beliefs we want to guide this important process?

The Life Cycle of an Emotion
We can imagine that all emotions play out on a timeline:

There is (1) the initiating event or situation, followed by (2) our conscious attention on that event. This is followed by (3) our own unique appraisal of that event, and (4) it's this appraisal (not the event itself) that results in us feeling an emotion. From there, the emotion may die down naturally or be prolonged. It may prompt action, or it may get repressed and sent into "the shadow" . . . perhaps to burst free at a later time.

So, for example, you have a long-haul flight booked for the following morning. You make an appraisal ("I hate flying! What if the plane crashes?"), and the resulting emotions are anxiety, panic, and fear.

We can step in to regulate our emotions at a few points in this process. Here's how it would look if you were trying to regulate the anxiety you faced when thinking about your upcoming flight:

Situation selection – This is where we choose which situations to enter according to the emotional outcomes we can expect for doing so (occurs *before* we encounter 1, the initiating situation).

In our example, this could look like simply avoiding situations we know will trigger and worsen panic. We decide not to watch an episode of *Air Crash Investigation* and deliberately avoid a friend who you know shares your anxiety and will only work you up into a froth if you talk to them too much before your flight. Another possibility is that, knowing how we'll respond, we avoid the trip entirely or find another way to get to our destination.

Situation modification – This is where we choose to change or alter the situation in some way (this is during 1, the initial situation).

In our example, let's say you do go on the flight. The situation can be modified to cause less anxiety, though. You take a mild tranquilizer and get an aisle seat and bring plenty of distractions as well as air-sickness medication if you need it. You practice breathing exercises and calming mantras.

Attentional deployment – This is where we choose to focus our attention on specific aspects of the situation (this is during 2, where we place our attention).

In our example, let's say you do get the flight, and despite your best efforts, you are still anxious. You consciously choose in that moment not to focus on and magnify the stress. Instead, you try to talk to the person next to you, play an immersive game, or try some challenging brain puzzles that take your mind off things—you only have a fixed mental bandwidth, and you'll have less available if you spend it all on another task!

Cognitive change – This is the choice to consciously modify the meaning we are ascribing to various aspects of the situation (this occurs at 3, when we make our appraisal).

In our example, the thoughts surrounding this flight might be very negative: "You can't avoid this, but it's unbearable." "You'll probably die." "You hate flying more than anything else in the world." But you can choose to make a different appraisal. You can reframe the situation like this: "I am being really brave facing my fears right now," or, "Ha ha, look at me! Isn't this silly fear of mine ridiculous?" or even, "Flying is annoying and uncomfortable, but it's far from the end of the world."

Response modulation – This is choosing to change the way we respond to our emotions physiologically, experientially, or behaviorally (this occurs at 4, the final response).

In our example, you still may find yourself enormously anxious. But you can still choose how you respond to this response itself. Let's say you notice your panic, but you are compassionate about it and accept it for what it is without judgment and resistance. Fearing a panic attack coming on, you call a flight attendant and discreetly explain the situation, asking if there is a private place onboard you can go for a few minutes to gather yourself.

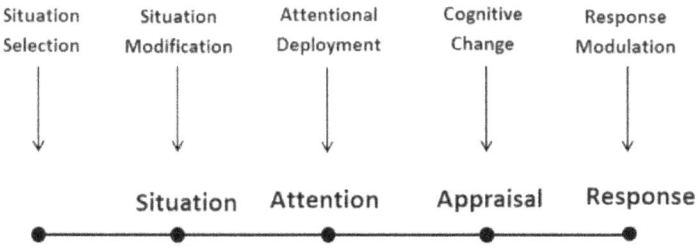

As you can tell, the point at which one aspect of the emotion ends and another begins is not clearcut, but this is not especially important. What is important is that you are aware and in control of the emotion as it unfolds, and taking steps to master that emotion at whatever stage that happens to be.

The above process may seem complicated when laid out all at once, but it's rather simple to learn it yourself. Here's how:

Step 1: Become aware
Ask yourself some of the following questions:

What am I experiencing?

Why am I experiencing it, or what came before?

Is this emotion helping or hindering me? What effect is it having overall?

What are my goals and values in this situation?

How does this emotion play into those goals and values?

Step 2: Consider context
Emotions don't occur in a vacuum. They're part of an unfolding situation in the external world and usually plugged into a social and physical environment. Look at the situation you're in and ask the following questions:

How does my emotion fit within this context?

Is any aspect of my situation changeable? How?

Can I make any changes that will help me achieve my goal or align with my values?

Step 3: Modify the situation
If the situation itself can't be changed, it can usually be shaped and modified somewhat. Become curious about how. Ask:

Would it be to my benefit to share my emotion with others?

If so, how best should I share it?

What changes to the situation would serve me best right now, given my goals and values?

Can I remove or introduce an object, a person, or an idea to change the dynamic in my favor?

Step 4: Put your focus where you choose
Don't just look at the situation, but look at how you're looking at the situation. What are you focusing on and what are you not paying any attention to? Become curious and notice what's happening both inside and outside your head, asking:

Where is my attention primarily going?

Is this focus helping or hindering?

Would it help me to focus on something different?

What is there currently in my situation that, if I focused on it, would help me increase positive emotions or reach my goal?

Is there anything that can distract me from a negative emotion right now?

Step 5: Modify the way you're appraising the situation
The way you are feeling is a direct result of how you are thinking about the situation. Once you become aware of how you're framing the situation, see if the following questions can bring some insight:

Is the current way you're thinking about this situation helping you achieve your goal?

Can both the emotion and the situation be looked at in another way?

Is it really that bad (i.e., have you correctly and usefully appraised the intensity of the emotion)?

Step 6: Modify how you're experiencing and expressing this emotion
The way you express your emotion will have an influence on the people around you, your environment, and the situation itself. Ask:

Do I want to share my experience—and if so, how?

If I don't wish to share it, how may I make that easier for myself?

What do I wish to change right now?

As you can see, with these questions, you are moving along the timeline of the emotion, looking for opportunities and areas along the way where you can intervene with action or reframing that speaks to your goals and values. You might do this *before* an anticipated situation, *after* the situation has already played out, or *during* the situation as it unfolds. Naturally, you will have more options the sooner you intervene. It's worth noting as well that it may be easier to take control the earlier along in the process you are. If the emotion is well underway, you may have to spend far more effort to modify it than if you had carefully avoided it in the first place. Prevention is always better than cure.

Not every situation will have an opportunity to make significant changes. Some situations will vary in how much you could possibly do at each stage. But, if you follow the above basic process, you are taking control of your emotional reality and steering it in the direction that suits you best, whatever the difficulties and limitations.

To recap:

1. Become aware of your emotion, your values, and your goals.
2. Consider your context and see how you are interacting with it
3. Take steps to change the situation
4. Notice where your attention is going and make changes
5. **Modify the way you're appraising the situation and the meaning you're giving it**
6. Take steps to change the way you are experiencing or expressing the emotion

As a brief example:

1. You become aware that you are experiencing fear and self-doubt after being asked to give a presentation the following day. You value bravery and confidence, and your overall goal is to do well at work.
2. You become aware of the context: You are well liked at work and being offered more responsibility. Your fear, however, might cause you to shy away from some of these opportunities.
3. You become aware of what you can change in the situation—you *could* refuse to do the presentation, but that may create a bad impression.
4. As you prepare, you notice that your thoughts tend to catastrophize. You deliberately steer your focus to other things—for example, the favorable

reports you've received so far and evidence from colleagues that you are doing a good job.
5. You deliberately choose to re-appraise the situation, going from: "This is a threatening and unpleasant event," to: "I am being given an exciting opportunity—how lucky for me!"
6. You decide to briefly confide in your boss, explaining your nervousness and asking for a day or two more to prepare the presentation. You express your fear very strategically, however, and express it only so far as to convey to your boss that you take the presentation seriously and want to do it properly (rather than treating the meeting as a mini therapy session!)

Usually, it is Step 5 that will have the most powerful impact, so if you can remember nothing of this process in the heat of the moment, try to remember to ask yourself simply, **"Is the way I'm thinking about this problem working for me right now?"** This alone will often open up doors of insight into other ways you can make modifications to the situation.

When we become good at mastering emotional regulation, we learn that our emotions are not in control of us—but it's not exactly true to say that *we* are one hundred percent in control of *them*, either. Rather, our emotions emerge as part of a broader situation, and they're caused and sustained by our beliefs and thought processes. Strictly speaking, we can never "control our emotions," but we can always take steps to control our environment, our thoughts, our reactions, and how we manage our emotions both internally and externally—which in turn will influence our emotions.

Summary

- Toxic positivity is a kind of cognitive distortion and is an overgeneralization of a positive and optimistic attitude. It consists of denial, minimization, and invalidation of your own experience. Toxic positivity grows with shame, silence, and judgment. Positivity itself isn't toxic, but denying our reality is. Human beings are wholes who contain both good and bad.
- We can embrace the *whole* instead of the *good* by watching the phrases we use, making friends with discomfort, being patient while we are in process, distinguishing between productive and unproductive negativity, and reconnecting to what we value and want to achieve in life. Ask yourself, "How does a person who values what I value behave when they experience what I'm experiencing?"
- Keeping a gratitude journal is a great way to create genuine feelings of positivity.
- Rather than creating good emotions and getting rid of negative ones, we can practice emotional self-regulation and become conscious masters of our own ever-unfolding emotional experience.
- What makes an emotion good or bad is the context and our own goals and values. We regulate when we decide which emotions to attend to, when, how, and for how long.
- Emotions have a life cycle, and we can manage those emotions at any point in the cycle—before the situation, during the situation, with our attention, with our

cognitive appraisal, and finally, with our emotional response. Generally, the sooner you intervene, the easier it is to modify the situation.
- Ask, "Is the way I'm thinking about this problem working for me right now?"

Chapter 6: But Where Does Negative Thinking Really Come From?

The more you work at identifying and rewriting your negative thought patterns, the better you'll come to understand this part of yourself—and realize how deep those roots really run. Why are some people so prone to negative thinking, pessimism, and a defeated attitude? Why do some of us dwell on anxieties and get embroiled in self-doubt, while others don't? Why do some people struggle with depression and low mood all their lives, while others seem to be functioning from a seemingly inexhaustible well of optimism?

These are big questions, and psychology has been trying to answer them for a long time. In this book, we've focused on possible answers at the psychological level—without getting too bogged down in overanalyzing what is in the past. We've explored how a critical and distorted inner dialogue encourages us to frame events according to a particular mental filter. And we've seen how thoughts and core beliefs influence the perspective we use to interpret everything around us. But then the question is, where did these thoughts come from? And what distorted those filters in the first place?

There are different levels at which we can think about the problem:

Physical – it's about hormones, genes, neurotransmitters, the food you eat, and the exercise you get (or don't)
Emotional – your unique feelings and responses to events that color and shape everything
Cognitive – the way you understand, explain, and conceptualize the world and yourself
Psychological – how your emotional and cognitive processing comes together into internal schemas and narratives
Social – the way your thoughts, feelings, and behaviors interact relationally with those around you, particularly your immediate family and early caregivers
Evolutionary – the fitness adaptations you've inherited from your ancestors
Cultural – the broader social and environmental significance of your life
Spiritual – the broader meaning of your life in relation to the divine or transcendental

Historical – your life as a developmental, and in the context of broader time scales relations

Political – the way your life interacts with the economy, the law, and the overarching power dynamics you live within

At *every* level, we can be influenced either toward a way of living that is predominantly pessimistic and negative, or one that supports our own conscious choice and agency. Though this book has focused mainly on the cognitive, emotional, and psychological dimensions, it doesn't take long to see that this is not the full story—if you were an impoverished peasant living in medieval times and suffered from malnutrition and disease all your life, it's hard to imagine how any of the techniques in this book could make a dent!

To return to the question of what causes a person's negative disposition—well, everything!

But the reason we've focused on the psychological/cognitive/emotional aspect is because, frankly, this is the area of life where we have the most control. In this final chapter, we'll look at two more sources of negativity and make an attempt to mitigate their impact on our daily life. The first is what's called "**negativity bias**," and the second is the **power of relationships** to create or counteract negativity in our lives (specifically, how toxic relationships can create and sustain negativity). This expands our examination of negative thinking to include some evolutionary and social causes, respectively.

Your Negativity May Be "Hardwired"

Simply, the negativity bias is the human tendency to register and focus more readily on negative stimuli while ignoring or downplaying positive ones. It means that we tend to remember negative experiences more vividly than happier ones, dwell on insults more than we do on praise, perceive loss as more painful than we perceive gain as pleasurable, and give more mental airtime to negative thoughts than to positive ones. In other words, we have a bias for the negative. Research has uncovered all sorts of ways this bias pops up:

- We tend to assume that very negative news must be more true or real
- We tend to be more motivated to avoid a loss than to win a gain
- We even tend to make decisions based more on negative information and learn more effectively after negative experiences instead of positive ones

Think about finding a fly in your soup—everything else about your evening out at a fancy restaurant may be perfect, but that single tiny fly is likely to receive the bulk of your attention! On an otherwise great date, your brain focuses on that one embarrassing thing you said, or the spinach stuck in the other person's teeth. On a report card, you gloss over all the praise and dwell on the single criticism you received (remember the "discounting" cognitive bias?).

It turns out that this is not just a psychological phenomenon or a question of a bad attitude. It's not about personality. It's not a reaction to trauma or a personal failing or some strange, unique thing that only happens to you. Rather, the human predisposition to zoom in on what's wrong has evolutionary roots—nothing could be more ordinary or predictable. Those of our ancestors who focused more heavily on the negative had a survival advantage on those who didn't. If a person is hypersensitive to potential threats in the environment, they may have a lot of false positives, but when something genuinely is a case of life and death, they're likely to survive. Those who ignored or downplayed that threat, however, would likely not.

. . . But that Doesn't Mean It's Written in Stone

The Negative Nancys of the world, in other words, lived to pass on those genes that would bias their offspring to focusing on the negative more than the positive. This tendency is so hardwired that neuroscientists have found heightened activity in response to negative stimuli compared to positive ones—this is true even for very young infants.

But, while our bias for the negative may have evolutionary roots, **that doesn't mean that we are pre-destined to have this orientation for all time**. With awareness and conscious effort, we can mitigate, pre-empt, or challenge our knee-jerk biases and make sure that this primal part of ourselves doesn't get the last word. The negativity bias served our ancestors well and did indeed keep us safe and alert to threats in our environment. In fact, it *still* serves this function today.

But that doesn't mean that we can't engage with it, double-check it, and factor in our own higher, conscious choice on the matter, too. As human beings, we have ancient, inborn biological tendencies. We also have an incredible organ that no other animal possesses: a human brain. With this we can become aware, choose, learn, create, adapt, and make meaning.

The great thing about understanding the negativity bias is that you *know* that you are always primed to look at the worst in a scenario—so you can do something about it. It's not unlike the way your leg will reflexively bounce up when a doctor taps your knee in just the right place.

Imagine an ordinary person in an ordinary relationship whose partner does something wrong and hurts them. Instantly, they're put on the defensive as this insult expands in their awareness to take up all their attention. This single negative action soon starts to be all that they can see—the countless positive things their partner has done for years on end seem to vanish, eclipsed by the single negative one. This focus on the negative is a cognitive distortion. The person ends up saying things like, "You always do this," and, "You don't care about me," (hello, generalization and mind-reading bias!). This is exactly the same as saying that *no part* of the entire fancy restaurant experience was good simply because there was a fly in the soup.

Resentment builds, miscommunications abound, and the relationship ends. However, had this person understood the negativity bias and observed that their own thought processes were being heavily influenced by this tendency, things might have played out differently. They might have been able to say, "I'm really angry right now, and all

I can see is the negative. What happened is bad, but I can also see that I'm fixating on it and that there are lots of good things in my relationship . . ." Consider how different conversations would be if the person held this attitude rather than unconsciously expecting and indeed seeking out the very worst in their partner.

But it's not just relationships where this bias plays out. Famed authors, researchers, and neuroscientists Kahneman and Tversky, in their Nobel Prize–winning work, explored the fact that people tend to place greater weight on the negative than the positive when making decisions. Their research helped them conclude that **people seem to fear loss more than they desire gain**—for example, people have a greater reaction to losing twenty dollars than to gaining twenty dollars.

This means that people often tend to prefer the status quo, even a negative status quo, simply because changing is perceived to incur too many potential losses—and the perceived gains are not enough to offset it. Negativity bias can influence our relationships, but it can also affect the way we process risk and reward.

As an example, we may be trying to make a decision between staying where we are or moving houses, or else keeping our job or accepting a new one. The thing is, we are not weighing up the options we have in a balanced, neutral way. Rather, we are placing more weight and emphasis on potential loss than we are on potential gain—and consequently we may stay in a suboptimal situation and miss out on good opportunities.

Here's an example. We might see that a new job pays twice as much and is way more fun but requires a month of intense training first, which we may potentially fail. We might also see that the current job doesn't pay much and is a bit boring but doesn't require any additional effort or take any risk. Objectively speaking, the new job is probably the better choice. But if we succumb to the negativity bias, we may overinflate the potential loss ("that month of training is just too risky!") and downplay the potential gain (a lot more money and more fun to be had), giving us a distorted picture of our options. **If we consciously recognize that the negativity bias is there, though, we can factor it in and make sure we're not unduly focusing on the negatives**.

Countering the Bias for the Negative

The good news is that you have already encountered (and hopefully tried) several powerful techniques for counteracting the human tendency to focus on the negative. Negative visualization and a gratitude journal especially can help you recalibrate so you are more aware of the good around you, not just the bad.

The solution is obvious—**if you cannot rely on your brain to automatically and unconsciously look for the positive, then you will have to *deliberately* draw your attention to it instead**. And it is there!

Pause to savor positive moments and register them fully. There is no evolutionary advantage to smelling the roses—but your life will be immeasurably improved if you can. Stay in the moment and relish all the lovely things that are actually happening all around you. If something positive is going on, literally imagine turning your mental antenna in its direction and paying it close attention. "This is positive. I'm enjoying this." Your mind will not do this for you—be deliberate instead and *choose* to see the good in things.

Mindfulness, presence, positivity, and gratitude all tend to go together. When we are conscious and awake to the moment—the full moment—we start to realize how fascinating and how lovely it is. And then we cannot help but feel grateful and content.

Try it tomorrow morning the moment you wake up.

Maybe you take a few seconds to really relish how comfortable your bed is, how soft the pillowcase. You stretch, and that long, taut feeling in your legs is just the most delicious thing ever. You yawn—that feels pretty good too, actually. You notice a pang in your stomach as you realize you have to get out of bed soon and go to work, a prospect you're dreading a little. But then you remind yourself of how you were unemployed a year ago, and how tense you were about money, and how it dented your self-esteem. This job isn't perfect, but you give yourself an internal pat on the back. You've made it this far, and you can keep going. You watch all that potential anxiety about your work just pass by. You feel thankful for this newfound ability you've developed. You're proud of yourself..

Some people claim that "happiness is a choice" and say that the secret to happiness is simply deciding that you want to be happy. This may not be true in the sense that we can change our mental state at will. But it is true in the sense that we can decide what we focus on, and we can decide *not* to have a bias that shuts out life's many blessings from our conscious awareness. We definitely have the choice not to go out of our way to interpret the world more negatively than it really is! **Happiness, then, is merely the choice to remove all those self-imposed filters and biases that keep us from enjoying what is already there**.

So much of every single day is automatic and unconscious. We resort to the same old patterns and habits without thinking about it or being aware that it's what we're doing. The negativity habit can be imprinted in our early formative years, sustained by our culture and society, and kept intact by our own set of narratives and core beliefs.

But people do not exist in a vacuum. No matter how personal and private your own thoughts, feelings, and core beliefs seem to you, they are in fact imbedded into the social environment around you. The relationships you have with others are constantly interacting with them, and there is mutual influence, for better or worse. All of this is to say that "negative thinking" can be like a house of cards—pull one card and you realize how many other cards fall as well because they were supported by it.

Your unique thought patterns and habits are in relationship with the unique thought patterns and habits of those around you. As you gain more awareness of the role that negativity plays in your life, you cannot help but notice how your relationships and general environment are all connected, too. To put it bluntly, if you have a problem with negativity, it's almost guaranteed that that negativity plays a role in your relationships with others.

A quick example will make this clear. Anne has worked really hard with a therapist to undo a whole complex web of negative core beliefs about herself. She can clearly see how her negative self-talk is jeopardizing her happiness, and how her distorted thought processes are making her miserable. She makes enormous strides and achieves genuine transformation, learning to defuse from difficult emotions and see herself—and the world—with completely different eyes. But somehow, it doesn't stick. She keeps finding herself back at square one and doesn't know why.

One day, her therapist gently suggests something: Could her husband be the reason? After gaining big insights into her behavior at every weekly therapy session, she then goes straight home and spends the remainder of the week with her husband, bickering. It's not that her husband is a bad person. Rather, it's that Anne has deeply entrenched patterns of negative behavior that *she plays out with him.*

Every day, there's a lot of complaining and fault finding, squabbles following some miscommunication, a little bit of sulking and stonewalling, a constant and low-grade level of irritation . . . all of it adding to a growing pile of resentment and negativity, every moment of every day. What chance did Anne's single therapy session have when pitched against all *that*?

The reason that Anne cannot make any improvements (or maintain the improvements she does make) is because she is not aware of the situations, relationships, and circumstances around her that are sustaining and creating her negativity. She is looking at the problem on one level (emotional, psychological, cognitive) and completely ignoring the other levels (social and relational). It's not that the work Anne is doing with her therapist is not useful—it's just that it doesn't go far enough. Importantly, it's not that Anne is a toxic person or that her husband is; rather, the relationship between them (i.e., their shared pattern of behavior) is toxic.

Once she realizes this, she goes back to her therapist, who encourages her to think strategically. What can she change, and what does she have to learn to cope with? How well is this pattern serving her life, and does she want to rewrite it?

To make the perspective shift that Anne has, you can ask yourself: what toxic behavioral patterns exist in your own life right now, and how do they interact with other people? **If relationships are shared patterns of behavior, what relationships in your life right now are part of a pattern of negativity**?

A Pattern Is Toxic; a Person Is Not

Before we go further, let's make a clear distinction: **There is no such thing as a "toxic person."** But the way a person relates to other people can certainly be toxic. After all, you may be reading this book because you have a pattern of negative thinking—but if you call yourself a "negative person," then you are saying that this pattern of behavior is fundamentally *who you are* . . . and that means that you cannot change. If you call yourself a person who has a pattern of negative thinking, then you are in control and can change. It's a big difference!

In the self-help realm, it has been trendy for a while now to go on "toxic person" witch hunts, i.e., identify anyone in your life who acts like a poison to you and forcefully remove them. While it may be one hundred percent true that another person treats you in abusive ways and negatively impacts your mental health and wellbeing, focusing exclusively on their role means you ignore your own. Thus, if Anne came to understand her husband as abusive, but called him "toxic" and simply left him . . . she might find herself in precisely the same kind of relationship once again. That's because she never understood and challenged her own patterns, so she promptly repeated them with someone else.

Remember that your unique thought patterns and habits *are in relationship* with the unique thought patterns and habits of those around you. If we think that the problem is merely that the other person is a jerk, we rob ourselves of a deeper understanding of our own ingrained relational patterns. For example, Anne might begin to understand that her negative thinking habit is actually part of a broader relational habit where she continually picks romantic partners who belittle and undermine her, because that fits with her core belief that she is worthless. If she merely blames her husband (who is, to be fair, to blame!), she never gives herself the chance to break that pattern within herself.

This is why it's so important to not lose sight of the fact that **relationships are shared patterns**. Anne's husband, should he find himself single again, may go back into the dating market and meet many new women . . . and none of them are interested in him because they are unwilling to tolerate his behavior. All alone in a room by himself, is he still "toxic"?

Anne might say, "He's an abuser; he makes me feel worthless," but this is not strictly true. It was Anne herself who first held the core belief that she was worthless. She then selected a partner who confirmed this and reflected it back to her. Again, neither Anne nor her husband are bad or toxic people. Rather, they both share in a mutual pattern of behavior that is toxic.

It's all too easy (and pretty tempting, if we're honest) to label people as toxic as though we didn't share equal responsibility for the quality of that relationship. But we do. And we commit to claiming our responsibility not because we want to take the "blame" but to better understand *why* our life is the way it is and what we can do to make it better.

What is a Toxic Relationship?

A toxic thought or feeling is one that has become so distorted and unhealthy that it is dramatically impairing your quality of life. A toxic relationship is the same. In CBT, you can challenge an unhelpful thought and rewrite it. But patterns are bigger than single thoughts, and they involve other people.

All relationships have some degree of difference, tension, and friction at times, but toxic relationships are more malignant; they amplify and recreate negativity in a way that is destructive and unhealthy for all parties involved. You'll know that you're in a toxic relationship if one or both of you

- Feels devalued, disrespected, or abused
- Feels utterly exhausted, drained emotionally, and defeated
- Feels unsafe, either physically or emotionally
- Experience a constant state of drama, angst, and conflict
- Experience a loss of self-esteem and dignity
- Feels their boundaries are repeatedly violated
- Experiences chronic deceit, lies, or manipulation
- Experiences violence and aggression

Trying to undo negative thinking patterns when you're in a relationship like this is like trying to train for a marathon when you have cancer . . . i.e., not easy! Instead, you need to first remove yourself from relationships that are amplifying and sustaining negativity so that you can start to work on those patterns within yourself.

Here are a few tips to keep in mind as you broaden your perspective:

Tip 1: Turn your focus from the relationship to the relationship *dynamic*

Look beyond the current situation or disagreement and become curious about recurrent patterns. What keeps happening over and over again? What is the bigger picture? Sometimes, negative behaviors are just a once-off, but look to see if any repeating cycles can be found.

It's not about identifying the good guy and the bad guy, or deciding where to place blame, but rather asking, "What is actually happening here?" and being genuinely curious about the answer. Look at this broader pattern and ask yourself where it might have originally come from. Did you share this pattern with a caregiver as a child? Is this a coping mechanism you picked up after a particularly traumatic event in your past?

Tip 2: Be accountable

Ask what your role in the ongoing dynamic is, bearing in mind that this is not an exercise in shame or judgment. Rather, be honest about the ways that you've enabled the pattern to play out—or at least didn't stop it from playing out. It is vital to be able to call out bad behavior and identify abuse, but if we cling too tightly to the victim identity, we may forget our own power to change the situation.

What are your core beliefs about your role in life? How does that assumption manifest in your relationships right now? How are your thoughts and feelings sustaining the dynamic, and how are they challenging it?

Tip 3: Examine your core beliefs

Our relationships with others are a reflection of our relationship with ourselves, and vice versa. *Ask honestly what a current relationship is revealing about the core beliefs you have about yourself.* For example, if you find yourself repeatedly complaining that nobody takes you seriously, become curious about whether *you* hold a core belief that plays into this, and whether you don't take yourself seriously, either. The disrespectful people in your life are just one half of the story. The other half is the unconscious core belief you hold that you are not, in fact, worth anyone's respect.

If you change the core belief but keep the disrespectful people in your life, you have only solved half the problem. Likewise, if you get rid of the disrespectful people but maintain the core belief, then sooner or later, you will just attract new people much like the old people, who will continue to reflect that core belief back at you. To make real progress, you need to tackle both.

When You're the Toxic One . . .

The internet is awash with advice on how to deal with negative family members, partners, and friends, and long checklists to help you identify the narcissists, energy vampires, and toxic people you need to cut out of your life. But if you're the one who's toxic? Well . . . let's just say there aren't as many people interested in *that* material.

We'll now consider a delicate topic that can be difficult to talk about or even think about. The truth is that if we have a problem with negative thinking, we have the potential to be "toxic people" ourselves and bring the lion's share of negativity to our relationships. Again, being aware of these patterns is not about blame and shame. Rather, the more we are conscious of, the more we can be in control of.

Here is an exercise to help you identify the toxic and negative patterns you may be contributing to the relationships around you.

Step 1: Make a list

Sit down and compile a list of behaviors you know that you engage in habitually, positive or negative, major or minor. This takes some self-knowledge and honesty, but the exercises in the preceding chapters may have given you some useful insight. Don't list single behaviors or events, but ongoing and recurrent patterns. For example, you may list

Complaining about the weather

Going for "bad boys"

Making jokes in awkward situations

Gossiping and spreading rumors

Overworking

Minimizing achievements

Step 2: Understand the behavior

Look at the list and explore the results you're getting with each pattern of behavior. Look beyond whether the pattern feels good or how inevitable it seems, and consider instead whether it's working for you or not. Also ask where the behavior might have originally come from and what purpose it serves. The big thing to understand is what core beliefs may be at the root of this behavior.

For example, you may realize that your pattern of minimizing your own achievements is having a very negative effect on your life. You may know that it stems from growing up with very strict and critical parents who were sparing with praise. The core belief behind it all is, "You're nothing special." Now, not all your patterns of behavior are going to be big and serious—some will be fairly minor and insignificant.

Step 3: Put the pattern in context

This is the most important step. Ask yourself how this pattern of behavior fits into your bigger world. How is it sustained and maintained by the relationships around you? In what way might your own core beliefs be amplified by certain key relationships?

For example, you may look at your work life and realize that your bosses are happy to take advantage of the fact that you are a workaholic . . . without properly compensating you. Inadvertently, they are taking part in the "you're nothing special" dynamic and are an extension of it.

Step 4: Make changes both inside and out

Once you understand your own core beliefs and how they fit into bigger patterns of behavior with other people, you can start making changes. Do this on both levels:

1. Commit to making one small change to your inner thought processes, but also
2. take a step to changing your environment or relationship.

For example, you may start working on your self-esteem and start each morning with a mantra that counters the "I'm nothing special" core belief. At the same time, you can start putting up more boundaries at work and not agreeing to work overtime. You might also consider asking for a raise.

Of course, a pattern like overworking is a lot less noxious than the pattern of, say, gossiping and starting rumors. It can be far more difficult to be honest about these less-than-flattering habits we might have. Overeating, being lazy, avoiding responsibility, petty addictions, seeking revenge... these patterns are difficult to face, but they offer the biggest opportunity for growth if we're brave enough to face them.

Step 5: Be proud of yourself

It's important to stop and take stock of the changes you do make, even if they're small. Celebrate those wins—it's not easy making this kind of change. Give yourself credit where it's due and you'll find that the momentum will build, and next time, the process will be easier.

Summary

- We can understand the problem of negativity on different levels, from the physical to the psychological to the spiritual, evolutionary, or cultural. The psychological and emotional level is the easiest for us to change.
- The negativity bias is an evolved human tendency that conferred a survival advantage on our ancestors. It's the tendency to register and focus more readily on negative stimuli while ignoring or downplaying positive ones. If we are aware of it, we can take steps to mitigate its influence in personal relationships and decision-making.
- If you cannot rely on your brain to automatically and unconsciously look for the positive, then you will have to *deliberately* draw your attention to it instead. Use a gratitude journal and deliberately choose to focus on the positive.
- No man is an island. Your unique thought patterns and habits are in a constant relationship with the unique thought patterns and habits of those around you. Relationships are shared patterns, and there is no such thing as a toxic person, only toxic patterns, behaviors, and relationships.
- All relationships are occasionally difficult, but toxic relationships amplify and recreate negativity in a way that is destructive and unhealthy for all parties involved. Focus on recurring dynamics and patterns rather than specific isolated behaviors, be accountable, and ask how your core beliefs are manifesting in the relationship.
- If you are bringing toxic patterns to a relationship, make a list of the behaviors, understand the function they are serving, put the pattern in context, then commit to making changes internally and externally.

Summary Guide

CHAPTER 1: REFRAME YOUR INTERNAL DIALOGUE AND TAKE CONTROL OF YOUR SELF-TALK

- How you think creates your life; negativity poisons everything in your world.
- Changing negativity requires a degree of metacognition (thinking about thinking) and a leap of faith to do something that hasn't been done before. Anyone can change their thought patterns; it requires only honest awareness and a willingness to take conscious and inspired action.
- Our mental shortcuts, assumptions, biases, and stereotypes are great at saving time and effort, but are not one hundred percent accurate one hundred percent of the time. The "all-or-nothing" disease is when we overextrapolate from one experience to other experiences we haven't had; we are making an error.
- Words have power, and our speech reflects our thought patterns. "Out of power" language is passive, self-victimizing, doubtful, angry, unconfident, fearful, excuse-making, or pessimistic, and can create a self-fulfilling prophesy.
- Become aware of your internal verbal habits. Then focus on what can be done, embrace nuance and shades of gray, and speak to yourself like you would a loved one.
- A cognitive distortion is a persistently incorrect belief, perception, or thought—for example, mental filtering, personalization, jumping to conclusions, mind-reading, catastrophizing, and using "should" statements and labels.
- Positive thinking is not just the absence of distortions, but thinking that helps you feel calm, hopeful, curious, grateful, stable, and confident.
- To challenge your inner critic, commit to not allowing your thoughts to dominate you. Gain psychological distance by labeling the thoughts as thoughts, not reality, and have self-compassion.
- Change happens outside your comfort zone, so realize that at some point, you'll need to take the leap and try something new.

CHAPTER 2: USE THE ABC METHOD AND WORK WITH A THOUGHT JOURNAL

- To rewrite our negative thought patterns, we "can't solve problems by using the same kind of thinking we used when we created them."
- We can use the ABCDE acronym (activating event, belief, consequence, disputation, and new event) and explore the stories we're telling in a thought journal. We can decide whether a new alternative is a good one according to its accuracy, helpfulness, and congruence with our values.

- Once you've identified your current thoughts, ask if there's a different way to think about things, and how you can bring that idea to life with concrete action. Seek out evidence for a new belief, practice self-compassion, and go into learning mode, asking questions instead of making statements.
- Negativity can be relieved by shifting perspectives and creating psychological distance. Remember that pessimism, negativity, and gloomy nihilism are all coping mechanisms and once served a purpose. But right now, we can choose to cope with adversity in different, healthier ways (and there always will be adversity!)
- Create spatial, temporal, and psychological distance from distressing thoughts, ask what others might do in our situation (role-switching), and turn your mind to concrete action instead of asking why. Focus on a small, concrete detail in the present and ask what you can **do**. Avoid identifying problems without seeking solutions—i.e., complaining!
- When we are stuck in intense emotions, we can try the ACT technique of defusion. Imagine that your Mind is something separate from you and that you can watch it.
- Remember that you are not your thoughts; you are just having thoughts. Make your thoughts earn their keep!

CHAPTER 3: MASTER THE ART OF DISTRESS TOLERANCE

- We need distress tolerance skills to help us cope with extremely trying or painful moments, or emergency situations. When we're distressed, it's easy to slip back into old patterns of behavior or default to clumsy, destructive, or unconscious ways of coping—these are false coping mechanisms.
- Self-soothing is a way to acknowledge and accept pain that is inevitable—without making it any bigger than it should be. It is not distraction or avoidance, but about anchoring in the present using your five senses—a technique called grounding.
- TIPP stands for temperature, intense exercise, paced breathing, and paired muscle relaxation, all of which can help lower physiological arousal. Try cold water, vigorous movement, or breathing exercises to calm the limbic system.
- Practice radical acceptance, which doesn't mean we like what is happening, only that we have agreed to not fight with reality. Acknowledge how you feel and the reality of the situation and remind yourself of what matters.
- The ACCEPTS acronym (Activities, Contribute, Comparisons, Emotions, Push away, Thoughts, and Sensations) can help you better tolerate momentary distress—although not for the longer term.
- With anxiety, our goal is not to force ourselves not to worry, but to worry more efficiently. Scheduling worry time puts you in proactive control and helps you gain distance.

- Notice the anxiety, write down the time you'll postpone to—with the duration and content—then follow through as agreed.
- Mental noting and focused mundane tasks can help you turn anxious moments into opportunities for mindfulness.

CHAPTER 4: UPGRADE YOUR PSYCHOLOGICAL TOOLKIT WITH STOIC TECHNIQUES

- The ancient Stoics were masters of living in the present.
- One way of rethinking your relationship to the past is to adopt the Stoic attitude of *amor fati*. This translates roughly to "love of one's fate." Whatever happens is embraced, wanting "nothing to be different." To practice it, look at events as neutrally as possible and then respond to them with a simple mantra like "good." By focusing on action and solutions, we are able to transform adversity.
- Negative visualization is where we occasionally spend a short amount of time imagining in detail the negative things that could happen in life. This renews appreciation and gratitude for what matters, allows us to prepare for the future, and creates psychological resilience.
- With the "what-if" technique, we write down a fear and ask, "What if this were true?" and explore the worst that could happen, showing ourselves that it is tolerable and not so bad after all. Likewise, remember *Memento mori*, Latin for, "remember that you will die" to help remind you of what matters.
- Problem-focused thinking zooms in on what's wrong. Solution-focused thinking zooms in on what *could* be right and looks to taking action to change the situation. Thinking needs to be balanced with action. Focus on the problem needs to be balanced with focus on the solution.
- Remember the Serenity Prayer and try the two-column exercise to help you identify what you can change and what you can't. Accept what you can't, act where you can. Ask what you want and value, then ask yourself, "Is what I'm doing, thinking, or feeling bringing me closer to that?"

CHAPTER 5: AVOID THE TRAP OF TOXIC POSITIVITY

- Toxic positivity is a kind of cognitive distortion and is an overgeneralization of a positive and optimistic attitude. It consists of denial, minimization, and invalidation of your own experience. Toxic positivity grows with shame, silence, and judgment. Positivity itself isn't toxic, but denying our reality is. Human beings are wholes who contain both good and bad.
- We can embrace the *whole* instead of the *good* by watching the phrases we use, making friends with discomfort, being patient while we are in process, distinguishing between productive and unproductive negativity, and reconnecting to what we value and want to achieve in life. Ask yourself, "How does a person who values what I value behave when they experience what I'm experiencing?"
- Keeping a gratitude journal is a great way to create genuine feelings of positivity.

- Rather than creating good emotions and getting rid of negative ones, we can practice emotional self-regulation and become conscious masters of our own ever-unfolding emotional experience.
- What makes an emotion good or bad is the context and our own goals and values. We regulate when we decide which emotions to attend to, when, how, and for how long.
- Emotions have a life cycle, and we can manage those emotions at any point in the cycle—before the situation, during the situation, with our attention, with our cognitive appraisal, and finally, with our emotional response. Generally, the sooner you intervene, the easier it is to modify the situation. Ask, "Is the way I'm thinking about this problem working for me right now?"

CHAPTER 6: WHERE DOES NEGATIVE THINKING REALLY COME FROM?

- We can understand the problem of negativity on different levels, from the physical to the psychological to the spiritual, evolutionary, or cultural. The psychological and emotional level is the easiest for us to change.
- The negativity bias is an evolved human tendency that conferred a survival advantage on our ancestors. It's the tendency to register and focus more readily on negative stimuli while ignoring or downplaying positive ones. If we are aware of it, we can take steps to mitigate its influence in personal relationships and decision-making.
- If you cannot rely on your brain to automatically and unconsciously look for the positive, then you will have to *deliberately* draw your attention to it instead. Use a gratitude journal and deliberately choose to focus on the positive.
- No man is an island. Your unique thought patterns and habits are in a constant relationship with the unique thought patterns and habits of those around you. Relationships are shared patterns, and there is no such thing as a toxic person, only toxic patterns, behaviors, and relationships.
- All relationships are occasionally difficult, but toxic relationships amplify and recreate negativity in a way that is destructive and unhealthy for all parties involved. Focus on recurring dynamics and patterns rather than specific isolated behaviors, be accountable, and ask how your core beliefs are manifesting in the relationship.
- If you are bringing toxic patterns to a relationship, make a list of the behaviors, understand the function they are serving, put the pattern in context, then commit to making changes internally and externally.

Bonus 10 Mental Health Worksheets and 30-Day Mental Health Action Plan

My Life Story

Take your time to reflect on your life journey and create an outline of your personal story using the steps and questions provided.

Create a Title

Title of Your Life Story:
Subtitle (optional):

Chapter Titles and Descriptions

Write at least six chapter titles that reflect significant moments in your life history. Focus on life stages or key pivotal events. Then, write one or two sentences to describe each chapter.

Chapter 1 Title:
Description:

Chapter 2 Title:
Description:

Chapter 3 Title:

Description:

Chapter 4 Title:

Description:

Chapter 5 Title:

Description:

Chapter 6 Title:
Description:

Step Three: Write Your Final Chapter

Write the final chapter of your life, which includes future dreams, aspirations, goals, and a game plan. This chapter should be longer and more detailed than the others because it is closest to the present and will likely contain themes and issues that are most relevant to you right now.

Final Chapter Title:

Description:

Step Four: Reflection and Analysis

After writing the final chapter, you can go back and add more sentences to the earlier chapters if you would like, but it's not necessary. Use the following questions to help you reflect on your life story:

Are there any recurring themes, symbols, or ideas in my chapters?

_____
_____
_____
_____
_____
_____

Is there a progression or development across all these chapters or events?

_____
_____
_____
_____
_____
_____

Does the story fit with how I think of myself today? Does it align with how other people view me?

_____
_____
_____
_____
_____
_____

Is there anything about myself that I used to think or believe but no longer do?

What do I want to change about my story moving forward? How would I prefer to think of myself?

If I were rewriting this story, how would I do it?

Where did this story or this theme come from? When did I first start thinking of myself this way?

_____
_____
_____
_____
_____

What chapters need to be added in order to bridge the gap between today and the final conclusion?

_____
_____
_____
_____
_____

Are there different ways to interpret or understand these events? Can I look at them through a different lens now that they are in the past?

_____
_____
_____
_____
_____

ABCD Model Worksheet

Use this worksheet to practice the ABCD model for identifying and re-engineering your ingrained thought patterns and cognitive distortions. Follow the steps outlined in the text and fill in the information as instructed.

Step 1: Start with the Activating Event

Describe the event, thought, feeling, gesture, situation, or dynamic that triggered the present situation.

↓

Step 2: Identify Your Beliefs

What are you saying to yourself about this trigger? Write down your interpretation of events and your thoughts.

↓

Step 3: Identify the Resulting Consequences

What do your thoughts and beliefs make you feel? How do you behave, given your thoughts and beliefs?

↓

Step 4: <u>Dispute</u> the Belief

In what ways can you adjust your belief? Is there a more realistic alternative?

Behavioral Experiments

Using the scientific method, we pose a hypothesis and then test it. We devise an experiment, gather data, interpret that data, and then check to see if the result allows us to reject our hypothesis or not. There is an infinite number of ways to conduct experiments, but they all follow this basic pattern of hypothesis testing.

Step 1: Identify the Belief You Want to Test

Try to write this belief or prediction down as a single sentence, looking for things that could be cognitive distortions.

Step 2: Assess the Strength of Your Belief

How strongly do you believe it on a scale of one to ten?

___/10

Step 3: Design Your Experiment

How are you planning to conduct your experiment? Write the details below.

Step 4: Proactively Identify Potential Obstacles

Before proceeding with your experiment, list down 3-5 obstacles that you might encounter and how you plan to solve them.

Potential Obstacle	Potential Solution
1.	
2.	
3.	
4.	
5.	

Step 5: Do the Experiment and Record Your Result

What is the outcome? Write it down below.

Compare your findings to your original hypothesis and rewrite the sentence accordingly.

Original Hypothesis	
Revised Hypothesis	

What's your rating after the experiment?

___/10

What have you learned from your behavioral experiment?

Socratic Method Worksheet

Anxiety often stems from our thoughts, which can be irrational or exaggerated. To help manage these anxious thoughts, follow these steps in the worksheet. By using Socratic dialogue, you can gain clarity and reduce anxiety.

Step 1: Describe the Anxious Thought

Start by putting your anxious thought into a clear sentence. For example, if your thought is, "He's probably going to die any day now, and I won't be able to cope when it happens,"

Step 2: Examine the Evidence

Check the thought's validity using these questions:

What evidence supports this belief?

↓

What do I know for sure about the situation?

↓

Am I making assumptions, exaggerating, or catastrophizing?

Step 3: Challenge Assumptions and Explore Alternatives

Is there a reason to believe that my thought will happen, or is this a worst-case scenario assumption?

↓

Are there alternative possibilities or counterexamples?

↓

What are others saying about my thought?

Step 4: Rewrite the Thought

Based on your answers, rewrite your anxious thought into something moderate.

Make a Mind Map

Creating a mind map can provide you with a clearer perspective, reduce overwhelm, and simplify your thoughts.

Mind Mapping

Begin by writing down a focus word or phrase inside the obligated shape below related to what's troubling you. Don't worry about being perfect or organized; the goal is to get everything out of your mind and onto the paper.

After that, create branches off the central word/phrase to explore different aspects of your concern. These branches can be related to your thoughts, feelings, and any associated elements. Feel free to add more.

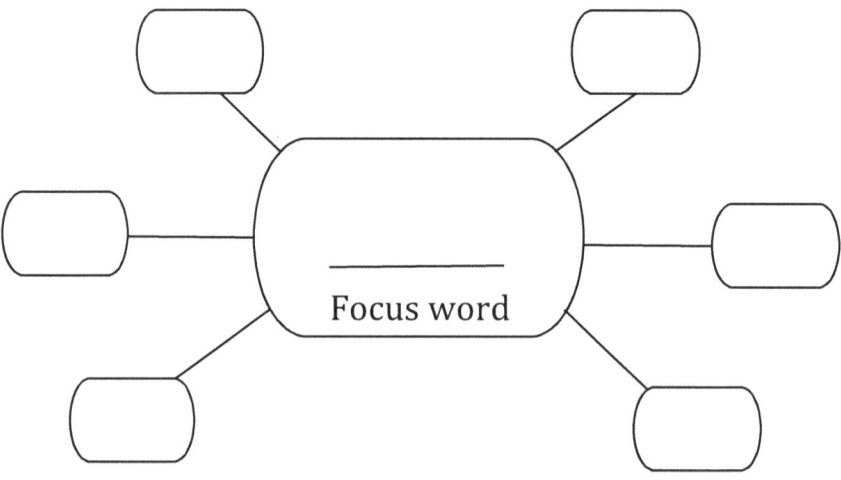

Organizing the Chaos

To simplify and declutter your mind, transition into a different mode. Ask your brain to help you cut through the chaos by answering these four questions:

What Can I Control?

What Can I Let Go Of?

What Are My Priorities?

What Are My Next Steps?

Five Levels of Self-Talk

Self-talk plays a significant role in shaping our self-concept and overall well-being. Complete the following worksheet to assess your current level of self-talk and set goals for improvement.

Level 1: Harmful Self-Talk

Level 1 self-talk is characterized by negative narratives and self-limiting beliefs. Reflect on your own self-talk and write down examples of Level 1 self-talk you may be engaging in.

1._____

2._____

3._____

Level 2: Recognizing the Need for Change

Level 2 self-talk acknowledges the need for improvement but may not provide solutions. Identify areas in your life where you recognize the need for change without taking decisive action.

1._____

2._____

3._____

Level 3: Taking Action

Level 3 self-talk involves actively working on self-improvement. Write down instances of Level 3 self-talk where you actively engage in positive changes.

1._____

2._____

3._____

Level 4: Comprehensive Self-Transformation

Level 4 self-talk involves replacing negative self-talk with self-respect and positivity. Identify areas where you have successfully replaced Level 1 and 2 self-talk with positive affirmations.

1._____

2._____

3._____

Level 5: Universal Affirmation and Acceptance

Level 5 self-talk encompasses broad acceptance and affirmation of yourself and others. Write down examples of Level 5 self-talk where you embrace life's complexities and affirm your values.

1._____

2._____

3._____

Reflection:

Which level of self-talk do you believe most of your mental effort and energy currently goes into?

Level: _____

Are you frequently caught in negative self-talk patterns, or do you actively work towards self-improvement and positive self-talk?

_____

_____
_____

_____
_____

What steps can you take to transition to a higher level of self-talk? List at least one action for each level of self-talk that you can implement in your life.

Level 2: _____

Level 3: _____

Level 4: _____

Level 5: _____

Rewriting Your Self-Talk with Self-Compassion

Instructions: Read the following and reflect on the concepts discussed in each section. Answer the questions to apply these concepts to your own life.

Understanding Self-Compassion

Self-compassion is deeper and more lasting than high confidence because it is not dependent on fleeting external factors.

Question 1:

Reflect on a time when you based your self-worth on external factors. How did it affect your self-esteem and well-being?

_____
_____
_____
_____
_____
_____

Benefits of Self-Compassion

Self-compassion is backed up by solid research as a way to achieve greater well-being, contentment, and resilience.

Question 2:

List the potential benefits of practicing self-compassion in your life and explain how it might improve your overall well-being.

_____
_____
_____
_____
_____
_____

Being Kind to Yourself

Imagine talking to yourself as you literally would to one of your dearest friends.

Question 3:

Recall a situation when you were hard on yourself. How might you change your self-talk if you treated yourself with the kindness and understanding you'd offer to a friend?

_____
_____
_____
_____
_____
_____

Your Inner Critic

A great exercise is to write out a 'job description' for your inner critic. What effect do they have on your life?

Question 4:

Write a job description for your inner critic and explain how it affects your self-esteem and well-being.

Applying Self-Compassion in Daily Life

When negative thoughts pop up, recognize that it's just the inner critic speaking. Listen if it's useful, but don't entertain any idea that damages your well-being.

Question 5:

Identify a recent negative thought you had about yourself. Is it constructive or harmful self-talk? How can you respond with self-compassion?

_____
_____
_____
_____
_____
_____

Your Inner Critic

Look at your inner critic as a separate entity who is only doing their job. You don't have to accept it.

Question 6:

Summarize how viewing your inner critic as a separate entity can help you distance yourself from negative self-talk. What strategies will you use to reject harmful self-criticism?

_____
_____
_____
_____
_____
_____

_____
_____

Identifying Cognitive Distortions

Understanding cognitive distortions is a vital step towards fostering better mental health and emotional resilience. By recognizing these distortions, individuals can develop the skills to challenge and reframe their negative thought patterns, leading to a more accurate, balanced, and optimistic view of themselves and the world.

Types of Cognitive Distortions

All-or-Nothing Thinking

Viewing situations in extreme black-and-white terms with no middle ground.

Examples: "If I'm not perfect, I'm a failure," or "It's either all good or all bad."

Mental Filtering

Focusing only on negative aspects while ignoring positive ones.

Examples: Only remembering criticism and forgetting praise or compliments.

Personalization

Incorrectly attributing external events to yourself.

Examples: Believing someone's bad mood is your fault, or assuming you caused someone to cheat on you.

Jumping to Conclusions and Mind-Reading

Making unfounded assumptions about others' thoughts and intentions.

Examples: Assuming someone's comment is about you when it may not be, or thinking you know why someone did something without evidence.

Catastrophizing

Magnifying the importance of negative events and predicting the worst outcomes.

Examples: Believing one mistake will ruin your life, or thinking that small issues will lead to total disaster.

"Shoulds" and Labels

Holding rigid expectations and applying arbitrary standards to yourself.

Examples: Thinking you should look a certain way, or believing you should always feel confident.

Instructions: In the following worksheet, you will be presented with various scenarios or statements. For each scenario or statement, identify the cognitive distortion being used. Use the meanings and examples provided to help you recognize the distortions. If a scenario or statement contains multiple distortions, identify all of them.

1. **After receiving a B on a test, Sarah thinks, "I'm a complete failure. I'll never be successful."**
   Cognitive Distortion(s): _____

2. **John's boss praised his work in front of the team, but he only remembers a coworker's criticism about a small mistake he made.**
   Cognitive Distortion(s): _____

3. Lisa's friend seemed upset, and Lisa immediately thought, "I must have done something to make her mad at me."
   Cognitive Distortion(s): _____

4. David saw a group of people whispering and assumed they were talking about him, even though he had no evidence for it.
   Cognitive Distortion(s): _____

5. After getting a parking ticket, Michael thought, "This is a disaster. I'll never be able to afford it, and I'll lose my job."
   Cognitive Distortion(s): _____

6. Emily believes she should always be happy and confident, and when she's not, she thinks she's failing at life.
   Cognitive Distortion(s): _____

7. Alex missed a call from his friend and immediately assumed that his friend no longer wanted to be friends with him.
   Cognitive Distortion(s): _____

8. Susan believes that if her partner cheated on her, it must be because she did something to cause it.
   Cognitive Distortion(s): _____

9. Tim believed that if he didn't win the competition, his entire future would be ruined.
   Cognitive Distortion(s): _____

10. **Jenny thinks she should always look perfect, and any imperfection makes her feel like a complete failure.**
    Cognitive Distortion(s): _____

Reflection: Distortion Detector

Review the scenarios or statements in the worksheet and identify 5 real-life situations where you've experienced similar distortions. Using the table below, briefly describe the situation and the cognitive distortion(s) involved. Reflect on how recognizing these distortions can lead to improved mental well-being.

	Situation	Cognitive Distortion	Reflection
1.			
2.			

3.		
4.		
5.		

Cognitive Fusion Exercise

This worksheet guides you through a cognitive defusion exercise, helping you gain distance from negative thoughts and regain control over your mind. Follow the steps below to practice this exercise.

Step 1: Identify What You Value

Ask yourself what you value most in life or what you are trying to achieve. It could be a big life goal, a personal value, or even something immediate. Hold that thought in your mind.

Value: _____

Step 2: Become Aware of Negative Thoughts

Like Ellen, become aware of any negative thoughts that are coming up for you. Write them down below.

Negative Thoughts:
1. _____
2. _____
3. _____

Step 3: Label and Create Distance

Take a closer look at one of the negative thoughts you've identified. Tell yourself, "I am having this thought." Also, give it a label, such as criticism, doubt, curiosity, fear, observation, resistance.

What's the name of your negative thought?
_____

Step 4: Assess Alignment with Your Values

Don't worry about whether the thought is "true" or not. Instead, ask if it matches up with what you identified in Step 1 as something you want or value.

Does this thought take you closer to or further away from that thing? Does this thought align with your values or desired outcome? (Circle one)

Yes   No   Neutral

Step 5: Make a Conscious Choice

If the thought takes you closer to your values, that's great. If it doesn't, or if it's neutral, you now have a choice. Will you actively choose something that goes against what you already know you want? Or will you let it pass by?

_____
_____
_____
_____
_____
_____

Step 6: Repeat as Needed

Repeat this exercise as often as you like. Just like buses, there's always another thought on its way. Practice cognitive defusion to gain control over your mind and make your thoughts work for you.

ACCEPTS SKILL

Instructions: The ACCEPTS skill is a valuable tool for coping with distressing emotions and situations. This acronym represents various strategies you can use to help manage your emotions and find relief during difficult times. For each letter in ACCEPTS, think about how you can apply the strategy to your own life.

A Activities	*List some activities that you can engage in to keep yourself busy and distracted from distressing emotions.*

	Identify ways in which you can contribute or help others, even when you're feeling down. This could be through volunteering or providing support to someone in need.

C Contribute	

C Comparisons	*Reflect on a challenging situation you've experienced. Can you find positive aspects or comparisons that help you put things in perspective?*

E Emotions	*Think about a situation that has made you feel intense negative emotions. How can you try on the opposite emotions or find humor in the situation to alleviate some of the distress?*

P Push away	*Recall a recent problem or decision that felt overwhelming. How can you temporarily set it aside to give yourself time to calm down before revisiting it?*

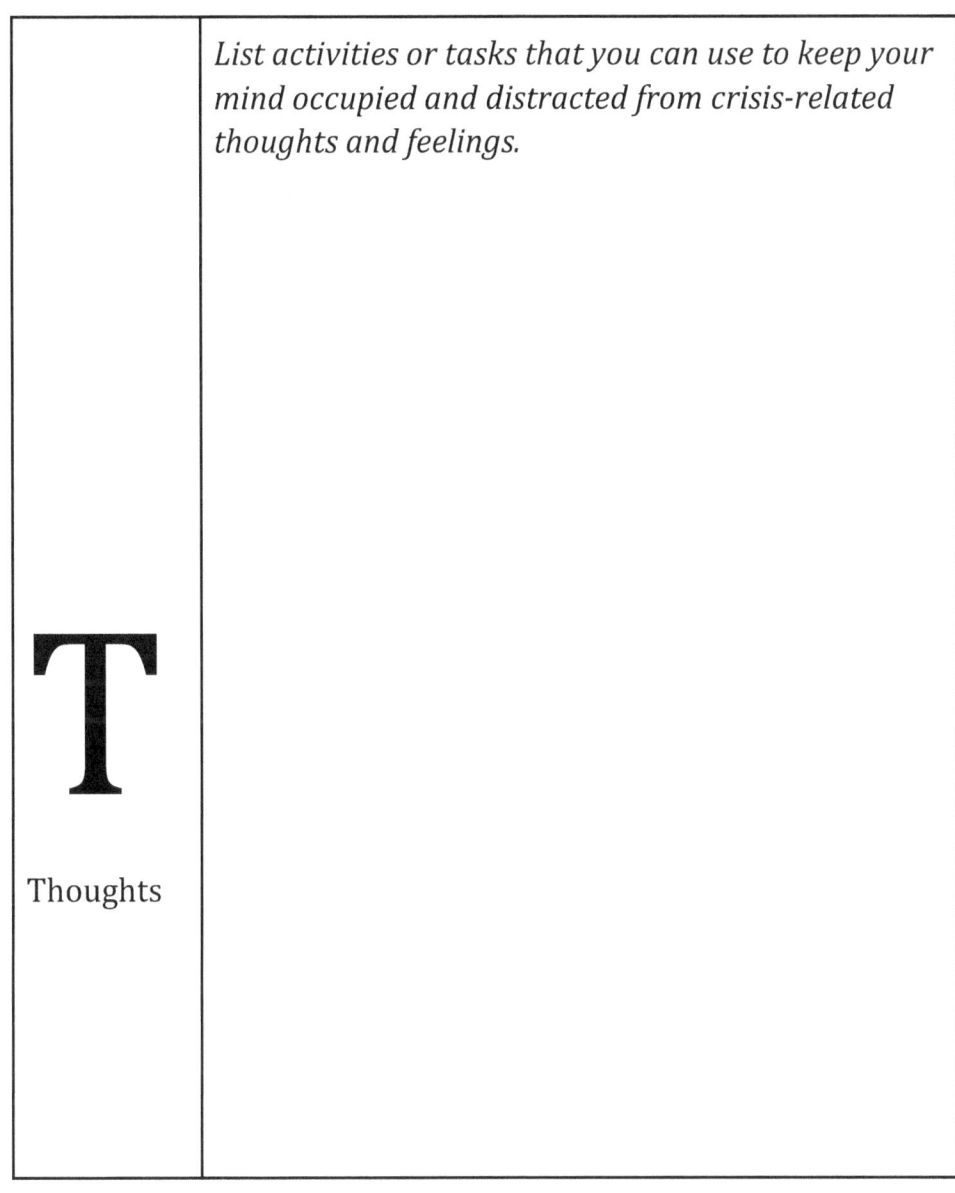

List activities or tasks that you can use to keep your mind occupied and distracted from crisis-related thoughts and feelings.

T

Thoughts

S Sensations	*Describe a grounding exercise you can use to connect with your five senses when you find yourself overwhelmed by negative thoughts and emotions.*

30-Day Plan for Better Mental Health & Self-Care

The 30-Day Mental Health and Self-Care Challenge is a program designed to enhance your mental well-being and promote self-care. Each day, you'll engage in simple tasks that prioritize your mental health and self-care practices. These tasks encompass various aspects of self-care, including relaxation techniques, gratitude exercises, mindfulness practices, and more.

By participating in this challenge, you'll discover that dedicating time to your mental health and well-being can have a profound impact on your overall quality of life. It's an opportunity to prioritize self-care, reduce stress, and build a healthier mindset, one day at a time. Throughout the challenge, you'll find that small, consistent efforts can lead to significant improvements in your mental health and self-care routine.

Day 1: Beginning Self-Exploration

Start a journal to record your thoughts, emotions, and experiences.

Day 2: Take a Walk on the Dark Side with Shadow Work

Identify and write down your shadow aspects or "dark side" and the emotions they evoke.

Day 3: Empty Chair

Visualize someone or something in an empty chair, engage in a dialogue, and release unresolved feelings to work through emotional challenges and change your perspective.

Day 4: Understanding Internal Family Systems

Find out if you're a firefighter, manager, or exile. Reflect on how your type shows up in relationships.

Day 5: What Is Your Attachment Style?

Take an attachment style quiz and reflect on your results.

Day 6: How to Reparent Your Inner Child

Write a letter to your inner child offering love and support.

Day 7: Rewrite the Story of Your Life

Rewrite a personal story from a more empowered perspective.

Day 8: Identify and Change Your Core Beliefs

Identify a negative core belief and reframe it positively.

Day 9: The ABCD Model

Use the ABCD model to analyze and challenge a negative thought.

Day 10: The Triple Column Technique

Create a triple-column chart to reframe negative thoughts.

Day 11: Cognitive Defusion

Practice cognitive defusion techniques to detach from negative thoughts.

Day 12: Systematic Desensitization

Create a fear hierarchy and start exposing yourself to things you fear.

Day 13: Behavioral Activation

Create a daily schedule with enjoyable activities.

Day 14: Behavioral Experiments

Design a small behavioral experiment to test your assumptions.

Day 15: Label Your Emotions

Practice labeling your emotions throughout the day.

Day 16: Build Self-Awareness

Reflect on your triggers and emotional responses.

Day 17: Question Yourself Using Socratic Method

Challenge irrational thoughts using Socratic questioning.

Day 18: Test Your False Beliefs

Test a belief about yourself or a situation.

Day 19: Limit Caffeine Intake

Reduce or eliminate caffeine from your diet.

Day 20: Schedule Your "Worry Time"

Allocate a specific time for worrying and stick to it.

Day 21: Cultivate Gratitude

Start a gratitude journal to focus on positive aspects of your life.

Day 22: Use "Mental Anchoring"

Select a desired state of mind, choose an anchor, relive a memory embodying that state, associate the emotion's peak with the anchor, and repeat the process several times to reinforce the connection.

Day 23: Belly Breathing

Practice deep belly breathing to reduce stress.

Day 24: The 5-4-3-2-1 Grounding Technique

Identify five things you can see, four things you can touch, three things you can hear, two things you can smell, and one thing you can taste to help recenter and alleviate stress or anxiety.

Day 25: Have a Mantra

Develop a personal mantra to boost confidence and calm.

Day 26: Scan Your Body

Perform a body scan meditation to release tension.

Day 27: Guided Imagery

Practice a guided imagery meditation to reduce anxiety.

Day 28: Metaphorize Your Anxiety

Create a metaphor for your anxiety and explore it.

Day 29: Talk About Yourself in Third Person

Speak about your concerns in the third person to gain perspective.

Day 30: Role-Playing

Practice role-playing by identifying a fear or threat, developing a desired behavior or mindset, and simulating situations with a therapist or a friend to enhance social skills or cope with anxieties.

www.ingramcontent.com/pod-product-compliance
Lightning Source LLC
Chambersburg PA
CBHW042357070526
44585CB00029B/2964